THE ROUTLEDGE COMPANION TO RUSSIAN LITERATURE

The Routledge Companion to Russian Literature is an engaging and accessible guide to Russian writing of the past thousand years.

The volume covers the entire span of Russian literature, from the Middle Ages to the post-Soviet period, and explores all the forms that have made it so famous: poetry, drama and, of course, the Russian novel. A particular emphasis is given to the works of the nineteenth and twentieth centuries, when Russian literature achieved world-wide recognition through the works of writers such as Pushkin, Dostoevsky, Tolstoy, Chekhov, Nabokov and Solzhenitsyn. Covering such diverse subjects as women's writing, Russian literary theory, socialist realism and *émigré* writing, leading international scholars open up the wonderful diversity of Russian literature.

With recommended lists of further reading and an excellent, up-to-date bibliography, *The Routledge Companion to Russian Literature* is the perfect guide for students and general readers alike.

Neil Cornwell is Professor of Russian and Comparative Literature at the University of Bristol. He has edited the *Reference Guide to Russian Literature* (1998) and is the author of two books on Vladimir Odoevsky, as well as *The Literary Fantastic* (1990), *James Joyce and the Russians* (1992) and *Vladimir Nabokov* (1999).

Routledge Companions

Routledge Companions are the perfect reference guides, providing everything the student or general reader needs to know. Authoritative and accessible, they combine the in-depth expertise of leading specialists with straightforward, jargon-free writing. In each book you'll find what you're looking for, clearly presented – whether through an extended article or an A–Z entry – in ways which the beginner can understand and even the expert will appreciate.

Routledge Companion to Global Economics
Edited by Robert Beynon

Routledge Companion to Feminism and Postfeminism
Edited by Sarah Gamble

Routledge Companion to The New Cosmology
Edited by Peter Coles

Routledge Companion to Postmodernism
Edited by Stuart Sim

Routledge Companion to Semiotics and Linguistics
Edited by Paul Cobley

Routledge Companion to Russian Literature
Edited by Neil Cornwell

THE ROUTLEDGE COMPANION TO RUSSIAN LITERATURE

Edited by
Neil Cornwell

London and New York

First published 2001
by Routledge
11 New Fetter Lane, London EC4P 4EE
Simultaneously published in the USA and Canada
by Routledge
29 West 35th Street, New York, NY 10001

Routledge is an imprint of the Taylor & Francis Group

Versions of chapters 2, 3, 6, 7, 9, 10, 13, 14, 15, 16, 18, 19 and 20 © 1998 Fitzroy
Dearborn; all additional material in these chapters © 2001 the authors;
chapters 1, 4, 5, 8, 11, 12 and 17 © 2001 the authors.

Typeset in Times New Roman by
Keystroke, Jacaranda Lodge, Wolverhampton
Printed and bound in Great Britain by
St Edmundsbury Press, Bury St Edmunds, Suffolk

British Library Cataloguing in Publication Data
A catalogue record for this book is available from the British Library

Library of Congress Cataloging in Publication Data
The Routledge companion to Russian literature / edited by Neil Cornwell.
p. cm.
Includes bibliographical references and index.
1. Russian literature–History and criticism. I. Title: Companion to Russian literature.
II. Cornwell, Neil

PG2951 .R68 2001
891.709–dc21 2001019769

ISBN 0–415–23365–8 (hbk)
ISBN 0–415–23366–6 (pbk)

CONTENTS

NOTES ON CONTRIBUTORS

Editor: **Neil Cornwell** is Professor of Russian and Comparative Literature at the University of Bristol. He is the editor of the *Reference Guide to Russian Literature* (1998) and author or editor of various studies in Russian and comparative literary fields.

Michael Basker is Reader in Russian Studies at the University of Bristol. He has written widely on Gumilev, Akhmatova and Pushkin.

David M. Bethea is Vilas Research Professor of Russian Literature at the University of Wisconsin, Madison. His books include *The Shape of Apocalypse in Modern Russian Fiction* (1989) and studies of Khodasevich, Brodsky and Pushkin.

Birgit Beumers is Senior Lecturer in Russian Studies at the University of Bristol. She has published books on contemporary Russian theatre and cinema.

A.D.P. Briggs was Professor of Russian at the University of Birmingham; now he is Senior Research Fellow at the University of Bristol. He has published a number of books on Pushkin, and is currently preparing a new translation of *War and Peace* for Penguin.

Ellen Chances is Professor of Russian Literature and Culture at Princeton University. She is the author of books on the superfluous man and Andrei Bitov.

Katerina Clark is Professor of Comparative Literature at Yale University. She is the author of books on the Soviet novel and cultural revolution in St Petersburg and co-author of the biography of Mikhail Bakhtin.

Ruth Coates is Lecturer in Russian Studies at the University of Bristol and author of *Christianity in Bakhtin* (1998).

Martin Dewhirst is Honorary Research Fellow, Department of Slavonic Studies, at the University of Glasgow. Specializing in post-war and contemporary Russian literary affairs, he was co-editor of *The Soviet Censorship* (1973) and *Russian Writing Today* (1977).

Richard Freeborn is Emeritus Professor of Russian Literature at the University of London. He is the author of several books on classical Russian literature and has translated works by Turgenev and Dostoevsky.

David Gillespie is Reader in Russian at the University of Bath and the author of several books on twentieth-century Russian literature.

W. Gareth Jones was Professor of Russian at the University of Wales, Bangor, and author of *Nikolay Novikov* (1984); he has written widely on eighteenth- and nineteenth-century Russia.

Catriona Kelly is Reader in Russian and Fellow of New College, Oxford and has published a number of books on women's writing and cultural studies in Russia.

Boris Lanin is Professor of Literature at the Russian Academy of education, Moscow. He has published widely on twentieth-century Russian literature.

Alla Latynina is a leading contemporary Moscow critic of modern Russian literature and columnist for *Literaturnaia gazeta*.

Robin Milner-Gulland is Professor of Russian and European Studies at the University of Sussex, and author of *The Russians* (1997) and many studies on Russian poetry, art and cultural history.

Derek Offord is Professor of Russian Intellectual History at the University of Bristol. He is the author of several books on Russian intellectual history and the Russian language.

Michael O'Toole is Professor of Communication Studies at Murdoch University, Perth, Australia. He is the author of *The Language of Displayed Art* (1994) and co-editor of *Russian Poetics in Translation* (1975–83).

Donald Rayfield is Professor of Russian and Georgian at Queen Mary and Westfield College, University of London. He is the author of several books on Chekhov and *The Literature of Georgia: A History* (1994).

G.S. Smith is Professor of Russian at the University of Oxford and author of *D.S. Mirsky: A Russian–English Life* (2000) and of many studies of Russian poetry and its versification.

Faith Wigzell is Reader in Russian at SSEES, University College London. She is the author of *Reading Russian Fortunes* (1998) and a number of studies of Russian folklore and medieval Russian literature.

PREFACE

An 'introductory' volume such as this naturally gives rise to the question: introductory to whom? The present book does assume a certain amount of literary knowledge and at least a vague familiarity with Russian history and culture. It is therefore intended to provide a reasonably comprehensive guide, or companion, to the development of Russian literature and to its main facets, in terms of period, genre and related topics. It is accordingly primarily aimed at students, at their teachers and at the informed or inquisitive general reader. It is hoped that it will also be of some interest to the more advanced scholar. While there is here a certain coverage of early Russian literature and a chapter surveying the eighteenth century, the bulk of this multi-authored study concentrates unashamedly on the nineteenth and twentieth centuries: the two-hundred-year period in which Russian literature first established and then confirmed itself as a prominent force in world culture.

Thirteen of the twenty essays comprising this book appeared as introductory contributions to the *Reference Guide to Russian Literature* (edited by Neil Cornwell with Nicole Christian as Associate Editor), published by Fitzroy Dearborn (London and Chicago, 1998). Those essays broaching the contemporary period have been updated or extended, to reach the end of the twentieth century. Others have undergone minor revisions. A further seven (the Introduction included) were newly commissioned for the present volume. Each essay is followed by an appropriate list of sources and suggested further reading. The present volume also contains a bibliography of recommended general studies and anthologies. For bibliographies of individual authors, readers may consult such sources as Proffer and Meyer's *Nineteenth-Century Russian Literature in English* (Ann Arbor, 1990), and relevant volumes in the *Dictionary of Literary Biography* series, as well as the main body of entries in the *Reference Guide to Russian Literature*.

The transliteration system used is that of the Library of Congress system (minus diacritics). Exceptions have been made for surnames ending in '-ii' or '-i' (hence the more familiar 'Dostoevsky' and 'Tolstoy'); certain other anglicizations or accustomed spellings have also been retained (e.g. 'glasnost', rather than *glasnost'*).

A brief word should perhaps be added about two of the essays. One solitary essay is devoted to a single author, albeit examining the impact on him of two key English figures; if any single Russian writer deserves such selectively individual attention, then surely that writer has to be Aleksandr Pushkin, the acknowledged 'father of Russian literature' and of the modern Russian literary language, whose bicentennial was celebrated in 1999. The final topic here presented, dealing with the first post-Soviet decade, is treated at slightly more generous length; this we justify on the grounds that material on this particular period is as yet less readily available.

Neil Cornwell
Bristol, January 2001

1

INTRODUCTION: RUSSIAN LITERATURE –
THE FIRST THOUSAND YEARS

NEIL CORNWELL

From the Kievan principality, founded according to the chronicles by Varangians (Vikings) under Rurik in the ninth century, and converting to the Greek form of Christianity in the tenth, there subsequently emerged the more centralized state of Muscovy. Having thrown off the so-called Tartar Yoke, the Moscow-centred power, stretching from Novgorod in the north to Kiev in the south, reverted to the name 'Rus'', and, in the early fifteenth century, its ruler adopted the title of Tsar (or Caesar). Conscious of its Byzantine heritage, and fortified by the notion of Moscow as 'the Third Rome', Rus' was soon pursuing a policy of territorial aggrandisement – sooner or later, in all directions. Unlike many empires, it has frequently been noted, Russia chose to concentrate on adjacent lands. Conquests over Tartars and Turks to the south, and Poland–Lithuania to the West, as well as expansion to the east (towards Siberia), were followed by rivalry with Sweden, the main military power of northern Europe, which culminated in the Great Northern War (1700–21). Peter the Great, the victor in this conflict, opening his 'window to the West' and founding his Baltic capital, assumed the Latinized title of *imperator* (emperor). He began an ambitious programme of westernization and attempted modernization, with technological advances drawn from Germany, Holland and England; this process was further pursued by Catherine the Great in the second half of the eighteenth century.

On its northern flank, Russia had chiefly prosecuted the acquisition of Finland and adjacent Baltic coastal territories at the expense of the Swedes, who had taken advantage of the Mongol invasions of Russia to push to the Neva. The Treaty of Täysinä in 1595 brought to an end one long period of conflict, leaving the Russians largely repulsed and an Arctic frontier and taxation rights favourable to Sweden, plus Swedish possession of Estonia. The Russians, who had founded isolated northern Orthodox monasteries to convert the Lapps, retained limited territorial and fishing rights. The Great Northern War saw the foundation of St Petersburg in 1703 on the edge of the empire amidst the Finnish marshes; it also led to Russian occupation of Finland, remembered as 'The Great Wrath'. The Treaty of Nystad (1721) ended the Russian occupation of Finland, but forced vital Baltic coastal territorial concessions from the Swedes and left Russia as the major northern power. Further hostilities broke out in 1741–3 and again in 1788–90. In the Napoleonic era, Russian armies again overran Finland and the settlement of 1809 led to the absorption of a 'Grand Duchy of Finland' within the Russian Empire, although with strong local legal and institutional autonomy. The Finno-Russian frontier, traditionally an oscillating blur,

1

was now fixed, and remained in place from 1812 until the Winter War of 1939–40, one of the events that unfolded from the Molotov–Ribbentrop Pact.

Annexation and absorption (both political and cultural) were the imperialist order of the day. Russian tsars and Soviet commissars alike, along with many even of their more progressive supporters, sought the forcible assimilation of minority peoples (Finns, Poles or Chechens) in pusuit of an imperial uniformity. In the mid-eighteenth century, however, at a time of diplomatic rapprochement, Russia – imperial aspirations notwithstanding – voluntarily underwent an astonishing process of reverse cultural imperialism by adopting French as the working and social language of court and aristocracy (by now largely a 'serving nobility', replacing or augmenting the old boyar élite who claimed descent from Rurik). This served, apart from anything else, as an aristocratic status symbol. The Russian aristocracy went through a veritable fever of French imitation in the second half of the eighteenth century: indeed, it became customary – even obligatory – in aristocratic homes for the children to be instructed in French almost from birth, and the habit of speaking and reading French trained them even to think in French. This exercise in Gallicization – in many ways a surprisingly neglected aspect of Russian cultural history – thus reached its peak following the French Revolution and around the turn of the nineteenth century (see the quantity of French used, or implied, in Tolstoy's *War and Peace* [*Voina i mir*]), but received a near-fatal setback with the Napoleonic invasion and, in more general cultural terms, suffered in the collapse of Russia's Enlightenment values associated with the failure of the 'Decembrist' adventure (see below). Nevertheless, the usage of French survived in court circles and the practice of employing western tutors to the children of the élite continued until the Revolution.

Meanwhile, the gains made by Catherine (largely superintended by her favourite and lover, Prince Potemkin), followed by the events of the Napoleonic era, meant that, from 1814, Russia's western frontiers were now fixed in a manner that was to last until the Great War of 1914–18. As a main victor of the Revolutionary and Napoleonic wars, Russia assumed, from the Congress of Vienna, its most commanding position yet as a European power. Russia's European policy was now to defend these existing frontiers, and indeed the established status quo in Europe, through the Holy Alliance. The colonial acquisition of the Caucasus, which had commenced at the end of the eighteenth century, continued unabated and provided a strong theme for Russian literature well into the nineteenth (in works by Pushkin, Lermontov and Tolstoy). The later years of Alexander I, and the accession of Nicholas I, greeted by the unsuccessful Decembrist revolt (of 14 December 1825) by more liberal elements of the nobility, together with repression in Poland and an implacable posture towards the European reform movements of 1830, ushered in a period of bleak reaction, at home and abroad, that was to be reinforced during the revolutionary period of 1848–9 and to last until its temporary and partial alleviation in the next reign, in the wake of military humiliation in Crimea.

It was in this period that the spectre of a serious Russian menace was perceived to arise over Europe; the second quarter of the nineteenth century has been called (by Martin Malia) 'the age par excellence of black literature about Russia'. Heinrich Heine saw within the Russian Empire the 'knout of tragedy', and Nicholas as 'a Russian wolf who has donned the moth-infested purple robe of the old Byzantine Empire, the time-worn imperial breeches of the Holy Roman Empire, and the diamond-studded old Frankish crown of Charlemagne' who would one day 'throw off this grandmotherly attire of the old empires and devour the Little Red Riding Hood of Freedom'. Not that Russia was ever entirely without its own dissonant or self-deprecating voices: Petr Chaadaev famously asserted that Russia existed only to teach the world some great lesson – apparently, that its example should be avoided at all costs.

It is surely not entirely coincidental, however, that this was precisely the period in which Russian literature first began to assert itself as a seriously recognized European cultural force. In the view of Ewa Thompson, for instance, Russian writers have almost invariably 'abetted the power of the centre so as to prevent the periphery from speaking in its own voice'. It was the career of Pushkin (in Thompson's view perhaps the greatest offender in this regard) that launched Russian literature on its 'Golden Age', which may be dated either (narrowly) to the poetic achievements of the 1820s and 30s, or (more broadly) to the half century of major literary creativity that extended to the 1880s. Significantly, perhaps, a number of commentators have dated the beginning of Russia's new cultural role to the climax of the Napoleonic wars; Dostoevsky, for instance, saw this period as 'the very inception of our true self-consciousness', the exact moment when 'Pushkin appeared'. Russia's growing convergence with the West was driven by its own mutations of the key European trends of Enlightenment and Romanticism: realism and romanticism in literature; Westernism (or 'progress') and Slavophilism (or 'the Russian soul') in thought; positivism and Symbolism with the approach of the *fin de siècle* 'Silver Age'.

Dante, Shakespeare and Cervantes all left their mark on Russian literature, as did Rousseau, Schiller, Goethe and Byron, Hoffmann, Poe and Dickens, the English Romantic poets and the French Symbolists. As Malia puts it, on the European scale: 'What France had done for secular rationalism and political radicalism in the previous century, Germany now did for aesthetic Romanticism and philosophical Idealism.' Accordingly, just as France had been the main cultural influence on eighteenth-century Russia, so did German thought and culture – from the Romantic philosophical systems of Schelling and Hegel to the materialism of Marx – provide the main ideological thrust for Russia in the nineteenth. Later still Dostoevsky and Nietzsche occasioned a kind of posthumous symbiotic impact on each other's national cultures. These two figures indeed became, along with Baudelaire and Wagner, what Malia calls 'the four evangels' of European culture as it moved into the twentieth century.

A further dichotomy within the Russian cultural psyche was (and, many would say, still is) the feeling of victimhood, backwardness or inferiority, as against future mastery or inherent superiority. On the one hand, the Russian state was constantly being ganged up on by the western powers; on the other, as Heine saw it, the blind obedience of the Russian people to the 'holy infallible power' of their tsar was in actuality 'a vehicle for their own self-glorification'. Culturally or ideologically, or perhaps politically and economically, Russia was likely to remain the suffering innocent, put upon by insidious horrors creeping in from East or West (be it, allegedly, devils, Mongols, capitalist predators, Jesuits or Jews). Then, as now: an unfathomably mysterious historical fate, or sheer paranoia?

Alongside western perceptions of Russia, therefore, the issue arises of Russian perceptions of the West – not just socio-philosophical (as in the case of Russian Westernisers or Slavophiles), but also military. It should be remembered that, in the period from 1812 to 1941, Russia was attacked five times by western powers: in the Napoleonic, Crimean and both world wars, as well as the intervention on behalf of the White forces in the Russian Civil War of 1918–21, in addition to two attacks by Japan. At the same time, the Russian Empire (subsequently the Soviet Union and now the still vast Russian Federation – albeit reduced in 1991 to a size comparable to that enjoyed in the seventeenth century), as we have seen, did not achieve its overwhelming scale without doing its own fair share of invading and subduing, including the invasions and annexations conducted under the cloak of the Nazi–Soviet pact. Peter the Great's wars apart, Russia had enthusiastically participated in European wars under Elizabeth (the Seven Years War) and Catherine II (the partition of Poland and Suvorov's campaigns against the French), up to and including the invasion of East Prussia and Austrian Galicia in the earlier stages of the First World War. As recently as 1979, on the occasion of the Soviet invasion of Afghanistan, Western strategists were concerning themselves with the (albeit unlikely) prospect of a Soviet-Russian pathway to the Indian Ocean (an old nineteenth-century fear, along with domination of the Bosphorus). Near the end of the twentieth century, the spectre of Pan-Slavism rose again over the former Yugoslavia (or rather Pan-Orthodoxy, as Russian sympathies appear to confine themselves to Serbia).

The rise of nationalism through the nineteenth and at the turn of the twentieth century, and renewed bouts of Russophobia, made their contribution to the causes of the massive European catastrophe of the First World War; the fall of the Old Regimes was vigorously fuelled too by what Malia notes as the 'device' of universal military service (which had come to Russia in 1874). In Russia's case, a disastrous entry and a fatal continued participation in this convulsion had been preceded by an attempted post-1906 reversion to the kind of national conservatism established under the reign of Nicholas I. The resulting process, in a climate of public unrest and thwarted constitutional reform, given the legacy of the trial run at revolution of 1905 and more than a little help after February 1917 from Lenin, was to terminate in the Bolshevik seizure of power in the October Revolution.

Throughout the Soviet era of Russian history (1917–91), ideology vied with power politics as the principal bone of contention between Russia and the Western powers, culminating in superpower rivalry and the protracted arms race with the US-dominated NATO of the post-World War Two period. The early 'revolutionary' political and relatively pluralist cultural phase of the new society was soon curbed into the Stalinist straitjackets of 'socialism in one country' and 'socialist realism' respectively, with worse to follow, in the shape of famine, the purges and 'the Great Patriotic War'. Peter the Great's window to the West was now blocked by the descent of the 'Iron Curtain'. A society based on the illusion of the masses in power revealed an increasing gap between pretension and performance. For decades all internal opposition in the Soviet Union remained eclipsed and critical analyses of its system could only be carried out in the West; from the late 1960s, however, this changed, as dissident Russian voices from within again began to be heard. Nevertheless, sovietologists of all persuasions failed to foresee the collapse of the USSR in anything like the form or the timing in which it occurred, and are still struggling towards comprehension and explanation.

What Malia classes as the four classical images of Russia pirouetted across decades of analysis of the the phenomenon of the Soviet Russian Communist state. Two of these may have largely fallen back into the realms of mythic fantasy; two others acquired more serious advocacy. The religious thinker Nikolai Berdiaev saw Bolshevik Communism as the Russian soul inverted (an 'upside-down Russian soul, the realm of cosmic demonism'). Others preferred to see in it a manifestation of 'eternal Russia', a permanently mutating Byzantine-Muscovite autocracy (which, of course, may well yet re-emerge in post-Soviet form). Greater academic following, however, has been achieved by the 'convergence' and the 'totalitarian-ism' models. The former tendency foresaw a medium- to long-term process of Soviet convergence with the economic and political ethos of the West: in other words, the system was reformable, with a form of 'enlightened despotism' inevitably bringing in modernization. This argument was favoured by 'revisionist' Marxists (such as the historian Roy Medvedev within Russia, and those Western commentators perceived as liberal-leftist 'doves'). The totalitarianist argument, propounded by the 'hawks', conservative Western politicians and their academic acolytes, often themselves of East European provenance, as well as by nationalists and traditionalists from within Russia (or its third wave of emigration, such as Solzhenitsyn) regarded the Soviet state as an 'Evil Empire' spawned by atheistic Marxism out of Oriental despotism: irredeemable and non-reformable, dangerous and utopian, it would remain essentially 'other'.

The convergence-reformist case, while hitting the hardline buffers of repression several times (Hungary in 1956, Czechoslovakia in 1968, Poland more than once), appeared finally to be on course for conceivable success with the development of Mikhail Gorbachev's policies of economic acceleration, *perestroika* and glasnost. However, ensuing economic chaos and the events of 1991 (the end of the USSR and the inauguration of a reduced Commonwealth of Independent States) were to leave this thesis abandoned, and at best unproven. The doctrine of full and immutable totalitarianism, consistently overstated (at least in the post-Stalin period), while producing tactics (surges in the arms race, especially the threat posed by the Strategic Defence Initiative) that undoubtedly helped precipitate economic problems, also turned out to be less than fully accurate, in that the Soviet 'experiment' ultimately showed itself at least to be reversible. Stalinist 'socialism in one country' had been economically viable in mid-century, albeit surrounded by a largely hostile world; Brezhnevite 'socialism in one imperial superpower bloc', however, later in the century eventually proved a busted flush.

Advocated more recently by commentators such as Vladimir Shlapentokh is the more 'detached' (and value-free) approach of regarding the Soviet Union as a 'normal totalitarian society' (though some might counter that that in itself was precisely *why* it collapsed so unexpectedly). The totalitarianism indubitably weakened over the second half of its existence; the 'normality' is attested by the ability of the system to function and reproduce itself over the duration of three quarters of a century, while the 'normal' aspirations of the regime were directed at self-preservation and enlargement of its geopolitical role. In addition, it might be added, successive Soviet governments behaved 'normally' by not precipitating a nuclear conflict. The two peaks in Soviet history, according to Shlapentokh, were reached in the late 1940s, with the expansion of empire after the defeat of Germany, and the mid 1970s, when military parity with the West was reached, along with the considerable Soviet achievements in education and science. However the Soviet economic system was unable in the longer run to compete with a developed Western market economy and it contained within itself the elements of corruption and criminality that were to burgeon over its last years – and massively so from 1991. Moreover, Malia points to a lack by the 1980s of a structured civil society. Other factors not to be left unstressed include the cultural and ideological impact of glasnost (the 'opening' up of media, culture and in particular literature from 1987) and the difficulty of preserving a 'closed' society against the march of the microchip.

It is debatable whether post-Soviet Russia, after several years of economic 'shock therapy', is now to be perceived as any more 'normal', with its reduced standard of living and quality of life (certain freedoms notwithstanding) for the vast bulk of the population. It may yet, nevertheless, maintain a sort of stability as a heterogeneous society with what are seen (by Shlapentokh) as four major interacting layers: the bureaucratic, the liberal (in the sense of free-market and 'democratic' institutions), the oligarchic (an élite class of tycoons) and the criminal. A stark warning of the international threat posed by the latter (collectively known as 'the Russian Mafia') was delivered in his last book by Andrei Siniavsky. What many historians now like to see as an interrupted transition to modernity was thus resumed, albeit in extremely haphazard fashion, under Boris Yeltsin, while President Putin – still against tremendous odds – is presumed to be pursuing the task of building, or rebuilding, an effective and independent centralized state. In some senses never conscious of having built an empire, the Russians still find it difficult in the extreme to relinquish their landlocked imperial possessions (as the Chechens will attest). Meanwhile, the more surreal aspects of life in the late Soviet and post-Soviet periods continue to offer rich raw material to Russia's artistic culture, while the grand narrative of Russian history, of course, had its counterpart throughout in the evolution of Russian literature.

The Scythian horsemen of ancient times, it is said, drank the blood of warriors they had slain. The blood of the Scythians, or at least their mythic aura, has retained a certain potency in the cultural ethos of Russia to this day. From similarly distant epochs, pagan and folkloric traditions have played an enduring role. The advent of literacy, with the conversion of the Kievan state to Greek Christianity in AD 988, brought Byzantine (Greek and early Christian) religious and secular texts into the orbit of the Eastern Slavs. It was to be some time, however, before further foreign influences penetrated Russian letters to any appreciable degree. Russia experienced no Renaissance and was more or less catapulted from medieval Rus' into 'modern' post-Petrine culture. The medieval period of Russian literature lasted, therefore, most commentators would say, until the end of the seventeenth century and European artistic movements, if they hit Russia at all, tended to do so with a considerable time-lag. Indigenous literary output, for much of this extended early and early modern period, was confined to sermons, saints' lives and chronicles – and subject, by and large, to the restrictions of devotional art (icon painting providing the obvious example). The notion of secular learning and even of devotional art itself – and certainly of any innovations therein – as 'potentially demonic or idolatrous' (as stressed by Pamela Davidson) was present from very nearly the earliest days of Russian culture.

The single acknowledged literary masterpiece (at least, on a European scale) is the anonymous twelfth-century epic poem, *The Lay* [or *Song*] *of Igor's Campaign* (*Slovo o polku Igoreve*), discovered only in the late eighteenth century, and described by Vladimir Nabokov (in the Foreword to his translation) as 'a harmonious, many leveled, many hued, uniquely poetical structure created in a sustained and controlled surge of inspiration by an artist with a fondness for pagan gods and a percipience of sensuous things'.

As time went on, travel tales and exotica entered the literature and, in the seventeenth century, the beginnings of a recognizable prose fiction, in the form of the picaresque tale and (via Polish influence) the syllabo-tonic verse of Simeon Polotsky. That century was above all momentous for the schism in the Russian Orthodox Church, leaving a rump population of 'Old Believers' that produced the literary work of the century (and one of the principal literary monuments of pre-Petrine Russia), *The Life of the Archpriest Avvakum by Himself* (*Zhitie protopopa Avvakuma, im samim napisannoe*), and had its own further lingering influence on Russian culture.

The eighteenth century, with the opening of Peter the Great's 'window on the West', saw a rapid influx of Western models and influences, especially of neo-classical literary forms imported from France. French, as we have seen, became the court language, while the next significant monarch, Catherine the Great, was herself a German (and a usurper) and a correspondent of the French Enlightenment's *philosophes*. In this period the Russian literary language (in something approaching its modern form) was struggling to establish itself. The poetic *oeuvre* of Derzhavin and the pre-Romantic prose of Karamzin (first as story-writer, then as court historian) supplied the most significant literary landmarks

7

until the advent of the first towering figure of Russian literature and master of many genres, Aleksandr Pushkin.

Literary styles were evolving in Russia, in the wake of various strands of European Romanticism, with native forms beginning to push out the translations and imitations (initially from the French, but increasingly also from the English and German) that had long dominated the reading habits of the Russian gentility. Historical novels, narrative poems, travel literature, adventure stories, society tales and Gothic stories all featured in the process that established Russian literature, in the second quarter of the nineteenth century, as the newly emerging and most vibrant national literature of Europe. This was soon evident in the lyric and narrative poetry of the 'Golden Age', and in at least a few isolated works of drama, but above all in the impressive prose forms of the short story (*rasskaz*), the novella (or longer story, the *povest'*) and, finally and most famously, the novel itself (*roman*).

At first this came in hybrid forms. Pushkin's *Evgenii Onegin* (a 'novel in verse'), was joined by Lermontov's *A Hero of Our Time* (*Geroi nashego vremeni*, structurally a cycle of stories), Gogol''s *Dead Souls* (*Mertvye dushi*, an un-completed trilogy, subtitled 'a poem'), Odoevsky's *Russian Nights* (*Russkie nochi*, a fictional-cum-philosophical frame-tale) and Dostoevsky's *Poor Folk* (*Bednye liudi*, an epistolary novel). However, all of these were engaged, in one fashion or another, with the Russia of their time and by mid-century the Russian novel as we know it was taking serious shape, at the hands of Goncharov, Turgenev, Dostoevsky and Tolstoy. The latter's epic *War and Peace* can be seen to encompass all the prose ingredients mentioned above, including more than a trace of the macaronic linguistic mélange still pertaining in Russian aristocratic circles, while *Anna Karenina* springs forth as the 'society-tale' novel *par excellence*. In the course of these same decades, such types as 'superfluous men', 'repentant noblemen', strong heroines, and then figures of mixed rank or origin (*raznochintsy*) were not only reflected fictionally, but were making their presence felt in the formation of what was becoming recognizable as the Russian intelligentsia. In this heyday of autocracy, Orthodoxy and nationality (*narodnost'* – at this stage a sort of crude 'kvass', or, as Nabokov might say, 'birch-stump' patriotism), the 'accursed questions' were being widely broached (the tsarist censorship notwithstanding) and the unstoppable rise of the Russian novel soon led it into renowned and unprecedented areas of psychological realism.

This period of major literary and political events gave way, as the last quarter of the century wore on, to a temporarily 'quieter' period, amid political reaction and a dominance of minor literary forms. The turn of the century, however, brought an artistic resurgence credited as the 'Silver Age', in which a strong neo-Romantic Russian Symbolist movement (of which Blok and Bely are commonly adjudged the leading exponents) embraced various strands of European modernism, while realism acquired a more naturalist hue. Russian theatre (graced with the innovations of Chekhov and Stanislavsky), music and painting came to world notice as a pan-European avant-gardism gathered pace. Again a generic and stylistic mix held sway as Symbolism yielded to the Acmeist and Futurist reactions in poetry, and 'revolutionary realism' or 'neo-realism' (a synthesis of materialist and idealist aesthetics) in prose. In the 'nightmarish atmosphere' of the interlude between the 1905 and 1917 revolutions, many writers and thinkers (as Aileen M. Kelly has put it), 'devoid of a sense of history, . . . lived in eschatological time'.

After the October Revolution, the well-established Russian relationship between literature and ideology (of whatever stripe) soon became menacingly overt. Artistic experimentation became increasingly suspect, and subsequently unacceptable, as the conservative artistic tastes of the new political and cultural élite regrouped under the banner of 'socialist realism' (recreating, under 'Party, ideological spirit and [now Soviet] nationality', an almost parodic version of the old nineteenth-century triadic mantra of 'autocracy, Orthodoxy and nationality'). For that matter, as Aileen Kelly has stressed, many of the proponents of a rationalist utopian idyll among the post-revolutionary avant-garde proved less tolerant of ideological deviation than the more sophisticated of the Bolshevik leadership in the 1920s (such as Trotsky, Lunacharsky or Bukharin) and, 'in their urge to harness art to political purposes, freely colluded in the mass manipulation that set the stage for Stalin's advent and their own destruction'. Official Soviet writing, while producing some works of artistic merit in the relatively tolerant twenties, and even in the much more inhibited thirties, had reached such a degree of tedium by the early fifties (fuelled by the introduction of 'conflictlessness' into literature and the so-called 'varnishing of reality') that even its own political sponsors felt moved to advocate a limited shake-up. Escapist genres (fantasy and science fiction) began to fill some of the gap. The Khrushchev 'Thaw' years and the long 'period of stagnation' under Brezhnev saw a moderate revival in worthwhile literary production, with a broadening of the socialist realist aesthetic (to encompass a kind of 'socialist realism of exposure', at least of minor 'shortcomings') and a selective tolerance of works paying lip-service (if any service) to a weakening ideological dominance: 'Youth Prose', 'Village Prose', 'Urban Prose', *mauvism* (or deliberately 'bad' prose) and a considerable resurgence of poetry. The 'literary process' was back in serious business.

Meanwhile, in most estimations, more significant literature was being produced either 'unofficially' within Soviet Russia, or by writers living in emigration. Publication of works in the former category (foremost novels and poetry by perceived political doubtfuls of past or present) was frequently delayed for decades – in many cases until the introduction of Gorbachev's policy of glasnost in the later years of the 1980s. Bulgakov's *The Master and Margarita* (*Master i Margarita*, written from 1928 to 1940), now widely considered the supreme Russian novel of the twentieth century, was unheard of until the 1960s and published in full only in 1973; it is now receiving wider recognition in the form of York Holler's opera, *Der Meister und Margarita*. *Doctor Zhivago*, Pasternak's novel of the revolutionary era, most widely known through David Lean's 1965 film, may be seen as a litmus test of Soviet cultural liberality in both the Thaw period (with its notorious prohibition in 1957–8) and, thirty years later, in that of glasnost (with, finally, its first Soviet publication in 1988). In emigration, Russian literature made certain advances, impeded only through its own auspices, under the first wave of emigration (following 1917), and to a lesser extent under the second (following the displacement of peoples occasioned by World War Two). Eminent writers (such as Ivan Bunin, soon to be a Nobel laureate) completed their careers in the émigré centres of Western Europe, where younger aspirants initiated or developed theirs (Vladimir Nabokov being the leading example). Emigré journals and publishing houses made a significant impact on the production of Russian literature. In the 1970s and early 80s, Soviet cultural policy of deporting or exiling dissident creative figures to the West gave rise to a prolific third wave (which included such leading lights as Brodsky, Siniavsky and Solzhenitsyn). Important new (or 'newish') writers who made their literary reputations in emigration include the novelists Vladimir Maksimov (who, after an earlier career as a Soviet writer, published his main works in the West and edited the influential literary and publicistic journal *Kontinent* in Paris), Sasha Sokolov and Zinovii Zinik. The question of the existence of 'one or two Russian literatures' (published 'here' or 'there', or disseminated illegally in the Soviet Union) was in the event resolved by the subsequent publication under glasnost of almost all writers previously banned, exiled, disgraced or ignored (first the safely dead, and then the living).

In 1991, shortly before the collapse of the Soviet Union as a political entity, the citizens of Leningrad voted to return to their city its original name. This, apart from anything else, ensured a revival of the singular tradition of the 'St Petersburg theme' of literary demonism in Russian literature, linked to the figure of Peter and to his city (established by Pushkin, Gogol', Odoevsky, Dostoevsky and Bely – to name but a few). The more innovative forms of dissident and third-wave émigré writing (as opposed to a more traditional mirror-image anti-socialist realism) gained ground too in the new openness within the metropolitan culture of the last Soviet years with something of a renaissance in experimental forms (although more hackneyed styles retain a certain popularity). Postmodernism soon became a buzz word in late Soviet and post-Soviet culture, with such groupings as the Conceptualists to the fore, and absurdism and the grotesque having made notable inroads. Nevertheless, Russian literature continues to weave a powerful and intricate tapestry of an almost narcissitic intertextuality, for which its own past and its own texts, as ever, supply the cardinal fibre. The irresistible relish for a belated appropriation and recapitulation of the artistic freedoms long available in the West soon saw the breaking of just about all the previous (seemingly eternal) taboos: moral and linguistic, as well as political. Perhaps the only traditional value (inherited from tsarist and Soviet culture alike) still to command any serious degree of artistic sacrosanctity is Russian patriotism.

As long ago as 1849, just a year after publication of the Communist Manifesto (we are reminded by Kelly), Aleksandr Herzen remarked that nobody should expect the victory of socialism to provide a conclusive solution to society's problems; instead, socialism would generate its own inner contradictions and absurdities, as a result of which 'a mortal struggle will begin, in which socialism will play the role of contemporary conservatism, and be overwhelmed in the subsequent revolution, as yet unknown to us'. However one may choose to regard the Soviet and East European brands of 'socialism' offered to the world between 1917 and 1989–91, Herzen's prescience would be hard to deny. We cannot know what surprises the new Russia must yet have in store; nor can we even begin to predict the course of Russian literature over its second millennium.

FURTHER READING

See the histories of Russian literature etc. in the General Bibliography, plus:

Barabtarlo, Gennady (ed.) *Cold Fusion: Aspects of the German Cultural Presence in Russia*, New York and Oxford: Berghahn Books, 2000.

Davidson, Pamela (ed.) *Russian Literature and its Demons*, New York and Oxford: Berghahn Books, 2000.

Haumant, Emile. *La Culture française en Russie (1700–1900)*, 2nd edition, Paris: Hachette, 1913. Reprinted Cambridge, Oriental Research Partners, 1971.

Hayward, Max. 'Introduction', to Chloe Obolensky, *The Russian Empire: A Portrait in Photographs*, London: Jonathan Cape, 1980, pp. 3–19. Reprinted in his *Writers in Russia, 1917–1978*, ed. Patricia Blake, London: Harvill Press, 1983.

Kelly, Aileen M. *Toward Another Shore: Russian Thinkers Between Necessity and Chance*, New Haven and London: Yale University Press, 1998.

Malia, Martin. *Russia Under Western Eyes: From the Bronze Horseman to the Lenin Mausoleum*, Cambridge, Mass.: The Belknap Press of Harvard University, 2000.

Shlapentokh, Vladimir. 'A Normal System? False and true explanations for the collapse of the USSR', *TLS* 15 December 2000, 11–13.

Sinyavsky, Andrei. *The Russian Intelligentsia*, trans. Lynn Visson, New York: Columbia University Press, 1997.

Thompson, Ewa M. *Imperial Knowledge: Russian Literature and Colonialism*, Westport, Connecticut: Greenwood Press, 2000.

2

OLD RUSSIAN LITERATURE AND ITS HERITAGE

ROBIN MILNER-GULLAND

In the eyes of the world Russian literature is perhaps the chief glory of Russian culture. What the world knows, above all, is the classic Russian novel, whose great age was amazingly brief – a mere quarter century, all within the reign of Alexander II (1855–81), which saw the publication of the best works of Tolstoy, Dostoevsky, Turgenev, and Goncharov. Those with a deeper interest might extend their knowledge back to the time of Pushkin and Lermontov in the early nineteenth century, and forward to Chekhov and the modernist Silver Age – around a century altogether – so becoming aware that Russian literature has more to it than blockbuster narratives: in particular an intensely-developed poetic tradition. Few outsiders (and not all Russians) understand, however, how deeply *literaturnost'* ('literariness') has been ingrained in Russian cultural consciousness over the thousand years since the Conversion, or realize that what is usually called Old Russian literature forms part of a distinctive tradition whose effects are far from being exhausted yet. Of course the forms of sophisticated literature, like the forms of upper-class behaviour, were changed radically and forcibly after Peter the Great's westernizing measures, but many underlying older principles remained intact, to be revealed in numerous ways as time went on.

Analogous situations can clearly be seen in the other sophisticated art-forms: painting, sculpture, architecture and music. In each, wholesale innovations of form, genre, and purpose apparently swept away 'medieval' artistic systems. It may be, however, that literature, embedded as it must be in practices of language, is less susceptible than other arts to the sudden and complete imposition of new methods. Whatever the reasons, mid-eighteenth-century writers such as Vasilii Trediakovsky and Mikhail Lomonosov, themselves propagators of western literary forms, had considerable interest in the literary tradition they were engaged in remodelling, an interest redoubled at the turn of the century with the generation of Aleksandr Radishchev, the Decembrists, and subsequently of Pushkin and his contemporaries, when the issue of 'Russianness' in literature came into sharp focus. It was then, too, that a growing antiquarian and historical interest in the manuscript heritage of Old Russia was galvanized by the sensational discovery (c. 1795) of a complex, subtle, and highly original work thought to date from the twelfth century, *The Lay of Igor's Campaign* (*Slovo o polku Igoreve*), raising questions about the nature and aesthetic qualities of Old Russian literature that have been with us ever since.

To discuss this literature in any detail would take a volume or several volumes. The purpose of the present essay is to fit it into the larger picture of Russian literary and cultural history: so I intend chiefly to give a fresh (if necessarily generalized) view of the diachronic nature of the literary experience in Russia.

First, some preliminary observations have to be made. The term Old Russian Literature, near-universal in scholarly usage, needs to be employed with caution. It (with its variants Early or Medieval Russian literature) is a temporal designation, tying literary development to historical periodization. Taken as implying that literature of the Old Russian period (i.e. up to Peter the Great's reforms) is quali-tatively separate from what came afterwards, the term is misleading. Modern literary forms (i.e. like those of the baroque in other parts of Europe) are observable in Russian literature from at least the early seventeenth century (even if they do not lead to masterpieces of European quality), within a still largely medieval literary system, whose after-effects, as suggested above, in turn long outlive the end of Old Russia itself. I propose instead the coinage Russian Traditional Literature as a conceptual rather than periodic term.

There is far more traditional (or Old) Russian literature than is usually thought, and plenty of it remains unpublished. Two works from the time of Ivan IV (ruled 1533–84) have more than 20,000 pages each in manuscript. More significantly, there are literally thousands of chronicles from the early twelfth to the eighteenth century originating from a large number of local centres, often small or remote; hundreds of versions of oral epic poems have been transcribed; and we must not forget the hundreds or thousands of translated religious and learned works, mostly of Byzantine origin, that were the bedrock of sophisticated traditional literature. Despite the large quantity of works that remain, we also know for certain of some that have not survived, and can postulate the former existence of many other lost works. There are probably still significant rediscoveries to be made: several important early works have been discovered in single copies in modern times. As for the durability of traditional Russian literature, one may mention as a curiosity the fact that there are still so-called Old Believer communities in out-of-the-way areas where a manuscript tradition of religious polemics in an essentially seventeenth-century vein has persisted to the present. More significantly, the guru of modernist Russian poetics, Velimir Khlebnikov (1885–1922), could claim to be the culminating 'Old' Russian writer (to the extent that he purged from his work all vocabulary of west European origin). The poet Osip Mandel'shtam wrote admiringly of him that 'he cannot distinguish which is nearer, the railway bridge or *The Lay of Igor's Campaign.*' Khlebnikov's followers, who extend to the present generation (e.g. Viktor Sosnora), have shown the continuing vitality of his example, and his influence has rippled outwards to affect much modern Russian writing. Even had Khlebnikov never lived, through Aleksei Remizov and other writers the older Russian traditions of 'literariness' would have been revived and given credibility for the twentieth century, and doubtless beyond.

The next general point that must be made about traditional Russian literature is that it existed in two great complementary spheres: the 'visible' and the 'invisible', in other words the written and the oral. Historians, for obvious reasons, concentrate on the former, admitting the latter only when (as with oral epics, the so-called *byliny*) it achieved permanent 'visible' embodiment by being written down – often in confusing multiple variants and probably several centuries after the work first arose. Early Russians perceived, it seems, the distinctiveness, but also the complementary nature of each of these spheres, allotting them separate roles (so that, for example, lyric poetry is absent from written literature until the seventeenth century, though evidently abundant in the Russian experience in the form of folksong). It would be tempting, but wrong, to equate these two spheres, written and oral, with the 'sacred' and 'profane' respectively. Although the written word often carried overtones of sacredness it was also used for entirely humdrum practical purposes (and the boundary between the literary and the non-literary is particularly hard to draw in a pre-modern age). Unwritten, oral literary creativity, by contrast, derives in direct descent from pre-Christian Rus', and never ceased to carry undertones of 'pagan' folk belief – though, as the centuries passed, it also acquired a multitude of Christian motifs, often strangely metamorphosed and 'folkified'. So while to some extent a sacred/profane, or more profoundly, a Christian/pagan dichotomy can be observed in Russian traditional literariness, it cannot wholly or permanently be equated with the written/unwritten spheres. In fact the conceptual world of oral literature subtly and significantly penetrated the writing in Christianized Rus', and lent a specifically Russian colouration to some of its best monuments: whether, for example, through turns of speech, proverbs or epic fragments in the early chronicles, through the stylized evocation of pagan divinities in *The Lay of Igor's Campaign*; through the wit and wordplay of *The Petition of Daniil the Exile* (*Molenie Daniila Zatochnika*); the ecstatic transformation of peasant lamentation in Epifanii's *The Life of St Stephen of Perm* (*Zhitie Stefana Permskogo*); the overtones of heroic epos in various military tales; the 'folkishness' of many aspects of Avvakum's autobiography; the chilling evocation and personification of the popular conception of human destiny in *Tale of Woe-Misfortune* (*Gore-Zlochastie*); or the fairy-tale motifs of *Peter and Fevronia of Murom* (*Povest' o Petre i Fevronii*). More generally, many stylistic features – types of antithesis and parallelisms, paratactic structures, riddling formulations, stock epithets – enter even sophisticated traditional literature from the folk sphere. The question of reverse influence, from the written to the oral, is harder to assess, but such influence was probably felt to some degree at least in the last century of Old Russia and indeed the first after Peter the Great; as Dmitrij Čiževskij writes, in the baroque age 'The novel turns into a fairy-tale in short-story form, the love poem into a popular song, the religious lyric into a "spiritual song."'

A corollary to my suggested way of perceiving traditional Russian 'literariness' is that literature is no longer to be regarded as simply the business of the literate segment of society. Much scholarly ingenuity has gone into trying to establish what proportion of the Old Russian population could read and write (in sixteenth-century Muscovy it may have been below five per cent, but much higher, for example in pre-Tartar Novgorod). Such figures, even if they could be reliably established, would not have any readily ascertainable cultural significance. The written sphere of literature – at least its dominant religious component – was suffused even among the illiterate through readings in churches, in monastic refectories, and in princely courts; oral literature – whether through folk-tales and songs, oral epos, the performance of itinerant minstrels (*skomorokhi*) – would have reached the entire population of pre-modern Russia without exception, however much it may have been frowned upon by the authorities and the Church.

The last, and largest, of these general observations concerns the most fundamental and individual aspect of the world of Russian traditional literature, that of its language. The arrival of Christianity in Rus' was accompanied by the new religion's inseparable concomitant, a fully fledged literary language known to us as Old Church Slavonic. The 'Apostles to the Slavs', Cyril and Methodius, with their assistants, devised Old Church Slavonic as a written language to express the conceptual world of the Bible, the Church Fathers, theology, and late-antique 'high culture' generally (through complex structures and a large abstract vocabulary, for example), basing this language on the South Slav speech of the hinterland of Thessaloniki, from which they came. At the time (mid-ninth century) the south, west, and east Slav dialects, later each to give birth to several distinct languages, were sufficiently close to be mutually comprehensible, and the apostles' translations (and, soon, original texts) were of equal use in Moravia – for which they were first commissioned – Bulgaria and, over a century later, Russia. Thus the written language for religious and translated literature generally was not exclusive to Rus': it constituted, in Likhachev's phrase, a 'Byzantine–Slav cultural milieu', 'a sort of common culture for the southern and eastern Orthodox Slav lands that evolved simultaneously as a single totality in various Slavonic countries as a result of the transplantation of Byzantine culture into them . . . a supra-national cultural milieu'. Riccardo Picchio and others have called this community *Slavia Orthodoxa*, 'Orthodox Slavdom'.

How did Church Slavonic relate to the spoken and eventually written language of the east Slavs, the progenitor of Russian, Ukrainian, and Belorussian? At the time of the Conversion they still had large areas of vocabulary, phonology, and morphology in common, while such differences as existed were of a regular and easily comprehended nature. Syntactically, Old Church Slavonic was partly based on the Greek from which most of its literature was derived. But while over the centuries Old Russian evolved in syntax and vocabulary, shedding some complexities of its grammar, Church Slavonic, fixed in the forms established in the canonical religious texts, underwent no significant changes. At the end of the Old Russian period, Ludolf's pioneering grammar of Russian (published in Oxford in 1696) could state in a famous formulation that 'loquendum est Russice & scribendum est Slavonice' (Russian is for speaking and Slavonic for writing), going on to point out that nowhere in the world was Slavonic actually a spoken language.

Ludolf's dictum, together with the modern perception of Russian and Church Slavonic as separate languages, can lead to a serious misunderstanding of the subtle and idiosyncratic linguistic situation in Rus'. In most European countries the early-medieval language of religion and scholarship was the international medium of Latin; vernacular literatures emerged only slowly and haphazardly towards the end of the Middle Ages (save where, as in some Nordic lands, oral epos and similar folk-works were transcribed in written versions). The role of Church Slavonic in Russia and other Orthodox Slav lands looks similar to that of Latin in the parts of Europe dominated by the patriarchate of Rome (the Papacy); but the resemblance is superficial. From its pre-Christian past, Latin carried the weighty baggage of the largest and most diverse literature the world had ever seen (leaving aside the socio-political pretensions wrapped up in this baggage): it was a fully-developed linguistic system usable in a multitude of registers from the poetic and rhetorical to the colloquial and legalistic. Church Slavonic, by contrast, was created to be a written language with the express purpose of transmitting the sacred Word to the Slavs. It proved in practice a flexible instrument for the creation of new words as well as the translation of pre-existing material, not all overtly religious. But it remained in its essence a sacred language, occasioning awe, respect, and considerable pride among the Orthodox Slavs – their main highway to salvation. Unlike Latin among west and central Europeans, it was not sensed by its users as 'other'. Specialists often still write as if an 'Old Russian literary language' existed side-by-side with Church Slavonic, the two available for use as the writer's choice or the task to be fulfilled dictated. But this would have astonished an early Russian, who did not even have the term Church Slavonic at his disposal. Far from being linguistically alien to him, what we call Church Slavonic was perceived as the time-hallowed, lofty register of Russian – its 'bookish' (without modern pejorative connotations) version.

The contemporary scholar Boris Uspensky has brilliantly analysed the fundamental 'diglossia' that characterized this linguistic situation, at any rate until the mid-seventeenth century when the modern attitude that gave rise to Ludolf's comment became widespread. Until then diglossia meant that translation (and parody) was impossible between Russian and Church Slavonic: they fulfilled functionally different roles within what was felt to be a single language. That does not mean, however, that the distinction between them was not powerfully felt; after all, the 'bookish' language had to be learnt, had fixed and 'correct' forms, was a microcosm of the divine order, while Russian vernacular language forms were unstable, unregulated, 'undivine', and hence potentially pagan or devilish. As Uspensky puts it:

> The specific character of the Russian linguistic, and more broadly cultural consciousness consists for the most part in the fact that here – in the functioning of diglossia as a linguistic and cultural mechanism – there exists no zone that is semantically neutral and which does not make reference to the sacred sphere. Hence, an absence of a connection with the sacred, the Divine, basically signifies a connection with its opposite, with the world of the Devil.

Uspensky gives some startling and thought-provoking examples (in Russian folk-tradition, we learn, the Devil loves to be called *chert*, the Russian word for him, and dreads the Slavonic term *bes*). Nonetheless there were perfectly legitimate areas for the use of written vernacular Russian: for practical purposes (decrees, laws, letters, ambassadorial messages, etc.) and – from the point of view of literary development most interestingly – in contexts where it is mixed to a greater or lesser degree with Slavonicisms. Sometimes this mixing is well-demarcated: thus in Epifanii's *The Life of St Stephen of Perm*, basically written in Slavonic, the Permian sorcerer who figures in its climactic scene speaks Russian (Uspensky likewise cites Russophone Chaldeans in the 'mystery play', derived from the Book of Daniel, that was performed in cathedrals). Often, though, such stylistic mixing could be more complicated, with subtler purposes: thus stylistically marked Slavonicisms can achieve lofty effects or suggest biblical reminiscences in chronicles or military tales whose language is fundamentally the Russian vernacular; the author who calls himself Daniil the Exile deliberately combines popular and learned (Slavonic) language to dazzle his audience with his wit; many other instances could be adduced, involving some of the most interesting and idiosyncratic Old Russian works and genres.

In the later seventeenth century the diglossia that has been described began to be questioned: vernacular Russian had moved far enough away from Church Slavonic for them to be perceived as distinct languages. Yet neither then, nor even in the eighteenth century, when in the wake of Peter the Great's reforms the entire west European literary system was imported piecemeal to Russia, did the Russian language turn its back on its Church Slavonic heritage. Following similar attempts in France, Germany, and elsewhere, the most influential mid-eighteenth-century theorist, Mikhail Lomonosov, codified what to eighteenth-century taste seemed the chaotic literary language into three stylistic levels – 'high', 'middle', and 'low' – suitable for various genres. For Lomonosov the defining factor was to be the quantity and nature of the Slavonicisms in the vocabulary employed at each level (Church Slavonic elements that had become incomprehensible to Russians on the one hand, and crudely colloquial or dialect forms on the other, were excluded from the system altogether).

Though Lomonosov's system was too fiddly and cumbersome to be a practical guide for long – and was alien to the spirit of simplicity and spontaneity that characterized the early-Romantic age that followed that of the baroque in Russia as elsewhere – its principles were not unsound. In Pushkin's age there were still 'archaists' for whom the Slavonic component was the truly literary element in Russian, and could be made a bulwark against the flood of west Europeanism (in vocabulary, syntax, and style) that inundated Russia from Peter's time onwards; needless to say, questions of national identity were closely linked with the language question.

The further history of the problematics of the literary language shows, very briefly, that the general nineteenth-century attempt to produce a neutral, middle-of-the-road, internationally based and homogenized all-purpose language was continually liable to be subverted by a Russian partiality for folk-elements (including semi-literate speech) on the one hand, and the continuing vitality of its Slavonic component on the other. The latter was indeed strengthened by a great deal of new abstract vocabulary, Slavonic in form and derivation. The modern scholar

Boris Unbegaun was tempted to speculate in print as to whether the Russian literary language is Russian or Slavonic in essence, coming down in favour of the latter.

This problem cannot really be resolved. All one can say is that modern written Russian is a hybrid, whose 'grandparents' are normalized Russian, folk and dialect Russian, west European imports, and Church Slavonic elements. Juggling the balance between them has given modern Russian literature an extraordinary richness of texture; the reader even of classic nineteenth-century writers such as Gogol' and Dostoevsky will miss much by not appreciating it – and in translation such things can all too easily be missed. In the twentieth century a host of writers – Bely, Remizov, Babel', Platonov, and Zoshchenko are merely among the outstanding names – play brilliantly and wittily with linguistic possibilities that are, after all, rooted in the age-old Russian tradition of 'literariness'.

Early Russia did not produce any of the select group of independently-standing masterpieces that have entered the canon of 'great works' of medieval literature, accessible in theory to readers of all cultures such as *The Divine Comedy*, *The Decameron*, *The Canterbury Tales*, the lyric poems of Dafydd ap Gwilym or Li Po, the Icelandic sagas, or the *Niebelungenlied*. As far as Russia is concerned, only *The Lay of Igor's Campaign* seems to have been occasionally promoted to such status, and it fills the role rather awkwardly, despite its undeniable individuality and poetic richness. The failure of this literature to engage the world's consciousness would seem to have distinctive causes that are not really to do with intrinsic literary merit or the lack of it. The problem is that there is something curiously ungraspable about Russian traditional literature and about the individual works within it. The boundaries between 'literary' and 'unliterary' texts are even more blurred than is usual in early literatures. Indeed, in my view, the chief masterpiece of early Russian literature, *The Tale of Bygone Years*, or *Primary Chronicle* (*Povest' vremennykh let*), is a work whose literary, 'shaped' qualities are often ignored altogether. Many of these texts are extremely unstable, and in the versions that have come down to us are clearly the result of multiple editing or rewritings; they can appear in such different guises that even identifying and naming them as separate works is a contentious business. This textual instability, incidentally, is a result of the purposes and methods of literary production in pre-modern Russia, and not merely of scribal sloppiness. By contrast, canonical religious works, whose wording carried divine authority, were copied and recopied through the centuries with few, if any, changes. When the ancient norms of Church Slavonic seemed in danger of being forgotten or ignored around the late fourteenth to fifteenth centuries a powerful (though not always well-informed) movement for the restoration of its correct orthographic and other principles spread through the Orthodox Slavs. It started in the Balkans and so was cumbersomely known to Russian literary historians as the 'Second South Slavonic Influence' (the first having been in the aftermath of the Conversion), but it was paradoxically really part of a great movement of cultural renewal in the Orthodox lands, still poorly understood in its totality.

The biggest problem in the appreciation of traditional Russian literature is that of contextualizing the works in question. An out-and-out 'new critical' or indeed

Formalist approach, concentrating on the text alone, can be of little help to our understanding. It takes a conscious effort for most westerners to enter into the civilizational context of early Russia; for Russians themselves the difficulties are much less, and Russians are often familiar with their own pre-modern literature – particularly the *Primary Chronicle* and *The Lay of Igor's Campaign* – to a degree that seems to be matched in English only from the age of Shakespeare and the 'Authorized Version' of the Bible onwards.

Our cursory survey of the traditions of Russian literature would be incomplete without a brief attempt to indicate how some of its characteristics have lived on to become determinants within the apparently very different circumstances of post-Petrine – and in particular twentieth-century – Russian literary culture. I make no claim, of course, that the points listed represent all the significant features of Russia's specific 'literariness', or indeed that they are exclusive to Russia, or add up to some fully integrated picture, or are very profound. But in each case they seem to me to relate both to pre- and post-Petrine literature; if we take them all together (and there are no doubt others that could be added), we may find that collectively they help us to map out a phenomenology or 'conceptosphere' of Russian literature in its *longue durée*: something that seems seldom if ever to have been attempted. I start from rather large, perhaps banal points and move on first to others that have a more specific connection with literariness and its embodiments, then to some underlying 'psycholiterary' factors.

Implicit in much early and subsequent Russian literature is the creation of landscapes that are really mental maps or chronotopes of Rus' (and of its boundaries, physical or mental, with outsiders). Note, too, the many 'idealized landscapes' of Russian literature, whether in the *Orison on the Downfall of Russia* (*Slovo o pogibeli russkoi zemli*), Avvakum's *Life* (*Zhitie*) or Goncharov's 'Oblomovka'. Complementing this, there has been a pervasive historical concern that is really rooted in 'mythistoricism' – the creation, often spontaneous, of national myth; but by the nineteenth century, often involving its ironic or tragic juxtaposition with 'real life'. Just as characteristic is a sort of dialogue between the competing claims of history and literature for the source material. No reader of *War and Peace* can be unaware of this, but it is equally pervasive in Pushkin, Solzhenitsyn, and much other literature, and is found as far back as early saints' lives and the *Primary Chronicle*.

The ideological saturation of much Russian literature ('ideology' is to be taken in the broad, Bakhtinian sense of a world-view; patriotic and political as much as religious) is particularly obvious in the pre-Petrine and Soviet periods, but is scarcely less apparent in the eighteenth and nineteenth centuries. This may not be unsubtle or monological. Bakhtin, for example, powerfully argued a view of Dostoevsky's mature novels (and more generally of the post-Dostoevskian novel) as a polyphony of incompatible ideologized voices.

Related to this point is a frequent concern with 'great questions' (in Russian often termed *prokliatye*, 'accursed' questions!) that may be of a moral or existential kind but are, perhaps, at their most interesting when they concern identity ('who/ where/what are we?', see, for example, the first lines of the *Primary Chronicle*). Of course there has been a reaction, explicit or implicit, against this all-too-obvious trait of Russian literature among some twentieth-century writers (such as Pasternak's remarks through the mouth of Doctor Zhivago on Pushkin and Chekhov as opposed to Gogol', Tolstoy, and Dostoevsky) – but it shows no sign of abating.

Unexpectedly perhaps, Russian literature has at all stages of its history been remarkably open to outside influences, or ready to absorb large numbers of translated works. This absorption has not been indiscriminate however, and the 'life' led by translated texts (whether, for example, the Byzantine Greek history of George Hamartolos, the Orthodox *Philokalia*, Alexander Pope's *Essay on Man*, the long poems of Byron, or the stories of H.G. Wells) can have a very different significance in a Russian context, where they fulfil new cultural needs, from their original existence.

The diglossia between the Old Russian and the Slavonic elements within the written Russian language has led to tensions, uncertainties (particularly in the eighteenth century) and great expressive possibilities for Russian writers, a peculiarly Russian situation that readers of Russian literature in other countries have not always understood. The consequent omnipresent awareness of the very materials of literature has often led to a sense of 'the word' itself being the real hero of the literary work (whether, to take a few examples, the pre-Tartar *Petition of Daniil the Exile*, in large medieval rhetorical works, in Gogol', the Futurists, Khlebnikov or Platonov).

A strong awareness of what Likhachev calls 'literary etiquette', of the 'behaviour' of literature *vis-à-vis* the reader, is perhaps related to the above. It is not quite the same as conventionality, though (particularly in Old Russia) it can manifest itself through commonplaces or stereotypes, and it can for instance make the forms of twentieth-century Russian poetry look curiously conventional to the western eye. Not surprisingly, disruption of literary etiquette, especially among some twentieth-century writers, can seem highly subversive – just as using not quite the right diction and phraseology in Soviet speech could do.

By contrast, there has always been instability and mixing of genre in Russian writing. Much Old Russian literature, especially where influenced by oral folkloric models, hovers tantalizingly on the boundary between prose and poetry (this is notoriously evident in *The Lay of Igor's Campaign*, irreducible to poetic metres yet sometimes included in anthologies of verse). The literature of the nineteenth and twentieth centuries is ostensibly well-defined generically, yet such definition is often skin-deep (even Gogol''s *Dead Souls* [*Mertvye dushi*], his only 'novel', is subtitled 'epic poem', while by contrast Pushkin's *Evgenii Onegin* is a 'novel in verse'; twentieth-century writers such as Khlebnikov and Kharms no longer try to conceal their freedom from generic constraints). Indeed this erasure of boundaries operates on a larger scale still. Russian writing has always had difficulty coping with the notion that clear distinctions can be made between the literary and non-literary use of language, and many of its most characteristic works seem (by western standards) awkwardly poised between 'literature' and 'non-literature' (the Chronicles, Avvakum's autobiography, Radishchev's *A Journey from St Petersburg to Moscow* [*Puteshestvie iz Peterburga v Moskvu*], *War and Peace*, Herzen's *My Past and Thoughts* [*Byloe i dumy*] are just a few examples.) The 'practical' orientation of much Russian literature has a distinctly medieval feel.

Literature has always been open to cross-fertilization and co-operation with the other arts. The remarkable development of Russian opera from the early nineteenth century, to take one example, is neither 'literature-led' nor 'music-led' but a real partnership of music, text, and spectacle. In the pre-Petrine period, sacred literature, art, architecture, and music tended towards a single totalizing iconic vision.

Narrative structure in Russian literature of all periods is often weak, or at least as seen from the viewpoint of the western preference for neat plot structures and the rigorous operation of causality. Originality of plot seems often to have been regarded as less important than the realization of mythic or archetypal situations (Katerina Clark has compared the 'quest' motif of the typical Soviet novel to folk-tales and saints' lives). The structural tendency is for *nanizivanie*, the stringing-together of plot elements, and the very language, particularly in the early period, favours paratactic structures (which can cause insuperable problems for translators of Old Russian literature). Comparisons can again be made with Russian music, and even such sophisticated nineteenth-century composers as Musorgsky and Tchaikovsky avoided sonata form, preferring the 'stringing-together' of thematic variations. Agglomerative works tend to be the result. It is significant that the first major 'novel' in Russia, Lermontov's *A Hero of Our Time* (*Geroi nashego vremeni*), is called by its narrator 'my chain of tales'; it also happens to be a remarkable generic mixture. Again we can cite Radishchev's *Journey* and Herzen's *My Past and Thoughts*, together with one of the longest and most memorable of all 'agglomerative' works, Dostoevsky's *The Brothers Karamazov*, a ragbag of tales and tales-within-tales. Pre-Petrine folk and sophisticated literature (not only chronicle-writing) is essentially episodic and agglutinative.

A further consequence is the 'open-endedness' of much Russian literature, with its admission of apparently extraneous material and 'unfinalized', even existentialist feel. Chekhov, in his mature plays and some late stories, is the obvious exemplar here. One recalls with astonishment in this context a historical novel to which the author, Solzhenitsyn, appended a note inviting readers to send him material that might serve to correct the text. The reader is a direct participant in the literary process (*A Hero of Our Time* with its two Prefaces is also relevant here); Bakhtin's principle of 'dialogism' in the best modern literature appears nakedly. This characteristic may well be a necessary corrective to the 'ideological saturation' mentioned earlier. In Old Russian literature, 'unfinishedness' is a normal feature of the text: new material can always be added.

There has always been in Russian literature a tendency towards large forms. At its simplest this may be a story (or lyric) cycle. More innovatively, it can mean the *sverkhpovest'* ('supertale') – a term devised by Khlebnikov – whose building-blocks are diverse ordinary poems or tales, 'like a sculpture made from different coloured blocks of different stone'. Again the novels of Dostoevsky and Tolstoy ('great baggy monsters', in Henry James's well-known formulation) can be cited. In Old Russian literature, the *Primary Chronicle* is an evident predecessor of the 'supertale', but it should also be noted that virtually every early Russian literary work that we consider independent came down to us as a component part of a larger manuscript, a miscellany comprising other texts; little scholarly work on the principles of compilation of such miscellanies appears yet to have been done.

Certain literary modes and forms have acquired a special coloration in Russia from early times onwards, for example lyric forms have tended towards lamentation, epic towards celebration. The role of literary humour has been particularly significant – the 'laughter world' of Rus' as Likhachev and Panchenko called it in a famous study. Laughter can be threatening, a form of 'anti-behaviour', associated for example with carnivalistic excesses and topsy-turveydom, the 'unmasking' absurdities of holy fools, or Ivan the Terrible's corrosive and theatrical sarcasm. This dangerous aspect of laughter is never far away in Gogol', Dostoevsky, or successors in the twentieth century such as Bely (*Petersburg*), and once again was analysed by Bakhtin, who saw it as deriving from the ancient genre of 'Menippean Satire' – though in Russia it clearly also has folkloric roots. As a milder phenomenon, laughter is often a mixed emotion in Russian literature (the characteristic 'laughter through tears' of Chekhov's plays and Goncharov's *Oblomov*); but the most typical vein of humour, going back to Old Russian, is inventive paronomasia and similar word-play, assisted by the varied and unstable registers and the notorious diglossia of the Russian language.

Self-consciousness about the literary process has often led Russian authors to 'metafiction' – the examination of the literary process itself within the literary work. We may cite as examples the self-questioning of the bard of *The Lay of Igor's Campaign* as to the best mode in which to recount his story, the obsessive interest of the narrator of *A Hero of Our Time* in his position *vis-à-vis* his readers, Shklovsky's remarkable pseudo-eighteenth-century (but very 'modern') novel *Zoo, or Letters Not about Love or the Third Héloise* (*Zoo. Pis'ma ne o liubvi, ili tret'ia Eloiza*).

'Publication' of literature in Russia has never meant exclusively the printing and dissemination of books through commercial channels. Naturally in Old Russia (even after printing was introduced in the mid-sixteenth century) written literature existed almost exclusively in the form of manuscripts that were copied *ad hoc* and usually collected into miscellanies. Texts other than those considered sacred would be revised, shortened, conflated with others, modernized for whatever reasons patrons and copyists thought fit. This kind of manuscript tradition has actually continued to modern times, for polemical purposes, among some remote Old Believer communities. But *samizdat* ('self-publishing') for a limited circle of readers, in manuscript or typescript form remained a characteristic aspect of Russian literary production through the eighteenth, nineteenth, and twentieth centuries. Actual copyings and recopyings could reach almost the entire educated public quite quickly, as happened in the nineteenth century with Griboedov's play

Woe from Wit (*Gore ot uma*), and in the later Soviet period with many works. While clearly such 'self-publishing' in post-Petrine times was primarily a means of bypassing censorship, it is also a signal of a Russian view of literature less as the production of a commodity, more as the intense dialogue of a literate class (sometimes disaffected from authority) with itself.

Perhaps because of this quality of literature as dialogue, an autonomous realm of debate, there is a powerful element of intertextuality – implicit or explicit reference to other writings the reader can be assumed to recognize – in modern Russian literature; after all, as Nabokov used to point out, the whole of classic Russian literature can be housed on a few bookshelves and be familiar to the average reader. But intertextuality was a vitally important feature of Old Russian literature too. The frequent quotations from the Bible (particularly the Psalms) and writings of the Church Fathers, even in works that we might consider primarily secular in orientation, do not represent mere padding or general edification, but are generally carefully chosen to provide an eternal context to counterpoint transitory events. Within the field of Old Russian writing itself there are intertextual echoes of, for example, Ilarion's *Sermon on Law and Grace* (*Slovo 'O zakone i blagodati'*) in many subsequent works; while an astonishing example is the dependence of the various works known collectively as *Zadonshchina* (about Dmitrii Donskoi's defeat of the Tartar Mamai, 1380) on the pre-Tartar *The Lay of Igor's Campaign*.

There is equally a reliance on subtextuality, as much in Old Russian as in twentieth-century Russian writing. Modern scholars such as Picchio have shown how hidden, as well as explicit, biblical references constitute 'thematic clues' that may determine the proper reading of early texts (such clues are normally placed near the text's opening). Late medieval literature in particular is fond of intricate puzzles, allegories, codes, of the riddling method (so well known too from folksong) of periphrasis, of *not* naming the object directly: features that readers of 'difficult' modern writers such as Khlebnikov will readily recognize.

A deep and widespread subtext to all Russian literature is that of Russian folk-belief, manifest even in explicitly Christian writers such as Gogol', Dostoevsky, Kharms or Soviet writers such as Zabolotsky and Platonov. Concern with the connected concepts of *dolia* (fate, lot) and *volia* (free will, liberty), with *onnyi svet*, the realm of the dead and its relation to that of the living is especially frequent.

Finally, an enduringly persistent tradition in Russian literature, whether ancient or modern, written or oral, is that of the word as magical – note that in Old Russia 'word', *slovo*, had a broader reference than in English, implying also 'discourse' or 'piece of literature'. The opening of St John's gospel, supposedly the first item to be translated in the missionary project of St Cyril and St Methodius, is of course 'In the beginning was the Word', immediately equating the Word with the divinity and divine order. Church Slavonic, which as we have seen was an inalienable element in the diglossia of Old Russian writing, was regarded as sacred in itself, and Russia as having been made holy after its adoption. But before Christianity (and persisting after it) there were the *zagovory*, magical spells or prayer – equivalents within folk-belief. Note also the magical significance of the Scandinavian runes known to Russia's early Viking rulers. Silence, too, had a sacred significance (particularly after Hesychasm, 'quietism', was adopted as Orthodox church doctrine in the fourteenth century) – see Dostoevsky's 'Legend of the Grand Inquisitor' in *The Brothers Karamazov*. It is striking how modernists such as the Russian Futurists gave 'the word' (often the 'self-valid' or 'self-sufficient word', *samotsennoe/samovitoe slovo*) an almost supernatural significance. Maiakovsky's last poem, opening 'I know the power of words, I know the tocsin of words', is an extraordinary example, while Kharms noted in the 1930s 'I know four kinds of word-machines: poems, prayers, songs and spells'. It is not too much to suggest that the obsessive attention paid by the Soviet authorities to verbal expression derived from a deep-seated fear of the word's magic power.

FURTHER READING

Birnbaum, H. and M. Flier (eds) *Medieval Russian Culture*, vol. 1, Berkeley: University of California Press, 1984.

Brown, William Edward. *A History of Seventeenth-Century Russian Literature*, Ann Arbor: Ardis, 1980.

Čiževskij, Dmitrij. *History of Russian Literature from the Eleventh Century to the End of the Baroque*, The Hague: Mouton, 1960.

Kuskov, Vladimir. *A History of Old Russian Literature*, trans. Ronald Vroon, Moscow: Progress, 1980.

Likhachev, D.S. *A History of Russian Literature 11th–17th Centuries*, Moscow: Raduga, 1989.

Zenkovsky, Serge A. (ed. and trans.) *Medieval Russia's Epics, Chronicles, and Tales*, revised and enlarged edition, New York: Dutton, 1974.

Zguta, R. *Russian Minstrels*, Oxford: Clarendon Press, 1978.

3

RUSSIAN LITERATURE IN THE EIGHTEENTH CENTURY

W. GARETH JONES

At the beginning of the eighteenth century, Russia had no secular literary culture to compare with that of western Europe. There were no acknowledged authors. Consequently there were no readers and no publishers and presses to cater for their needs. There was a lack not only of a literary Russian language, but even of a modern typography. By the end of the century the situation had been transformed. Russia now possessed a vibrant literary culture that was part of Europe's and would produce and sustain a literary genius destined to become her national poet. Significantly Aleksandr Pushkin was born in the closing year of the eighteenth century on 6 June 1799.

What accounted for this remarkable transformation? The prime mover was Peter the Great who took over the government in 1694 with a mission to westernize his Empire and make it an equal of the most advanced states of Europe. Peter himself was no writer – unlike his later successor Catherine the Great – and few literary works appeared during his reign. His policy of rapid westernization, however, inevitably led to the emergence of a literary culture modelled on that of Europe and recognizable as 'European'. That process determined the particular development of Russian literature in the eighteenth century.

The Russia inherited by Peter had not been immune to western influence. Earlier in the seventeenth century Catholic Poles had occupied Moscow during the Time of Troubles, and the Protestant Swedish armies of Charles XII had marched through Russian lands at the beginning of Peter's reign. It was the foreign colony of western craftsmen, merchants, and mercenaries established in Moscow's Nemetskaia Sloboda (Foreign Quarter) that nurtured Peter's own enthusiasm for western ways. Peter regained for his empire extensive areas of traditional Russian lands in today's Belarus and Ukraine that had been deeply influenced by Catholic and Latin culture during long years of Polish domination.

What have come to be recognized as 'Petrine' reforms had certainly been under way before Peter's accession. But it was Peter who was acknowledged by both the contemporary opponents of his reform and its supporters to have made a decisive break with the past.

During his reign there was little evidence of the birth of a new literature. But by obliging the influential upper classes to dress in western style, attend social assemblies and acquaint themselves with western mores, Peter sought to change their outlook. By ordering the boyars to shave off their beards, Peter altered the very appearance of Russian faces. Likewise he changed the appearance of the traditional typeface used by the Russian Orthodox Church: in 1708 he created the new *grazhdanskii shrift* (civil typography) which could be used not only for technical and didactic works, but, in principle, for secular, entertaining literature. A new typeface was not the sole fundamental requirement supplied by Peter for a literary culture: other rudiments were basic education and the translation of standard textbooks. He encouraged the transformation of the Moscow Academy, previously a Church school, into a modern academy based on the one in Kiev with its tradition of teaching the classical languages and philosophy.

Russian literature developed not only under the press of these reforms but also in response to the towering personality of Peter himself, which was to act as a focus for Russian writers until the end of the century and beyond. 'Grant health, power, peace, security! / Grant this to Tsar Peter, crowned by Thee, / And to his most loyal chieftain, Ivan!' was the concluding chorus of Feofan Prokopovich's *Vladimir*, a five-act tragi-comedy on the Christianization of the Russian lands in the tenth century. Performed at the Kiev Academy in July 1705, in the presence of Peter the Great's henchman Ivan Mazeppa, *Vladimir* was a major literary *tour de force* by a young 24-year-old cleric with modern, westernizing views. Some of its salient features would remain characteristic of Russian literature throughout the century. In form, it imitated a European exemplar; in this case it drew on the established Jesuit tradition of school drama. In content, it combined eulogy of an active, reforming tsar and his supporters with a satirical attack on those obscurantist backsliders who opposed reform.

Prokopovich's *Vladimir* railed against the superstitious, ignorant, drunken, and gluttonous pagan priests of pre-Christian Russia, but these also manifested the failings of the Orthodox clerics of contemporary Russia; consequently *Vladimir* had a distinct anti-clerical and secular bias. The play, therefore, was political in its thrust, as much of eighteenth-century Russian literature would prove to be. Significantly Prokopovich's outlook had been determined by his background and education. Born in Kiev in 1681, he had received his early education at the city's Academy which had long been subject to Latinate influences. Like other brilliant students, he then pursued his studies at Jesuit colleges in Polish territory before being sent to Rome; here he completed in 1701 three years of study at the 'Greek College', where the Vatican trained men for its mission in eastern Europe. He returned to Kiev to re-embrace Orthodoxy, critical of the Papacy yet deeply influenced by western ways of thought and committed to support for the Petrine plans for modernizing Russia to enable her to rank alongside other European nations.

The pattern of Prokopovich's upbringing and education was repeated in the lives of the other prominent and influential Russian writers in the next generation. Also coming from the periphery of the Russian Empire with ready access to the outside world, they would spend a vital, shaping period of their life in western Europe. These were Antiokh Kantemir (1708–44), Vasilii Trediakovsky (1703–69), and Mikhail Lomonosov (1711–65).

Kantemir was the son of a Moldavian prince, Dmitrii Kantemir, a renowned scholar who had written a Latin history of the Ottoman Empire and had come to

Moscow as a political émigré. Naturally gifted, nurtured in a cultured home and acquainted with classical Greek and Latin literature, Antiokh Kantemir was exceptional enough to be sent first to London in 1732 as Russian envoy, and then as Ambassador to Paris in 1738. Trediakovsky was the son of a priest in Astrakhan on the Caspian Sea where Italian Capuchins had established a Catholic mission. It was from them that he received his early education, a grounding in Greek and Latin and exposure to western culture. After two years in Moscow at the Slavo-Greco-Latin Academy, he went abroad in 1725 to study first at The Hague and then from 1726–30 at the University of Paris. Here he came to know and even participated in French literary life, an experience that would be crucial not only for his personal career but for the development of Russian literature. Lomonosov, like Trediakovsky, was born in a place with ready access to sea routes that brought western influence to bear on Russians. His home was a village near Archangel on the Severnaia Dvina river that ran into the White Sea. Like Trediakovsky, Lomonosov used the Slavo-Greco-Latin Academy as a staging post on a journey that would lead to European universities, first at Marburg and then at Freiburg. Although his mission was to study chemistry and mining, his acquaintance with the literary life of Germany enabled him to make a crucial contribution to Russian letters after his return to St Petersburg's Academy of Sciences in 1741.

If direct acquaintanceship with European literary life was one experience that Prokopovich, Kantemir, Trediakovsky, and Lomonosov shared, another feature common to all four was that they were not rooted in the traditional noble families of Russia. Their families were either displaced or belonged to social strata of low esteem. Consequently, the young men recognized that their ambition could best be sustained by Petrine values that exalted talent, merit, and devotion to the strengthening of the state above birth and inherited station. Literature was used by them, as it had been used by Prokopovich with his *Vladimir*, as a political weapon to defend the Petrine reforms by praising their author and to attack the reactionaries who attempted after Peter's death to undermine the advances made under his reign.

It is not Peter's own epoch that saw the emergence in print of a secular European-style literature in Russia. The 1730s was the decade that witnessed the flowering of a literature consciously modelled on European exemplars. Kantemir wrote six satires between 1729 and 1731 in response to the danger he saw coming from obscurantist clerics and backwoods noblemen who rejected Peter's inheritance, particularly the introduction of modern science and technology and the encouragement of European classical Latin education at the expense of the traditional Greek-orientated learning of Muscovite Orthodoxy. But his negative satire was balanced by his attempt in 1730 to write an epic poem on Peter, his *Petrida*. The *Petrida*, like other attempts by Russian eighteenth-century poets to compose epics, remained unfinished. The eulogy of Petrine values was more commonly conveyed in the Russian solemn ode, developed in particular by Lomonosov, which remained the most esteemed poetic genre until the end of the century.

Both satire and ode were poetic forms for which classical and French Neoclassical models were readily available. At this early stage in the establishment of modern secular Russian literature, reliance on such well-defined canonical models was essential. The new literature would be based on western techniques and methods, as surely as the technology and procedures of the reformed army and administration would be founded on those of Europe. Kantemir indeed drew attention to the technical sources of his satires by accompanying his verse with copious notes to explain in detail what he was about and whose example he was following. The Latin satirists Juvenal, Persius, and Horace were all acknowledged as precursors in his fourth satire, but it was the supreme legislator of French seventeenth-century Neoclassicism, Nicolas Boileau, who was indicated as Kantemir's main mentor and guide. Whenever Kantemir directly copied from these satirists, the source of his 'imitations' was dutifully registered in the accompanying reference. The opening note of Kantemir's fifth satire confessed that a previous version had all been taken from Boileau's eighth satire. It was Boileau's *Odes* too that served as models for their Russian imitators. Trediakovsky's *Solemn Ode on the Surrender of the City of Gdansk* (*Oda torzhestvennaia o sdache goroda Gdanska*, 1734), which he claimed in an afterword to be the very first ode in Russian, was in places a direct translation of Boileau's *Ode on the Capture of Namur* (*Ode sur la prise de Namur*, 1693), and the *Discourse on the Ode in General* (*Rassuzhdenie ob ode voobshche*) which constituted the afterword, was a reworking of Boileau's *Discours sur l'ode* that had introduced his own ode. Lomonosov's 1739 *Ode on the Capture of Khotin* (*Oda na vziatie Khotina*) in turn followed the pattern of Boileau's *Ode sur la prise de Namur*, although another western exemplar also made its presence felt – Johann Christian Günther's German ode on the peace of Passowitz between the Austrian and Ottoman Empires in 1718.

It was the metre of Günther's ode, the accentual iambic tetrameter, which accounted for the depth of its imprint on that of Lomonosov. The latter's 'A Letter on Russian Versification' ('Pis'mo o pravilakh rossiiskogo stikhotvorstva', 1739), had been composed in Freiburg and sent to the Russian Academy of Sciences in St Petersburg together with the *Ode on the capture of Khotin*, which served as an example of the new form of versification that he proposed. The establishment of a system of versification, generally acceptable and which has lasted to this day, was one of the most important achievements of the eighteenth century. Since the late seventeenth century, the dominant system of prosody used by Russians in their writings was syllabic verse, a method borrowed from Polish poetry. In syllabic verse there were rhymed pairs of lines with a fixed number of syllables in each line. It was a system well suited to a language, such as Polish, with its regular penultimate stress on words. Russian, however, with its characteristic mobile stress was unsuited to verse organized in this way. Nevertheless Kantemir's satires had been written according to the rules of Polish syllabic verse with an obligatory penultimate stress in each line mimicking the penultimate stress automatically produced by a Polish word ending a line. Trediakovsky also composed his early verse, including the *Solemn Ode on the Surrender of the City of Gdansk*, in accordance with the syllabic system, but he grew uneasy at its inadequacy for the Russian language. Lacking the musical attributes of 'measure and cadence', argued

Trediakovsky, syllabic verse did not sing to the Russian ear and deserved to be called 'mere prose'. Consequently he wrote a treatise, *A New and Brief Method for Composing Russian Verse* (*Novyi i kratkii sposob k slozheniiu rossiiskikh stikhov*, 1735), which proposed a new rhythmical principle, a regular alternation of stressed and unstressed syllables that was appropriate to a language such as Russian with its mobile but very marked stress.

As in other fields, Trediakovsky was a trail-blazer who hacked away at outworn tradition in order to show the way forward, but it was often others who strode out boldly along the new path. Lomonosov's 'A Letter on Russian Versification' seemed to present a more thoroughgoing reform as it expanded greatly the possibilities of accentual verse but it relied essentially on Trediakovsky's radical break with the prevailing system. Eventually a comprehensive theory of Russian syllabo-tonic prosody was produced by Trediakovsky, in 1752, in his revised *A Method for Composing Russian Verse*, which drew on the experience of Russian poets in using the new metrics in the preceding decade.

Not only were Russian metrics refined by the combined efforts of Trediakovsky and Lomonosov but the literary language itself. One of the effects of Peter the Great's stress on secular reforms was that Church Slavonic was fast losing its role as the vehicle of literature and culture. Peter himself used as simple and direct a colloquial language as possible in his own writings, but his spoken Russian was incoherent, invaded by new military and administrative terms of foreign origin. There was no court or cultural centres and salons to cultivate a polite society language on the basis of this clumsy vehicle of everyday intercourse. For the generation of writers who appeared after Peter, however, with their new conception of literature and new techniques, the forging of a complementary new literary language was essential. Trediakovsky had returned to Russia in 1730 from Paris anxious to introduce to his fellow countrymen the light-hearted fiction and lyrical love poetry of French *galant* literature. While abroad, he had translated Paul Tallemant's *Voyage de L'Isle d'Amour* and his realization of a new kind of literary Russian was made plain in his preface:

I humbly beg you not to be angry with me for not translating this book into Church Slavonic but into almost the most ordinary Russian such as we speak among ourselves. I have done this for the following reasons: firstly, Church Slavonic is for us an ecclesiastical language, whereas this is a secular book; secondly, Church Slavonic in the present age is for us very obscure and many of us cannot read it, whereas this is a book about sweet love which should be understood by everybody; thirdly . . . Church Slavonic sounds harsh to my ears.

His practice, unfortunately, could not match the clarity of his theory. Sweet love was rendered not only by simple, colloquial speech, 'such as we speak among ourselves'; it was mingled with bureaucratic officialese, strange-sounding Gallicisms and Slavonicisms, and the lexical muddle was further deformed by a clumsy syntax and dislocated word order. Trediakovsky nevertheless contributed to the elaboration of a literary language indirectly by his conscious transplantation of the generic system of French Neoclassical literature into Russia. As Russians were initiated into a hierarchy of genres – epic, ode, elegy, satire, eclogue, lyric, *précieux* romances, comedies, epigrams, and songs – they realized that gradations of language might best suit each genre. The practice and taste of Russian writers in the 1730s and 1740s ensured that lines of demarcation would begin to emerge in the mass of Church Slavonic and Russian vocabulary. The 'high style', reserved for epic and ode, was marked by a large admixture of Slavonicisms which, however, had to be understandable to Russians. The 'low style', shunning all Slavonicisms, could embrace vulgar colloquialisms. The 'middle style', drawing on the vocabulary stock common to both Church Slavonic and Russian, was allowed a discreet tinge of Slavonicisms. It was this growing refinement of usage that was reflected in Lomonosov's theory of the three styles expressed in his *Rhetoric* (*Ritorika*, 1748), *Russian Grammar* (*Rossiiskaia grammatika*) (1755), and in his 1757 essay 'On the Usefulness of Church Books in the Russian Language' ('O pol'ze knig tserkovnykh v rossiiskom iazyke'). This 'theory of the three styles' was not original; it adapted the current conventional linguistic theory of France to the Russian situation that Lomonosov observed. But the effect of his essays on his contemporaries was beneficial in that it gave theoretical justification to what was happening in practice. He enabled writers in the second half of the eighteenth century to align their writings consciously with a neutral, middle style.

Initially, the foundations of a Russian literary culture had been laid by talented individuals who strove to impose European criteria on their countrymen. They laboured almost in isolation, relying on a coterie of like-minded enthusiasts for their readership. That audience, however, was significantly broadened by the enthusiastic patronage bestowed on the theatre by the Empress Elizabeth during her reign (1741–62). A degree of compulsion was still necessary to turn Russians into theatre-goers: Elizabeth made attendance at her court theatre mandatory for her courtiers. Equally indicative of the progress in spreading the appeal of Russia's literary culture was the success of an amateur troupe of actors in the provincial city of Iaroslavl led by a merchant's son, Fedor Volkov. After ordering Volkov's company to St Petersburg to give a command performance at court, the Empress Elizabeth decided to polish the provincial enthusiasts by enrolling them in the Kadetskii korpus, a state school for privileged young noblemen.

It was from this establishment that the third prominent Russian poet of the time had graduated. Aleksandr Sumarokov (1717–77) ranked himself alongside his senior contemporaries Trediakovsky and Lomonosov, whose disciple he had originally been. Between 1747 and 1751 he wrote five tragedies, all constructed according to the dictates of the Neoclassical form of drama, derived from Racine and Corneille and still acknowledged as the only way of composing serious drama by contemporaries such as Voltaire in France and Gottsched in Germany. *Khorev, Hamlet, Sinav i Truvor, Artistona*, and *Semira* were to be the kernel of the Russian theatrical repertoire for a generation. Formulaic in plot – the relationship between a pair of lovers close to a sovereign is subverted by a clash between social duty and personal passion, and then resolved – the plays nevertheless had a novel appeal in their portrayal on stage of human emotions. Sumarokov's *Khorev* was one of the four plays performed by Volkov for Elizabeth at her court, and when the Empress instituted a public theatre in St Petersburg in 1756 from Volkov's men who had been sufficiently refined at the Kadetskii korpus, Sumarokov was appointed its director. He thus became the first in a long line of Russian noblemen to devote himself exclusively to a profession of literature. Confident of his superiority as a writer, he accepted as completely justified the title bestowed on him of the Russian Racine. It was partly this sense of being guardian of a high European tradition that prompted him to return to the writing of Neoclassical tragedies in the late 1760s in response to the vogue for the new sentimental bourgeois drama of France that he deplored. A feature of these later tragedies, best exemplified by his *Dmitrii the Imposter* (*Dmitrii samozvanets*, 1771), was their intention, in deference to Voltaire's example, to preach civic virtue and warn of the dangers of private passion.

The didactic impulse that was reinforced by the growth of the bourgeois drama in contemporary France was also apparent in the Russian comedies and sentimental drama that flourished in Catherine the Great's reign (1762–96). Play-writing then enjoyed particular prestige since Catherine herself, aided by her literary secretaries, was a prolific composer of comedies whose satirical targets were social misdemeanours such as gossiping and hypochondria, although her sights were occasionally raised to attack parental tyranny and religious bigotry. Her distaste for any religious enthusiasm was further manifested in a group of comedies she wrote in 1785–6 directed against exponents of Russian Freemasonry.

One of Catherine's collaborators was Ivan Elagin (1725–94) who replaced Sumarokov as director of the Imperial Theatres in 1766, and encouraged young disciples who would make their mark on Russian drama, such as Denis Fonvizin (1745–92), Vladimir Lukin (1737–94), and Bogdan Elchaninov (1744–70). Lukin's *The Haberdasher* (*Shchepetil'nik*, 1765), based on Robert Dodsley's *The Toy-Shop* (1735), was an example of his policy of 'adapting to our customs' foreign plays. In his dramas Lukin attempted to Russianize characters, situations, surroundings, and social relationships while, at the same time, transferring to the Russian context the overt social moralizing and sermonizing of his European sources. It was on the pioneering foundations of Lukin and Elchaninov that Fonvizin was able to compose *The Brigadier* (*Brigadir*) in 1769, which became one of the most acclaimed Russian eighteenth-century comedies mainly because of its masterly portrayal of society and the naive, long-suffering, comically humble Russian woman in the role of the Brigadier's wife. In 1781 Fonvizin completed his masterpiece, *The Minor*, (*Nedorosl'*) the only eighteenth-century play that has retained a permanent place in the Russian theatrical repertoire. In *The Minor* a group of *raisonneurs*, spokesmen for Petrine and enlightened values, prevail against a motley of provincial boors and ignoramuses who, nevertheless, with their crude energy and ripe colloquial parlance form the abiding dramatic interest.

The butts of Fonvizin's satire were not new. They had been paraded in most of the comedies of the previous two decades, including the plays composed by Catherine the Great. The satirical targets had also been set up in the moral weeklies that were a crucial stage in the creation of Russian prose literature. Again Catherine herself took the initiative by launching in 1769 a weekly paper, *All Sorts* (*Vsiakaia vsiachina*), modelled on the renowned English journals of Joseph Addison and Richard Steele, the *Spectator* and the *Tatler*.

Literature for Catherine was a means of furthering her policy of encouraging the Russian nobility to become agents of Enlightenment. So in 1768 she established her Society for the Translation of Foreign Books that gave a stamp of approval to modern writers such as Montesquieu, Voltaire, Diderot, D'Alembert, Blackstone, Swift, Fielding, Gellert, and Goldoni. Enlightenment thought had already been distilled in translation into the famous *Nakaz*, or Instruction, to the deputies summoned to a legislative commission in 1767. The assembly itself, only suspended on the outbreak of hostilities with Turkey two years later, formed a rudimentary public opinion and was a demonstration of how the freedom of thought, speech and the press – all prerequisites for a flourishing literary culture – had been expanded.

The moral weeklies were another demonstration of the concept of freedom of expression promulgated in the *Nakaz*. *Vsiakaia vsiachina* called on other writers to join with it in satirizing the anti-Enlightenment elements that still frustrated Peter the Great's objective of transforming Russian society, and several new journals sprang up in response to the imperial summons. The most successful by far was *Truten'*, edited by Nikolai Novikov (1744–1818) who followed it with the equally impressive *Zhivopisets* (1772–3) and *Koshelek* (1774). Not content with being editor of these moral weeklies, Novikov became a historiographer and published sketches of leading Russian writers in his *An Essay on the Historical Dictionary of Russian Writers* (*Opyt istoricheskogo slovaria o rossiiskikh pisateliakh*, 1772), reflecting the extent of the emergence of a distinctive Russian literary culture. From 1779 to 1789 he held the lease of Moscow University Press and, benefiting from Catherine the Great's 1783 decree permitting independent presses, he became Russia's leading publisher.

That Novikov had sufficient material to feed his presses in the 1780s was due, to a great extent, to the impetus given to prose writing by his own satirical journals of 1769–74. In them he was able – in letters, pen-portraits, dialogues, and stories – to practise a literary prose style that proved adequate to express the concerns of his age. Travel sketches from supposed 'correspondents' foreshadowed the vogue for travel literature, closely linked with the epistolary mode, that flourished towards the close of the eighteenth century. The fashion gave rise to some of the most significant Russian prose works of the century: Fonvizin's letters from abroad during his journeys of 1777–8 and 1784–5; the radically critical *A Journey from St Petersburg to Moscow* (*Puteshestvie iz Peterburga v Moskvu*) by Aleksandr Radishchev (1749–1802); and *Letters of a Russian Traveller* (*Pis'ma russkogo puteshestvennika*) by Nikolai Karamzin (1766–1826).

Editors of some of the 1769–74 moral weeklies such as Fedor Emin (1735–70) and Mikhail Chulkov (1734–92) made the first attempts at producing extended prose fiction. Emin, editor of *Adskaia pochta*, as well as translating romances from

Spanish, Italian, and Portuguese, tried his hand at novel writing and is credited with the first original Russian novel with *Inconstant Fortune* (*Nepostoiannaia fortuna*, 1763). It initiated a short but productive period of novel writing: further novels by Emin, Chulkov, Popov and a series of Neoclassical and allegorical novels by Mikhail Kheraskov (1733–1807) whose cultivation of a wide array of genres, both within and without the Neoclassical canon, and role in organizing and inspiring young literary talent made him an outstanding figure of Catherine's reign. One of the most distinguished novels of the eighteenth century was Chulkov's *The Comely Cook* (*Prigozhaia povarikha, ili Pokhozhdenie razvratnoi zhenshchiny*, 1770), with its rumbustious narrative of contemporary life and manners. Russian fiction, however, had a hard struggle to make any headway against the stream of translated novels available to the Russian reader in the last third of the century: Fanny Burney, Henry Fielding, Madame de Genlis, Oliver Goldsmith, Samuel Richardson, Jean-Jacques Rousseau, Laurence Sterne, and Jonathan Swift eclipsed the earnest pioneers of Russian fiction.

It was not until the last decade of the century that a Russian writer of prose fiction appeared whose work could stand comparison with that of his European contemporaries. This was Nikolai Karamzin, whose first novella *Eugene and Julia* (*Evgenii i Iuliia*) appeared in 1789 in Russia's first magazine for children. Soon his original fiction filled the pages of literary journals and almanacs founded and edited by him. The first Russian Sentimentalist story, *Poor Liza* (*Bednaia Liza*), published in 1792, enjoyed outstanding success and signalled a new stage in Russian literature. In 1794–5 the almanac *Aglaia* carried the stories *The Island of Bornholm* (*Ostrov Borngol'm*) and *Sierra Morena*. The success of the journals won for Karamzin the right to be called Russia's first modern journalist. Prose fiction, inspired by European Sentimentalism, and journalism were not the only fields in which Karamzin indicated fresh paths for Russian literature to follow. Prompted by the growing enthusiasm for Shakespeare in Germany, Karamzin was the first to reveal the genius of Shakespeare to the Russian reader with his translation from the original of *Julius Caesar* and preface that sought to explain the particular qualities of the Shakespearean drama. Another prompt to which Karamzin responded was the vogue for the poetry of Ossian, the Gaelic bard of antiquity whom James Macpherson had claimed to have translated. Karamzin's poetry, hinting at folk-song and singing of the pure emotions of the human heart, anticipated the romantic lyricism of the following century. New themes were accompanied by daring technical playfulness, such as his teasing use of near rhymes and blank verse. In his verse, as in his supple prose, are heard the colloquial intonations and lucid syntax with which Karamzin transformed literary Russian at the close of the century. No theoretical treatises on the nature of Russian, however, were left by him; his Russian was based on his own personal appreciation of the sound and significance of living speech, the fittingness of words and expressions from common parlance or foreign borrowings.

Above all, Karamzin was guided in all that he did by his conviction of the standing of the individual author. It is worth comparing Karamzin's self-image as an author with that of his contemporary Gavrila Derzhavin (1743–1816), the greatest poet before Pushkin. Throughout his work, Derzhavin had demonstrated unrivalled creative inventiveness and independence. Not shackled by the dictates of Neoclassical canons, by playfully mixing light satire and lyricism into the pattern of the Lomonosovian solemn ode, he produced dazzling hybrids. His bold innovation was evident in the mock ode *Felitsa* (1782), a lightly veiled allusion to Catherine the Great, that established his renown. Derzhavin went on to write poems of genius in which his own personality, his exuberance in the richness of life's pleasures and anguish at the brevity of his own span were manifested in brilliantly innovative verse. Yet Derzhavin retained the modest view of his own poetry as an adjunct to the more important service he could render his sovereign as a high official in the Russian administration.

For Karamzin, however, the calling of author was the highest possible and had no need to be buttressed by other services outside literature. Dedicated to the sole profession of author, he did not limit himself to poetry alone, but played his part in all possible fields – fiction, drama, philosophical essays, poetry – and as editor and publisher as well as writer. While acknowledging the role that Catherine the Great had played in enhancing the prestige of writers, Karamzin drew pointed attention to the essentially amateur nature of her own pastimes with her pen. What distinguished the truly committed professional writer in Karamzin's eyes was his gift of being a unique vessel to hold genius. A writer's personality should be projected in his works, not out of vanity, but as a focus for genius. Behind that confident assertion of the writer's standing in society lay all the strivings to establish foundations of a national Russian literature in the eighteenth century.

The influence now exercised by the individual author on his society had its darker side. The last decade of the century, it is true, would be known as Karamzin's period in recognition of his intellectual and moral leadership. Those closing years would also be remembered as the time when the Russian state, in the person of Catherine the Great, alarmed by the French Revolution of 1789, moved to silence authors suspected, however unjustly, of being threats to the established political order. Radishchev, whose *A Journey from St Petersburg to Moscow* might well have been welcomed by Catherine earlier in her reign as an argument in favour of enlightenment, was exiled to Siberia for publishing a book now perceived as seditious. Novikov, whose whole career had been devoted to succouring Catherine's enlightened literary enterprises, was sentenced in 1792 to twenty years' incarceration in the Schlüsselburg fortress, and suspect publications impounded in his presses and bookshops were condemned to be burnt in 1793–4.

As the new century dawned, Russian literature already possessed its martyrs, casting a dark shadow on the triumphal achievements of those pioneers who had discovered a supple literary language, new literary forms, and a confidence to break free from the restraints of foreign Neoclassical models. Russian literature had revealed the power of the individual conscience in the Russian writer.

FURTHER READING

Baehr, Stephen Lessing. *The Paradise Myth in Eighteenth-Century Russia: Utopian Patterns in Early Secular Russian Literature and Culture*, Stanford: Stanford University Press, 1991.

Brown, William Edward. *A History of 18th Century Russian Literature*, Ann Arbor: Ardis, 1980.

Cross, A.G. (ed.) *Russian Literature in the Age of Catherine the Great: A Collection of Essays*, Oxford: Meeuws, 1976.

Drage, C.L. *Russian Literature in the Eighteenth Century*, London, published by the author, 1978.

Garrard, J.G. (ed.) *The Eighteenth Century in Russia*, Oxford: Clarendon Press, 1973.

Gasperetti, David. *The Rise of the Russian Novel: Carnival, Stylization and Mockery of the West*, DeKalb, Illinois: Northern Illinois University Press, 1998.

Morris, Marcia A. *The Literature of Roguery in Seventeenth and Eighteenth-Century Russia*, Evanston, Illinois: Northwestern University Press, 2000.

Segel, Harold B. (ed. and trans.) *The Literature of Eighteenth-Century Russia: An Anthology of Russian Literary Materials of the Age of Classicism and the Enlightenment from the Reign of Peter the Great (1689–1725) to the Reign of Alexander I (1801–1825)*, 2 vols., New York: E.P. Dutton, 1967.

Study Group on Eighteenth-Century Russia Newsletter (1973–)

4

FOLKLORE AND RUSSIAN LITERATURE

FAITH WIGZELL

Outside Russia the folk heritage of the country is best known in its operatic, musical and balletic guise. Stravinsky's *Firebird* (*Zhar Ptitsa*), Rimsky-Korsakov's operas *Sadko* and *The Snow Maiden* (*Snegurochka*), Vaznetsov's monumental paintings of legendary folk heroes or the elegant reworked folk images of the illustrator Bilibin and the neoprimitivist paintings of Goncharova, Larionov and Malevich at the beginning of the twentieth century all brought folkloric material, if not folklore itself, to the West. Although it is often not obvious in translation, the impact of folklore on literature is no less significant. This fact reflects the overall importance of oral tradition in Russian life. Up until the Revolution the great majority of the population depended upon an oral culture and, despite socialist protestations and efforts at eradication, things changed only gradually. Economic backwardness possesses few advantages, but in Russia where, additionally, the great geographical expanses resulted in the isolation of communities, it helped to maintain the peasants' premodern world-view. *Inter alia* their views found expression in songs, tales, folk beliefs, rituals, laments and legends. Then as towns grew in the course of the nineteenth century, rural migrants were drawn to them; in 1864 in westernized Petersburg, for example, half the population were peasants, most of them illiterate. The new arrivals brought with them their folklore, which was modified in the new context and fed into a developing urban folklore. The oral heritage in Russia is as a result both rich and varied.

It represented, however, a world from which the élite classes had become alienated following the adoption of Western manners during the eighteenth century. From the end of the eighteenth century on, despite élite prejudice about folklore's presumed lack of refinement, it increasingly became seen as the exotic 'other', something strange and different and yet at the same time 'ours'. For writers and other creative artists it became a resource, and through the nineteenth and early twentieth centuries they evolved a literary relationship with the parallel oral culture. As the century advanced, their understanding deepened, leading to greater sophistication in their creative use of folklore (though, naturally, with exceptions and considerable individual variation). More specifically, nineteenth-century literature started from Romantic aesthetics with its view of folklore as decoration (for example in Zhukovsky's ballad *Svetlana*), or a source of a supernatural frisson and local colour (as, for example, in Gogol' 's early stories, even if here the folklore was Ukrainian rather than Russian). Starting with Pushkin writers became collectors of folklore not just out of a desire to turn amateur ethnographer, but also because of the sense that vast folk-poetic treasures lay untapped – hardly any serious collections of Russian folklore existed. Pushkin collected folk-songs in the 1820s and early 1830s. Gogol', too, moved from the use of colourful folkloric material as literary material in *Evenings on a Farm near Dikanka* (*Vechera na khutore bliz Dikan'ki*) to collecting folk-songs in the early 1830s as examples of oral history. For his part Zhukovsky proposed an anthology of Russian folk-tales to his daughters in 1816, but it was not until the 1840s that the task of recording folklore in a serious way was taken up by his nephew Petr Kireevsky along with other Slavophile sympathizers. It is unfortunate that their efforts, like much of Kireevsky's material, only reached a wider public much later.

The deeper knowledge of folklore possessed by writers like Leskov and Dostoevsky, and later by Zamiatin and Remizov sprang both from personal experience and familiarity with the standard collections of folk-poetic texts that appeared from the 1850s on. Apart from Afanas'ev's collection of folk-tales and Christian legends (1855–63, 1859), Dal' 's proverbs (1862) and incantations or charms (1869), there were major publications of sung poetry, especially the epic (the *bylina*) and historical songs (1861–7 and 1873), spiritual songs (1860 and 1861–4), lyric songs (1870–7, 1895–1902 and 1898) and folk laments (1872). Round the country peasant rituals, beliefs and superstitions were eagerly noted down by amateur and professional ethnographers. The enthusiasm with which the educated public greeted these national treasures sparked a renewed interest in folklore as source material in all the arts, one which lasted into the twentieth century. The poet Blok, for example, was fascinated by folk incantations, magic spells traditionally used to try to drive out or ward off illnesses and afflictions (impotence, toothache, love, the evil eye etc.). For him the magic words uttered by the sorcerer or folk healer represented true poetry in their combination of utility, beauty and power, while reflecting primitive man's unity with nature. After the Revolution, despite having to find itself a 'progressive' role in a Marxist society, folklore continued to be collected and published and remains an important source for many writers, especially the exponents of Village Prose such as Shukshin, whose knowledge is based on personal familiarity much more than printed collections.

Over the decades writers have drawn on a huge range of folk genres. No brief survey can be comprehensive. This one, therefore, will concentrate, first, on those forms of verbal folklore which possess obvious aesthetic qualities, and second, on folk belief, in each case briefly indicating some examples of their creative use by nineteenth- and twentieth-century writers.

The artistic principles that underlie oral literature everywhere present a sharp contrast to the conventions of its written counterpart. Oral literature in Russia emerges from an environment with a magical world-view, which is to say that human beings, seeing themselves as vulnerable in the face of a natural world over which they have little control, not only tend to conceive of this threat in mythological form as spirits, evil forces or gods, but also to evolve magic rituals to placate these forces, activate their help and guarantee the survival of the community. Failure to perform the correct actions, or utter the right words at the right time could lead to disaster. Consequently, adherence to tradition rather than change and innovation was what brought success. Folklore reflects this in its reliance on linguistic formulae and repetitive structural patterns, its typical characters, situations and themes. No weight is given to originality. However, traditionalism does not result in creative ossification. In folk-tales, epics or ballads the singer or teller of tales composes by blending the poetic conventions, stylistic features and commonplaces of the given genre, such that each rendering (known as a variant) differs. There is therefore no canonical form of any song or tale, though some short forms like proverbs are closer to being fixed in form. Artistry lies in each performer's skill in combining traditional elements.

Among the best known forms of oral literature are folk-tales, particularly numerous in the Russian tradition. Of these the best loved are the wondertales (or fairy tales as they are conventionally called in English). The theme of these may be said to be the young man's (less often a girl's) initial sortie into the adult world and involve his or her transformation. As the famous folklorist Vladimir Propp argued, all such tales have essentially the same structure, defined not by the character who performs an action, but by what is done, what he termed functions. All wondertales (in Russian the *volshebnaia skazka*), he said, began with an initial lack caused by the disappearance of an object or person, a parent's death, or the desire for a bride. Any of these may prompt the hero's departure on a quest. Along the way he (rarely she) encounters various human or animal figures to whom he must behave correctly (assist, speak civilly to, etc.) in order either to gain some magic object or the direct assistance of the magic helper in the subsequent stage of the quest located in the thrice-ninth kingdom. Here he or she must defeat the ogre and gain the object of the quest. Further tribulations may follow, usually a consequence of the theft of object of the quest by the hero's brothers, but the tale concludes with victorious return and marriage. Although the validity of Propp's structure for all such tales in all cultures has been contested, it provides a useful way of bringing out the patterning of Russian wondertales and has been frequently and intriguingly applied to written literature. Propp's point was that there was nothing intrinsically Russian about wondertale structure and, one could equally argue, about their heroes, the passive Prince Ivan, Ivanushka the Fool, or victim heroines such as Vasilisa the Beautiful.

National distinctiveness lies elsewhere. Although Ivanushka the Fool, a dirty creature with snot running down his face, is dramatically more repulsive than his west European simpleton counterpart, what really marks out the Russian wondertale is its stylistic ornamentation and its range of frightening ogres. Of the latter the best known is the Baba Iaga, no ordinary witch, but, it would seem, mistress of the animals and guardian of the other world, and hence connected with death. She has cannibalistic tendencies and a hideous appearance; a long nose, greasy hair, breasts made of iron or long and dangling. She rides in her mortar and pestle or sits legs spread grotesquely wide in her hut on chicken legs located deep in the forest. One leg is made of bone and the other of excrement. Less gruesome but still frightening are the twelve-headed dragon, Chudo-Iudo, who grows back more heads every time any are cut off, and the evil Koshchei, whose death is elaborately concealed inside an egg, inside a duck, inside a hare in a trunk beneath an oak tree on an island in the sea. Find it and he can be killed. In these figures, as in the quest motif, we may be able to glimpse the origin of these tales in ancient initiation rites, shamanistic beliefs and concepts of death and the world beyond. In initiation rites, for example, the initiate is usually isolated from the community where he is believed to pass through a state of death before emerging into a new stage of existence. The tales could be said to represent that journey to the other world of death where the initiate must perform tasks before returning to an adult life. So the visit to the thrice-ninth kingdom in the tales, success in the quest and ultimate prize of a bride may reflect these ancient patterns. Others have suggested that the visit of the shaman in a trance to the land of dead ancestors may also lie behind some tales. Nothing, however, can be established for certain.

On the other hand some aspects of the tales do seem to reflect peasant rituals and beliefs recorded in the nineteenth century, such as a bear cult, veneration of ancestors and female initiation rites (which may have their roots in antiquity). What is more, when one remembers that the milieu from which these tales came was one that believed in magic, mythological spirits and an 'other world' not entirely of a Christian nature, the brilliant fantastic world of the Russian tale seems more comprehensible. Listeners are led into the fantastic world of the wondertale and kept there by a distinct folk-poetic language. The tale opens with a rhyming formula (*v tridesiatom tsarstve, v tridesiatom gosudarstve*), includes rhyming names (e.g. *Mar'ia Morevna, prekrasnaia korolevna*), various narrative formulae (*skoro skazka skazyvaetsia, ne skoro delo delaetsia*) and a rhyming conclusion that brings the listener back into the here and now. Although in the nineteenth century among peasants these tales were told mainly by men to adults, in the educated circles that produced the country's writers, these tales, more than any other kind, were a treasured part of childhood and for many a source for their adult writing. Goncharov's hero Oblomov, a case of arrested development, has based his own poetic ideals on the wondertales told by his nanny, in particular 'Emelia the Simpleton' ('Emel'ia durak') about the layabout who achieves his heart's desire without ever having to move off his beloved stove. Pushkin, too, admired the charm of folk-tales and even recorded some, but his own literary folk-tales in verse, though liberally dotted with folkloric phrases learnt from his nanny or from cheap woodcut books, are largely based on foreign, mainly French models. Purism was to come later.

The two other main categories of tales (though some scholars would divide tales into further groups) are the animal tales and the tales of everyday life. The former, which correspond to the Black American Brer Rabbit tales, feature animals with man, if present, in a subsidiary role. The animals possess certain fixed human characteristics and behave in accordance with them, with cruelly humorous results. Most of the tales are structured on a meeting in which one animal, often the smooth-talking Little Sister Fox (*lisichka-sestrichka*) proceeds to outwit the stupid bear, the clumsy wolf, the vain cockerel, the trembling hare and so on. Although the world distribution of such stories suggests great antiquity, nothing can be stated with certainty about their original form or function. In their current guise, they are stories for children told by women (unlike other types of tale which at least until the latter part of the nineteenth century were told by men). What gives them a distinctive Russian flavour is a narrative style incorporating rhyming diminutives and little songs which allowed for a considerable performance element in the telling. As children's literature they rarely reached literature except in the form of the literary fable, which in the case of the early nineteenth-century writer, Krylov, drew far more on the literary precedent of Aesop than on popular Russian animal tales.

The third category, the tales of everyday life, deal with social foibles of various kinds and are set in the world of peasants, masters, merchants, priests and other social groups. Characters are stereotyped and the interest is on colourful, fast-moving action, often culminating in the victory of the underdog over the stupid and gullible or else the humiliation of figures of authority. They may, therefore, possess an element of subversion: priests, for example, are inevitably greedy and avaricious, lecherous and drunken. One of their major functions was to perform a wish-fulfilment role for the peasant audience by showing the poor getting rich, the mean and powerful being defeated. Equally they might serve to reinforce community values by laughing at those who ignored its rules. By poking fun at the stupid they instructed the young in the ways of the world. Though tales of everyday life are generally said to lack magic, small devils and other supernatural figures feature extensively, but, whereas peasants feared them in real life, here the wish-fulfilment function of these stories reversed the roles; here foolish and gullible devils are outwitted by the clever hero. The hero of this type of tale might be a soldier (stereotypically a person who lived by his wits) or a smith (reputed to have some control over supernatural powers). Others are the apparently stupid youngest brother or the poor peasant with initiative and cunning. Told in a racy style, these tales are often crude, even obscene, and were hugely popular. They reappear in Russian literature in the works of writers like Gogol' and Leskov, who, coming from relatively modest backgrounds, knew oral tradition better than writers from the élite, whose nannies would have deemed these stories unsuitable for their charges. In the case of Gogol', his early stories featuring stock characters like the lecherous cleric (the priest's son in 'The Fair at Sorochintsy' ['Sorochinskaia iamarka']) or the clever smith who outwits devils and witches ('Christmas Eve' ['Noch' pered Rozhdestvom']) draw indirectly on the tales via popular theatrical interludes and puppet theatre. In Leskov's *Cathedral Folk* (*Soboriane*) the sympathetic portrait of the three members of the clergy in the novel needs to be seen as an attempt to rescue the tarnished image of the clergy in the tales, and in the same work Leskov inverts the traditional folk-tale motif of the priest tricked by a mock devil when his heroic deacon bravely unmasks the character who is terrrifying the townsfolk with his impersonation of the devil.

More important for their impact on Russian culture are the epic songs of Russia (the *bylina*). These are the best known of several types of narrative sung verse. Composed in tonic metre with a set number of stresses in the line, but a varying number of unstressed syllables and without rhyme, most appear to have been composed between the tenth and fourteenth centuries, albeit with some older material (dragons and other supernatural figures). They seem to have been based on some historical event, but whatever their original setting and date, the majority are now set in a mythologized ancient Kiev, the first Russian state, where Prince Vladimir, an amalgam perhaps of the two famous Kievan rulers, Vladimir I and Vladimir Monomakh, is surrounded by a group of warrior heroes, the *bogatyri*. Of the Kievan heroes the best-loved is brave Il'ia of Murom, followed by the diplomat and dragon-slayer Dobrynia Nikitich and Alesha Popovich who is something of a trickster. Although these heroes owe their fame to their single-handed defeat of the enemies of Orthodox Rus', hideous monsters and huge armies, not to mention their capacity to down huge quantities of 'green wine', it would be wrong to regard the Russian *bylina* as solely devoted to heroic martial exploits. A smaller cycle of epic songs featuring the gusli-player Sadko and the rumbustious Vasilii Buslaev is set in the medieval republic of Novgorod, and reflects its commercial interests and more plebeian ideals. Elsewhere other subjects include fashion contests (*Diuk Stepanovich*), the tragic killing of an Amazonian wife by her husband in an archery contest (*Dunai*), a journey to the bottom of the sea (*Sadko*) and a sorceress who turns young men into aurochs (*Dobrynia and Marinka*).

It seems probable that folk epics were originally sung by professional minstrels and entertainers, the *skomorokhi*, as a form of entertainment for Kievan princes and their retinues and later to a wider audience. In the seventeenth century they were banned and dispersed, in particular to the territory of the former republic of Novgorod. It was here in 1860 that the *bylina* was discovered to have survived around Lake Onega and, later, also along the White Sea. The removal of these epic songs from their original aristocratic milieu may well have prompted the downgrading of the figure of Prince Vladimir into a coward and fool, his wife Apraxia into a faithless woman, as well as introducing elements of comedy. Nonetheless, the *bylina* retains its hyperbole and mythologizing; for example, when Nightingale the Robber sings, the trees bow to the ground and the flowers lose their petals. Not only the subject matter but also the highly stylized poetic manner, what is termed epic ceremonialism, mark it out. Prominent in the poetics are stock phrases such as the greeting 'Hail to thee' (*goi esi*), stock episodes (the hero saddles his horse, adversaries exchange taunts, for example), extensive use of repetition and parallelism, as well as epithet-noun phrases: 'the bright falcon' (*iasnyi sokol*) for the hero, 'green wine' (*zeleno-vino*), 'the good horse' (*dobryi kon'*), or, for Vladimir, 'the fair sun' (*krasnoe solnyshko*).

So well known is the *bylina* in Russia today that its language forms a distinct sub-code of literary Russian and as such may appear in all manner of literary works. No less important are the heroes, though here it is not so much the figures themselves who are the inspiration for literary characters as the qualities they embody, which are seen as quintessentially Russian: patriotism, strength, endurance and great capacity for drink. One writer who did model some of his characters after them is Leskov. He made the parallel plain by openly calling both Akhilla Desnitsyn in *Cathedral Folk* and Ivan Fliagin in *The Enchanted Pilgrim* (*Ocharovannyi strannik*) *bogatyrs*. In each case Leskov wished to highlight what he saw as both the virtues and the failings of the ordinary Russian, full of potential but ill equipped for the modern world. Both are flawed modern versions of the epic hero, whose decency, spontaneity and utter devotion to Russia and her people cannot adequately compensate for their binge drinking, brawling and reckless behaviour.

The dividing line between the various types of sung verse is hard to make (singers themselves made no distinction), but the main features delineating the historical song from the *bylina* are the absence of epic hyperbole and supernatural elements as well as much of the epic ceremonialism. Historical songs have a clearer relationship to historical events and with isolated exceptions date from no earlier than the sixteenth century. As a form of oral history, the songs reflect popular attitudes to rulers and events, and not necessarily those of the period in which the song was originally composed. The episodes in these and other songs are not historically accurate, or even verifiable; their truth lies in the popular attitudes they embody. Perhaps not surprisingly, of all the Russian tsars it is Ivan the Terrible and Peter the Great who feature most in the songs. Ivan is celebrated for his impulsive, violent nature as well as his essential fairness when proved wrong, Peter for his physical prowess and empathy with ordinary folk. These popular images have strongly influenced literary, cinematic and artistic depictions of the two tsars. A further group of songs celebrates Cossack oral history, especially famous leaders like Ermak, Stenka Razin and Pugachev, or else express their martial ethos and love of freedom, while justifying the Cossack claim to historic rights and lands. Some of the more popular historical songs focus on the tragic fate of individuals, such as the tragic death of the young Prince Mikhail Skopin-Shuisky, poisoned at a banquet in 1610 by the wife of a relative who was jealous of his military successes and popularity.

The emphasis on personal tragedy and dramatic death links historic songs with folk ballads. Some of these may have started life as songs about specific events but subsequently lost any connection with history. They were not recognized as a separate genre in the nineteenth century, and even now scholars argue about the inclusion of one or other song in the different categories of sung narrative verse. Known throughout Russia in the pre-revolutionary period, ballads frequently depict personal or family conflicts that result in violence, brutal murder or unwitting incest. No motivation or reaction to events is offered, thereby adding to the starkness of the drama. Some may be Russian variants of well-known European tales or ballads. The theme of 'Vasilii and Sof'ia', for example, is the common European one of lovers reunited after death when trees grow miraculously intertwined on their adjacent graves. In some of the Russian variants instead of the conventional ending on a romantic note, the angry and vengeful mother rips out the trees, illustrating the stark lack of sentimentality so characteristic of Russian ballads. Perhaps the best known ballad, thanks to its constant republication in songbooks, was 'Prince Volkonsky and Vania the Steward' ('Kniaz' Volkonsky i Vania kliuchnik'), which depicts the cruel vengeance the prince takes on his young wife and her lover, the dashing Vania. It was reworked by the minor poet Krestovsky in 1862 and used as the subject of a play by Fedor Sologub as well as acting as part of the folkloric subtext to Leskov's story *Lady Macbeth of Mtsensk* (*Ledi Makbet mtsenskogo uezda*). There it was combined with motifs from another ballad, 'The wife killed her husband' ('Zhena muzha zarezala').

Love is always unhappy in the ballads, a situation all too often repeated in the lyric folk-song tradition, but here the singer must endure the situation. Many songs are connected with calendar festivals or life cycle rituals, especially marriage, which was an elaborate affair lasting up to a week. The category of ritual songs includes poetic laments sung in memory of a dead person, usually by an older female member of the family or occasionally by a local woman famed for poetic improvisation. In the eighteenth and nineteenth centuries laments also accompanied the departure of a son to the army – not surprising when the period of compulsory service for a recruit was twenty years or more. They were also sung by the bride during the wedding ritual. She obligatorily lamented her impending separation from her parents and the end of her unmarried state. Lyric songs not tied to ritual events frequently depict separation, unhappy love or a hard, lonely life. They included songs that are the property of social groups like barge-haulers, soldiers, or carters, whose occupations took them away from home for long periods. Other categories are essentially joyful or jocular, particularly those sung to dance rhythms, or to while away the time as girls sat over their sewing at *posidelki* (social gatherings), and flirted with the young lads of the village.

It was folk-songs that first began to attract the upper classes to folklore in the mid-eighteenth century. Lyric folk-songs were perceived initially as pastoral charm, but in the early nineteenth century, when verse dominated literature, they came to be seen as rustic poetry and the essence of russianness. Pushkin's use was more varied than most, ranging from local colour to ironical counterpoint (for example, the song sung by the peasant girls picking raspberries while Tat'iana awaits Evgenii's answer), or elsewhere functioning as emotional emphasis (as in the epigraph from a wedding song to Chapter 12 of *The Captain's Daughter* (*Kapitanskaia dochka*)). In the same novel a Cossack sings Pugachev's favourite song, 'Do not rustle, mother-forest green...' ('Ne shumi, mati zelenaia dubravushka'). This song, which expresses traditional Cossack acceptance of official retribution for reckless military endeavours, offers a bitter commentary on the fate awaiting the rebels. Generally speaking, however, the most significant impact of the folk-song was on poetry. The lyric folk-song often uses parallelism, perhaps introducing the human subject of the song with a symbolic picture of nature in which the symbols are traditional (for example, 'Over the lake stands a willow/Beneath the willow a stone/Sitting on the stone a maiden/So bitterly is she weeping'). As is clear from this quotation the singer does not usually speak in the first person but chooses a subject which reflects her (or his) mood. Like other genres of sung folk poetry, lyric songs are full of constant epithets ('silken grass' *trava shelkovaia*), 'azure flower' (*lazurevyi tsvetok*)), and are noted for a device known as the progressive contraction of images which means that the song focuses in from the larger setting or most important details down to the smallest or least. From the Romantic period onwards poets borrowed folk-song devices or composed mock folk lyrics. Among those most influenced by folk-song were Kol'tsov and Nekrasov in the nineteenth century and Esenin in the twentieth.

Unlike the categories of folk verse described above, which are secular, the spiritual songs of Russia encapsulate the spirit of popular Orthodoxy. Before the Revolution they were sung mainly by two separate groups, the Old Believers and itinerant blind beggars, the *kaleki perekhozhie*. They could be heard at fairs, on market places, by monastery gates, church doorways or beneath the windows of the rich. The best time to hear them was Lent, since the Church frowned on secular songs at this period and Old Believer communities banned them entirely. After the Revolution the *kaleki perekhozhie* disappeared and spiritual songs were deemed to have died out, though they survive still among Old Believer communities. Observers relate how profound was the emotional impact on audiences as they listened to those songs of lamentation and repentance permeated by a profound consciousness of the sinfulness of earthly life. Songs may depict the suffering of martyrs and saints (Saints Boris and Gleb, St Alexis or St George), or the lamentation of mothers (Rachel or, in particular Mary, Mother of God). Others praise the virtues of poverty or have cosmological and eschatological themes, such as the famous song based on a popular apocryphal text *The Descent of the Mother of God to Hell* (*Khozhdenie Bogoroditsy po mukam*).

Although in *War and Peace* (*Voina i mir*) Tolstoy shows the *kaleki perekhozhie* being welcomed at the back door of the Bolkonsky house by Princess Mar'ia, it is Dostoevsky who made the greatest creative use of spiritual songs. This is not so surprising given his interest in the spirituality of the common folk. For him the songs were a distillation of the traditional values of the Russian people. As a general principle he chose to embed folkloric material into the text along with material from other sources in such a way that it is integral but not easily recognized, especially by those not familiar with the sources. In particular he found in the songs a Christianized version of the cult of Mother Damp Earth, the repository of moral purity and the all-forgiving mother who must be approached with humility and love. In the songs the earth's role as the embodiment of moral purity is explicit. For example in the 'Lament of the Earth' ('Plach' zemli') the burden of bearing so many sinful people causes Mother Earth to cry out to the Lord. Thus, when Raskol'nikov obeys Sonia's instruction to bow to the ground and kiss the earth, he makes the first move towards repentance and moral regeneration. Sonia herself represents poverty, suffering, humility and love, all key values in the spiritual songs. In one of the best known songs 'The two Lazars' ('Dva Lazaria') it is the younger completely destitute Lazar who upon death enters the kingdom of heaven unlike his rich but hard-hearted older brother. When Sonia reads the gospel story of the raising of Lazarus, she is not only referring to Raskol'nikov's need to raise himself from his spiritually crippled condition, but also pointing to the values expressed in the song that will assist him. The image of the earth as mother reappears in *The Devils* (*Besy*) notably in the figure of Mar'ia Lebiadkina, crippled herself like the singers of the spiritual songs. Despite her dementia her equation of Mary Mother of God and Mother Moist Earth, one found in the spiritual songs, is evidently meant to be taken seriously. The impact of the songs is felt too in the image of Alesha Karamazov which depends partially on the popular spiritual song about St Alexis, Man of God.

Although some forms of folklore that have been discussed were not exclusively rural, in particular ballads and spiritual songs, none mentioned so far are primarily urban products. Of those that are the most famous is probably the puppet theatre, Petrushka, which illustrates the processes of cultural reception and russification manifested in high culture in Russia after Peter the Great. Brought to Russia by travelling Italian puppeteers in his original guise of Pulcinella some time between 1810 and 1840, Petrushka acquired local features and by 1880 was seen as quintessentially Russian. Resemblances to other European versions of Pulcinella such as Punch remain, notably the crude humour, grotesque figures and actions and some of the character types, but in his Russian guise the propensity of the hero to violence is developed at the expense of the sexual innuendo common in some west European versions. Petrushka's popularity rested also on the essentially subversive nature of the play, which mocked and undermined authority of any kind. Through the nineteenth century Petrushka made his way into literature rarely, usually viewed with a degree of educated contempt for his vulgarity, though the poet Nekrasov enjoyed the energy and wit of the puppet plays. Generally, his irreverent attitude to authority was appropriated for political purposes or distorted. The Symbolists, for example, ignored the violent and subversive elements in favour of an interpretation of the Petrushka figure as a tragic mythical archetype representing human suffering (and best known in Stravinsky's ballet *Petrouchka*).

With all the folk genres discussed so far both form and content might be imitated, reworked or parodied in literature. The same is not true of the other major area of folklore that influenced high culture, folk belief. Although beliefs may be and often are verbalized, the interest lies not in the form these take but in the beliefs themselves. For Russian peasants, whose world centred on home and village community, everything outside presented a potential danger. They believed in the 'unclean force' (*nechistaia sila*), whose primary location was the other world (*tot svet*), but who might take various forms and inhabit this world. The most famous manifestations are those of the house spirit (*domovoi*), the forest spirit (*leshii*), the water demon (*vodianoi*) and the *rusalka* (largely a water spirit), but others lurked in the bathhouse, the threshing barn, the marsh, the fields and so on. Though the spirits varied in the degree of hostility they displayed towards human beings, ranging from the generally benign house spirit to the water demon who enjoyed drowning people, they were not exclusively evil, only punishing man when he showed insufficient respect (for example ignored the housespirit's culinary prefer-ences) or invaded the spirit's territory without taking appropriate precautions, such as wearing clothes inside out before venturing into the forest. In the case of the house spirit his more favourable image probably depends partly on links with an ancestor cult; he was usually believed to be old and even to look like a dead master of the house. It was essential when moving house to take a coal from the old house so that the *domovoi* would come along too. Without his protective help it was believed the family would perish.

Like the *domovoi*, the forest spirit was as much playful as malicious. He might lead peasants astray in the forest by calling out to them or even kidnap babies, but those who met him could placate him using various methods such as making him laugh by uttering obscenities. Many believed that forest spirits lived in large family groups much like the peasants themselves; they had wives and children, lived in houses, herded animals and played cards. The appearance of the *leshii* varied, but most often was believed to resemble a tall peasant carrying a knout or cudgel over his shoulder, though he could at will metamorphose into an animal or vary his size. Ultimately he was less harmful than the water demon, partly because peasants could not swim and hence death by drowning was a real possibility, especially after a night out and when one remembers that villages were normally built near water. Though the *vodianoi* was usually said to resemble an old man, with green slime-covered hair and beard, his hostility towards humans led to his image becoming confused with that of the devil (horns, glowing eyes and a tail). His home was in deep pools from which he would emerge to drag the unwary under the waters.

No nature spirit achieved more prominence in high literature than the other water spirit, the *rusalka*. Except in the north of Russia, where she was envisioned as a hideous creature with grotesquely large breasts, water sprites were seen as beautiful young maidens. They were believed to be the souls of drowned maidens or unbaptized children who, having died an unnatural death, were in a liminal state between life and death. They would emerge from the water at night to sing, dance and entice male passers-by. Then they would drown them or tickle them to death, though there were also accounts of marriages between water sprites and humans. Pushkin, Lermontov, Gogol' and Turgenev were all drawn to this image, because it corresponded to the *ondine* of French and German folklore, so popular in the period of Romanticism, while at the same time being distinctively Russian. In Gogol''s 'May Night' ('Maiskaia noch'') the motif of the dangerous drowned maiden enticing the young hero Levko is woven into a story full of motifs from Ukrainian folklore. There was, however, much more to the image of the *rusalka*. Many located her in the fields. In particular she featured in the rites of Rusal'naia Week in late spring. From these it would appear that she was connected to a cult of vegetation and fertility, and as she emerged from the waters, she brought life-giving moisture. At the end of the week an effigy of the *rusalka* was ritually destroyed in the fields, perhaps as a way of negating her danger to man or perhaps as fertility magic to bring a good harvest.

Nature spirits were perhaps too redolent of folksy charm to feature extensively in Russian literature after the period of Romanticism; an exception can be found in early Zamiatin stories such as *The North* (*Sever*), where the past history of Marei plays on the *rusalka* conceit. Where spirits were seen as evil, writers even more than peasants tended to equate them with devils; Blok, for example, wrote about marsh devils in his cycle *Bubbles of the Earth* (*Puzyri zemli*). In general, the folk devil invades many areas of Russian literature, though most openly in Romantic writing. Of course, given his Christian origins, separating the folk devil from his ecclesiastical counterpart is complicated, especially as folk mythology influenced the image of the devil throughout Christian history. Nonetheless, in Russia the concept of the 'unclean force' and its many manifestations may well have prompted the particular emphasis on demonic multiplicity and ubiquity; peasants were more keenly aware of the hordes of small devils than a single Devil. This sense of ubiquitous evil apparently not only influenced Gogol' in his vision of a demonically infected Petersburg, but also provided a national context for the literary demonism of the Symbolists. Although the spirits rarely left their own habitats, whereas devils insinuated themselves everywhere, devils resembled spirits in having dwelling places, holes or cracks in the earth's surface and watery places, which led to the equation of the *vodianoi* and the marsh spirit (*bolotnik*) with the devil. Since any opening or body of water would suffice, it was essential to cross oneself when yawning or place sticks in the form of a cross on bowls of water. Simply mentioning the devil could cause him to appear, a motif employed to effect by both Gogol' (in *The Overcoat* [*Shinel'*] and 'The Fair at Sorochintsy') and Dostoevsky (in *The Double* [*Dvoinik*], *The Devils* and *The Brothers Karamazov* [*Brat'ia Karamazovy*]). Both writers also made extensive use of the association of laughter with the demonic: witness the transformation of the folk image of the devil as prankster in *The Devils*, where Petr Verkhovensky calls himself by the common term for the devil, 'joker' (*shut*). In *Crime and Punishment* (*Prestuplenie i nakazanie*) Svidrigailov bursts out into mirthless laughter when he first meets Raskol'nikov.

Mythological creatures were only the most colourful aspects of folk belief. The peasants' concept of time was essentially circular (as illustrated by the hero of the novel *Oblomov*, who is permanently locked into circular rather than linear temporal structures). The agricultural year and the concept of man's life as a series of stages before a final return to the earth, the ultimate source of all fertility, further reinforced ideas of circularity. The benevolence of Mother Damp Earth was sought in rituals that dotted the folk calendar. Most had lost real meaning for urban and literate Russians, such that folk festivals appear in literature mainly as ethnographic references with little understanding of the world-view that lay behind them. Aspects of Shrovetide carnival festivities, such as sliding down ice hills and, above all, Yuletide customs, became a beloved part of Russian identity for all classes. Thus in *War and Peace* Tolstoy describes Yuletide as celebrated by his archetypal Russian family, the Rostovs. Similarly, in *Evgenii Onegin* Pushkin depicts his very Russian heroine, Tat'iana, following Yuletide tradition and trying to tell her fortune.

Only the most important aspects of Russian folklore and literary folklorization have been covered here. While folklore was an integral part of the peasant way of life in the nineteenth century, and to a decreasing extent in the twentieth, the élite classes happily separated from its social context and viewed it as charming, often artistic, curiously, colourful, essentially Russian, and, though some refused to admit it, often crude or cruel. Depending on attitudes, social background and period, writers not only made the most varied creative use of folklore, but also often unconsciously incorporated traditional oral culture into their work, even if it was just the occasional proverb. The battle to drag peasants into the modern world, with the consequential loss of the world-view that generated the old artistic and colourful forms of folklore, inevitably caused and still causes objections; a relatively recent attempt to reassert old values was made by Soviet Village Prose writers. Old ways still hang on in rural backwaters, but Russians today have an active contemporary folklore (songs, anecdotes, urban legends and so on), which is of less literary than sociological interest. It is unlikely this new subculture will seriously impact upon the dominant literate culture of Russia, but artistic folkore collected over the last two centuries remains part of every Russian's upbringing and will doubtless continue to serve as rich source material for writers.

FURTHER READING

Afanas'ev, A. *Russian Fairy Tales, collected by Aleksandr Afanas'ev*, trans. Norbert Guterman, New York: Pantheon, 1973.

Bailey, James, and Tatyana Ivanova (ed. and trans.), *An Anthology of Russian Folk Epics*, New York and London: M.E. Sharpe, 1999.

Haney, Jack V., *An Introduction to the Russian Folktale* (*The Complete Russian Folktale*, vol. I), Armonk, New York and London: M.E. Sharpe, 1999.

Haney, Jack V. (ed. and trans.), *Russian Animal Tales* (*The Complete Russian Folktale*, vol. II), Armonk, New York and London, M.E. Sharpe, 1999.

Ivanits, Linda J., *Russian Folk Belief*, Armonk, New York and London: M.E. Sharpe, 1989.

Kelly, Catriona, *Petrushka, The Russian Carnival Puppet Theatre*, Cambridge: Cambridge University Press, 1990.

Oinas, Felix J., *Essays on Russian Folklore and Mythology*, Columbus, Ohio: Slavica, 1985.

Propp, V., *Morphology of the Folktale*, trans. Laurence Scott. Second revised edition, Austin, Texas and London: University of Texas Press, 1968.

Reeder, Roberta (ed. and trans.), *Russian Folk Lyrics*, Bloomington and Indianapolis: Indiana University Press (a reprint of *Down Along the Mother Volga*, 1975), 1993.

Ryan, W.F., *The Bathhouse at Midnight: Magic in Russia*, Stroud: Sutton Publishing, 1999.

Stangé-Zhivirova, N., *Une autre Russie: Fêtes et rites traditionelles du peuple russe*, Paris, Peeters, 1998.

Thompson, Ewa M., *Understanding Russia: The Holy Fool in Russian Culture*, Lanham, Maryland: University Press of America, 1987.

Warner, Elizabeth A., *The Russian Folk Theatre*, The Hague: Mouton, 1977.

Warner, E.A. and Evgenii Kustovsky, *Russian Folk Lyrics*, Hull: Hull University Press, 1989.

Wigzell, Faith, *Reading Russian Fortunes: Print Culture, Magic and Divination in Russia from 1765*, Cambridge, Cambridge University Press, 1998.

5

RELIGIOUS WRITING IN POST-PETRINE RUSSIA

RUTH COATES

This essay looks at the tradition of religious writing in Russia and attempts to draw out some of its major themes. It is not concerned with theology as such, insofar as the writers under review here, with rare exceptions, were neither official representatives of the Church nor academic theologians. Historically, in Russia the discipline of theology was confined to the seminaries, the traditional channel for young men who wished to take holy orders. In fact, there was a huge social and cultural gulf between the Orthodox priesthood and the educated classes in Russia, a gulf reflected in and perpetuated by the parallel existence of two educational systems: the seminaries and the universities. Ever since the reign of Peter the Great (reigned 1696–1725), who first introduced secular, western-style education in Russia, it was as though two worlds existed side by side. One, the rural, peasant world, contained the Church and breathed its ancient and traditional values. The other, much smaller world, predominantly urban, and for a long time aristocratic, was modelled on western forms – the state bureaucracy, the education system – and eventually assimilated the West's secular, post-Enlightenment values.

It was out of this second micro-world that the Russian intelligentsia arose in the first half of the nineteenth century. Yet the intelligentsia, strictly defined, consisted only of those intellectuals who dedicated themselves to taking Peter's cultural revolution to its logical social and political conclusion: the overthrow of the tsarist regime and the adoption of some form of socialism in Russia. And crucially, since, despite Peter's successful technical subordination of the Church to the state, the autocracy and the Church had remained ideologically hopelessly intertwined, this meant the rejection of Orthodoxy also. Those intellectuals whose religious beliefs excluded them from the intelligentsia proper therefore found themselves playing an ambiguous role as interpreters of an alien culture to their secularized peers. Hence the peculiar generic status of religious writing in Russia: neither theology, nor philosophy, it occupies a space all of its own. Nevertheless, precisely because of its function as bridge, it affords the western reader unique access to aspects of what I should like to call the Orthodox Russian consciousness, on the grounds that even those Russian religious writers who disown Orthodoxy betray the religious sensibility which they have inherited in the manner of their disownment.

The eighteenth century in Russia witnessed the labour and birth pangs of high culture in the western European mode. A tiny élite of artists and intellectuals strove to adapt a still essentially medieval cultural and linguistic sensibility to alien literary forms, and thereby to change that sensibility for ever. They were supported in their goal of forging a European identity for Russia culturally by the historical coincidence that this difficult, conscious turning towards the West took place during the Enlightenment, whose values strongly reinforced their modernizing impulse.

Particularly relevant is the cosmopolitan flavour of the period, its emphasis on the universal direction of the illuminating beam of reason onto benighted humanity as such, and the relative disregard of merely national cultural concerns. In the Russian context, this was bound to manifest itself as insensitivity to, or hostility towards, the function fulfilled by Russian Orthodoxy in the constitution of the national psyche which the 'Enlighteners' were seeking to mould. The differences between Eastern and Western confessions so important to nineteenth-century debates about Russia's relationship to Europe were irrelevant in the eighteenth, when the idea was to become an enlightened citizen of the world by taking up the struggle with institutionalized religion *per se*. The satirical literature of the period, predictably, attacks the Church in this anti-obscurantist spirit (Kantemir's Satires, Fonvizin's drama). Religious belief, where it is manifested, is deistic: Church tradition is discarded in favour of a vision of God as the creator of a harmonious rational universe, with man in his appointed place as master of all he surveys, relying exclusively on the inner light of reason for guidance (see the odes of Lomonosov and Derzhavin and Radishchev's *Journey from St Petersburg to Moscow*). The rise of Freemasonry in Russia in the eighteenth century, with its emphasis on brotherly love, faith, and charity, and its esoteric interpretation of Christianity, echoes the trend away from the established Church.

In the first decades of the nineteenth century Russian artists began to liberate themselves from western literary models and to articulate a rapidly developing cultural sensibility that was at once European and uniquely Russian. Again, cultural developments in the West helped to bring this about: the Neoclassical paradigm of the Enlightenment era, which privileged the principle of imitation of classical models and thereby impeded the progress of the Russians in overcoming imitative practices of their own, gave way to Romanticism, with its rejection of generic and linguistic hierarchies and its deliberate replacement of Enlightenment universalism with the principle of national identity, ethnicity, and folk. This latter, as promoted by the ideologues of Romanticism, the German Idealists, was to prove immensely fruitful for Russian religious thought throughout the nineteenth century and beyond.

Under the influence of Romantic philosophy, the significance of Russian Orthodoxy for Russian national culture became a relevant and even pressing question, given the ongoing quest of Russia to define itself *vis-à-vis* Western Europe. Petr Chaadaev (1793–1856) famously defined the terms of the debate in his first *Philosophical Letter* (1836), in which he subjects his country to a devastating critique. The Orthodox Church is held responsible for subjecting Russia to a centuries-long static and stagnant existence beyond the boundaries of the civilized European world by its rejection of the Catholic Church, under whose aegis a united West had made steady progress towards the realization of a common, Christian, goal. By contrast, Russia had contributed nothing to the history of humanity, and indeed had no history of her own, since history was only possible where there was a shared set of ideals. In *Apology of a Madman* (*Apologiia sumasshedshego*, 1837), Chaadaev modified this position in response to the outcry the *Letter* had provoked, crediting the Orthodox Church with holding Russia together in times of national disaster, and turning the absence of a past into a potential advantage by predicting a glorious future for Russia who, should she only resolve to join the European family, could bring the fresh perspective of youth to bear on the problems of the ageing West and find solutions for them.

The defence of Russian history and the role of Orthodoxy in it was mounted by a group who came to be known as the Slavophiles. Its leading ideologists were Ivan Kireevsky (1806–56), Aleksei Khomiakov (1804–60), and Konstantin Aksakov (1817–60). The Slavophiles accepted the essential structure of Chaadaev's position – the fundamental divide between Russia and the West, the central role of institutional Christianity in history, and the evaluative distinction between the Western (Catholic) and Eastern (Orthodox) Churches – but inverted his basic argument, contending that Russia's historical isolation from western Europe, taken in combination with the unique qualities of the Eastern confession which had shaped the Russian psyche as well as her political and social structures, meant that Russia had been able to preserve something precious which the West had lost. Chaadaev's vision of a future healing mission for Russia was also adopted: the spiritual and social health of the West was Russia's to restore, though not with the light touch of a child, but with the healing hands of an old sage.

The something precious can best be described as 'wholeness' or 'integrity', as the Slavophiles sought to establish in several interrelated spheres. In their reading of western history, those very cultural developments which had passed Russia by – the ancient civilizations, the Renaissance, the Reformation – were actually milestones on a road to spiritual impoverishment, driven by the ascendancy of rationalism, the *bête noir* of the Slavophiles. The deadening, formalizing spirit of rationalism had been bequeathed to western Christianity by Rome, in the political and legal spheres, and in philosophy by Aristotle, whose thought informed medieval scholasticism. The great failure of the Roman Catholic Church had been to allow reason to oust faith, and the formal principle of external authority to replace the inner integrity of a freely shared communion. The Protestant Reformation was a rebellion against this principle, but, as Khomiakov put it, it merely resulted in a barren inversion of Catholicism: where the Roman Church had known unity, but not freedom, Protestantism knew freedom, but not unity. Without a unifying Church, believers were thrown back on their own individual mental resources in the interpretation of Scripture and doctrine, which situation had led directly to the Enlightenment, the Age of Reason. In Hegel the rational principle had reached its apogee.

In philosophy, Kireevsky opposed rationalism with the principle of 'integral reason', according to which the cognitive function should not dominate but complement the other faculties – feeling, intuition, and the will – in an 'organic' approach to truth. Truth was a matter for the whole human being, not just one isolated aspect of mental life. Ultimately, Kireevsky believed that philosophy should emanate from within a life of faith. His 'new principle' in philosophy was not in fact new for Russia, where the Orthodox tradition, nourished on the Greek Fathers and not 'tainted' by Western developments, had never experienced the conflict between reason and faith. Thus true Russian culture (as opposed to the thin veneer of European culture borrowed from the West) did not know the fragmentation, the isolation, and the loneliness of western Europe.

In theology, Khomiakov contrasted the formal and hierarchical authority of the Roman Church with the Orthodox principle of *sobornost'*, or 'conciliarity'. He represented the Eastern Church as an organic community of equals, with authority invested only in Christ, in which decisions on matters of faith and dogma were made in the ancient conciliar manner, on the basis of the unanimity of all the Church's members. Deriving ultimately from the Trinity, *sobornost'* was seen to have penetrated, through the Orthodox Church, to the very communal foundations of Russian agrarian society: Aksakov in particular did much to promote the idea that the peasant commune, the *obshchina*, and its ancient form of self-government, the council of elders known as the mir, embodied the conciliar principle. *Sobornost'* was not to be confused either with democracy (freedom without true unity) or collectivism (unity without freedom): rather it expressed the perfect harmony of freedom within unity, or the many in the one.

The founders of Slavophilism were idealistic aristocrats who shared a conservative utopian vision of a Russia uncontaminated by the West. Thus they did not wholeheartedly stand behind the autocratic regime as it existed under Nicholas I (ruled 1825–55). Although monarchists, they had strong reservations about the post-Petrine bureaucracy which, as they saw it, distorted and corrupted the traditional relationship between the tsar and his people; they opposed the subordination of Church to state, the institution of serfdom, and the suppression of free speech which intensified so unbearably in the aftermath of the Decembrist rebellion of 1825.

After their deaths, however, Slavophilism developed in a different, less romantic and utopian, but at the same time far less philosophically fruitful direction. Their epigones were hard-headed political pragmatists, who espoused an imperialistic and chauvinistic political platform. The movement degenerated into Pan-Slavism, the political aspiration to the unification of all the Slav peoples into one mighty Orthodox empire and the recapture of the Byzantine capital of Constantinople from the Turks. The most representative theoretical exposition of Pan-Slavism can be found in Nikolai Danilevsky's *Russia and Europe* (*Rossiia i Evropa*, 1869).

A distorted and extreme version of the Slavophile world-view emerged in the later work of the brilliant prose writer Nikolai Gogol' (1809–52), as his aesthetic idealism was transformed into a tortured religious didacticism. This development is reflected in the production history of his novel *Dead Souls* (*Mertvye dushi*, 1842), originally conceived as a satirical picaresque exposure of the vices of Russian provincial society, but becoming for Gogol' the first of a three-part project of epic proportions designed to show the path to the complete moral regeneration of

Russia. The task eventually destroyed him: after a decade of intensive work he proved unable to write the second volume to his own satisfaction and twice burned the manuscript, the second time ten days before his death. Instead he produced *Selected Passages from a Correspondence with Friends* (*Vybrannye mesta iz perepiski s druz'iami*, 1847), a semi-confessional, semi-didactic collection of 'letters' and articles in which the full extent and nature of his messianic Orthodox nationalism was laid bare to a totally unsuspecting public, and whose moralizing tone and extreme reactionary force alienated even his Slavophile friends.

Russia's foremost metaphysical poet Fedor Tiutchev (1803–73) occupies an interesting place in relation to Slavophilism. By political persuasion Tiutchev was a conservative nationalist and Pan-Slavist, and these attitudes are reflected in the rather significant proportion of his verse which is overtly political, often written in heated response to contemporary events. Yet the critical consensus is that he lacked a personal religious faith, Orthodoxy being for him primarily an ideological necessity. On the other hand, his (superior) philosophical verse shows an intense personal apprehension of metaphysical chaos underlying the apparently stable order of things, which one is tempted to designate religious, though certainly not Christian (Schelling's influence is apparent here). Again, however, it has been argued that this terrifying dualism is more an expression of the poet's own psyche than of a philosophical or religious system.

The next truly fertile literary reworking of Slavophile insights came with Fedor Dostoevsky (1821–81). In his youth Dostoevsky was a socialist sympathizer, attending the underground, radical Petrashevsky circle, which famously led to his arrest, mock execution, and eventual internment in Siberian labour camps for a public reading of Belinsky's *Letter to Gogol'* (1847). However he emerged from exile in 1859 a convert to Orthodoxy, and devoted all his journalistic energy thereafter to fierce polemic with the radicals, whilst in his great novels, for the first time in Russian literature, he gave the intuitions and religious yearnings of the Slavophiles concrete form, at the same time taking them forward in his own unique way.

In the 1860s Dostoevsky was part of a group of like-minded thinkers and artists known as the *pochvenniki* (from the Russian word *pochva*, meaning 'soil'). These included his brother, Mikhail, the poet and critic Apollon Grigor'ev, and Nikolai Strakhov. The *pochvenniki* stood for reintegration, a recognizable Slavophile theme, though the greater turbulence of the times lent it a new pathos. With the ideological inroads made by the radicals, and the socio-economic inroads made by advancing capitalism and the proletarianization of the peasantry in the wake of the Emancipation of 1861, the old Orthodox feudal Russia was no longer merely under threat, as it had been in the early Slavophiles' day, but was rapidly and tangibly disintegrating. It was already impossible simply to turn one's back on the West. The *pochvenniki* read the situation apocalyptically, calling for the reconciliation of West and East, the westernized intelligentsia and the people, before it was too late. However, as their name clearly implies, the *pochvenniki* felt it was for the West (more particularly the spirit of the West in Russia) to humble itself (to 'return to the soil') before the people, who would receive it as a prodigal son.

Of course the concept of 'soil' denotes the *soborny* life of the people who worked the land. But it is important to grasp the profound symbolic and religious connotations of the term. This was damp, black, fertile Mother Earth, the supreme object of worship of the Slavs in pre-Christian times, and still in the nineteenth century identified with the all-embracing, synthesizing spirit of Mother Russia. Moreover, the soil was intimately connected with the Orthodox Church, which had absorbed its symbolic energy into the veneration of Mary, the Mother of God, and the importance attached by the Orthodox to the feminine image of Sophia, the Holy Wisdom. A return to the soil thus meant the reintegration of the masculine, rational principle into a very feminine spirituality.

The consequences of a rationalism which has lost contact with its unconscious roots are a dominant theme in Dostoevsky's fiction. In *Notes from Underground* (*Zapiski iz podpol'ia*, 1864) the anti-hero is the ultimate uprooted superfluous man who attacks the rationalist world order from a position of enraged impotence. His helplessness derives from the fact that there is no alternative set of values in which he might place his trust. Ironically, the censor prevented Dostoevsky from presenting that alternative in the novel in the form of Christianity. As a result, *Notes from Underground* is perhaps the starkest presentation of psychological disintegration he ever produced. The various outcomes of such disintegration – complete moral degeneration, madness, and suicide – are counterposed in his later works with the potential for healing. For example, in *Crime and Punishment* (*Prestuplenie i nakazanie*, 1866) a rootless young intellectual commits murder in order to prove a theory, but is ultimately saved from the blind alley he has driven himself into by the devout prostitute Sonia, an embodiment of Hagia Sophia. In a passage of central importance in the novel, Sonia is represented reading the Gospel story of Christ's raising of Lazarus from the dead to Raskol'nikov, presaging his own symbolic resurrection.

Christ was supremely significant to Dostoevsky, who once famously declared that if he had to choose between Christ and the truth he would choose Christ. Christ was the image of the perfect human being, the God-man, to which Dostoevsky opposed his antithesis, the man-God, a concept ultimately deriving from his reading of Feuerbach with the Petrashevsky circle and denoting the idol made of man by the promotion of human reason above all other standards of truth. Napoleon, whom Raskol'nikov seeks to emulate in *Crime and Punishment*, is one image of the man-God in Dostoevsky: a person who permitted himself to overstep all moral boundaries in the pursuit of a 'great idea', with complete disregard for his victims.

Dostoevsky was in broad agreement with the Slavophiles about the historical route followed by rationalism in its ascendency, but went much further than they had done in the demonization of the Roman Catholic Church, of which he wrote in apocalyptic terms as the Antichrist. He saw a direct link between Catholicism and the atheistic socialism which he now feared and hated so much: to his mind, socialism was a secular re-enactment of Catholicism, an attempt to regain the unity, also the unifying idea (the establishment of heaven on earth) which had been lost with the Reformation. Yet he was convinced that such unity could only be attained through violence and at the cost of the moral freedom of the individual which was more precious to him than any paradise. The most sophisticated treatment of this view is found in the 'Legend of the Grand Inquisitor' of *The Brothers Karamazov* (*Brat'ia Karamazovy*, 1880), a parable related by Ivan Karamazov to his brother Alesha portraying a society which has voluntarily surrendered its freedom to the Grand Inquisitor (another man-God) in return for happiness. The philosophical complexity of the story arises from the persuasiveness of the Inquisitor's defence of his actions; he casts himself as a noble and suffering saviour figure who has taken on the burden of freedom for the sake of his subjects, and from the ambiguity of the silent kiss with which Christ receives the heretic.

Dostoevsky's view of the Orthodox Church surpasses the Slavophiles in its messianism. Russia alone had preserved the image of Christ in all its purity. She was the God-bearing nation which was destined to save the West. This paradox of arrogant humility and nationalistic universalism is clearly expressed in the celebrated speech he delivered in 1880 at the unveiling of the Pushkin monument in Moscow. Here Dostoevsky represents Pushkin as the supreme embodiment of Russia's 'unique' spirit of universal brotherhood, and calls upon all Russians to humble themselves for service to the West.

Dostoevsky attained widespread fame, if not acceptance, in his own lifetime. Two of his contemporaries, Konstantin Leont'ev (1831–94) and Nikolai Fedorov (1828–1903), did not, but have since come to be appreciated for the originality and fruitfulness of their ideas. Leont'ev was a prose writer and a playwright, but unlike Dostoevsky never managed to capture the extraordinary flavour of his world-view in his fiction. For this we must turn to his essays, in particular *Byzantinism and Slavdom* (*Vizantinizm i slavianstvo*, 1871–2). Here he elaborates his quasi-biological theory of the development of civilizations from 'primitive simplicity' through flourishing complexity to degeneration into a secondary simplification. An aesthete above all else, he was fiercely opposed to contemporary western developments, which showed all the symptoms of third-phase decay, on the grounds that the bourgeois aspiration to material prosperity and the socialist ideal of equality were resulting in an aesthetically impoverished, monotonous cultural sameness. His political arch-conservatism and appreciation of the Russian autocracy were motivated partly by the aesthetic wealth of stratified and brazenly unequal societies, but also had a religious basis: paradoxically, Leont'ev's Orthodoxy was of the most ascetic Byzantine variety, a religion of fear which believed in the purgative value of the suffering which violent authoritarian regimes could be trusted to deliver.

Nikolai Fedorov's ideas, set out in *The Philosophy of the Common Task* (*Filosofiia obshchego dela*, 1906 and 1913), tapped another root of the Russian religious sensibility and at the same time gave an extreme and unique twist to the utopian theme. Fedorov's vision was for no less than the transformation of the mortal universe into an immortal cosmos by the concerted effort of humankind, which he felt to be no more than the logical outcome of human evolution. To attain this goal would be finally to cast off the suffering occasioned by our consciousness of mortality and thus to arrive at a state of perfect happiness. But to Fedorov it was axiomatic that such happiness was psychologically impossible unless it could be shared by the many generations who had died on the path to its realization. Thus it was imperative that the present generation should utilize all the resources of science and technology available to it bodily to resurrect all of its predecessors. This extraordinary supposed reverence of the sons for the fathers represents a modern resurfacing of the ancient, pre-Christian, Slavic practice of ancestor worship, which in Fedorov's view accounted for the importance attached by Russians to *rod*, the 'clan', and ultimately for Russian collectivism. On being made acquainted with Fedorov's ideas, Dostoevsky declared that he had never read anything more logical; critics have demonstrated a clear connection to them of the central, patricidal motif of *The Brothers Karamazov*.

Lev Tolstoy (1828–1910) occupies a peculiar place in the Russian religious tradition. He underwent an existential crisis in mid-career, culminating in religious conversion in 1878, a year after the publication of *Anna Karenina*. This had an enormous, mostly deleterious, impact on his creative writing as he embraced a view of art as decadent wherever it does not serve a clear moral purpose (see *What is Art?*, 1898): almost all of his post-crisis work suffers from this unapologetic didacticism, though some might argue that this is mitigated by its undeniable moral power. As a religious thinker Tolstoy is something of a maverick. This is because of the rationalist spirit in which he arrived at his final religious world-view. There is a paradox here: Tolstoy's crisis was the result of his inability to arrive at the meaning of life through the use of his reason, yet no sooner had he been saved by accepting the 'irrational' faith of the people than reason kicked back in, with Tolstoy systematically rejecting all those rather crucial aspects of Christianity which were not amenable to rational explanation – the incarnation and resurrection of Christ, for example, and the belief in an after-life – eventually arriving at a view of Christ as little more than a great moral teacher. In this he is far closer to developments in Protestant theology in the West than he is to Orthodoxy, whose sacramental and liturgical life he could not accept, with the inevitable result that he was excommunicated by the Orthodox Church in 1901. Tolstoy has been described as a Christian anarchist: he rejected the very concept of the state and therefore of the institutionalized religion which shored it up ideologically, instead placing his faith in a brotherhood of man united in love and practising non-resistance to evil for the realization of heaven on earth. It is this extreme utopianism which does in the end mark him out as a *Russian* religious thinker.

In terms of a direct reworking of major themes bequeathed by the Slavophiles (wholeness, the religious significance of the relationship between East and West) and reinterpreted by Dostoevsky (the feminine principle, Godmanhood and the centrality of Christ, apocalypse and Antichrist), the most important figure to succeed Dostoevsky was undoubtedly Vladimir Solov'ev (1853–1900).

Solov'ev is a pivotal figure in the history of Russian religious culture. A trained philosopher who for some time worked within the academic establishment, Solov'ev gave systematic philosophical form to theories and ideas which the Slavophiles had sketched out in letters and essays, and which Dostoevsky had developed in journalistic polemic and prose fiction. He thus marks the apogee of the Slavophile tradition. At the same time, he is also the forerunner who paved the way for, indeed made possible, the profound cultural shift – designated the Russian religious renaissance by Zernov – which was to take place at the turn of the nineteenth and twentieth centuries, and which found artistic expression in Russian Symbolism. In this role as forerunner, Solov'ev's poetry is as important as his thought.

Yet Solov'ev was first and foremost a mystic, whose profound intuitive sense of the perfect oneness of the universe, divine and created, beyond the veil of imperfect appearances, was the starting point for his thought. Indeed, it has been argued that the excessively dry abstraction of his philosophical system, so foreign to other Russian religious thinkers, and seemingly paradoxical in the light of their concern – shared by Solov'ev himself – to overcome rationalism in philosophy, is a kind of compensation for, an attempt to contain, the unsettling power of his mystic experiences. Even in his poetry, life-changing visions are described in a self-deprecating, ironical spirit, as though deliberately to defuse their ecstatic charge. In any event, Solov'ev's theory of 'all-unity' (*vseedinstvo*) was founded on mystical perception. It may be said that he dedicated his whole life to actually bringing about the restoration of that cosmic unity which he had first glimpsed in a vision in early childhood.

In this project of reintegration we clearly recognize a hallmark of Russian religious thought, here manifesting itself for the first time in a mystical way. Solov'ev's life falls into three distinct phases which have been defined as theosophy, theocracy, and theurgy, or eschatology. Crudely speaking, Solov'ev devoted the first decade of his career to establishing all-unity theoretically, in his philosophy, the second to working for the reunification of the Churches, whilst towards the end of his life he confronted the possibility of failure for the first time and his writing took a dark, eschatological turn.

In the philosophical works of the first phase Solov'ev adopts and expands Kireevsky's historical critique of rationalism, but takes it further by contextualizing it as the second part of a three-stage dialectic. Long ago there existed a primitive form of primeval unity, when humanity lived an unconscious collective spiritual life. In due course individual consciousness, the ego, emerged, only to become over time fatally detached from nature: this is described, following Schelling, as a Fall. But civilization was now on the brink of a third phase: the synthesis of western rational formalism with eastern spiritual content in a new and higher unity. Thus, unlike the Slavophiles, Solov'ev accounted the development of western rationalism a necessary and ultimately productive event but, like them, believed that only the East could show the way to synthesis.

Solov'ev's presentation of the task of philosophy also represents a reworking of Kireevsky's 'integral reason'. Philosophy had disintegrated into fragmented disciplines; metaphysics, ethics, and aesthetics had lost sight of one another; rationalism and empiricism had exhausted themselves in isolation. Solov'ev proposed, and attempted systematically to theorize, the reintegration of the practical, intellectual, and religious manifestations of thought, will, and feeling, into a dynamic whole: 'integral life' (*tsel'naia zhizn'*). Nevertheless his system displays a clear hierarchy of values, with the religious manifestation of these three functions elevated over the others. For example, theology was superior to philosophy and science in the manifestation of the cognitive function. Thus the boundaries between philosophy and faith in Solov'ev are blurred. Perhaps the simplest way of summarizing their relationship is to say that for him philosophy was the rational presentation of Christian truth, and at the same time the vehicle for making that truth real: like Marx, he believed it was the task of philosophy to change the world.

In 1878 Solov'ev captivated educated Russian society with his *Lectures on Godmanhood* (*Chteniia o bogochelovechestve*). In these he took up Dostoevsky's pet theme and elaborated on its theoretical basis, demonstrating the need, as he saw it, for a new anthropology based on the synthesis of the socialist conception of the divine potential of man with the Christian understanding of his insignificance in the light of his mortality. The truth of Godmanhood had always been known to the Eastern Church and was expressed in the formula arrived at by the Council of Chalcedon concerning the 'unmerged and undivided' relation of the divine and human natures in Christ. Christ's Incarnation is the guarantee of the divine-human process in history, whereby humanity is called upon to know God and, together with the whole creation, achieve union with him. Solov'ev went on to trace the stages of development of this divine-human process and show how it reached its highest expression in the Incarnation.

In the second phase of Solov'ev's career he dramatically broke with the Slavophiles and challenged Dostoevsky's favourite prejudices by committing Chaadaev's great sin of identifying with the aspiration of the Catholic Church to establish the rule of God on earth. Abandoning philosophy, for a decade Solov'ev worked hard to prepare the ground for the reunification of the Christian Church, both by active collaboration with sympathetic Catholics abroad, and at home by a ruthless attack on Pan-Slavic ethnic chauvinism and Orthodox nationalism, which he exposed as inconsistent with universal Christian values. His ecumenism made him as isolated from the conservatives as he already was from the radicals by dint of his faith, and so he came to occupy a position rather similar to that of Chaadaev half a century before.

Solov'ev's efforts to concretize his theory of the historical divine-human process in a theocracy inevitably ended in disillusionment. His increasing pessimism about the Christian project was articulated in his last work, *Three Conversations: a Tale of the Antichrist* (*Tri razgovora: povest' ob antikhriste*, 1900). This apocalyptic piece brings him close to Dostoevsky once again, and carries strong echoes of the latter's 'Legend': an idealistic young man, impatient with Christ, succumbs to the Devil's temptations and, once he has become ruler of the world and satisfied the needs of humanity for food and miracles, tries to bribe a Christian rump to offer him allegiance. Since he refuses to acknowledge Christ, they decline, but emerge victorious from the subsequent Armageddon to be reunited with the returning Messiah.

Solov'ev lived to witness the early stages of a cultural revolution in Russia, the dawn of modernism, which was to challenge the very foundations of mainstream Russian culture – positivism, materialism, realism. Of course, this was happening all over Europe, but in Russia the process had a flavour and edge all of its own, due partly to the unprecedented upsurge in religious awareness which Solov'ev had himself in large measure brought about, and partly to the atmosphere of social and political unrest which intensified precipitously in the run-up to the 1917 Revolutions. But the religious response of the period was extraordinarily diverse, and after Solov'ev it becomes impossible to look at religious thought as an essentially linear development of Slavophile ideas. A striking characteristic of this time, for example, was the explosion of interest in non-Christian religions – Eastern spirituality, Judaism, and in particular pagan mythologies, the latter receiving added impetus from exposure to Nietzsche, whose work was supremely influential in this period. Yet simultaneously many intellectuals began to engage seriously with Orthodoxy for the first time, some actively working towards a rapprochement of the intelligentsia and the Church, a few even taking holy orders. It was this generation, too, who first fully appreciated the genius of Dostoevsky, rehabilitating him in a series of important critical works. In particular he was appreciated as a prophet who had foreseen the crisis to come, and indeed in these terrifying years the themes of apocalypse and Antichrist which had engaged him, and with which Solov'ev had ended, were restated again and again.

One of the most important initiators of the new sensibility – Dmitrii Merezhkovsky (1865–1941) – was also one of its most representative exponents. As poet, novelist, and critic his work exhibited the confluence of art and thought which was a hallmark of Russian Symbolism. His novel trilogy, *Christ and Antichrist* (*Khristos i Antikhrist*, 1896–1905), wrestles with the typical dilemma of whether and how paganism could be reconciled with Christianity. Merezhkovsky is drawn to the life-affirming ethos of paganism and to the romantic figure of the Nietzschean superman-antichrist (man-God!) in his various historical incarnations, and regrets the world-renouncing spirit of Christianity whilst recognizing its spiritual beauty. Ultimately, however, he was to embrace the religion of Christ and devote his considerable energies to promoting a Christian spiritual revival. Together with Zinaida Hippius and Dmitrii Filosofov he set up a series of Religio-philosophical Assemblies (1901–03) where representatives of the Church convened with St Petersburg's intellectual élite in an unprecedented manner in an effort to bridge the cultural gulf between them and establish a common language. After the 1905 Revolution Merezhkovsky became politicized. Like many others he interpreted it as a sign of imminent Apocalypse, and he became an enemy of socialism in the Dostoevskian manner, believing it would result only in despotism.

The religious passion and contradictions of the Silver Age found extreme expression in the person of Vasilii Rozanov (1856–1919). Rozanov was repelled by Christianity as a religion of death, and resented Christ for turning God, whom he loved, against the world and establishing a religion which, as he saw it, was both asexual and anti-sexual. 'Have nothing to do with women' was how he summed up the message of the New Testament. Rozanov loved both the feminine earthy fecundity of the world and the masculine principle, the seed. He celebrated the intimate sphere of the family (seed-*semia*/family-*sem'ia*) and, echoing Fedorov, attributed particular significance to clan and race. For this reason he greatly admired Judaism (whilst simultaneously expressing grossly anti-Semitic views in the conservative press), yet also, paradoxically, cherished the liturgical life of the Orthodox Church, so intimately interwoven with the daily life (*byt*) of the nation. Nevertheless, when faced with the suffering of a loved one, or indeed his own death, Rozanov drew close to Christ, refusing to apologise for the contradiction. It is typical of him that he should die with the words 'Christ is risen' on his lips, having spent the last months of his life working on *The Apocalypse of our Time* (*Apokalipsis nashego vremeni*, 1917–18), in which he lays the blame for the Revolution, which was sweeping away everything he loved about Russia, on Christianity, on the grounds that Christ had taken God away from the world, leaving a vacuum into which the forces of revolution inevitably had to rush.

The anti-rationalist legacy of the nineteenth-century religious tradition was assimilated in a variety of different ways by artists and philosophers. The defining characteristic of the literary movement of Symbolism, which flourished between 1890 and 1910, was a rejection of the rational order apparent on the surface of things and an attempt to capture the unseen, higher metaphysical reality in art. In the religious interpretation of their quest, Solov'ev was of primary importance in particular to the second generation of Symbolists – Viacheslav Ivanov (1866–1949), Andrei Bely (1880–1934), and Aleksandr Blok (1880–1921). Specifically, they identified with his engagement with Sophia, the Holy Wisdom or Divine Feminine. In his youth Solov'ev had received three mystical visions of Sophia, which persuaded him experientially of the existence of a perfect world beyond the veil of appearances. In his philosophy he interpreted Her variously as the world soul, the divine principle which animated the created cosmos, or else as the protectress of creation and mediator between heaven and earth. She was a major theme in his poetry, which Blok read at the time he was writing his *Verses on a Beautiful Lady* (*Stikhi o Prekrasnoi Dame*, 1901), his own first and purest treatment of the Sophia theme.

The Jewish philosopher Lev Shestov (1866–1938) abandoned the attempts of his forebears to integrate reason with faith, declaring the two to be irreconcilable opposites. Persuaded by Nietzsche of the meaninglessness of all so-called universal ethical standards, he held that all systems of knowledge and belief devised by human beings were nothing more than constructs erected to enable them to avoid facing the existential chaos within, the only genuine reality of human experience. This was the basis of his attack on Tolstoy's rationalistic moralism in an early study of that writer, and in *Dostoevsky and Nietzsche: The Philosophy of Tragedy* (*Dostoevskii i Nitche: filosofiia tragedii*, 1903) he championed the man from the Underground as the first of Dostoevsky's heroes to take up a new, existential and rebellious stance against the lie of common-sense truths and rationalist utopias. He saw the Underground Man and his heirs – Ippolit, Ivan Karamazov, etc. – as Dostoevsky's mouthpieces and the proof of his greatness, not the religious characters, who represented a retreat into ignoble dishonesty on Dostoevsky's part. Yet the absurdity of existence was not proof of the death of God: on the contrary, it was the token of our absolute need of God, but of God himself rather than any of his rationalizations. Genuine freedom was only attainable through the irrational act of faith.

Another form which the opposition to rationalism took was the evolution of the convictions of numerous intellectuals at this time from revolutionary Marxism through neo-Kantian Idealism to Orthodox Christianity. Four prominent representatives of this trend are Petr Struve (1870–1944), Semen Frank (1877–1950), Nikolai Berdiaev (1874–1948), and Sergei Bulgakov (1871–1944). These became widely known to the reading public through their collaboration in a project called *Signposts* (*Vekhi*, 1909), a collection of essays which launched a concerted attack on the radical intelligentsia in the wake of the 1905 Revolution from a Christian-humanist perspective. Its critique is the more potent because so many of the authors knew the world-view they were deconstructing from the inside. But what is really original about this collection is the combination of a defence of spiritual values with a sophisticated political awareness and a social conscience. The contributors were not reactionaries or even conservatives, but reformists: a number of them participated actively in the democratic experiment of 1905 to 1917.

The return to Orthodoxy took different forms, and people started from different places. Frank was a Jew from the professional class who looked on Christianity as the completion of his religious upbringing. Berdiaev was an aristocrat from a family which was nominally Orthodox but had a relaxed attitude to matters of faith. He himself remained on the margins of confessional loyalty, which he never allowed to compromise his highest value: personal freedom. Like Shestov, he was philosophically closest to the Existentialists, though he claimed to go beyond them in rejecting ontology in favour of freedom as a starting point for philosophy. He made use of the Slavophile concept of *sobornost'* and Solov'ev's divine-human process in his thought, but for his central concern is indebted to Dostoevsky: in his late book, *Dostoevsky's World Conception* (*Mirosozertsanie Dostoevskogo*, 1923; translated as *Dostoevsky*, 1934), he deplores the novelist's nationalistic chauvinism, but celebrates him as a metaphysician concerned with tracing 'the tragedy of the human spirit' arising from the fact of freedom – a thinker, in fact, rather like himself.

Bulgakov's was a return to the Church in the full sense of the word: coming from a priestly family, he in due course joined their number, renouncing his post as Professor of Political Economy to take orders in 1918. In exile he was to produce a body of theology which was deeply indebted to Solov'ev's meditations on Sophia and Godmanhood. Other philosophers directly influenced by Solov'ev are the brothers Trubetskoy, Sergei (1862–1905) and Evgenii (1863–1920), Lev Lopatin (1855–1929) and, from a younger generation, Vladimir Ern (1881–1915) and the brilliant mathematician and later priest Pavel Florensky (1882–*c*.1939), whose major work, *The Pillar and Ground of Truth* (*Stolp i utverzhdenie istiny*, 1914) broke new ground in Russian theology and was another important influence on Bulgakov's later work.

The October Revolution of 1917 unceremoniously brought down the curtain on the Russian religious renaissance. Some of its leading players – Rozanov, Blok – died within years of causes not unrelated to the upheaval. Many went into exile in the wave of enforced expulsions of 1922. Florensky perished in a labour camp. Others survived in the Soviet Union. In the diaspora the tradition of religious thought continued to develop, despite its alien environment, in both its philosophical and its theological incarnations. At home in Russia, it was left to artists to preserve the memory of a Russian spirituality until such time as it could be resurrected: Anna Akhmatova, Osip Mandel'shtam, Boris Pasternak, Mikhail Bulgakov, Andrei Platonov, Aleksandr Solzhenitsyn. Among philosophers, a thread of continuity was provided by Mikhail Bakhtin (1895–1975), who was rehabilitated from internal exile in the 1960s after the rediscovery his 1929 book on Dostoevsky by young admirers, and therefore survived to exert a personal influence on what was to become the first post-Soviet generation of religiously minded scholars.

FURTHER READING

(See also some items listed following Chapters 11 and 12)

Berdyaev, Nicolas, *The Russian Idea*, trans. R.M. French, London: Geoffrey Bles, 1947.

Bulgakov, Sergius, *A Bulgakov Anthology*, ed. James Pain and Nicolas Zernov, Philadelphia: Westminster Press, 1976.

Coates, Ruth. *Christianity in Bakhtin: God and the Exiled Author*, Cambridge: Cambridge University Press, 1998.

Copleston, Frederick C. *Philosophy in Russia: From Herzen to Lenin and Berdyaev*, Tunbridge Wells: Search Press; Notre Dame, Indiana: University of Notre Dame Press, 1986.

Copleston, Frederick C. *Russian Religious Philosophy: Selected Aspects*, Notre Dame, Indiana: University of Notre Dame Press, 1988.

Crone, Anne Lisa. *Rozanov and the End of Literature: Polyphony and the Dissolution of Genre in Solitaria and Fallen Leaves*, Würzburg: JAL Verlag, 1978.

Duncan, Peter J.S. *Russian Messianism: Third Rome, Revolution, Communism and After*, London and New York: Routledge, 2000.

Fedorov, N.F. *What Was Man Created For? The Philosophy of the Common Task*, trans. Elisabeth Koutaissoff and Marilyn Minto, London: Honeyglen, 1990.

Fedotov, G.P. *The Russian Religious Mind*, 2 vols., Cambridge, Mass.: Harvard University Press, 1966.

Florovsky, Georges. *Ways of Russian Theology*, 2 vols., Belmont, Mass.: Nordland, 1979.

Frank, S.L. (ed.) *A Solovyev Anthology*, trans. N. A. Duddington, London: SCM Press; New York: Scribner, 1950.

Martin, Bernard (ed.) *A Shestov Anthology*, Athens, Ohio: Ohio University Press, 1970.

Shragin, Boris, and Albert Todd (eds) *Landmarks: A Collection of Essays on the Russian Intelligentsia – 1909*, translated by Marian Schwartz, New York: Karz Howard, 1977.

Williams, Rowan (ed.) *Sergii Bulgakov: Towards a Russian Political Theology*, Edinburgh: T & T Clark, 1999.

Zenkovsky, V.V. *A History of Russian Philosophy*, trans. George L. Kline, 2 vols., New York: Columbia University Press; London: Routledge and Kegan Paul, 1953.

Zernov, Nicolas. *Three Russian Prophets: Khomyakov, Dostoevsky, Solovyev*, London: SCM Press, 1944.

Zernov, Nicolas. *The Russian Religious Renaissance of the Twentieth Century*, London: Darton, Longman and Todd, 1963.

6

PRE-REVOLUTIONARY RUSSIAN THEATRE

A.D.P. BRIGGS

In the late seventeenth century, when the French professional theatre was at its zenith and England and Spain looked back over several generations to the heyday of their theatre, drama in Russia first tottered into official existence. Wishing to please his new wife and mark the birth of their first child (the future Peter the Great), Tsar Alexei ordered the court performance of a play, the biblical story of Esther, entitled *Artaxerxes*. This was the same tsar who, in 1648, had decreed the destruction of all musical instruments and theatrical properties, with severe punishment for anyone using them. Now, in 1672 (when Paris was watching the première of Racine's *Bajazet*), the stilted, day-long play received royal approval, and the German producer Johann Gregory (1631–75), was encouraged to form a small Court Theatre. The enterprise began well, extolling the Monarchy and glorifying the Christian Church as instructed, but it staged only nine productions and fizzled out in less than three years. This miserable false start, ill-conceived, artificial and un-Russian as it was, typifies the desultory beginnings of the Russian theatre, which would not achieve any real stature or permanence for nearly another century. Its early story is one of sporadic outbursts in various directions, followed by persecution, indifference or uncontainable competition from foreigners.

The earliest sources of Russian theatre are similar to those in other countries, deriving from either folk arts or both pagan and liturgical ceremony. Peripatetic entertainers – minstrels, clowns, animal-trainers, puppeteers, musicians and the like – were in demand from the earliest times of Russian history to perform at holidays and festivals, weddings and funerals. (The Russian *skomorokh* combined many of these functions.) Despite their natural popularity with ordinary Russians, they were distrusted by both the monarchy and the Church, cruelly persecuted and driven to the outer regions of the country. Ecclesiastical drama, while more acceptable, failed to develop in any meaningful direction. One or two morality pieces became established in annual performances, particularly 'The Fiery Furnace', an adaptation of the famous third chapter of Daniel, in which three youths are rescued at the last moment from death in the flames as punishment for refusing to worship the Golden Calf. Church schools also borrowed from abroad, imitating first Byzantine religious drama and then the theatrical practices of Jesuit schools in Poland, which even permitted diverting interludes (usually improvised) to enliven the familiar morality pieces. From this sub-genre emerged at least one or two seventeenth-century plays written in Russian that have a modest claim to interesting characters and stories, the best of them generally considered to be *The*

Prodigal Son (*Komediia pritchi o bludnom syne*) by Simeon Polotsky (1628/29–80). These separate streams, however, never fed into each other to produce an early current of indigenous drama, and all the attempts to assimilate western theatrical culture petered out after 1676, when Alexei died and the small Court Theatre was closed. Three decades of indifference ensued.

Early in the eighteenth century Peter the Great, seeing the propaganda potential of drama, made some attempts to institute a popular theatre using secular materials. His coercive measures brought in some hundreds of spectators but killed off any genuine enthusiasm; attention reverted to the court where imported ballet and opera became fashionable in Moscow and even in the newly-constructed St Petersburg. Some historical plays were written and produced by Feofan Prokopovich (1681–1736), but the actors were always non-Russian, and the spirit of the age – strictly moral when prescribed by the Church and flippant within the royal precincts – discouraged new theatrical practices. Once again a halting start came to nothing much.

The next beginning was a real one. Several factors came together by the middle of the century to initiate a truly Russian theatrical tradition. A professional company was created by royal edict in 1756, its chief performer being Fedor Volkov (1729–63), a celebrated young actor-manager whose reputation had been made in the provinces (Iaroslavl); his impact was such that Belinsky would one day describe him as 'the father of the Russian theatre'. He put money, talent, and effort into the company, eventually becoming its director and leaving it, when he died, in good health. His arrival coincided with the mature work of Russia's first serious playwright, Aleksei Sumarokov (1717–77), the author of a dozen derivative comedies and nine more substantial tragedies, which provided good roles for Volkov. Apart from an interesting adaptation of *Hamlet*, which transformed the play into a political allegory with a happy ending, the most striking of his plays was *Dmitrii the Imposter* (*Dmitrii samozvanets*, 1771), the Russian subject-matter of which won immediate popularity and also invited imitation, notably by Iakov Kniazhnin (1740–91) in *Vadim of Novgorod* (*Vadim Novgorodsky*, 1789). For the first time Russian plays were being well performed by Russian actors. Along with the serious plays a wide range of entertainment through comedy and opera also became available, much of it along lines dictated by France and Germany. The Empress herself, Catherine the Great (1729–96), contributed numerous works, now regarded as undistinguished, but some of them imaginative enough to break with the ruling Neoclassical tradition and involve the adaptation of Shakespeare. This age also produced one dramatist of enduring significance, Denis Fonvizin (1745–92), whose satirical comedies posed serious questions about the responsibilities of the landowning class. His first original play was *The Brigadier* (*Brigadir*, 1780), an entertaining satire directed against the over-Frenchified manners of polite Russian society; the characters speak an absurd language half-way between French and Russian, coining ludicrous gallicisms in every other sentence to avoid the ostensible vulgarity of their native language. His masterpiece, *The Minor* (*Nedorosl'*, 1782), creates a group of amusingly negative characters not far removed from the archetypes of Molière but recognizably Russian; this is the earliest Russian play that is still performed in the twentieth century.

By the end of the century Russia had created a theatrical tradition which, for all its old-fashioned spirit, consisted of original Russian works, well-written and ably performed by Russian actors. The strongest development of all was in the theatre itself, which had grown rapidly in popularity at all levels of society. Encouragement came from the top. Catherine herself had ordered the beginning of a Grand Theatre, later called the Bolshoi, in 1773, and six years later she founded the Imperial Theatre School. All of this involved much expenditure, which Catherine may be credited with underwriting for good artistic reasons as well as for the possibilities of autocratic control that naturally ensued. At the same time, all the major provincial towns now wanted to introduce and encourage this new medium; many did so successfully without subsidy. Privately owned theatres also flourished, serf companies proliferating both in the mansions of Moscow and on the landowners' country estates. Wealthy neighbours sought to outdo each other in the lavishness of provision and production; the buying and selling of serf artists, sometimes *en masse*, has produced legendary stories of exploitation and excess. Standards of achievement must have varied from rustic enthusiasm to a high degree of metropolitan professional expertise; large numbers of people were involved in the performances, and still larger ones enjoyed watching them. In this way a broad theatrical infrastructure was laid down during a few short decades, in buildings and boards, artistic texts and commercial expertise, but also in the Russian mentality. When the nineteenth century dawned Russia at last possessed the potential for rich development and serious achievement. So appealing was the theatre now that most of Russia's greatest literary artists, as well as many less gifted, would soon want to write for it.

Not that the national investment paid immediate dividends. Conservative tastes prevailed for a couple of decades, the most popular dramatists looking back to the examples of their predecessors. Historical drama enjoyed a popularity beyond its intrinsic merits as purveyed by Russian writers. The plays of Vladislav Ozerov (1769–1816), for instance, packed the theatres past the limits of safety and ran for years to thunderous applause. Written in creaky hexameters and declaimed with a brash pomposity, they nevertheless captured the contemporary imagination that was more concerned with national pride than artistic niceties, cultural innovation or profound ideas. *Oedipus in Athens* (*Edip v Afinakh*, 1804), began and ended with a rousing tribute to the tsar; *Dmitrii of the Don* (*Dmitrii Donskoi*, 1806) presented historical characters who could be easily translated into their modern counterparts, Napoleon, Alexander I and his aides, so that the audience could cheer the triumphs of Old Russia and at the same time invoke new ones. More extreme still were the offerings of an outright chauvinist, Nestor Kukol'nik (1809–68), whose drama *The Hand of the Almighty Has Saved Our Fatherland* (*Ruka Vsevyshnego otechestvo spasla*, 1832) lavished praise on the Romanov dynasty for their historic role as saviours of Russia. The author even 'improved' his text by incorporating a list of amendments proposed by Nicholas I. Writers of successful plays like these were raised to wealth and short-lived glory; their works are read now only by devoted specialists.

Russia has no great tradition of classical, tragic or historical drama able to claim unalloyed quality and international renown. It was in the flourishing field of Russian comedy that artistic advances were soon made and then multiplied. Comedy came in many different forms; light opera, *comédie larmoyante*, satirical drama, melodrama, vaudeville, and every kind of comic translation or adaptation all enjoyed their hours on the Russian stage of the early nineteenth century. Vaudeville was especially popular. This theatrical hybrid, born of light opera and French comedy, began as a one-act play and gathered some complexity as the years went by, adding acts and increasing the amount of improvisation. With interpolated songs and dances, it was an agreeable form of relaxation, light-hearted, gently satirical, and not without the odd touch of naughtiness. It could even accommodate a mild form of political and social criticism, though it never so much as brushed against subversiveness or sedition. A close eye was kept on everything said or done on stage, Nicholas I exercising personal control over the repertory and even the casting of plays. In vaudeville what mattered more than ideas, music or character-portrayal was the speedy story-line with its stream of jokes and the inevitable snappy ending. Musical quality was not a priority. Many hundreds of vaudevilles were enjoyed over several decades, ranging in quality from dire vulgarity to a polished style that has kept one or two of them alive still in the modern repertory. The father of the genre was Aleksandr Shakhovskoy (1777–1846), a name to conjure with in the annals of Russian theatre. Having written Russia's first vaudeville, *The Cossack Poet* (*Kazak-stikhotvorets*), in 1812, he went on to serve as impresario, director, theatre manager, talent-spotter, and eventually elder statesman of the profession. His versatile career spanned five decades, beginning under Catherine, seeing the Russian theatre through to full maturity, and leaving its own legacy of well over a hundred plays. His early masterpiece *A Lesson for Coquettes, or Lipetsk Spa* (*Urok koketkam, ili Lipetskie vody*, 1815), for all its old-fashioned appearance, was strikingly modern in action, story, characters, and especially language, the verse medium permitting for perhaps the first time plausible-sounding conversation. The modernization of the Russian literary language, for which Pushkin is usually given exclusive credit, was initiated by Shakhovskoy and a handful of similar writers, the stage being an important vehicle for its implementation.

The new age soon began to produce a dynasty of famous actors and actresses, as well as the first Russian plays of real consequence. By mid-century Aleksandr Griboedov (1795–1829), Aleksandr Pushkin (1799–1837), Nikolai Gogol' (1809–52), and Ivan Turgenev (1818–83) had each written a play of such quality that, in one form or another, it still appears on the national, even the international, stage. Griboedov's *Woe from Wit* (*Gore ot uma*, 1825), was a satirical verse comedy in four acts, using free iambic lines. The satire was acerbic and direct, contemporary manners in St Petersburg being castigated by the sullen, anti-social hero Chatsky, whose pungent diatribes are among the most memorable declamatory pieces in the language. Without naming names they left no doubt in the audience's mind; everyone could identify, for instance, the brutish plutocrat who was rumoured to have swapped some of his long-serving serf retainers for four borzois. All Russians acknowledge the striking quality of the language of this play; Pushkin's famous prophecy that half of its lines would become Russian proverbs was rapidly vindicated. Pushkin's own play, *Boris Godunov* (1831), was conceived as nothing less than an epoch-making innovation in historical drama. Away went the conventions and artificialities of the Neoclassical stage; the author turned to his beloved Shakespeare in a deliberate search for historical authenticity and, above all, psychological consistency. Written in a curious form of blank verse (with a French-style caesura after the fourth syllable of every line), the play may have originally been conceived as a five-act tragedy, but the author chose to do away with divisions into anything other than twenty-three varied tableaux. These attempts to create distance from the English master have done the play a disservice, emphasizing a fault that already exists; in its keenness to look original it appears like a collage of brilliant scenes that fail to cohere into a proper piece of theatre. Despite containing many examples of Pushkin's most effective poetry in the grand style, *Boris Godunov* is now best-known in its simplified operatic version (1874) by Musorgsky. Similarly, *Woe from Wit*, for all its qualities, has never succeeded abroad, not even on the London stage in 1993 with the most excellent of translators and staging.

This is not true of the plays by Gogol' and Turgenev. The former's *The Government Inspector* (*Revizor*, 1836), is hilariously successful wherever it is performed. This work, in four acts of modern (if provincial) prose, has no serious rival for acceptance as Russia's greatest play. A penniless opportunist, Khlestakov, takes advantage of a misunderstanding to pass himself off as a Government Inspector in a scruffy backwoods town, whose tatty officials scurry round in one silly antic after another in order to ingratiate themselves with him. The wonderful processions of tawdry supplicators, the dramatic irony that builds a succession of amusing crises, the wide range of comedy from slapstick–pantomime upwards – all of this gives the play a universal appeal that has little to do with the dreadful state of particular institutions of rural Russia. The many attempts at imposing deep meanings on this play – moral, sexual, political – are best discounted. This is comedy at its purest, far transcending the satirical purpose from which it first grew.

Turgenev's play *A Month in the Country* (*Mesiats v derevne*), well-known though it may be, is a more substantial achievement than most people realize. Written at the very point of mid-century, it belongs really to the following century, demonstrating how much ground had been traversed since the days of Ozerov and Kukol'nik. The action takes place on a country estate. A young tutor, Beliaev, turns the head of the mistress, Mme Islaeva, and also her seventeen-year-old ward, Vera. The older woman is a *tour de force* of theatrical characterization. Neglected by a busy husband and conscious (at twenty-nine) of the first signs of ageing, she permits her lower instincts of self-interest to prevail over everything else in a ruthless attempt to gain favour with the young man. There is little overt action and no outright catastrophe results from her selfish conduct, but the destinies of a dozen characters have been changed, mostly for the worse, by the end of the play. Turgenev has demonstrated his pessimistic vision (deriving from personal experience) of the power of Eros to disrupt and ruin ordinary lives. This apparently light comedy – there is much amusement in it – prefigures psychological drama by at least a generation, which is why the play was undervalued by everyone (including the diffident author himself) in its day. It is a most accomplished work, ever popular around the world, and the unacknowledged debt owed to this work by Anton Chekhov is only now coming to full acknowledgement; the borrowings, general and particular, are remarkable. Turgenev's play therefore enjoys a double distinction; celebrated in its own right, it is also the founder of a famous tradition in Russian drama.

These four plays show how far Russian theatre was able to progress in the first half of the nineteenth century. The rise of Russian actors was equally impressive. By the 1840s a cult of personality had been spun effectively around several accomplished performers; the names of Karatygin (1802–53), Mochalov (1800–48), and Shchepkin (1788–1863) became legendary. The first two were polar opposites, professional-classical versus amateur-romantic; the handsome and dedicated Karatygin acted impressively, deploying meticulous and dependable skills, whereas the stooping, impulsive Mochalov worked by instinct and emotion, sometimes attaining sublime heights of inspiration but often sinking back into dull recitation. Russia was lucky to have them both at the same time, and sometimes (as in *Woe from Wit*) they performed together. Mikhail Shchepkin, who was born more than a decade before them and outlived them by a similar period, in some ways combined their qualities and rose to even greater popularity, particularly in the 1860s. His acting career began in the late eighteenth-century manner, with a strong declamatory style of acting accompanied by emphatic gesticulation. Convinced of the ineffectiveness of such artificial strutting about the stage, he worked consciously to evolve a style of acting that would parallel the 'natural school' affected by literature itself in the early nineteenth century. Realism became the order of his day, based on close observation and detailed imitation of actual people. Empathy and intelligence were brought to bear on each role, along with the most scrupulous preparation. It is not difficult to discern the beginnings of the Stanislavsky method in these mid-century preparations for what we now know as modern drama.

The career of Aleksandr Ostrovsky (1823–86) thoroughly exemplifies the new sense of realism. He is unique among front-rank Russian playwrights in writing for the theatre alone, his fifty plays constituting a broad study of contemporary Russian life centred on the middle class, such as it was, or on classless people. Owners of small businesses are well represented and this new capitalist community turned attention repeatedly to the subject of money. Ostrovsky's other main preoccupation is of a more general kind: the nasty tendency for some small-minded people blessed with a little power to misuse it by oppressing less fortunate individuals. The petty tyrant (often a woman) who operates only on a domestic or local scale but with cruel and tragic consequences for his or her dependants, known to Russians as a *samodur*, appears in a number of Ostrovsky's plays, notably in his best-known work, *The Storm* (*Groza*, 1859, the subject of Janáček's opera *Katia Kabanova*). Here the oppressive Kabanikha impels her son into grovelling obedience and her daughter-in-law into a brief love affair followed by repentance, confession, and suicide. This pessimistic play ruthlessly exposes family despotism against a background of demeaning Russian provincialism. The socio-political implications of Ostrovsky's work have emerged with some clarity, but to the detriment of his overall reputation, which depends excessively on his being defined as a realist. It is a mystery why he has so far not proved amenable to export through translation, unlike many of his compatriots, though this is unlikely to be redressed until the broad universality of his themes is properly substantiated in criticism and new translations recommend themselves to modern directors. Ostrovsky's rehabilitation on the world stage is long overdue.

Other mid-century Russian dramatists of significance include Aleksei Pisemsky (1821–81), whose peasant tragedy *A Bitter Fate* (*Gor'kaia sud'bina*), shared a national prize for excellence in the theatre with *The Storm* in 1859, and Aleksandr Sukhovo-Kobylin (1817–1903), whose personal problems (including a long-standing threat of indictment for murder) long overshadowed his work, to the temporary detriment of a powerful trilogy, *Krechinsky's Wedding* (*Svad'ba Krechinskogo*), *The Case* (*Delo*), and *The Death of Tarelkin* (*Smert' Tarelkina*, 1854–69), which spirals down through the dark depiction of administrative corruption in the provinces to a kind of early black comedy in a St Petersburg strongly reminiscent of Gogol'. Towards the end of the century two different Tolstoys came to prominence in the theatre. First, A.K. Tolstoy (1817–75) completed a historical trilogy in blank verse: *The Death of Ivan the Terrible* (*Smert' Ioanna Groznogo*, 1866), *Tsar' Fedor Ioannovich* (1868), and *Tsar' Boris* (1870). Not for the first time his sense of timing was out; having, earlier in the century, written a historical novel just when the genre itself was going out of favour, now he presented further historical materials that were not particularly wanted by the public, nor were they immediately acceptable to the establishment, since they seemed to adopt an anti-monarchical stance. Performance was delayed until the 1890s. Along with Pushkin's version of *Boris Godunov*, Tolstoy's plays are considered to be the outstanding representatives of Russian historical drama. The more famous Lev Tolstoy made at least ten attempts to write for the stage, producing one drama of remarkable strength and quality, *The Power of Darkness* (*Vlast' t'my*, 1888), in which the obvious didactic spirit is, fortunately, overwhelmed by a disturbing story, which involves nothing less than infanticide on stage. The mature writer also makes careful use of closely-studied peasant language, as well as showing a true sense of both characterization and construction; a strong impression of reality derives from the origin of this tragedy in real-life events.

Apart from these writers, and a good number of minor figures, the Russian theatre in the second half of the nineteenth century sustained itself on many translations and adaptations from abroad. Also from the West came the impetus for a brilliant new start to theatrical life in Russia. Impressed by the forces of naturalism that were sweeping across the continent, and aware of naturalist tendencies already maturing in their own country, two great figures came together to form what would soon become one of Russia's most celebrated cultural institutions, the Moscow Arts Theatre. Konstantin Stanislavsky (1863–1938) joined with Vladimir Nemirovich-Danchenko (1858–1943) under the auspices of the amateur Society for Art and Literature, and within a short time their new ideas were bearing rich fruit. It is still a cause for astonishment for us to contemplate the originality and sheer quality that went into the production of their fifth offering, a revival of Chekhov's unsuccessful play *The Seagull* (*Chaika*) in 1898. Ol'ga Knipper (soon to be the author's wife), Stanislavsky himself, and the up-and-coming, imaginative Vsevolod Meierkhol'd (1874–1940) all took part, and the remarkable innovation was that not one of them could be regarded as a star. Personality was submerged in a sense of communal contribution and achievement; what mattered now was the total effect of verisimilitude conveyed at a slow pace by the steady build-up of atmosphere as opposed to remarkable incidents, all of this sustained by the closest attention to production detail. Chekhov would stage his last three dramas, *Uncle Vania* (*Diadia Vania*), *The Three Sisters* (*Tri sestry*), and *The Cherry Orchard* (*Vishnevyi sad*), at the Moscow Arts Theatre, and the two main directors, especially Stanislavsky, would soon rise to lasting celebrity with their assiduous writings on the training and direction of actors and plays. The 'Stanislavsky Method' became a byword for professionalism and excellence in the modern theatre. As to Chekhov, he has become everyone's favourite, enduringly popular in all countries. His great success was to remove the last vestiges of artificiality from the stage, blurring the distinction between tragedy and comedy, so that his plays cannot be forced into either category. It had now become less interesting to see someone struck down by the gods than worn down by the gentle abrasion of everyday existence and the growing awareness that time has moved faster than might seem possible, taking with it many lost possibilities. There is some oblique criticism of contemporary Russia in all of this, but Chekhov's aimless or misdirected characters do not belong to a single nation. The sadness of unfulfilled opportunity, misapplied effort, recurrent ill-fortune and empty existence, as well as the difficulty of intimate communication with other people – this mood of melancholic disappointment is recognizable to all audiences, as is the call for a renewal of strength that is also implicit in Chekhov's plays.

One other important new Russian play was produced by the Moscow Arts Theatre in 1905, when Gor'ky's remarkable tragedy of the dosshouse, *The Lower Depths* (*Na dne*), with all its striking political undertones, rose to instant fame before going off around the world on a tide of popularity that has yet to run its full course. Like Chekhov's work this play may be seen as a piece of contemporary social criticism, and one that happened to get off to a good start by being so well-presented. In fact it has more quality than any such narrow judgement might suggest, dealing as it does with universal concepts such as the nature of truth and the immorality of misjudging people by surface appearances. Like Tolstoy's *The*

Power of Darkness, from which it partly derives, this play achieves its broad didactic purpose by dissolving it in strongly interesting language, characters, and situations. The delicacy of this achievement is borne out by the lack of any such subtlety in Gor'ky's other half-dozen plays, which by comparison seem tendentious in their treatment of too-obvious political content. Another playwright of the period, Leonid Andreev (1871–1919), began his career in a similarly Neorealistic manner with *To the Stars* (*K zvezdam*) in 1905, but soon developed a taste for a more rhetorical style and allegorical range of meanings. One or two of his later plays, particularly *He Who Gets Slapped* (*Tot, kto poluchaet poshchechinu*, 1915), found short-lived success at home and even abroad, though a rapid decline in his popularity (applying also to his reputation as a story writer) was never arrested. Andreev now rests in obscurity and his plays are unlikely to be revived.

By the end of the century, the country had entered a period of economic and social turmoil that would culminate in the violent political events of 1905 and 1917. The cultural scene reflected the same spirit of instability, uncertainty, and yearning for change. In theatrical circles a new tendency arose, more diffuse and much less successful in box-office terms than Neorealism, towards a broader expressiveness supposedly achieveable through new experiments with symbol, enchanting or mystifying language, and the representation of a greater reality than that which the five senses crudely perceive. Meierkhol'd first attempted to stage Symbolist works at the Moscow Arts Theatre, in the hope that the challenging ideas of Maeterlinck might catch on; when they did not he transferred his attentions to St Petersburg, working with the famous actress Vera Komissarzhevskaia (1864–1910) in the theatre that she had founded. Typical of his more successful work there was the startling triumph of a poetic drama by a young poet, Aleksandr Blok (1880–1921), entitled *The Puppet Show* (*Balaganchik*) and described as a 'mystical satire'. A puzzling work, this story of Pierrot and Columbine appears to relate both love and death to a transcendent reality, or perhaps to ridicule writers who try to do this sort of thing. Wildly controversial in its day, it achieved a *succès de scandale*, making the poet's name as well as confirming the director in his role as the country's leading theatrical experimentalist.

For many people novelty was the order of the day. Valerii Briusov (1873–1924) and Nikolai Evreinov (1879–1953), among other less well-known theoreticians and directors, condemned the Stanislavsky school as narrow-minded, backward-looking, and stultifying. Taking over from Meierkhol'd at Komissarzhevskaia's theatre in 1908, Evreinov advanced the anti-realist cause still further in his writings, adaptations, and many productions. He also directed a small experimental theatre called 'The Crooked Mirror' that captivated rapturous, if sometimes bemused, audiences from 1908 to 1918. Elsewhere up and down the country theatrical experimentation, often overlapping with avant-garde poetry readings, flowed out from small private theatres into cafés, night-clubs, cabaret rooms, parks, and other public places. The Futurists were shocking the bourgeoisie and everyone else with their crazy stunts and outrageous manifesto pronouncements, bringing iconoclasm, insult, and self-advertisement to a fine art. The poetry readings of Vladimir

Maiakovsky (1893–1930) were memorable theatrical performances in themselves and some of his works were plays more than poems. His *Vladimir Maiakovsky: A Tragedy* (*Vladimir Maiakovskii: tragediia*) carried on where Blok's *The Puppet Show* had left off; performed in Luna Park, St Petersburg, in December 1913, it began with an open statement by the poet-actor-director that no one was going to understand what was about to happen, and few did. It is possible retrospectively to view this piece as a 'monodrama of suffering' in which the poet emerges as a scapegoat for the sins of mankind, but contemporary audiences, lacking the hindsight that we now enjoy, were left bemused. Alternating with *Vladimir Maiakovsky* was *Victory Over the Sun* (*Pobeda nad solntsem*), a kind of opera written by the Futurist most committed to 'transrational' language, Aleksei Kruchenykh (1886–1968), with a prologue by Khlebnikov, music by Matiushin, and sets by Malevich; when the Futurists caught the sun and dragged it down from the sky the onlookers may have been able to take this as a satirical thrust against the Symbolists, but the words and details of the piece must have bewildered them.

Most people, enjoying the spectacle and scandal, did not mind the obscurity; many were conscious of witnessing significant experiments that could only enrich the cultural achievement of their country. Everyone could feel the intensity of the new theatrical experience; travelling companies took the experimental words out into the far provinces. The nation was shocked, puzzled, disturbed, and impressed by turns; no one could remain indifferent. A kind of excitement bordering on hysteria had taken over the Russian cultural scene, reflecting and prefiguring the apocalyptic political changes about to engulf the nation and its art. The outside world knew about this. Along with Russian art and music (especially ballet), the late-coming theatre of that country, standing now for high professionalism on the one hand and amazing creativity on the other, had risen to such prominence that it had captured the world's imagination, delivering a confident challenge to Europe and America. Then came the Revolution.

FURTHER READING

Cooper, Joshua (trans.) *Four Russian Plays*, Harmondsworth: Penguin, 1972; reprinted as *The Government Inspector and Other Russian Plays*, 1990.

Green, Michael (ed. and trans.) *The Russian Symbolist Theater: An Anthology of Plays and Critical Texts*, Ann Arbor: Ardis, 1986.

Karlinsky, Simon. *Russian Drama from Its Beginnings to the Age of Pushkin*, Berkeley: University of California Press, 1985.

Reeve, F.D. (trans.) *An Anthology of Russian Plays*, 2 vols., New York: Vintage, 1963.

Senelick, Laurence (trans.) *Russian Comedy of the Nikolaian Era*, Amsterdam: Harwood Academic, 1996.

Slonim, Marc. *Russian Theater, from the Empire to the Soviets*, Cleveland: World Publishing Co., 1961.

Varneke, B.H. *History of the Russian Theater (Seventeenth through Nineteenth Century)*, trans. Boris Brasol, ed. Belle Martin, New York: Macmillan, 1951.

Welsh, David J. *Russian Comedy, 1765–1823*, The Hague: Mouton, 1966.

7

PUSHKIN: FROM BYRON
TO SHAKESPEARE

DAVID M. BETHEA

It is something of a textbook topos that different national literatures have their own quite different national poets – father figures who are considered seminal or originary (the 'origin without origin') to the nation's culture and world-view. What is less easily explained is how and why a certain national poet should appear on the scene precisely when he does. Why, for example, should Dante epitomize Italian Catholic culture in the thirteenth–fourteenth centuries, Shakespeare Anglo-Saxon culture in the sixteenth–seventeenth centuries, and Goethe German culture in the eighteenth–nineteenth centuries? Clearly, the problem is more complicated than the serviceable apophthegm of genius 'being in the right place at the right time', for what we are dealing with in these special instances is the combination (two-way, mutually interpenetrating) of an individual and a culture/national identity both coming of age, and knowing or sensing, they are coming of age, at the same time. The young man who may have been involved in a libellous deer-poaching incident or the wealthy senior citizen who mysteriously wills his wife a 'second-best bed' becomes Shakespeare, going to his grave, as a recent biographer phrases it, 'not knowing, and possibly not caring, whether *Macbeth* or *The Tempest or Antony and Cleopatra* ever achieved the permanence of print' (S. Schoenbaum). Great contemporaries such as Spenser or Jonson become instead, on the scales of history, foils of genius – Laertes to the Hamlet whose play-within-the-play contains them, rather than the other way around.

One ingredient in this coming-of-age formula is the awareness of the necessity of a mature inside/outside perspective: what is 'ours', beginning with a national poetic tradition, has sufficient internal dignity and grandeur that it can, now for the first time, take on the challenge of the larger, supranational context (here European high culture, the classical and Judaeo-Christian traditions, and so on) as an equal. Poised on this inside/outside, ours/theirs seam, the culture, through the creations of this gifted individual, comes to value its own unique character in a manner that seems not parochial but universal. (This is what Dostoevsky was alluding to with reference to universal *otzyvchivost'*, 'responsiveness', in his famous Pushkin speech.) A poet's 'source material', broadly defined, including historical person-ages and famous characters from literature, plots, genre conventions, rules of style, rhyme schemes and metres, are no longer simply 'imitated' or copied (the relation of the lesser to the greater), but are borrowed freely and boldly and reworked in accordance with this new mature outlook. Shakespeare uses Holinshed respectfully but creatively; Pushkin uses his teacher Karamzin in precisely the same way.

The present essay is an attempt to place Russia's national poet in a correct alignment along this inside/outside seam. My argument, in brief, will be that for Pushkin, Byron and Shakespeare, as creative writers and personalities, represented a crucial choice in the period 1824–6; and furthermore, that being English, these figures offered the 'Frenchman' (his nickname at the Lycée) Pushkin a choice of romantic personality (*lichnost'*) versus 'romantic' art, but romantic art defined in a special, non- or anti-Byronic way. Pushkin needed the Byronic personality up to a point to define his emerging authorial 'I', and in a real sense he never stopped being interested in that personality and never stopped, in his typically masked, indirect way, applying the lessons of that personality to his own life and artistic career. However, at a rather precise juncture, by now pored over by literary historians, Pushkin turned from Byron to Shakespeare, and he did so not only because Byron had by then died (1824). There were other reasons, ones that had to do with Pushkin's own beginnings and points of orientation. The names of Byron and Napoleon had become inevitably linked in the young poet's mind (and indeed in those of his entire generation) since the early 1820s: the first exercising a mythical authority in the sphere of art, and the second an equally mesmerizing authority on the stage of history. Here the core text was the third canto of *Childe Harold*, where the 'self-exiled' hero broods on the defeat ('thou fatal Waterloo!') of the great man 'whose spirit, antithetically mixt . . . [was] extreme in all things', and 'quenchless evermore, preys upon high adventure'. 'The joining of himself [Byron] with Napoleon appealed to his self-esteem', writes Pushkin of the author-hero dynamics of *The Corsair*, and of that work's otherwise inexplicable success ('On Olin's Tragedy *Korser*' [1827, unpublished]). Pushkin had begun his career by celebrating Russia's victory over Napoleon in *Reminiscences at Tsarskoe Selo* (*Vospominaniia v Tsarskom Sele*, 1814), yet throughout these early years the myth of the *muzh sudeb* ('man of fate'), whose success on the battlefield coexisted in the schoolboy's mind with the prestige of eighteenth-century French literary models and tastes that had informed his first reading, continued to cast a powerful spell. With the death of the *echt*-romantic personality in history and art came the simultaneous urge to 'de-Gallicize' his own work and its tradition and to find an inside/outside path that better accorded with the Russian language and with Russian history, thought, and culture.

Pushkin came to Byron and Shakespeare primarily through the French, and this, for a creative personality as linguistically sensitive as his, was immensely problematic. As he wrote to his friend Prince Viazemsky apropos possible linguistic indiscretions in his Byronic poem *The Fountain of Bakhchisarai* (*Bakhchisaraiskii fontan*) in December 1823, on the verge of his transition away from Byron and toward Shakespeare: 'I hate to see in our primitive language traces of European affectation and French refinement. Rudeness and simplicity are more becoming to it. I preach from internal conviction, but as is my custom I write otherwise.' Here we find the always independent Pushkin chafing not only at the lacquered *bon goût* of his first teachers Voltaire and Parny, but also at the salon-inspired speech, with its 'feminine' circumlocutions, of the Karamzinian school, among whose senior members numbered the poet's own relatives (his francophile uncle Vasilii L'vovich, for example), and whose most brilliant graduate he was. The young poet wanted, in short, to find a way to practise what he preached.

Various Soviet Pushkin scholars, including Tomashevsky, Alekseev, and Levin, have studied aspects of the poet's 'Shakespearism' with great philological care and insight. The one thing persistently missing in their treatments, however is what Pushkin felt personally, in terms of his own challenges and anxieties, as he took on first Byron and then, more crucially, Shakespeare, perhaps the central figure in the western canon. Because Pushkin is, as the famous cliché goes, 'our everything' (*nashe vse*), there is the unavoidable tendency to treat him as an invulnerable god who enters into these sub- and con-textual tugs-of-war with nothing to lose. Indeed, according to Soviet 'philological' argument, he borrows and makes his own effortlessly, with little or no personal investment. However, I here suggest that Pushkin consciously and a times even hotly, plays Shakespeare off against the French and, in so doing, he creates an analogous niche for himself along the Russo-French cultural axis.

PUSHKIN AND BYRON

Pushkin was introduced to European Romanticism largely through Byron, his older contemporary. Traditionally it has been argued that the 'naive' phase of Pushkin's infatuation with Byron coincided with his southern exile (1820–4): it was in these years that the impressionable poet modelled certain aspects of his political and amorous behaviour on the cult of the alienated Byronic hero; that he wrote his narrative poems, especially the hugely popular *The Prisoner in the Caucasus* (*Kavkazskii plennik*), written 1820–1 and published in 1822, and *The Fountain of Bakhchisarai* (written 1821–3 and published 1824), as Russian versions of Byron's oriental tales (*The Giaour*, *The Bride of Abydos*, *The Corsair*, etc.); and that this infatuation grew increasingly complex until *The Gypsies* (*Tsygany*, written 1824, published 1827) – Pushkin's last *poema* based on 'early' Byronic models of characterization – where the treatment of the central hero becomes so ambiguous and ironic as to lead commentators to conclude that the poet has now passed beyond Byron, and developed a polemical as opposed to pupilary relationship to him.

Much evidence to support this view can be gleaned from Pushkin's biography and from his correspondence. On the one hand, Byron was obviously the *kumir* ('idol') during this period when Pushkin, in forced physical exile (Byron's was ultimately voluntary), challenged social norms with politically incendiary verse and reputedly stormy liaisons with married women (Amalia Riznich, Karolina Sobańska, and Elizaveta Vorontsova). On the other hand, Viktor Zhirmunsky in his classic work (*Bairon i Pushkin: iz istorii romanticheskoi poemy*, 1924) has shown how Pushkin learned a great deal from the form of the Byronic verse tale: its fragmentariness (*otryvochnost'*), its creation of exotic/oriental setting, its rapid transitions and plot dynamics, its fluid relationship between hero and narrator, its telescoping of sexual conquest and military exploits – all became, mutatis mutandis, aspects of Pushkin's southern *poemy*. But even here Pushkin never follows Byron completely: in *The Fountain of Bakhchisarai* his female characters (Zarema and Mariia) are more complex than Byron's; and in *The Prisoner in the Caucasus* the narrator shows a strange, un-Byronic tendency to paint the natural beauty of the 'others' (the Circassians) within the story, but to celebrate Russia's imperial right to conquer such indigenous peoples in the epilogue. By the same token, and despite the famous 'Don Juan list', the small and ugly (or, as he liked to think, 'satyr-like') Pushkin was an imprecise replica of the dashing Byronic lover: too trusting, too hot-tempered and given to fits of jealousy, he could be (in his own recounting) manipulated by cunning rivals or, just as likely, by the beautiful women who took pleasure in tormenting him.

As mentioned, Byron's life, like Napoleon's, had left an enduring impression on Pushkin. He needed to see that life as a finished secular *vita* ('the life of the poet'), as something he could feel himself outside or beyond, before he could move on. The nearest the reader comes to seeing Pushkin speak candidly about Byron's life is not in his correspondence, where he tends to wrestle with a friend or contemporary (Petr Viazemsky, Aleksandr Marlinsky) over the great man's significance in a kind of sibling rivalry, but in an 1835 draft of a biographical article he had planned to write based on Byron's memoirs (*Letters and Journals of Lord Byron*), published by Thomas Moore in 1830 and cited by Pushkin in their French edition. This draft is fascinating because in it Pushkin speaks warmly about aspects of the biography that are almost self-referential – that is, the parallels are so clear that the author must, at some level, be speaking about himself. (Typically, Pushkin is most self-revealing when he discusses a privileged other, and most guarded when he talks directly about himself.) For example, not only is the age and historical significance of the Byron family noteworthy, but so, more importantly, is the fact that 'Byron valued his genealogy more than his literary works. A completely understandable feeling! The brilliance and the hereditary honours of his ancestors elevated the poet, while his own acquired [literary] fame brought him petty insults, ones that often humiliated the noble lord and yielded his name up to the whim of gossip.' Here the Pushkin of *My Genealogy* (*Moia rodoslovnaia*, 1830), is both describing a former hero's struggle with his own social context from the point of view of that hero's nobility (Byron's *blagorodtsvo* [nobility], a spiritual quality related to a proud past; see Pushkin's famous line about 'leaving the hero [Napoleon] his heart' in his poem *The Hero* [*Geroi*, 1830]), and thinking about his own similar difficulties – an ancient noble family fallen on hard times, subject to gossip, intrigue, the petty insults of his *kameriunkerstvo* (his court position as 'the gentleman of the bedchamber'), and so on.

Likewise, Byron's unhappy childhood and family life (mention of which would be too 'humiliating' to include in one's published writing); his desultory record as a student but his love of athletics, games, and competitions; his 'playful, hot-tempered, grudge-bearing' (*rezvyi, vspyl'chivyi i zlopamiatnyi*) character; his passion for the 'severe beauties' of Scottish nature and his eerily unattainable first love (see Pushkin's famous *potaennaia liubov'*); and his distinguished and eccentric naval ancestors. All these biographical details are not random to Pushkin, but selected and commented on because they resonate powerfully with his own past and sense of *amour-propre*. Even the discussion in the draft of Byron's eccentric grandfather, who isolated himself in Newstead Abbey with only his housekeeper and servant for company and who whiled away the time 'feeding and instructing' crickets (Pushkin's Arzamasian nickname ironically being *sverchok*, 'cricket') seems almost foreordained, playfully suggestive of Pushkin's own creation Ivan Petrovich Belkin, himself a humorous *alter ego* for the poet holed away in Boldino. Last but not least, there is poetic justice to the fact that Pushkin ends this draft with reference to Byron's 'wounded pride' (*iazvlennoe samoliubie*), to his fatal combination of 'magnanimity' (*velikodushie*) and 'unbridled passions' (*neobuzdannye strasti*), and to the limp, his physical mark of Cain, an accident of birth that he blamed on his highly-strung mother and with which she hurt him by calling him once, in a scornful tone, a 'lame boy' (*khromoi mal'chishka*). Pushkin himself did not suffer any such obviously symbolic physical defect, but he was ugly and unloved as a child in ways that left their own mark of Cain. The defiant last sentence of this abandoned homage to Byron's life is as close as Pushkin will ever come to explaining his own will to succeed and turn adversity to advantage: 'This very defect [of the club foot] increased [the boy's] desire to distinguish himself in all exercises demanding physical strength and agility.' Within months of writing these lines Pushkin would be dying in terrible pain with D'Anthès's bullet lodged in his abdomen; when Dal', the doctor-friend overseeing the patient's last hours, suggested he cry out to relieve the agony, the poet answered, 'It would be ridiculous to allow this trifle to overpower me!'

But this was Byron's *life*. Its rebellious heroism could be bracing and inspiring, a way to measure one's own actions with an eye to their place in history, but not necessarily a means of understanding the world outside oneself. 'I want to understand you, / I search for meaning in you', Pushkin writes in his famous insomnia poem *Lines Written at Night During Insomnia* (*Stikhi, sochinennye noch'iu vo vremia bessonitsy*, 1830). Ultimately the Byronic hero, the product of words, whether he be Childe Harold or Conrad or Manfred, did not leave Pushkin and his emerging tradition enough to work with. Indeed, the life appears to have obstructed the work, so that by approximately 1828 when Pushkin's English was sufficient to read both Byron and Shakespeare in the original, he seems to have become much more interested in the figure whose life will permanently remain in the shadows, whose every recorded action will always be contested by scholars, and whose greatest works exist in a relationship of permanent mystery to their creator's biography. To borrow a distinction first made by the Milton scholar Douglas Bush, 'alienation' is a distinctly modern concept, while 'isolation' is the only possible status for the outlaw hero of Renaissance drama. Macbeth is 'isolated', and deservedly so, from the society whose laws he has traduced; Manfred also has terrible crimes on his conscience, but the grandeur of his titanic personality is supposed to counterbalance, if not ultimately outweigh, the cost of alienation. To put it crudely, society itself has to be sufficiently advanced and secularized in order to produce the notion of 'alienation' in the first place.

Despite his remarkable sophistication, Pushkin grew impatient with the Byronic model and its magnificent egotism. Without knowing it, he sensed that Russian literature, and the world that literature reflected, would be better served by the lessons Byron's younger colleague Keats first associated with the name of Shakespeare and gathered under another heading: 'At once it struck me, what quality went to form a Man of Achievement especially in Literature and which Shakespeare possessed so enormously – I mean *Negative Capability*, that is when man is capable of being in uncertainties, mysteries, doubts, without any irritable reaching after fact and reason.' Pushkin could have used Keats's term when he said, in another letter to Viazemsky (June 1824) describing his hero's Achilles' heel:

> I see that . . . you are sad about Byron, but I am very glad of his death, as a sublime theme for poetry. Byron's genius paled with his youth. In his tragedies, not excluding even *Cain*, he is no longer that flaming demon who created *The Giaour* and *Childe Harold*. The first two cantos of *Don Juan* are superior to the following ones. His poetry noticeably changed. He was created completely topsy-turvy; there was no gradualness in him, he suddenly matured and attained manhood, sang his song, and fell silent; and his first sounds did not return to him again.

In 1824 Pushkin could hardly have read Byron in the original with any serious understanding; moreover, it is not at all clear how carefully he has read the other cantos of *Don Juan* that he here so summarily dismisses. Even so, he has caught a fatal lack of development ('there was no gradualness in him') in all the shimmering variety. As the narrator hastens to tell the reader in the first chapter of *Evgenii Onegin*, he, as opposed to Byron, 'the poet of pride' (*gordosti poet*), 'can write tales in verse about something other than oneself' ('Pisat' poemy o drugom, / Kak tol'ko o sebe samom').

It has been suggested more than once that Byron's *sprezzatura* ease and brilliance, his love of 'chatter' and action-delaying digression, his urbanity and even complaisant cynicism, and above all his deployment of a stanzaic form designed to give his mercurial genius free rein, were adopted by Pushkin and put to use in the greatest work of his middle phase, *Evgenii Onegin* (written 1823–31). Pushkin did not hesitate to make use of certain formal features characteristic of the later Byron of *Beppo* and *Don Juan*: his most ambitious work is named after a peripatetic hero, it is organized in a loosely expandable canto/chapter format, the narrator has a playfully foregrounded role, and so on. Pushkin did, therefore, have his eye on *Don Juan* when he first started working on his *roman v stikhakh* ('novel in verse'). But the likeness abruptly stops at the level of character/ personality. Byron, particularly after 1824, is useful to Pushkin only on a comedic level (compare the links between *Beppo* and *The Little House in Kolomna* [*Domik v Kolomne*, 1830], also written in *ottava rima*). As Pushkin says in his correspondence, *Evgenii Onegin* is more unlike *Don Juan* than like; its universalizing irony – a tantalizing 'hovering' between the poetic and the prosaic, wonder and disappointment – veers away from Byronic satire. Likewise, the Onegin stanza is much more flexible than *ottava rima* in English (it is in effect a quicksilver combination of Petrarchan and Elizabethan sonnet), has virtually none of the latter's 'burlesque' effect (poetry, especially rhymes, making fun of their doggerel sounds), and can be genuinely lyrical or *bel canto*. Onegin himself does have Byronic tendencies, beginning with an arrested personality, but is far from celebrated for them by his narrator, while Tat'iana is neither Donna Julia nor Haidée, but a genuine muse figure created out of provincial everyday life who comes to occupy a central, rather than episodic, place in the story. In sum, Byron could be of no use to Pushkin in the creation of serious, much less tragic, portraits (even without knowing English well, Pushkin sensed, as we can tell from the aforementioned quotation, how weak Byron's verse tragedies were) or in his turn toward history, broadly defined. Here his guide would have to be Shakespeare.

PUSHKIN AND SHAKESPEARE

Pushkin freely adopted, with breathtaking virtuosity and almost always with a playfulness that underscored the self-conscious nature of the gesture, the formal features and narrative strategies of the major literary figures of his time or of the past, such as Voltaire, Ariosto, Anacreon, Chénier, Parny, Byron, Ovid, Scott, Dante, Goethe, Batiushkov, Zhukovsky, Bogdanovich, Karamzin, and Derzhavin. But in this group Shakespeare occupies a special position, for it is my hypothesis that Pushkin's mature aspiration was to become nothing less than the Shakespeare of Russian culture. By the mid-1820s his correspondence is increasingly punctuated by admiring references to 'our father Shakespeare':

> Verisimilitude of situations and truth of dialogue – here is the real rule of tragedy. (I have not read Calderón or Vega) but what a man this Shakespeare is! I can't get over it. How paltry is Byron as a tragedian in comparison with him! This Byron who never conceived but one sole character . . . this Byron, then, has parceled out among his characters such-and-such a trait of his own character; his pride to one, his hate to another, his melancholy to a third, etc., and thus out of one complete, gloomy, and energetic character he has made several insignificant characters – there is no tragedy in that.
>
> (Letter to N.N. Raevsky *fils*, July 1825)

In a draft of the same letter Pushkin writes: 'Read Sh[akespeare] . . . he never fears compromising his hero/character [*deistvuiushchee litso*]; he has him speak with all the naturalness of life [*so vseiu zhiznennoi neprinuzhdennost'iu*] because he is certain that at the appropriate time and place he can make that hero find a language consistent with his character.'

As already suggested, however, these first ecstatic comments about Shakespeare were mediated by their French source: the 1821 Paris edition (Chez Ladvocat) of the *Oeuvres complètes de Shakespeare*. This popular edition, based on the eighteenth-century prose translations of Letourneur that François Guizot and

Amedée Pichot had recently revised, came supplied with a 150-page essay by Guizot on Shakespeare's life and times that Pushkin studied thoroughly as he proceeded to read the poetry and plays. As the Guizot essay was Pushkin's first and most immediate introduction to Shakespeare and his historical-literary context, its importance as a document cannot be overstated. (There were other sources that Pushkin used to become better acquainted with Shakespeare, including a French translation of August Schlegel's *Vorlesungen über dramatische Kunst und Literatur* [*A Course of Lectures on Dramatic Art and Literature*] and Madame de Staël's *De la littérature considérée dans ses rapports avec les institutions sociales* [*The Influence of Literature upon Society*]. The focus here, however, is on Guizot and the 'La Harpe/Voltaire' tradition of French Shakespeare criticism represented by him.) This is the same historian Guizot, author of *Histoire générale de la civilisation en Europe* (1828), that Pushkin would take issue with in his 1830 review(s) of Nikolai Polevoy's *A History of the Russian People* (*Istoriia russkogo naroda*, 1829–33): by slavishly following Guizot and the latter's notion of historical determinism leading inevitably to 'European' (read French-dominated) Enlightenment and the emergence of the *tiers-état*, Polevoy (himself a commoner) not only insulted the memory of a better historian (Karamzin, who taught first and foremost respect for one's past), but fatally misread the unique, saving difference of Russian history – its *sluchainost'* (its 'chance' or unpredict-able, random quality) – that which distinguishes it from the neat French model. It was these same Euro- and Franco-centric assumptions about the shape of history and national genius in Guizot's otherwise informative and admiring essay on Shakespeare that must have made Pushkin pause to contemplate his own fate, during his northern exile in Mikhailovskoe (1824–6). Buried in the woods, looked after only by his ageing nanny and the 'oak groves', he again made a virtue of necessity – the thoughts of flight abroad that had been his farewell to the south: for example the watery escape route and Byronic and Napoleonic heroics of *To the Sea* (*K moriu*, 1824), became his figurative greeting to the Russian historical imagination, the Shakespeare- and Karamzin-inspired 'romantic tragedy' *Boris Godunov* (written 1824–5, published 1831).

Guizot's essay came with its own cultural bias, which the 'responsive' (*otzyvchivyi*) Pushkin would have noticed immediately, and seen as turned on himself, the 'barbarous' Russian. Not only would he have to find the 'real' Shakespeare through the Gallicizing prism, he would in his own work have to project a 'Russianness' that was smart enough, and self-aware enough to stave off such reductionist thrusts. Guizot writes, for example, that 'We live in the time of civilization and foresight, in which everything has its place and its order, in which the destiny of each individual is determined by circumstances more or less imperious.' This must have sounded absolutely absurd (and condescending) to Pushkin, who in his own position would have felt very far from a society and history 'where everything has its place'. Furthermore, Guizot goes on to explain the phenomenon of Shakespeare by alluding to two types of poet – the one who develops logically, as an extension of this orderly civilization: 'A poet begins by being a poet; he who is to become one knows it almost from his infancy'; and the one who develops 'in difficult and the most vulgar of times', as an extension of nature, or as Guizot seemed to be saying, a brute, uncivilized man ('the poet who is formed by nature alone'). Shakespeare – and Pushkin himself – clearly belong to the second group with its raw, unpredictable genius and its 'fougueuse [impetuous] imagination'. Lacking 'the universal and profound imprint of Roman civilization', Great Britain became a melting pot of non-distinguishable conqueror and conquered (Saxons, Danes, Normans, and so on) – all 'également barbares'; and whereas the Franks found in Gaul a well-established Roman Catholic clergy capable of modifying the institutions, ideas, and way of life of the victors, the Christian priest of the Saxons 'was Saxon himself, long since vulgar and barbarous, like his congregation'.

The point, as one imagines Pushkin reading such lines, is not that Great Britain (or Russia for that matter) *is* civilized by European standards during these early centuries prior to the appearance of its national genius, but that its 'lack' cannot be judged from the vantage of French 'fullness' (romantic historiography, clichés about elemental genius, and so on). The following lines in particular can be perceived as a challenge to a great Russian writer who also happens to possess a 'native' command of French: 'Thus the young civilization of the North grows, in England, in simplicity as well as with the energy of its own nature, independent of borrowed forms and of the foreign vitality received elsewhere from the old civilization of the South.' Pushkin, representing another 'civilisation du Nord', would use Shakespeare to show not only how 'unsimple' was his own genius, but also how it could borrow the forms of other European cultures, including the French, in a way that was by no means 'natural' or unconscious. Many of the arguments that Guizot makes in his long essay would be taken up by Pushkin precisely as a challenge – how to turn these potential anomalies or 'defects' of Shakespearean dramaturgy (such as the shattering of classical unities, the mixing of 'pure' comedic and tragic genre expectations, the undermining of consistent character 'types') into the productive principle of a new *Russian* theatre liberated from French Neoclassical principles. Guizot, however, would see the hypocritical essence ('la fourberie menaçante de l'hypocrite') of Molière's *Tartuffe* as confirmation of its classical heritage and a source of national pride. Pushkin would point out the artificiality, and the lack of verisimilitude in that notion of character:

In Molière the hypocrite [Tartuffe] chases after the wife of his benefactor, while acting the hypocrite; takes the estate under protection, while acting the hypocrite; asks for a glass of water, while acting the hypocrite. In Shakespeare the hypocrite [Angelo in *Measure for Measure*] pronounces sentence with vainglorious severity, but fairly; justifies his cruelty with the profound reasoning of a statesman; seduces innocence with powerful, attractive sophistries, not a ridiculous combination of piety and cheap charm [*volokitstvo*].

('Table-Talk')

In short, while Guizot has many positive things to say about Shakespeare, his tone and his ready-made juxtapositions (such as French–English, classical–popular, orderly–chaotic) continue in a lesser key the earlier generalizations of La Harpe, who in commenting about Letourneur's translations seemed perplexed that a people having such exemplars as Corneille, Racine, and Voltaire could take seriously the works of 'un auteur barbare' whose 'monstrous' plays are, despite patches of talent, bereft of common sense and plausibility. It was presumably not only the more notorious statements of La Harpe (and Voltaire) but also those of Guizot that Pushkin had in mind when he wrote, in a note of 1832, that 'It is well-known that the French are the most anti-poetic people.' What he meant by this was that Shakespeare was the essence both of true 'poetry' (imaginative empathy) and true 'historical' consciousness, that the French tendency to find an elegant, abstracting argument or 'plot' (*vymysel*) for everything was inadequate to explain Shakespeare (and hence 'unpoetic', in the sense of ungifted, imperceptive), and that, as far as Russia's troubled history was concerned, including the 1825 Decembrist Uprising, Pushkin would try to approach it, as he urged his friend Anton Del'vig to do, 'with the glance of Shakespeare'.

The extent to which Shakespeare informs the works of the second half of Pushkin's career, beginning with *Boris Godunov*, is truly astonishing: naming only those with an obvious Shakespeare connection, one finds *Count Nulin* (*Graf Nulin*), *The Blackamoor of Peter the Great* (*Arap Petra Velikogo*), *Poltava*, *The Little Tragedies* (*Malen'kie tragedii*), *The Tales of Belkin* (*Povesti Belkina*), and *Andzhelo*. Three aspects of Pushkin's mature 'borrowing' of Shakespeare are noteworthy for our purposes. First, the life itself, although gleaned by Pushkin from Guizot and other sources, seems to have been of limited interest, as opposed to the case of Byron. Where certain parallels could be used and where the poetic narrator (subject) and romantic hero (object) formed a seam that was the essence of romantic irony ('life is a work of art and the poet its creator'), Shakespeare could not be 'got at', and this turned out to be liberating. What was, in modern and postmodern terms, a theatrical metaphor in Byron, something originating in the words and role-playing of the speaker, was in Shakespeare nothing more or less than a fact of life. 'All the world's a stage', yes, but that stage was not perceived as a figure of speech. There was no way to join up, other than through sheer speculation, the voice inside the poems (too hermetic) or inside the plays (too much belonging to the 'voice zones' of individual characters) with the voice (virtually unrecorded) and the actions outside them. Second, Pushkin is principally interested in the lessons of Shakespearean character, especially verisimilitude and the 'unpredictability' of life, but what is striking is that this newly flexible, utterly un-Byronic notion of character coexists with a powerful appreciation of 'classical' form (here Pushkin's roots in eighteenth-century French culture would never be fully transcended). And third, the oppositions of poetry/prose and history/fiction, so crucial to Pushkin's later works, would now be filtered through a Shakespearean lens as well: Shakespeare's magical ability to blend, within the covers of one play, the antithetical stylistic registers of a Master Elbow and an Angelo/Isabella as well as the forms of poetry and prose (metre, rhyme, etc.), all of which had been lost in the Letourneur translations, would find an analogue in some of Pushkin's greatest poems, stories, and plays.

Of all the works that demonstrate Pushkin's new-found admiration for Shakespeare, perhaps none is more bold, more 'epochal' in its inspiration, than *Boris Godunov*. The play is a goldmine of reinvented and thoroughly 'russified' Shakespearean characters, episodes, vying levels of diction, genre telescoping (tragedy and history), and spirited dialogue with sources (especially Karamzin's tenth and eleventh volumes of *The History of the Russian State* (*Istoriia gosudarstva rossiiskogo*), which had appeared in March 1824). Pushkin the poet clearly knew what he was doing:

> Being completely certain that the outmoded forms of our theatre were in need of reshaping, I organized my tragedy according to the system of Our Father Shakespeare, and I sacrificed at his altar two of the classical unities [time and place], while barely preserving the third [action]. In addition to these famous three unities there is another, that of style [*edinstvo sloga*], about which the French critical literature is silent (probably because they assume its necessity cannot be contested) ... [Here too] I followed this very seductive example [of Shakespeare].
> (Draft letter to the publisher of *Moskovskii vestnik*, 1828).

Thus, in Boris's staged rejection of the crown one can readily see echoes of *Julius Caesar* and *Richard III*; in the cynical comments of Shuisky and Vorotynsky that open Pushkin's drama against the backdrop of the artificially wailing *narod*, a recasting of the tribunes Flavius and Marullus and the benighted commoners of *Julius Caesar*; in the Pretender's light-hearted ability to recreate himself anew in different roles and with different addressees, a play on the Hal character of *Henry IV* Parts 1 and 2, just as his disarmingly sound, saddle-cradling sleep on the losing field of battle is a playful inversion of Richard III's famous 'A horse! a horse! my kingdom for a horse!'; and in the famous love scene between the Pretender and Marina Mniszek at the fountain, a return to the balcony scene of *Romeo and Juliet*, but with this powerfully ironic difference – Marina is not a swooning, innocent Juliet, but a scheming, utterly cool Lady Macbeth, and so on. The connections are rich and almost endlessly multiplying. As Pushkin brought these characters to life from the pages of Karamzin, he looked at them all 'with the glance of Shakespeare' – he did not hold them to an overarching plot (the dramatist's idea of how history 'exfoliated'), but made them all full-blooded personalities, with often conflicting motivations, and with words that constantly shifted their meanings depending on the *Realpolitik* of context.

But not even Pushkin could create the equivalent of Shakespearean drama in a vacuum. That he used the French as a negative point of departure, but still used them, is the real marvel of this new invention of Russian 'romantic tragedy'. For what Pushkin achieved, for all his sincere statements about dispensing with the unities, was a remarkably classical concept of form played off against a dynamic new Shakespearean understanding of character. With regard to the formal aspects of the play, Pushkin was typically self-concealing while appearing to be self-revealing: he says in the same draft letter quoted above that 'I replaced the honourable alexandrine with blank verse, I demeaned myself in several scenes with despised prose, and I did not divide my tragedy into acts.' However, as a recent scholar, I. Ronen, has posited (following D. Blagoy and others), the play is constructed in an elegant mirror symmetry, with the themes (Russia/Poland, east/west, secular love/primitive patriarchy, legitimacy/imposture, death of children/dynastic succession, and so on), characters (Boris/Pretender), and episodes of its first ten scenes lined up, pyramid-like, with those of the last ten (14–23), leaving the scenes 11–13, those involving Poland and culminating with the Pretender's declaration of love to Marina at the fountain, as the peak of the pyramid and the point at which all fortunes turn. But this numbering has to be added by the reader: it is not there in the text. In other words, Pushkin has consciously removed those formal markers of the historical tragedy, such as mention of large and small divisions (acts/scenes) or listing of dramatis personae, that draw attention to their artificiality, their *staged* quality. Why? Because he is bringing history to life, actually not metaphorically – the ultimate Shakespearean magic. At the same time, however, his work is subtly structured within a framework of homeostatic tensions and releases that reveals the strength of an opposing tradition – the French Neoclassical.

The centre of Pushkin's play and the height of its romantic tension is the fountain scene, where the Pretender is forced by circumstances to decide between two roles – the resilient Hal who is Henry V *in statu nascendi* and the pining Romeo who longs to hear words of love from the lips of his Juliet. This is indeed the juncture where the love plot and the political plot come together and vie for supremacy, where issues of erotic role-playing and 'power' blur into those of martial prowess and legitimate right to govern. This is also the point where Pushkin's understanding of Shakespearean disinterestedness or 'negative capability' comes most to the fore. 'Thanks to the French', writes Pushkin in the previously cited draft letter, 'we do not understand how a dramatic author can reject his own mode of thought [*obraz myslei*] in order to transpose himself to the age that he imagines.' Thus the genuinely romantic is not the filtering through the thought patterns of intervening generations and cultures (here the French), but the attempt to shed those patterns in order to come as close as possible to re-entering the still 'open' and future-laden experiences of a former age. Historical personages are not actors on some dramatist's or director's stage; at the time they speak and act, there is no denouement, other than their own fears and desires, pulling them forward into the future.

In this respect, the fountain scene has been both brilliantly read and, in my opinion, misread by recent critics of a postmodern stance. Monika Greenleaf, for example, argues for a provocative homology between Hal's 'theatrical talent', where his 'princely assumption' is that 'everything is as counterfeit to his own behaviour', and the Pretender's 'understanding of the contingency of his being' – 'There *is* no referential basis for Dmitry's language. . . . His pure verbal invention is their [the Pretender's and Marina's] entrée into history'. Likewise, Juliet's famous 'What's in a name?' becomes the deadly ironic play with the Pretender's different names in this erotic duel. However, where Greenleaf and the postmoderns err is in their treatment of the theatrical imagery and role-playing as metaphorical *tout court*, as linguistic habiliments that can be donned risk-free – worn (thus the emphasis on 'fashion') for the duration of the performance and then placed calmly among the other costumes and stage decorations. But Pushkin and Shakespeare lived in worlds where life and language were continually filled with risk. In the fountain scene Pushkin was not only embedding some of his own very vulnerable feelings about strong, calculating women who use their beauty to gain power outside the domestic sphere; he was also showing the full romantic potential of the Pretender's character, who becomes a kind of 'poet in life/history'. When the Pretender finally understands the limits of the crisis he has cast himself into by trying to reach Marina through the 'truth', self-exposure, and 'honest' love, he gathers himself together and makes his most powerful speech: 'The shade of [Ivan] the Terrible adopted me, / Named me Dimitrii from the grave, / Incited people around me / And doomed Boris to be sacrificed to me / – I am the Tsarevich'.

Two things draw attention away from a postmodern (or 'post-Byronic') reading and towards a 'Shakespearean' one: first, the Pretender breaks into rhymed verse (*usynovíla + nareklá + vozmutíla + obreklá + tsarévich ia*) as he declares these lines – these are the formal markers of his sudden rising in grandeur in Marina's and the audience's eyes, and Pushkin never questions the ontological reality of language, its ability to say what it means; and second, for the only time in the scene, the voice 'proudly' (*gordo*) delivering these words is named as 'Dmitrii', and not as the *Samozvanets* ('Pretender'). In other words, at this point the Pretender fully assumes the identity of the Tsarevich, not on a stage he can walk away from but in life, in history, with all the risks attendant on that move (one day in the future his ashes will be shot from the Kremlin back in the direction of Poland). And when he does this, Marina backs down for now she respects and fears him, which is her condition (since she understands that her beauty and his 'love' are worth nothing in the abstract) for any amorous reciprocity in the first place. If Pushkin has not shown how this erotic battle actually happened (if it ever did), he has shown how it could have happened, and he has shown brilliantly how the different 'Pretenders' ('lover', 'fugitive monk', 'tsarevich', and so on) can coexist fully in one very tense and pivotal 'historical' situation.

In conclusion, this Shakespearean notion of disinterestedness in character portrayal coupled with a powerful, though never foregrounded, appreciation of inhering form, stayed with Pushkin throughout the remainder of his career. On the level of character, for example, we find the Othello-Desdemona situation in Mariia's inexplicable and ultimately self-destructive passion for the older Mazepa in *Poltava* (a theme that the author of course knew in his family history – see for example *The Blackamoor of Peter the Great*, and his own choice of bride). Likewise, several of the characters and situations in *The Little Tragedies* suggest Shakespearean sources and transpositions: in 'The Avaricious Knight' ('Skupoi rytsar'') Pushkin has split Shylock's trade and passion between the parodic Jew (*zhid*) and the noble baron, just as in 'Mozart and Salieri' ('Motsart i Sal'eri') he has given us an Iago figure in the deeply and mysteriously offended Salieri, but one transferred from the sphere of martial skill (Iago is angered because he has been passed over by Othello for Cassio – 'mere prattle without practice is all his soldiership') to that of art. So too might one see the central plot device of 'The Stone Guest' ('Kamennyi gost'') – Don Juan's most 'impossible' (and thus maximally arousing) suit yet, that of the pious widow Donna Anna, whose husband he has slain – as a reprise of the great wooing scene in *Richard III*, when Richard, Duke of Gloucester offers the weapon and bares his breast to the newly widowed Anne, whose feelings, because she believes the villain's ploy ('Your beauty was the cause of that effect [the killing of her husband Edward]'), go from fierce invective to the beginnings of love in the space of a single scene. One might even go so far as to speculate that Pushkin's famous 'descent to prose' in *The Tales of Belkin* is a playful reversal, or 'de-tragification', of several of the most famous Shakespearean plots: the outer limits of revenge in 'The Shot' ('Vystrel') (*Othello*); a storm-induced case of mistaken identity among young lovers and a strangely magical fate in 'The Blizzard' ('Metel'') (*The Tempest*); graveside humour and metapoetic thoughts involving Eros and Thanatos in 'The Coffin-Maker' ('Grobovshchik') (*Hamlet*); a beloved daughter who 'betrays' a proud and vulnerable father in 'The Stationmaster' ('Stantsionnyi smotritel'') (*King Lear*), and a feud between two families whose children are carrying on a secret romance in 'The Peasant Lady' ('Baryshnia-Krest'ianka') (*Romeo and Juliet*). The essence of all these various inversions, however, is that human potential is always greater than the ability of any pre-ordained plot to contain it. Thus, in *The Little Tragedies*, at the centre of whose title page Pushkin sketched the head of Shakespeare, we are constantly confronted with contradictions: a knight (noble) who is covetous (ignoble), a guest (a human presence invited in) that is stone (immobile, inhuman), and so on. By the same token, as Pushkin shifted to prose and the language of everyday life, he wanted to focus on those characters who step out of the roles assigned to them by the 'plots' of western literature – the 'eternally fortunate' count of 'The Shot' must now live with a sense of guilt and dishonour (he has taken an unearned shot against Silvio); the 'prodigal daughter' Dunia of 'The Stationmaster' does succeed at escaping her biblically-imposed destiny, but at the cost of hurting her father, whose death she comes to mourn at the end.

Last but not least, the Angelo that Guizot and his tradition saw as flawed and inconsistent is in Pushkin's work of the same name one of the greatest, and psychologically realistic, characters in world literature. That this epitome of justice, rectitude, and the law could 'fall' for Isabella's virtue, just as Isabella's passionate chastity could in the end 'rise' to make a case for mercy on behalf of her tormentor, seemed to Pushkin the very essence of human plot potential: neither honour nor mercy has meaning outside the other. One can easily imagine, for example, the poet who urged the new tsar (Nicholas) to be lenient toward his Decembrist friends in *Stanzas* (*Stansy*, 1826), and who named as one of his singular virtues in his great valedictory poem 'I have erected a monument not made by hand', (1836) ('Ia pamiatnik sebe vozdvig nerukotvornyi') the fact that he 'called for mercy toward the fallen', remembering the eloquent pleas for mercy delivered by Isabella and her sister character Portia from *The Merchant of Venice*. It was not by chance that a brave virgin (Masha Mironova), whose 'honour' is at stake at various points in the story and whose call for mercy before the Empress Catherine on behalf of a tainted loved one (Petr Grinev) saves the day, becomes the prosaic muse figure of Pushkin's last major work, the Scottian historical romance *The Captain's Daughter*, 1836 (*Kapitanskaia dochka*). It was precisely this exceptional gesture of mercy, from a position of moral and/or political authority, that broke the predictable form of justice and thereby gave it vitality. By the end of his life Pushkin had left a Russian legacy of Shakespearism never to be duplicated but which took time to be understood and appreciated. He had borrowed without imitating; he had written of imagined others without speaking 'only about himself'; he had passed beyond Byron to a salutary self-consciousness that would, as the 'origin without origins', feed his tradition indefinitely.

FURTHER READING

Barzun, Jacques (ed.) *European Writers: The Romantic Century. Vol. 5: Goethe to Pushkin*, New York: Scribner's, 1985.

Bayley, John. *Pushkin: A Comparative Commentary*, Cambridge: Cambridge University Press, 1971.

Greenleaf, Monika. *Pushkin and Romantic Fashion: Fragment, Elegy, Orient, Irony*, Stanford: Stanford University Press, 1994.

Makolkina, Anna. 'On the Poetics of Biography: Transformations in Some Biographies of Byron and Pushkin' (Dissertation). University of Toronto, 1988.

Mirsky, D.S. *Pushkin*, New York: Dutton, 1963.

Simmons, E.J. *English Literature and Culture in Russia (1553–1840)*, Harvard Studies in Contemporary Literature, Vol. 12, Cambridge, MA: Harvard University Press, 1935.

Trueblood, Paul Graham (ed.) *Byron's Political and Cultural Influences in Nineteenth-Century Europe*, London: Macmillan, 1981.

Plus the following specialist works in Russian:

Alekseev, M.P. *Pushkin: Sravnitel'no-istoricheskie issledovaniia*, Leningrad: Nauka, 1972.

Alekseev, M.P. (ed.) *Shekspir i russkaia kul'tura*, Moscow–Leningrad, Nauka, 1965.

Zhirmunskii, V.M. *Bairon i Pushkin: Iz istorii romanticheskoi poemy*, Leningrad: Academia, 1924. Reprinted as *Bairon i Pushkin. Pushkin i zapadnye literatury*, Leningrad: Nauka, 1978.

8

THE GOLDEN AGE OF RUSSIAN POETRY

DONALD RAYFIELD

'Golden Ages' are recognized only in hindsight: not until the 1880s, when Russian poetry and prose seemed to be in the doldrums, did it become usual to refer to the age of Pushkin, and particularly to its poetry, as a Golden Age. When Russian poetry revived in the 1900s to create a Silver Age, the term implied the emulation of a Golden Age a century before. For our purposes, the Golden Age begins in 1813, with the surge of creative optimism that followed on Russia's defeat of Napoleon, reaches its climax in 1825 at the end of Alexander I's reign and persists until about 1845, when Nicholas I's censorship, the emergence of a wider readership and the triumph of prose genres over verse marks the Age's demise. The Golden Age, inevitably, is studied as though it were a planetary system of poets revolving around Pushkin the Sun and, although the Golden Age marks the appearance of the first truly great works of prose fiction and verse comedy in Russian literature, we shall nevertheless here survey the age as primarily one of poetry, when lyric poets incorporated into an already established Russian verse canon all that European Neoclassicism and Romanticism could give, and gave poetry not just a proliferation of originality and musicality but a public importance that it would take many decades to regain.

The Golden Age built on the achievements of the eighteenth century in arriving at a literary language that could bridge the colloquial speech of educated Russians and the official Church Slavonic patois that had been cobbled together as the language of administration and commerce. Technical questions of poetic form, metre, rhyme had been solved by the middle of the eighteenth century. In its choice of genre (elegy, ode, fable and so on), however, the eighteenth century had been motivated primarily by the fact that poetry's main function was to be a response to patronage, its role as a court entertainment. The Golden Age moved away from genres subservient to the state and the patron, such as the ode, and thus from the ruler as patron. As educated circles broadened, poets could find readers among their peers, even if the Russian reading public was still too small to make a poet, or any journal he or she published in, financially independent. The confidence of a poet that he was an autonomous being, even the romantic pretension to being an unacknowledged legislator of the world, was a precondition of the Golden Age.

The generation of young officers returning from the Napoleonic wars included two key poets in the first years of the Golden Age: Konstantin Batiushkov and Vasilii Zhukovsky. Those who sojourned in Paris and London brought with them not just the fruits of Romanticism, the verse of André Chénier, Walter Scott and Friedrich Schiller: they brought back the concept of a poet's independence. Those who did not fight but were educated in St Petersburg and Moscow did not lag behind. The *lycée* at Tsarskoe Selo, where so many poets were schooled, was staffed by many a survivor of the French Revolution or refugee from Napoleon, who gave their pupils a sense of history and an intellectual's role in shaping it. Moscow University numbered among its teachers such refugees as Baron Stein, future Foreign Minister of Prussia. The education of poets to come – who, by some enigmatic demographic wave, were born in unprecedented numbers in the late 1790s and early 1800s – was thus not just infused by printed examples of Romanticism and its beliefs in the primacy of nature, folk poetry, the rights of man and the power of art: it was stimulated by a living generation of revolutionaries, royalists and renegades. The one element of Romanticism that is strikingly absent in the poetry of Russia's Golden Age is the renewed Christianity that infuses so much English and French Romantic poetry. In this respect the Neoclassical and Voltairean eighteenth-century spirit remained undimmed.

The poetry of Konstantin Batiushkov (1787–1855) was the main bridge from the eighteenth century to the Golden Age. Batiushkov could write satire in the same mode as eighteenth-century radicals such as Radishchev; but his Neo-classicism went further, with his elegies which mourned not just the loss of life but the loss of love and of inspiration. First an officer in the Napoleonic wars, then a diplomatic official in Italy, Batiushkov saw in western Europe an Arcadia, from which he was very soon expelled. In his earlier verse he took plasticity of syntax and melodiousness of phonetic line further, emulating the virtues of the two main works of the unjustly neglected French hedonist and free-thinker Evariste Parny: *La Guerre des dieux* and *Les Déguisements de Vénus*. Without incorporating any new system of beliefs into his work, Batiushkov's extraordinary gift for cadences gives his work a deep melancholy which approximates it to Romantic 'spleen'. As disasters struck him – he was dismissed from the service, jilted by his fiancée, prone to more and more persistent bouts of clinical depression, Batiushkov's elegiac mood deepens: his poem of 1815, *The Shade of a Friend* (*Ten' druga*), in which the ghost of a warrior companion appears during a journey at sea, has the Romantic conviction in the reality of the otherworldly which is to infuse the best of the Golden Age. Like his successors, however, Batiushkov was to discover that no Romantic beliefs in the numinous could overcome the tragic Hellenic outlook that Russian poets had inherited from their eighteenth-century predecessors. Batiushkov's light touch with the sounds of Russian, miraculously approximating it to Italian, was emulated by Pushkin. But by the time Pushkin had matured, Batiushkov was in an asylum, and the example of his melancholy was to act as a *memento mori* for the next decade of the Golden Age. Batiushkov's only partly demented *Imitations of the Ancients* (*Podrazhanie drevnim*) shows a remarkable synthesis of Hellenic pessimism and Romantic aspirations which is typical of the Golden Age: numbers 4 and 6 of the elegies run:

When the maiden departs in suffering and the livid corpse grows cold, – vainly love pours ambergris and flings a cover of flowers over it. She is pale as a lily in the cornflowers' azure, as a wax cast; limp fingers take no joy in flowers, and fragrance is vain . . .

Do you want honey, son? then fear not the sting; a crown of victory? – boldly to battle! You long for pearls? – then go down to the bottom where the crocodile gapes under the water, do not be afraid! God will decide. He is a father only to the bold: only the bold win pearls, honey or perdition . . . or a crown.

Batiushkov had mined deeper the French (and Italian) vein which permeates the Golden Age; Vasilii Andreevich Zhukovsky (1783–1852), another returning officer, turned Russian poetry in a direction that was primarily German and secondarily British. Zhukovsky's work was mostly translation or adaptation, but was nonetheless influential for that, however much his imitation provoked his contemporaries to parody and even mockery. Germanic maidens borne off to the other world by their dead lovers are given their Russian equivalents by Zhukovsky:

And Minvana is no more . . . When mists rise from the currents, hills and fields, and the moon shines without rays, as through smoke – two shades can be seen: merging, they fly to the shelter they know . . . and the oak moves and the strings sound.

But these popular Romantic ballads of ghostly love are only part of the baggage that Zhukovsky had brought back from the West. He also presented Russia's poets with a new role, as a demiurge, as a mouthpiece for the people. As well as pursuing melodiousness, Zhukovsky widened the genres available with pseudo-folk ballads and songs, with the concept of effusion and fragment to replace the symmetrical ordered classical poem. If Zhukovsky, appointed by Nicholas I to sift through Pushkin's heritage, to compose a national anthem and even a ceremony for carrying out capital punishment, and to tutor the heir to the throne, seemed in the 1830s to betray the role of the free spirit, then we must remember those other Romantics who failed to die young: Wordsworth with his *Sonnets on the Death Penalty* or Lamartine with his candidacy for the Presidency. Zhukovsky for most of his life set the younger poets of the Golden Age an example of idealism: 'Blessed is he who amid life's destructive disturbance has . . . scorned and forgotten the vileness of the real'.

From 1815 to 1818 Batiushkov and Zhukovsky, together with Pushkin's uncle Vasilii, became closely linked with their successors, especially Pushkin, when they became founder-members of the Arzamas circle: the society was founded in the name of a tavern in the provincial town of Arzamas, known for its fat geese, and was meant to satirise the 'Conversation of Lovers of the Russian Word' ('Beseda liubitelei russkogo slova'), a conservative, chauvinist group of writers surrounding the now forgotten Admiral Shishkov. These innovative and disrespectful poets were known by nicknames: Batiushkov was called 'Achilles', Zhukovsky was known as 'Svetlana', Petr Viazemsky was 'Asmodeus', the adolescent Pushkin was 'Cricket'. In its short existence (which ended when Shishkov's group melted away), Arzamas became a centre not just for burlesque mockery of the establishment but for the propagation of Romantic ideas and Romantic genres. It brought together many

St Petersburg poets of the Golden Age – notably, Petr Viazemsky – and its mock-conspiratorial aura led many members into the more ominous secret societies that fomented the Decembrist revolt of 1825.

If Batiushkov and Zhukovsky widened poets' horizons, out of the Napoleonic wars came a new confidence in the intellectual's ability to see further than the statesman. The poetry of the Golden Age is inseparable from the *Lettres philosophiques* circulated by Petr Chaadaev, Russia's first original political thinker (until he, too, like Batiushkov was overcome by depression – in his case a self-fulfilling diagnosis of madness made by an indignant Tsar). Chaadaev's mission was to infuse Pushkin and his circle with a belief in the flame of history, in Providence: a cornerstone of Romanticism being its conviction that history was not a series of senseless recurrences, but the unfolding of Providence, a journey from the fall to paradise. The prospects of western Europe, spiritually free even in political turmoil, were articulated so well by Chaadaev that almost all the poets of the Golden Age became, at least for a while, convinced of man's ability and duty not just to understand but to change the world with the word.

If the officers returning from the Napoleonic wars were responsible for the import of new ideas and modes of poetry, a new model of the poet-rebel and poet-innovator came a decade later, when many of the poets of the Golden Age were scattered over Russia. Byron's reputation (largely because of the common sympathies of Russian and British poets for the Greeks' struggle to win independence) spread all over Russia, as it had over Europe in the 1820s, a reputation that became godlike when Byron died of fever at Missolonghi. When we consider that Pushkin and the other Golden Age poets who were influenced by Byron read him not in English, but in a mediocre French prose version by Pichot, the extent to which Byron influenced Russian poetry is astounding. Byron showed how to develop intuitively, almost cinematically constructed narrative poems, and gave Russian poets, if only for a few years, new themes: doomed love that transcended the boundaries of Christian and Moslem; the poet as an unrepentant Faust, Don Juan and Don Quixote all rolled into one.

If the Golden Age is a solar system, then we should begin by examining the work of the poets who were closest to the sun – those who were educated in close proximity to Pushkin and whose work is often a dialogue with him: the poetry of Del'vig, Iazykov and (although he is almost a decade older) Viazemsky.

Anton Antonovich Del'vig (1798–1831), Pushkin's closest friend, has been somewhat underestimated: a short and slothful life left a slender *œuvre*: one volume of verse published two years before his death, a narrow range of vocabulary and images have led critics to consign him to the rank of a minor poet. His theme, however, was the end of a private and poetic idyll, the death of Arcadia, and was best expressed in a poem *The End of the Golden Age* (*Konets zolotogo veka*) – written, ironically, at the very climax of what was to be known as Russia's Golden Age. Del'vig seems to have welded Shakespearean tragedy into the Neoclassical games of Daphnis and Chloe: in Del'vig's Arcadia, the nymph drowns as she sings, like Ophelia:

Amarylla was borne by the current, singing her song, not feeling perdition close, as if born to be in water by her ancient father Ocean, without finishing her sad song, she drowned.

The death of an abandoned heroine was a theme inherited by the Golden Age from Karamzin's sentimental prose tale *Poor Liza* (*Bednaia Liza*), but Del'vig raised it to a far greater significance, which we find echoed in Pushkin's narrative poems – *The Prisoner of the Caucasus* (*Kavkazskii plennik*), *The Fountain of Bakhchisarai* (*Bakhchisaraiskii fontan*). Del'vig's last elegies, inviting death to dinner and to bed, foreshadow the elegies of Pushkin's last period: Del'vig's death affected Pushkin perhaps more deeply than that of any of his circle. In one aspect Del'vig went further than even Pushkin: he was the first Russian poet to master sonnet form, and his sonnet *Inspiration* (*Vdokhnovenie*) is not only a perfect example of a form which succeeds relatively rarely in Russian but quintessentially Del'vigian in its stress on a private morality in an amoral world, for Del'vig places the poet even higher than his fellow Golden Age poets:

> Wandering alone under the skies, He speaks with ages yet to come; He puts honour above all other parts, His fame takes vengeance on slander And he shares immortality with the gods.

Del'vig's techniques and themes were a century later to exert an influence on Mandel'shtam. Even better than avowedly folk poets, such as Kol'tsov, Del'vig was able to catch the tone and subtly displaced rhythms of folk poetry in a number of pastiches; he was also one of the most successful poets of his day in providing texts for the Russian equivalent of *Lieder*: a number of his poems are now best known as *romansy* set to music by Glinka.

Petr Andreevich Viazemsky (1792–1878) appears to be the opposite of Del'vig, and not only in longevity. He was more heavily influenced by his cosmopolitan background. Irish–Swedish on his mother's side, he was influenced by a Voltaire-francophile father. Although seven years older than Pushkin and (like Batiushkov and Zhukovsky) a veteran of the Napoleonic wars, Viazemsky mixed with Pushkin and his fellow lycéens on equal terms. Viazemsky was (with Baratynsky and Iazykov) one of the Golden Age poets who for reasons not entirely of his own choice moved to Moscow – a move which seemed to almost all Russian poets, in the 1920s even more than in the 1820s, to be an exile from Europe and order into Asia and chaos. Unlike the depressive Del'vig, Viazemsky was combative, dissident to the point of physical discordance. In Gogol''s essay of 1846 'What is Actually the Essence of Russian Poetry . . .', the first thorough appreciation of the Golden Age's achievement, Viazemsky comes in for harsh criticism; Gogol''s main point still stands:

> next to a verse which is stronger and firmer than any other poet's, we find another sort, quite unlike the first; at one moment he will show the pain of living flesh ripped from the heart, at another he will repel with a sound that is almost alien to the heart,

which is quite out of tune with the subject; you can feel his lack of inner consistency, a life which is not filled with strength.

Pushkin, as a close friend, was bold enough to tell Viazemsky in 1826: 'Your verse is too clever. Poetry, God forgive me, has to be a bit stupid.' To this criticism might be added Viazemsky's refusal to make concessions to melodiousness: he is perhaps the only poet of the Golden Age whose texts no composer was able or willing to set to music.

Like Fedor Tiutchev, Viazemsky was the only poet of the Golden Age to live his full three score and ten; unlike Tiutchev, he was not restored to the canon by the critical re-evaluations of the early twentieth century. His life-long disgruntled and uncompromising stance made him unattractive: to write on Russia (*The Russian God* [*Russkii bog*], 1828) as he did, as unpatriotically as Turgenev in the novel *Smoke* (*Dym*) was not to court popularity:

> Full of grace to the stupid, mercilessly strict to the clever, God of everything inappropriate, that is him, the Russian God. God of everything that is outlandish, unseemly, out of place, God of mustard after supper, that is him, the Russian God.

The death of Pushkin (not to speak of five of his own children) led Viazemsky into a pessimism bleaker than even Pushkin's darkest moments. Though he was to know Europe and modern times better than any other survivor of the Golden Age, progress only deepened Viazemsky's gloom. A train journey from Prague to Vienna left his convictions unaltered:

> Man has been armed with a bold and rebellious force; he is burning for ever with an insatiable, uncontrollable passion. The battle of elements, of contradictions, the discord of conflicting forces has all been trampled down by the human mind and subordinated to calculation. Thus ploughing through the universe, because of his passions and plans the master of limited days arrogantly forgets himself. But if the slightest mishap occurs and our mighty giant goes off the tracks, if only by a hair's breadth, Then all the calculation, all the wisdom of the age is just zero, and the same zero and nonentity of man will fly off its stilts into dust and ashes.

Viazemsky, unlike the other rebellious spirits of the Golden Age, consistently saw life as an old dressing-gown, a comforting membrane that could never be discarded. His *Farewell to the Dressing-Gown* (*Proshchanie s khalatom*) of 1817 is echoed in 1877 with the lines: 'Our life in old age is a worn-out dressing-gown . . . The two of us have long since grown together like brothers; We can't be repaired or renovated.'

If Viazemsky represented the irredentist intellect, then Pushkin's friend Nikolai Mikhailovich Iazykov (1803–46) was all instinct and impressionable emotion. Although he knew Del'vig and Zhukovsky from his student days and mixed with Pushkin's friends and relatives during his university years at Dorpat (Tartu), he did not actually meet Pushkin until the Golden Age had endured its great crisis, the retribution exacted in 1826 by Nicholas I on real and suspected Decembrists. At Trigorskoe, next to Pushkin's estate Mikhailovskoe, the two poets met and in his poem *Trigorskoe* Iazykov celebrated one of the most productive encounters in Russian poetry: Iazykov expresses Pushkin's feelings at having escaped exile to the south or, worse, to Siberia with an effusiveness that Pushkin's reserve would not have allowed:

> How sweet for the young prisoner, leaving the darkness and weight of chains, to look at daylight, at the shine of the rippling water, to walk along the meadow shore, to sate himself on the fields' air. How comforting for the poet to escape the world of cold vanity, where numerous hopes and dreams run to the Lethe, where in a heart beloved of the muse, sometimes, like a stream of flame extinguished by thick smoke, because of the unbearable roar of passions, the life forces weaken, – to take refuge, a free man, in the beautiful world, in nature's gardens and suddenly and proudly forget his lost years.

Iazykov's poetic fire was dampened very soon after this climax. His elegies on love are full of erotic fire, and his poetry from his years of travelling Europe's spas being treated for syphilis produces some memorable scenic poetry in a Byronic genre. But Iazykov's burning radicalism, despite the execution of friends such as Ryleev, cooled and he even began to deplore Pushkin's free-thinking and narrative fecundity.

Those poets who took an active role in the revolt of December 1825 ran on an orbit more distant from Pushkin's closest circles. Nevertheless, two of them, Kondratii Fedorovich Ryleev(1795–1826) and Vil'gel'm Karlovich Kiukhel'beker (1797–1846) were poets of note, if not of genius. Ryleev was one of the youngest veterans of the Napoleonic wars, but what he had learnt and wished to propagate was more political than literary. Patriotism and civic courage were ideals blazed by the heroes of his narrative poems, and of modern poets only Byron influenced him, more as a fighter than a poetic innovator. Before his fatal involvement with revolution, however, Ryleev and a co-conspirator founded an annual almanac, *Poliarnaia zvezda* (*The Polar Star*) which was to be the model for Russia's 'thick' periodicals which, from the 1830s to this day have been – even more than book-publishing – the mainstay of all imaginative literature in Russia and can be regarded, together with the monthly *Sovremennik* (*The Contemporary*) that Pushkin subsequently founded, as the most durable of the Golden Age's bequests to posterity. Ryleev's political views, like most of the Decembrists', were eclectic and contradictory; his high regard for the constitution of the United States of America was at odds with both the aristocratic constitutionalism of the 'northern' rebels and the totalitarian dictatorial views of the 'southerners' – views which were, unfortunately, to prevail among Russia's opposition thinkers.

Although Kiukhel'beker fired a pistol at a Grand Duke and was sentenced to beheading, he paid for his involvement with the Decembrists not with his neck but with his liberty and, eventually, his eyesight. More naive and independent than Ryleev, he was the more original and productive poet. Although his family was

German-speaking and he was heavily influenced by Goethe's mythopœia, he was (perhaps in compensation for his Germanic surname) an ardent Slavist, adhering more to the archaicists in his determination to write a purely 'Slavonic' Russian. He was a fellow-pupil of Pushkin's and his traits were copied to create the naive poet Lensky in *Evgenii Onegin*. It might be said that he was Pushkin's polar opposite, as Lensky was Onegin's, and his departure for hard labour and exile in Siberia affected Pushkin as deeply as Lensky's death is described as affecting Onegin. Classical Hellenic values, as much as Byronic romanticism, underlie Kiukhel'beker's radical stance. Like many Russian intellectuals of the Golden Age he saw no contradiction between his defence of Greek national self-determination and his valiant military service in the Caucasus in the early 1820s, waging under General Ermolov a genocidal war against Chechens and Dagestanis.

In solitary confinement Kiukhel'beker was allowed to continue writing. Arguably, his best poetry came from reflection. Of all the Golden Age poets he was the most ambitious: his long verse work *Izhorsky* is a mystery play that appears to emulate Goethe's *Faust Part II* and he produced two very long historical verse epics. In his lyric verse, however, Kiukhel'beker remains close to the best of the Golden Age. He remained convinced of ultimate justice and, in a poem *To a Slanderer* (*Klevetniku*) attacking the officers in charge of his fate, warned:

> Believe me, there is Nemesis in the world, and she notes any offence and enters it in a book, and silently a mysterious maiden reads this book day and night and chooses victims and punishes them without wrath, but without pity too. Lies and slander will eventually be paid for with the same slander, and the murderous arrow of evil lies will penetrate your heart too . . .

His poem on *The Fate of Russian Poets* (*Uchast' russkikh poetov*) remains a harsh but well-judged model for later poets' self-induction:

> Bitter is the fate of poets of all races; fate punishes Russia worst of all . . . God gave their hearts fire, their minds light, yes, their feelings were inspired and ardent – What then? They are hurled into dark prisons, killed by the freezing cold of hopeless exile . . . Either disease brings night and fog to the eyes of the far-sighted and inspired; or the hand of despicable favourites puts a bullet in their sacred brows; Or else rebellion rouses the deaf rabble, and the rabble tears to bits him whose flight, dazzling us with thunderbolts, would have flooded his native land with radiance.

Many Russian poets were to be threatened with execution and punished with exile; when, a hundred years later, Stalin made it the normal fate for almost any poet worth his salt, none was so eloquent in his self-defence as Kiukhel'beker had been.

The Golden Age's greatest poets, it might be argued, are those who escaped Pushkin's orbit and became luminaries in their own right. Those who lived and wrote in Moscow escaped the Pushkinian influences that were particularly overpowering after 1827, the year of Pushkin's return from exile. Of all Pushkin's cohort Evgenii Abramovich Baratynsky (1800–44) was most clearly an equal. He too began his literary career writing melodious elegies under the influence of Batiushkov and Parny; he too was exiled (but to Finland rather than the South). Like Pushkin, Baratynsky developed the narrative poem, with a Finnish rather than a Crimean or Caucasian setting, as his main genre. But Baratynsky's often touching narrative poems are no longer widely read, even though Pushkin praised them; his early elegies – despite the fact that some, for example 'Do not tempt me with the return of your affection', are still treasured as the texts for the most affecting Russian *Lieder* – have been superseded in critical esteem by his later work. Baratynsky was alienated first from Moscow life and then from life in general. His increasing discontent led him to a language which is more and more austere and precise and to a conviction that art was the only salvation:

Chisel, organ, brush – happy is he who is drawn to them as to sensual things, not stepping across their boundary. He has intoxication at the world's feast-day. But before you, as before a naked sword, o word, bright ray, earth's life goes pale.

Particularly after Pushkin's death, Baratynsky became a poet very modern for his times: the poems of his 1842 collection, *Twilight* (*Sumerki*) compare with Théophile Gautier's *Émaux et camées* in their pursuit of pure form in art and thought, and his conviction in the power of death to divest all experience of any meaning anticipates the world-view of the Symbolist and Decadent. Like Gautier, Baratynsky symbolized the destruction of poetry by technology by the image of a steamboat crushing water nymphs. Baratynsky was the first to foresee the nineteenth century ousting the aesthetic from life. In his poem *The Last Poet* (*Poslednii poet*) he declares: 'The age marches along its iron path, acquisitiveness is in hearts, and the common dream is every hour more obviously and shamelessly about the everyday and the useful.' His economy of language echoes his idealization of the sculptor as the ideal artist, adding and making nothing, merely removing surplus material. Baratynsky achieved greatness towards the end of his life and that of the Golden Age: it was left to the Symbolists, on the centenary of his birth, to recognize his extraordinary importance. The frequent and vibrant echoes of Baratynsky in Mandel'shtam's work suggest that of all Golden Age poets Baratynsky has most to communicate to the twentieth century.

Those Golden Age poets for whom Moscow was home, rather than exile from St Petersburg, lived in an atmosphere imbued with German Romantic mysticism rather than French Classical rationalism: Schelling meant more to them than Voltaire. They were relatively immune to radical political ideas or to the Byronic model, and out of their ranks would come the Orthodox theology and Pan-Slavist political ideals of the Slavophiles. The most charismatic of these poets was Dmitrii Vladimirovich Venevitinov (1805–27) whose short life, terminated by tuberculosis and pneumonia, has led readers to infer from the handful of poems he left a potential genius. For a brief time, surrounded by a circle of friends to whom his poems were addressed, Venevitinov played the same solar role in Moscow as Pushkin did in St Petersburg, but the impassioned rhetoric of his valedictory verse is valuable mostly as a harbinger of unrealized greatness.

Far more significant was Venevitinov's fellow Muscovite, a lowly poet, the illegitimate son of a merchant, Aleksandr Ivanovich Polezhaev (1804–37). Because of his bawdy masterpiece *Sashka* (which has never been published in full), Polezhaev was both famed and destroyed. A pastiche of Chapter One of Pushkin's *Evgenii Onegin*, its hero Sashka is likewise a roué dependent on his uncle; Polezhaev's witty verse evokes the debauchery of Moscow's students and whores. Polezhaev shows all the talent for graphic burlesque of the eighteenth-century erotic poet Ivan Barkov and of Pushkin's uncle Vasilii. The poem's notoriety led to an interview with Nicholas I and the Minister of Education. Polezhaev was forced to recite the poem in full, after which he was sentenced to serve as a rank and file soldier in the Caucasus. Although Polezhaev fought bravely, his plebeian status deprived him of protection. Floggings and military prison wrecked his health and before he died of tuberculosis his achievement was limited to little more than one fine narrative poem, *Chir-Yurt*, on the vicious war of attrition against Chechens and Circassians – a poem which anticipates Lev Tolstoy's sketches of the Caucasian wars – and a valedictory poem entitled *Consumption* (*Chakhotka*): its portrayal of a doomed poet anticipates Apollon Grigor'ev's record of self-destruction thirty years later and the despair of the Symbolists:

> Fateful consumption stares me in the eyes and, distorting its pale face, I can hear, it hoarsely says: 'My dear friend, you have long invited me to come with the ringing of bottles. Thus I appear with a bow – give your slave a corner to live in. We shan't live a boring life, believe me: you will cough and groan, and I shall always, inseparably, be ready to console you.'

The Golden Age was not ready for Polezhaev, and like Pushkin's and Lermontov's bawdy verse, his work was consigned to the foreign or private press and to manuscript circulation.

If Polezhaev was a Moscow parodist of Pushkin, Russia's greatest metaphysical poet, Fedor Ivanovich Tiutchev (1803–73), took as his point of departure Pushkin's lyrics on the otherworldly nature of inspiration, on the indifference of nature to man and on the fatal, unrequitable nature of love. In the 1830s some of Tiutchev's lyrics were published by Pushkin in *Sovremennik*. Tiutchev's work, however, followed other directions; his Moscow education and his diplomatic career took him into a Germanic orbit. In Munich he met Heinrich Heine and an improbable mutual respect sprang up between the left-wing German Jew and the right-wing Russian aristocrat, a respect founded on their common pessimism about the outcome of their poetic and political struggle. In 1833 Tiutchev, an intensely self-critical poet, whose surviving lyrical poetry (if we exclude political and translated verse) barely amounts to a hundred poems, destroyed a large amount of what he had written. Publication in 1836 attracted little attention – a subsequent edition in 1854 passed almost unnoticed. Tiutchev may belong to Pushkin's generation, but his poetry, so scandalously ignored in his lifetime, is not really part of the Golden Age: its dawn came posthumously and his poetry, based on a systematic opposition of light and dark, order and chaos, male and female, belatedly found its place in the twentieth century's Symbolist and Acmeist schools. In his metaphysical poetry, Tiutchev did not scorn the dissonant sounds and displaced rhythms of the eighteenth century's first experimenters; in his later love poetry, chronicling the distress and death of his mistress, Tiutchev found a simple tone, breathtakingly dangerous in its closeness to banality, a tone which is not to recur in Russian poetry until Pasternak's last lyrics. Tiutchev thus does not belong to the Golden Age – he is too much a timeless poet even to belong to the nineteenth century.

The Golden Age's last generation was born in the mid-1810s: writers such as Turgenev were soon to abandon verse for prose fiction and belong to the so-called Realist school of the 1850s and 1860s. The only major poet of this generation is Mikhaíl Iur'evich Lermontov (1814–41). Lermontov is linked to Pushkin primarily by his obsessively (however much denied) Byronic poetic persona and by his insistence on hiding his deepest feelings, outside the parameters of his verse, behind the mask of an officer and gentleman. His permanent adolescence meant that Lermontov's thought, a refusal to accept a world governed by a hostile God and despicable humanity, developed little; his outlook was never matured by observation or experience, even though at the end of his life he was able to produce a novel *A Hero of Our Time* (*Geroi nashego vremeni*) which is one of the most original pieces of psychological prose ever written and stands, together with *Evgenii Onegin*, as the Golden Age's main achievements in the novel. Conversely, Lermontov's verse became more and more plastic in the last four years of his life, reaching its extraordinary combination of evocative musicality and hypnotic narrative in his two poems of the Caucasus, *The Demon* (*Demon*) and *The Novice Monk* (*Mtsyri*). Lermontov and Pushkin, alone of the Golden Age poets, raised the narrative poem to parity with the lyric.

The Golden Age did not die a sudden death. From the mid-1840s poetry began to recede from public esteem. The only estimable woman poet of the Golden Age, Karolina Pavlova, emigrated to Germany. By a strange demographic response, nature seemed to have dried up the supply of poets. The late 1810s–1820s gave birth only to Afanasii Fet, Nekrasov and Aleksei Konstantinovich Tolstoy. Afanasii Fet, like Tiutchev, was to be largely ignored, even mocked, in his own century, and his daring love lyrics, sometimes verbless, sometimes shaped vertically as if a translation from the Chinese, had to wait until the twentieth century to make their impact. Nikolai Nekrasov, on the other hand, was to be idolized from the middle of the century to his death in 1877, but only as a honorary prose writer, because of his laudable democratic sentiments and his choice of subject matter among the impoverished peasantry and urban poor. His poetic genius, which at its best was extraordinarily innovative in rhythm, passed with little comment. Aleksei Tolstoy was one of the few poets of the nineteenth century to articulate Christianity – both Orthodox in his recreation of the hymns of St John Damascene, and evangelistic in his cruel *Ballad of Delarue* (*Ballada o Delariu*) about the gruesome fate of the altruist. Alone, he revived the eighteenth-century genre of historical verse drama. Like Fet, Aleksei Tolstoy was to be valued only posthumously.

In the forty years after 1825, even fewer poets were born: only six major poets, compared with, say, two dozen in the preceding forty. True, 'junk' poetry (by poets now largely forgotten, such as Maikov, Benediktov, and Mei), not to mention a still overrated pseudo-folk poetry by the Voronezh poets Kol'tsov and Nikitin, commanded a somewhat Philistine following, in the same way as the neo-Romantics of the late nineteenth century in England, France and Germany provided a diluted bourgeois version of the true Romanticism of the Napoleonic era.

The heritage of the Golden Age is a dual one. The Russian novel took from poets many of the themes first explored by poets: Pushkin's Onegin and Lermontov's Pechorin are models for superfluous heroes in Turgenev and Tolstoy; the intuitions of Tiutchev's love poetry are the underlying force behind the tragic fate of *Anna Karenina*. Baratynsky and Iazykov in Italy outline the reactions to be found in Russian novelists' peripatetic heroes. The less immediate heritage came into force with the birth of the Silver Age. Without the rediscovery of Batiushkov, Tiutchev and Baratynsky at the beginning of the twentieth century, the development of Aleksandr Blok or Osip Mandel'shtam would have been unthinkable; and, at a broader level, Russian poets would have not been able to foresee and cope with their ephemeral role, had they not had before them the example of their forefathers a century earlier.

FURTHER READING

Austin, Paul M. *The Exotic Prisoner in Russian Romanticism*, New York: Peter Lang, 1997.

Beaudoin, Luc J. *Resetting the Margins: Russian Romantic Verse Tales and the Idealized Woman*, New York: Peter Lang, 1997.

Brown, William Edward. *A History of Russian Literature of the Romantic Period*, 4 vols., Ann Arbor: Ardis, 1986.

Greenleaf, Monika and Stephen Moeller-Sally (eds) *Russian Subjects: Empire, Nation, and the Culture of the Golden Age*, Evanston, Illinois: Northwestern University Press, 1998.

Offord, Derek (ed.) *The Golden Age of Russian Literature and Thought*, London: Macmillan; New York: St Martin's Press, 1992.

Rayfield, Donald, Hicks, Jeremy, Makarova, Olga and Pilkington, Anna (eds and trans.) *The Garnett Book of Russian Verse*, London: Garnett Press, 2000.

9

THE CLASSIC RUSSIAN NOVEL

RICHARD FREEBORN

The classic Russian novel comprises the major Russian novels published between 1830 and 1880. They form a body of writing in the genre that can be shown to have certain specific characteristics that we nowadays think of as 'Russian'. These works are classic not in the sense of any 'classic-romantic' opposition, but in the straightfoward sense of being accepted as standard or definitive both within the framework of Russian literature and in terms of its influence. They are the works of Turgenev, Tolstoy, and Dostoevsky and their immediate predecessors, or near-contemporaries, Pushkin, Lermontov, Gogol', and Goncharov. In short, barely more than half-a-dozen men of outstanding genius, born in the thirty years between 1799 and 1828, created what we can now regard as the Russian novel. In the case of Tolstoy and Dostoevsky their achievement has become traditionally so associated with perfection in the genre that it has earned the Russian novel the distinction of being considered in relation to classical norms of the Homeric, of Attic Tragedy, of Menippean satire, the medieval mystery play, and so on. Their novels have come to be regarded with the same esteem as the classical works of world literature and for this reason alone deserve to be treated as classics in their own right.

It has been a commonplace of criticism to talk about 'realism' in relation to the Russian novel. Soviet treatments tended to stress such 'realism' in a socio-political *dirigiste* spirit to the exclusion of practically any other kind of approach. Undoubtedly valuable for its historicity, such a blinkered treatment found difficulty dealing with the greatest works of Russian literature, such as Dostoevsky's major novels and the religious, anti-revolutionary ideas, not to mention the aberrant human behaviour, contained in them. Restricted by the official tenets of socialist realism, scholarly Soviet treatments of the Russian novel were usually so uninspired that they left plenty of room for other approaches to flourish in the non-Soviet world.

Curiously enough, this led to a diktat of an opposite kind. Emphasis came to be placed on such issues as polyphonism (*pace* Bakhtin) in a spirit that tended to regard the polyphonic or 'multi-voiced' novel as somehow superior to the single-voiced novel, with its obvious authorial presence. Formalist considerations, concentration on specific features of the Tolstoyan or Dostoevskian novel, quasi-structuralist approaches, no doubt valuable and illuminating in their own right, tended to be as limited in their appraisal of the Russian novel as the politically prescriptive emphasis on 'realism'.

There is no doubt that the novel in its Russian context reflected social issues, portrayed heroes and heroines characteristic of Russian society, and came to play a more important role than its European counterparts in giving expression to a range of substantive moral issues and choices facing the society of its time. It existed and evolved in a climate of official government censorship largely unknown in the West. Yet it passed through the crucible of that censorship and emerged so strengthened and assertive of its own right to govern opinion that it made censorship seem a futile official irrelevancy.

It is worth pointing out that the creators of the classic Russian novel were for the most part privileged members of Russian society who were not in any radical sense anti-establishment. They were all patriots. They all enjoyed the right to travel, whether in Russia (excluding, naturally, the enforced travel of exile) or in Europe (with the exception of Pushkin and Lermontov); and the freedom to travel in Europe was vitally enriching to Gogol', Turgenev, and Goncharov, if for very different reasons, whereas for Dostoevsky and Tolstoy it had a profound influence in stimulating and defining their work and their attitudes. Intellectually and culturally all those who helped to create the classic Russian novel wrote as Russians, both deeply conscious of being part of a European heritage and aware that they wrote for a Europeanized, if not for a specifically European, readership.

They wrote to justify as well as to expose. They were concerned more with portraiture than plotting, more with ideas than adventure narratives. They made reality seem strange or 'defamiliarized' (as in Tolstoy's case) or explored meta-physical reality (as in Dostoevsky's epileptic 'penetration of the real') by a propensity for assuming, above all, that fact and fiction need not be distinct entities.

The classic Russian novel asserted detachment as its prerogative from the very start. This was Pushkin's gift to Russian literature. Though always urged in one or another direction by partisan critics, the greatest of the Russian nineteenth-century novelists asserted a freedom to bear their own witness. A prophetic role may gradually have obtruded, lending the classic Russian novel near-biblical powers of moral edification; yet its penetrative honesty and its humanistic concerns are the ultimate touchstone by which its greatness is to be judged.

Pushkin's novel in verse *Evgenii Onegin* (written 1823–31) has to be regarded as the first Russian novel and is thematically of a classic simplicity. Pushkin, as narrator and first-person participant, may never be absent from his work but he contrives throughout to maintain a historian's detachment in telling the simple story of his hero Onegin's relationship with his heroine, Tat'iana. Places, seasons, foods, pastimes, and activities seem to have a verifiable contemporary authenticity.

As a novel in verse, inspired by Byron's *Don Juan*, *Evgenii Onegin* must seem derivative; yet it achieved a uniquely formulaic role in determining the evolution of the classic Russian novel. Concerned principally with portraiture, through the medium of Pushkin's delightful stanzas that have such a beautifully sustained, dance-like vitality, the novel opens with an elaborate picture of Onegin's daily life as a typical St Petersburg dandy. He is exceptional only in suffering from Byronic disillusionment. He therefore leaves St Petersburg and moves to the country, a stranger to its ways. Here he encounters the pensive, impressionable Tat'iana. She falls in love with him, apparently confusing him with the hero of a romantic novel, and he, in rejecting her love, reveals himself as cold, superfluous, and dangerous.

After killing his close friend, the young poet Lensky, in a duel, Onegin departs on travels that eventually bring him back to St Petersburg four years later where he finds Tat'iana married and an admired adornment of the *beau monde*. After falling desperately in love with her, he is humiliated to learn that she, having discovered so much about him and his world, can speak with a definitive authority about her own duty of fidelity as a wife and in so doing assert a morality clearly superior to the norm prevailing in high society.

The last meeting between hero and heroine provides both a dramatic climax and a final moral test of the hero's worth. In so doing it establishes the classic Russian novel as one characterized by dramatic encounters in which the truth of people's lives is suddenly laid bare.

In the prose work *A Hero of Our Time* (*Geroi nashego vremeni*, 1840), Lermontov used his dramatic sense to explore a similar kind of Byronic portraiture but in a manner that was less detached, more subjective than Pushkin's; the 'novel', comprising the linked short stories 'Bela', 'Maksim Maksimych', 'Taman', 'Princess Mary', and 'The Fatalist', was termed a 'chain of stories' by its author. The hero Pechorin was intended as a successor to Onegin but has much in him that might be ascribed directly to Lermontov himself. The autobiographical impulse, though, is cleverly concealed by the use of three narrators; and the work falls into two parts: the first two stories offer a portrayal of Pechorin seen through others' eyes; the final three stories comprise Pechorin's 'journal' and aspire to give a private picture.

A discernible air of irony and mystification surrounds this 'hero of our time' despite Lermontov's claim that it is a portrait 'composed of the vices of our entire generation in their full development'. Though supposedly offering such a generalized portrayal of a Byronic type, the work diagnoses the dilemma of its hero at a much deeper level. Man as the plaything of fate or master of his destiny is the issue that forms the psychological and ideological focus of Pechorin's activity. Crippled morally – or so he claims – he compensates with a defiance of law and convention that pits him against society and against fate.

Clearly a psychological study, and full of intriguing complexities, particularly in its chronology, Lermontov's 'novel' has little coherence beyond its purpose as portraiture. The enfranchising of the ordinary, the non-Byronic, in the Russian novel, its 'democratizing' in a loose sense, occurred first through the comic, word-rich genius of Gogol'. *Dead Souls* (*Mertvye dushi*, 1842), can lay claim to be the first true prose novel in Russian literature even though Gogol' entitled it a 'poem' (partly for censorship reasons).

A picaresque work, in that it describes the travels of its hero, Chichikov, in search of 'dead souls' (that is, the serfs still subject to poll tax though they had died since the last census), the novel owes much to theatrical principles of presentation in depicting the essentially comic encounters between the hero and the respective serf-owners. Each encounter occurs within a grotesquely detailed setting, a miniature world of incongruously characterizing possessions, and the humour largely derives from ignorance of the visitor's intentions. It is a classic work of comedy, often deviously satirical, both in its characterization and in its tendency to digressions and extended metaphors.

Suggestively, as if in the corners of its Bosch-like vision of rural Russia, the novel enfranchises hosts of partially glimpsed characters. But the foreground grotesques – Korobochka, Manilov, Nozdrev, Sobakevich, Pliushkin, the serf-owners whom the hero visits – have a dreadful ordinariness and *poshlost'* (Pushkin's definition of them, so Gogol' claimed, meaning vulgar acquisitiveness). None is more evidently characteristic of this than Chichikov himself, even though he may be mistaken for Antichrist, Napoleon or a certain mysterious Captain Kopeikin.

Gogol' himself might also be mistaken for a great comic genius, but he wished to be mistaken for a prophet of a new, morally rejuvenated Russia. So at the magnificent climax of *Dead Souls*, Chichikov in his carriage drawn by a troika of horses is transformed into a vision of Russia racing into the future. At this point the classic Russian novel came of age and acquired purpose as well as stature.

During the 1840s prose became the dominant medium in Russian writing. The purpose prescribed for it by the leading critic of the decade, Vissarion Belinsky – to offer an exposure and diagnosis of the ills of society (of which serfdom was the most conspicuous and the most proscribed by the censorship) – found reflection in only two works that could be seriously called finished novels: Aleksandr Herzen's *Who is to Blame?* (*Kto vinovat?*) and Ivan Goncharov's *A Common Story* (*Obyknovennaia istoriia*) both of 1847. Herzen's *Who is to Blame?* is a study of the superfluous intellectual and the damage such a type can inflict. Of greater literary value is Goncharov's sardonic, understated portrait of an ordinary young nobleman from the provinces, callow in his romanticism, who receives a lesson in the harsh realities of life from his uncle, a prominent St Petersburg bureaucrat and learns it so well that he ends up more self-seeking and cynical even than his mentor.

In the immediate post-Crimean War period the writer most responsible for enlarging the scope of the Russian novel was Ivan Turgenev. Although he had made his name initially through his famous sketches of rural life, *Sketches from a Hunter's Album* (*Zapiski okhotnika*), it was after being exiled to his country estate for the publication of his work in a separate edition (1852) that he turned to writing novels. *Rudin* (1856), his first work in the genre, portrayed an eloquent intellectual, a so-called 'superfluous man' of the 1840s, who fails to live up to his words when faced by the strong-minded young heroine Natal'ia. Rudin is portrayed, for all his weakness, as gifted with an enthusiasm for ideas. In 1860 Turgenev added an epilogue in which his 'eternal wanderer' of a hero dies the death of a revolutionary on a Paris barricade in 1848.

The novel has theatrical antecedents and is so composed that each of the principal characters is introduced with an explanatory biography of some sort and placed in a particular setting. The only unknown quantity is the hero who arrives (like Onegin) as a stranger from outside. As portraiture, the novel explores the hero's meaning in socio-political terms: as a cosmopolitan advocate of western ideas, and also in terms of his emotional fallibility.

As a conjuror of atmosphere Turgenev had no equal. He succeeded in evoking the world of the Russian country estate so perfectly that no other writer has surpassed him. In his second novel, *A Nest of the Gentry* (*Dvorianskoe gnezdo*, 1859), he produced a picture of a summer idyll as backdrop to the sad story of Lavretsky's return to his gentry home after a self-imposed exile in Europe and the failure of his love for Liza, a religious heroine who may be said to epitomize a spiritual ideal that Turgenev, ever the agnostic, could admire but never share.

The purposeful role of the classic Russian novel found expression in Turgenev's case as a chronicle of the Russian intelligentsia. In Goncharov's second novel, his masterpiece, *Oblomov* (1859), the portrait of the hero epitomized the indolence and stagnation of the nobility against which the intelligentsia had to struggle. Immured more firmly in his theatrically elaborate setting than any Gogolian character, coddled in his St Petersburg apartment by his ineptly devoted servant and the self-delusion of his patrician idleness, Oblomov is a masterly – not to say loving – study of a disease, diagnosed by the radical critic Nikolai Dobroliubov as 'Oblomovism' (his famous critique 'What is Oblomovism?' ['Chto takoe Obmolovshchina?']). Although in part a love-story, the novel is chiefly memorable as the greatest monument to sloth in literature. The efforts of the ostensible 'positive' hero, Shtolts, to persuade Oblomov to lead a fuller life seem ultimately meaningless when compared with the child-like purity of heart and soul that Oblomov succeeds in retaining to the end.

But the critical clamour for positive images in literature could not be ignored. Turgenev responded in his third novel, *On the Eve* (*Nakanune*, 1860) – the title anticipates the Emancipation of the Serfs scheduled for 1861 – by portraying his heroine Elena as unable to choose between her two Russian suitors since neither is sufficiently positive for her. She finally chooses a Bulgarian patriot and accompanies him to Venice where he dies. Less satisfactory in structure than his previous novels, it offered the first major study of a heroine capable of renouncing her heritage and liberating herself even if the consequences were tragic.

The image of the liberated woman became central to the seminal propagandist novel *What is to be Done?* (*Chto delat'?*, 1863), by Nikolai Chernyshevsky, a work exemplifying the need for literature (and art generally) to be a 'textbook on life' and therefore to serve a recognizable civic purpose. Banned immediately after publication, the novel's Utopian socialist vision of a humanity liberated through co-operative work may seem comic in its earnestness, but it undoubtedly concentrated minds by projecting an image of revolutionary change.

Turgenev picked up on such an image in his greatest novel, *Fathers and Sons* (*Ottsy i deti*, 1862), in which he created the figure of the nihilist Bazarov. Bazarov may not be the portrait of a revolutionary in a strictly political sense. He is radical only in his cast of mind and social attitude as one who abrogates everything that is not justifiable according to the laws of the natural sciences. The figure of Bazarov has never ceased to arouse controversy. A series of different settings serve as a means of gradually revealing important facets of the hero, his ideological significance, for instance, his romanticism and, in the end, his flawed humanity. Though a materialist, an extrovert, Quixotic in his desire for action, he is forced to acknowledge an introspective, Hamlet-like quality in himself when he falls in love with a wealthy widow. Returning eventually to his parental home once his attempts to find love have failed, he dies from typhus poisoning contracted after performing an autopsy.

Bazarov, representative of the younger generation, proves victorious in a ridiculous duel with his older opponent, Pavel Kirsanov, a dandyish anglicized Russian of Turgenev's generation. Even though his own destiny was to be that of a tragic hero who dies with his potential unrealized, Bazarov's outspoken, plebeian honesty contains a Promethean arrogance in the name of science that could imply root-and-branch Jacobinism as well as disdain for the established order. His nihilism might seem ultimately to contain a challenge to divine justice in the name of human freedom.

No Russian novelist was more conscious of this aspect of nihilism than Fedor Dostoevsky. His major novels explore it as an obsessive pathology afflicting the Russian intelligentsia, yet always in the light of a dramatic debate between opposed ideas. His first treatment of these issues took the form of a monologue attributable to an 'underground man' (in Part I of *Notes from Underground* [*Zapiski iz podpol'ia*] 1864). The author of this profoundly paradoxical work asserts that man is not naturally inclined to act rationally in his own best interests and that he demonstrates his individuality by the exercise of his caprice or free will.

The *Notes from Underground* open the way, ideologically speaking, to Dostoevsky's first important achievement as a novelist, the portrayal of the dropout student Raskol'nikov, hero of his first masterpiece, *Crime and Punishment* (*Prestuplenie i nakazanie*, 1866). During some two weeks of a hot St Petersburg summer Raskol'nikov murders a shrewish old moneylender and her sister and succeeds in evading suspicion until an examining magistrate puts pressure on him and the young prostitute, Sonia, who loves Raskol'nikov and eventually persuades him to confess.

Why did he commit murder? The novel analyses his motives and for the purpose makes dramatic use of a unity of time, place, and action in the novel form through Raskol'nikov's own sick, hallucinatory apprehension of reality. There is no doubt that this is a crowded, fetid, urban ant-heap of a world, packed with 'voices' and given a baroquely detailed authenticity. But the 'crime' is what excites and horrifies. It is a planned, deliberate killing committed for what superficially appears to be a two-fold motivation: altruistically to rid society of the moneylender's malign influence; egotistically to prove that he, Raskol'nikov, is a latter-day Napoleon, one of the 'extraordinary' men who can usurp the place of God in the moral universe.

Such a Promethean ideal is parodied in the figure of Svidrigailov, who demonstrates the ultimately nihilistic meaning of such supposed free will by committing suicide. In the course of revealing what Dostoevsky called 'the psychological process of the crime', Raskol'nikov realizes that his motives were all flawed. But whether or not he abandons his satanic arrogance must remain in doubt.

Profoundly complex and multifaceted, *Crime and Punishment* established new standards of psychological portraiture and ideological debate in the Russian novel. The world it depicted was essentially in flux; even notions of the real were imperilled; and divine judgement, like any obvious authorial moral, was absent. It was unique as an example of detective fiction, but equally unique, if in a quite different genre, was the work during the 1860s of Dostoevsky's great contemporary, Lev Tolstoy. In the course of the decade he created the greatest historical novel ever written, *War and Peace* (*Voina i mir*, 1869).

As a historical narrative this epic work deals with Russia's two main confrontations with Napoleon (Austerlitz in 1805 and Borodino in 1812), but in other respects it may be considered a family chronicle novel devoted to the two main families of Bolkonskys and Rostovs. The ideological meaning of the work is personalized through the lives and evolving ideas of its two main heroes, Prince Andrei Bolkonsky and his friend Pierre Bezukhov.

The apparently seamless way in which history and fiction coalesce, the range of episode and social scene are all facets testifying to Tolstoy's genius for evoking character and suggesting, in a pictorial sense, an active, vital replica of reality. Sometimes, however, a moral coloration is given to events through the way the observer-narrator's candid eye 'defamiliarizes' what is seen, as in the famous example of Natasha Rostov's visit to the opera.

Although an epic novel about violent events and the 'swarm life' of human beings stricken by war, in its fundamental assumptions *War and Peace* ultimately stresses the role of the Russian nobility as a mainstay of the status quo. The major heroines become matriarchs, and their husbands, family men, given only to oblique thoughts about political change.

In terms of personal ideas the novel is about the search for God. If, for Prince Andrei, God is finally identified with love as an eternal unifying source to which he will return at his death, for Pierre, under the influence of the only peasant figure in the novel, Platon Karataev, life itself, in all its multiplicity, is a manifestation of the divine. In historical terms, the novel is concerned with debunking the Napoleonic myth and nowhere is this more obvious than in the second epilogue where Tolstoy argues a case for assuming that power in history rests less with the so-called leaders than with those who participate directly in events.

Russia's relationship with Europe was of paramount importance for Turgenev at this time. In 1867, for example, in his fifth novel *Smoke* (*Dym*), set in Baden-Baden, he urged the need for Russia to become more civilized and European. To Dostoevsky, on the other hand, this was anathema. Driven into exile in Europe by his creditors, he now saw his native country as in need of a new image of Christ to protect it from European influences.

He conceived such an image in his second great novel *The Idiot* (*Idiot*) of 1868 in the figure of the epileptic Prince Myshkin. Plunged into a mill-race of events upon his return to Russia, Myshkin encounters a metropolitan world of financial greed, nihilism, and hysteria. The image of the beautiful Nastasia Filippovna is the most memorable in a striking array of female figures attracted to him; she is also the ultimate victim of the murderous world of St Petersburg avarice surrounding her. Among several brilliantly executed scenes in the novel the most outstanding is the final one when Myshkin and Nastasia's murderer, Rogozhin, spend a nightmarish wake beside her corpse.

In a publicistic sense *The Idiot* attempts too much. Sub-plots and secondary issues have a clogging effect. The message of the 'positively beautiful man', Prince Myshkin, changes from that of the world redeemed by beauty to the anti-Catholic notion of a Russian Christ destined to bring salvation to a corrupt Europe.

In his third great novel *Besy*, translated as *The Devils* or *The Possessed*, European ideas can be seen to have entered into sections of the Russian intelligentsia on the pattern of the story from St Luke's gospel about the man possessed of devils. Set in a small Russian provincial town and ostensibly filtered through the observations of a know-all narrator, the novel describes how Stavrogin, a young scion of the local nobility originally tutored by an elderly liberal, Verkhovensky, returns after a period abroad to renew his acquaintance with his 'disciples', Shatov and Kirillov. The central theme of the novel is derived from the notorious affair of Nechaev (1847–82) who, in 1869, organized the murder of a member of a revolutionary cell to guarantee other members' loyalty.

A loose familial relationship of ideas can be seen to exist between Stavrogin's 'disciples'. Shatov, paradoxically uncommitted in his beliefs, advocates the notion of a people or nation as God-bearing, while Kirillov is obsessed with suicide as a means of overcoming the fear of death and ensuring for mankind the freedom of man-godhood. Both 'disciples' die – Shatov as the victim of a plot like Nechaev's, designed by Verkhovensky's son, Petr, to guarantee loyalty to his revolutionary cell, and Kirillov by his own hand after signing a false confession to Shatov's murder. Stavrogin, the 'father' of their ideas, is cast by Petr in the role of revolutionary leader but eventually is proved impotent, both sexually and ideologically, and hangs himself.

A sinister, very dark novel, manifestly anti-revolutionary in intent, *The Devils* nevertheless contains some of the funniest scenes in Dostoevsky's *oeuvre*. It also originally contained a horrific chapter (unpublished in Dostoevsky's lifetime) in which Stavrogin confesses to the rape of a young girl who subsequently kills herself from shame.

Violence, mayhem, murder, and suicide, the strong ingredients of Dostoevsky's fiction, reflected an increasing malaise in Russian society during the 1870s. As the younger intelligentsia gradually united under the banner of 'freedom for the people' or Populism (*Narodnichestvo*) and resorted finally to terrorism in the struggle against the autocracy, the leading novelists treated the incipient unrest as posing a serious danger above all to the family and the moral health of the nation.

Dostoevsky's first contribution in this respect was his novel of 1875, *Podrostok* (translated as *A Raw Youth* and as *An Accidental Family*). Generally acknowledged to be the least successful of his major novels, it describes a young man's attempt to establish his legitimacy as the member of an 'accidental family' of the Russian nobility. The cause of family breakdown in this instance was attributed largely to intelligentsia free-thinking, personified by the father, Versilov. In Mikhail Saltykov-Shchedrin's relentlessly harsh satire *The Golovlevs* (*Gospoda Golovlevy*), published serially 1875–80, the focus is on the greed of the mother and the hypocrisy of the son. So far as the politics of the decade were concerned, the only novel to offer an understanding picture of revolutionary Populism was Turgenev's *Virgin Soil* (*Nov'*) of 1877, but its lukewarm appraisal of the revolutionaries' aims while celebrating their self-sacrifice made it seem ambiguous and dated.

The age of the classic Russian novel concludes with two masterpieces, Tolstoy's *Anna Karenina* (1875–7), and Dostoevsky's *The Brothers Karamazov* (*Brat'ia Karamazovy*, 1880). Both reflect closely the dominant issues of the decade – in Tolstoy's case, the emancipation of women, the new role of the landowning nobility, the threat posed by the urban to the rural, the Russo-Turkish War; in Dostoevsky's, the issue of justice, faith versus free will, the power of money, the incipient terrorism – all within the framework of the damage done to the moral fibre of society and particularly to the family.

Anna Karenina may seem a triumph of authorial detachment in a technical sense, though there is no denying that the famous epigraph 'Vengeance is mine and I will repay' presupposes some degree of authorial judgement. This does not mean that Anna's is not a portrait of deeply engaging vitality, and her tragedy the more poignant for that reason. Her high-society world has an equally strong allure. Driven by a need for love in her infatuation with Vronsky and turned into a social pariah by her husband's refusal of a divorce, she is seen moving brilliantly through her world, deserving better than its superficiality and yet never able to achieve a spiritual focus. Her suicide can seem as inevitable in its tragedy as the railway lines on which she immolates herself, but it is also all-too-humanly understandable in its futility and despair.

Structurally a novel of twin strands divided into eight parts, Anna's story is complemented by the parallel story of Konstantin Levin, which clearly enough reflects the author's own spiritual quest. Insufferably opinionated and serious-minded though Levin is, he possesses a truthful eye and can see Anna for what she is on the only occasion they meet – a vital, beautiful woman consumed by the tragedy of her loveless situation. His own marriage, if uneven, at least permits him the security of love and the chance to reach beyond rational causes to a belief in the popular wisdom that one should live for one's soul, thereby discovering a concept of God that can reconcile all men. His discovery, set as it is against the background of the Russo-Turkish War of 1877–8, the first so-called 'War of Liberation', has a pacifist appeal no doubt suited to its time; it lacks, however, the contentious challenge that Dostoevsky brought to his classic study of the meaning of justice.

The Brothers Karamazov, though conceived much earlier, sprang from Dostoevsky's attendance at the trial of the terrorist Vera Zasulich in 1878 and has as its climax the trial of Dmitrii Karamazov for the killing of his father. Pronounced guilty by the jury, Dmitrii is shown in the first three parts of this four-part novel to be the victim of a miscarriage of justice. The reasons are explored in a supposedly narrated account of what actually happened in the three days immediately preceding the parricide.

Set in a small town suspiciously like Staraia Russa (Dostoevsky's vacation resort not far from Novgorod) and at a remove of thirteen years before the supposed time of writing, the novel challenges notions of the real, and of truth and justice in many complex ways. On one level, it is about money. At a deeper level, it is about the choices facing Russia. These take two principal forms in the opposed ideas of Dmitrii's brothers, Ivan and Alesha.

Ivan seeks to liberate mankind from God and his unjust world by decrying the notion of a hell for evil-doers and offering a brilliant critique of Christ's teaching (in the famous chapter 'The Grand Inquisitor'). He ends with the nihilistic assertion that there is no virtue and 'all is permissible'. Ironically Smerdiakov, his illegitimate brother, acts on such permissiveness to commit the parricide. The irony is compounded when Ivan is confronted on the eve of Dmitrii's trial by his personal devil who challenges him to tell the truth. But Ivan, for whom truth has become so deeply penetrated by paradox, cannot do more at the trial than declare that 'We all desire our father's death', and a miscarriage of justice becomes inevitable.

Alesha, studying to be a monk at a local monastery, offers the teaching of his spiritual father, Zosima, as an antidote to Ivan. He advocates a Christian responsibility for all other men's sins. The killing of the father, however reprobate, becomes in this context a heinously nihilistic act that destroys both the unity of generations and the idea of justice as inseparable from universal responsibility for sin.

The ideas must seem incomplete, as the novel was incomplete, but in their boldness, as in the exploration of the tenuous line between the real and the unreal, the rational and irrational, Dostoevsky expanded the limits of the novel as a genre. His legacy of the ideological novel was the summit of achievement in the classic Russian novel. No other half-century of novel-writing in any literature has been able to match it.

FURTHER READING

Freeborn, Richard. *The Rise of the Russian Novel: Studies in the Russian Novel from "Eugene Onegin" to "War and Peace"*, Cambridge, Cambridge University Press, 1973.

Jones, Malcolm V. and Miller, Robin Feuer (eds) *The Cambridge Companion to the Russian Classic Novel*, Cambridge: Cambridge University Press, 1998.

Mersereau, John, Jr. *Russian Romantic Fiction*, Ann Arbor: Ardis, 1983.

Todd, William Mills III. *Fiction and Society in the Age of Pushkin: Ideology, Institutions and Narrative*, Cambridge, MA: Harvard University Press, 1986.

Valentino, Russell Scott. *Vicissitudes of Genre in the Russian Novel*, New York: Peter Lang, 2000.

10

THE SUPERFLUOUS MAN IN RUSSIAN LITERATURE

ELLEN CHANCES

The 'superfluous man' (*lishnii chelovek*) is a term that, since the mid-nineteenth century, has been applied to a particular type of character in Russian literature. Ivan Turgenev's work of 1850, *The Diary of a Superfluous Man* (*Dnevnik lishnego cheloveka*), popularized the term 'superfluous man', which came to be used to identify literary characters of an earlier period of the nineteenth century as well as those in the middle years of the century and beyond, into the twentieth century. Often, the end of the tradition of 'superfluous men' was earmarked as the mid-nineteenth century, with characters such as the eponymous Oblomov in Ivan Goncharov's novel, many of Turgenev's characters, including Chulkaturin, in *The Diary of a Superfluous Man*, and Bazarov in *Fathers and Sons* (*Ottsy i deti*).

Although the idea of the superfluous man is specific to Russia, it is also part of a broader phenomenon in terms of the ways in which cultures, past and present, have viewed nonconformists and conformists. Whether we examine a southern woman writer from the United States, Kate Chopin, in her novel, *The Awakening* (1899); or the German writer, Friedrich Schiller, in his play, *The Robbers* (*Die Räuber*, 1871); or the French director Eric Rohmer, in his film, *L'Amour l'après-midi* (*Chloë in the Afternoon*, 1972), like the Russian writers we shall explore in the superfluous man tradition, these artists, disparate in time and place, have created works in which, explicitly or implicitly, conformity to the status quo is presented as a virtue. Certain writers, from different cultures, weave the same patterns, often portraying those who dare to be different as literal or spiritual losers. Characters who submit to the status quo, who conform to social or religious values, are often portrayed as the moral victors.

Sometimes the nonconformist can be seen as a noble, tragic figure, but sometimes he or she can be seen as being explicitly or implicitly condemned. The authorial disapproval of nonconformist behaviour, or an ambivalent attitude toward nonconformity, marks the life and art of diverse cultures.

The psychologist Erich Fromm, in *Escape from Freedom* (1941), observed that a desire for freedom coexists with a desire for submission. Psychological experiments, by Stanley Milgram and Solomon Asch, have shown that people think that they support individualism more than they do. This pattern fits the Russian superfluous man tradition in that certain writers, hailed as individualists, actually reflect, in their works, an ambivalent attitude toward their nonconformist protagonists.

The late eighteenth-century *Bildungsroman* taught the importance of learning to reconcile oneself to society. Both rugged individualism and a will to conform have been observed as distinctive features of the culture of the United States. A children's book by the American writer Gertrude Crampton, *Tootle*, stars a young train who loves going off the tracks to romp and play in a flower-filled meadow. The final message conveyed to young readers is that the train must never go off the tracks.

In Russia, we see that Boris and Gleb, the first saints to be canonized by the Russian Church, were admired for their refusal to rebel. In Russian Orthodoxy, human beings are viewed more as an integral part of a larger community rather than as individuals. The collective is emphasized. Salvation is attained by remaining within the community rather than by individual effort. The concept of 'universality' (*sobornost'*) emphasizes the collective nature of the human being's life and religion. Russian Orthodoxy condemns the human being's attempts to lead an isolated or independent existence.

These values were reflected in the beliefs of the Slavophiles, a group of the nineteenth-century intellectuals who believed that the path to Russia's salvation lay in the values of the simple Russian people, in the ideal of communality, Russian religion, the irrational, and the peasant commune with its communal ownership of property. Others among the educated, the westernizers, felt that Russia's salvation resided in the adoption of west European laws, innovations, and values such as individualism and rational thought. The experience of the westernized Russians, who often studied in western Europe and then returned to their homeland, was indirectly reflected in portrayals of the superfluous man. Here were people who, because of their western education, felt that they did not fit into Russia, yet in western Europe, they felt they were Russians who did not fit into Europe.

Just who were the superfluous men who inhabited so many works of Russian literature? Let us first turn to a general description of the literary type. As I have written elsewhere, the superfluous man has been described as

> an ineffectual aristocrat at odds with society . . . 'dreamy, useless', . . . an 'intellectual incapable of action', an 'ineffective idealist', 'a hero who is sensitive to social and ethical problems, but who fails to act, partly because of personal weakness, partly because of political and social restraints on his freedom of action'.
> (Ellen B. Chances, *Conformity's Children*, 1978).

A typical description of the type appeared in a Soviet literary encyclopedia, where the superfluous man's essence was described as his 'alienation from his environment, eventually leading to a complete break from and falling out with it' (*Literaturnaia entsiklopediia*, vol. 6, 1932).

Often, this type of weak outsider misfit man was juxtaposed to a strong woman who did fit into society, who could act, and who could become involved in the life around her. Accounts frequently turn to the juxtaposition of the weak, ineffectual Evgenii Onegin, protagonist of Aleksandr Pushkin's novel in verse, *Evgenii Onegin*, and Tat'iana, the novel's strong, effective heroine. Sometimes, like Onegin, the superfluous men came from the 'tainted', false atmosphere of the city, often from the westernized city of St Petersburg. Conversely, the female foils, like Tat'iana, had strong roots in and ties to the Russian countryside.

The term 'superfluous man' was most commonly used to refer to certain characters, beginning with Pushkin's *Evgenii Onegin* and extending to Turgenev's *The Diary of a Superfluous Man*. Critical evaluation of such characters sometimes focused on them as tragic or romantic heroes, unsuccessful because of society's inability to respect or to understand the individualist who is an outsider on account of his superior qualities. Consequently the writers themselves could be seen as favouring their alienated, outsider figures by pointing to the flaws within society that led to this alienation of such talented 'superfluous' characters.

Examples of this kind of structure include one of the earliest depictions of the superfluous man in Russian literature, the character of Chatsky in Aleksandr Griboedov's play, *Woe from Wit* (*Gore ot uma*). Chatsky is shown to have a strong moral compass, a feature that makes him stand out in the society in which he lives. He is an utter misfit, but his qualities are those that are shown to be worthwhile, in spite of the fact that society considers him to be crazy.

Another example of the virtues of the misfit being upheld is in a novel that comes much later, but which fits into the tradition of the romantic hero. Boris Pasternak's *Doctor Zhivago* (*Doktor Zhivago*) features an eponymous hero whose 'superfluity' to society is hailed by the author as being a positive characteristic. His difference from most members of society, his individualism, and his independent thinking are qualities to be admired. All of this is something that the world needs, according to Pasternak, in order to maintain and uphold the most important values of human life. Iurii Zhivago is able therefore, to tap into his own inner talents and create powerful, lasting poems. Even though Zhivago sacrifices his life, Pasternak makes it clear, by the end of the novel, that Zhivago's poetry will continue to live.

Here Pasternak, in creating his superfluous man, reflects the nineteenth- and twentieth-century tradition of the Russian intelligentsia. In describing his misfit hero, Pasternak is drawing upon the strong tradition, within the nineteenth century, of the special calling of the Russian writer. The writer is regarded as someone who is different from the rest of society, but who is more noble. This is a tradition whose roots can be found in the nineteenth-century romantic attitude ennobling the artist. It is a tradition that lasted longer in Russia and the Soviet Union than in western Europe, perhaps, paradoxically, precisely because the Soviet Union, with its Iron Curtain and its isolation from the rest of the world, 'froze' in place many features of nineteenth-century culture.

Pasternak's description of Iurii Zhivago, the poet, resonates with Pushkin's depiction of the poet in his famous poem of the 1820s, *The Prophet* (*Prorok*). In Pushkin's poem, an angel appears to a man, touches his eyes and ears, and substitutes the tongue of a wise serpent for his own tongue. The angel takes out the man's heart and instead inserts flaming coal. God then instructs him to burn people's hearts with His Word. In Pasternak's novel, Zhivago, the doctor, spiritually heals people with the words of his poetry.

Pushkin's poem about the special calling of the poet continued to live in Russian culture well into the 1980s. For example, the film director Andrei Tarkovsky quoted Pushkin's poem in his book *Sculpting in Time* (*Zapechatlennoe vremia*, 1981), to explain the role of the artist, and *The Prophet* appeared in an article written by the protagonist of Andrei Bitov's novel, *Pushkin House* (*Pushkinskii dom*).

In his novel, Bitov speaks of Russian literature from the eighteenth century to the early pre-revolutionary years of the twentieth century as still being in place in the 1960s and early 1970s, preserved like a 'nature preserve', precisely because of the rupture that Stalin had caused in social and cultural life. Moreover, Bitov himself, in *Pushkin House*, offers the reader a character, Modest Platonovich Odoevtsev, whose virtues are shown to be his independence of spirit and his individualism in the face of pressures to conform to the demands of the Soviet system. Odoevtsev's grandson, Leva Odoevtsev, is criticized for his dependence on the system, for the fact that he does not even know how dependent he is on the system, for the fact that, even if he were set free from the system, he himself would ask to return.

Most depictions of superfluous men in the nineteenth and twentieth centuries differed from those one might observe in Griboedov's play or in the novels of Pasternak and Bitov. While Griboedov, Pasternak, and Bitov praised their misfit protagonists for daring to challenge the dictates of society, a close examination of *Evgenii Onegin* reveals the fact that Pushkin has an ambivalent attitude towards his hero. He implicitly and explicitly criticizes him precisely because he is a nonconformist. And Tat'iana's virtues are praised precisely because, by the end of the novel, she submits to the flow of life and does not rebel against the status quo. At the beginning of the novel, Tat'iana is a nonconformist. She prefers reading to passing her time with the empty upper-crust society set of the countryside. Describing Tat'iana after she moves to St Petersburg, Pushkin praises her for having learned how to live according to the dictates of society. In his depiction of his heroine, Pushkin has chosen to praise the characteristics of submission to society rather than those of the individualist. Onegin is described as fitting nowhere, neither in St Petersburg society nor in the countryside, and this quality, the reader surmises, is a negative one. Pushkin is ambivalent in his attitude towards the conformist in that while he praises Tat'iana for finally conforming to society, he criticizes her sister Ol'ga for her failure to distinguish herself from the majority.

Another early depiction of the superfluous man, Mikhail Lermontov's *A Hero of Our Time* (*Geroi nashego vremeni*, 1840), offers a negative attitude toward Pechorin, the 'hero' of his time. Lermontov's Pechorin, a Byronic, romantic figure, a rebellious loner, is constantly shown as a disruptive force, wherever he goes. In contrast, another character in the novel, Maksim Maksimich, a kindly, straight-forward man, is shown as a positive force. Maksim Maksimich does not question fate, as Pechorin does. He accepts whatever life doles out to him. Quite simply, Lermontov praises Maksim Maksimich and condemns Pechorin.

In Pushkin's and Lermontov's early depictions of superfluous men, we can discern patterns that will continue to appear in later novels containing the same types of protagonists. *Evgenii Onegin* contains a character, Onegin, who rebels against society. *A Hero of Our Time* describes a character, Pechorin, who is a metaphysical rebel. (It is no coincidence that the French writer Albert Camus, a century later, chose a quotation from Lermontov's novel as the epigraph to his Existential novel, *The Fall* [*La Chute*], about a metaphysical rebel.) From this time on, many Russian writers who described superfluous men wrote about social or metaphysical outsiders.

Aleksandr Herzen's *Who is to Blame?* (*Kto vinovat?*) is a social novel, describing the origins of a Russian social dreamer type. Herzen's protagonist, Bel'tov, is shown to have been brought up on large doses of literature, cut off from real life. What Herzen has done is to take the type of dreamer common in German romanticism (such as E.T.A. Hoffmann's Anselmus in *Der goldene Topf* [*The Golden Pot*]), in which characters prefer (and are praised for preferring) the realm of imagination to the less colourful, bland routines of daily living. In the creation of his superfluous man, a Russian social dreamer, Herzen cross-breeds a German romantic dreamer hero, following the models of Romanticism, with the hero of a social novel, following the models of novels by French urban social writers like Balzac and Russian writers of naturalist works. Critics have pointed out that Herzen was so impressed with Gogol''s naturalistic setting in *Dead Souls* (*Mertvye dushi*) that he chose his own locale with Gogol''s example in mind. In addition, Herzen had as precedents the misfit types of Pechorin and Onegin.

Herzen's contribution to the tradition of the superfluous man lay in his combination of all these models, which led him to create a superfluous man who wants to help society in some way. By placing a dreamer in a social novel, by describing a dreamer type who wants to help change society, Herzen had put forward a Russian 'social dreamer', a character who is transformed into a superfluous man with socio-political overtones. He is an outcast from society because he wants to, but cannot, play an active role in changing society. Thus Bel'tov, like many real-life Russian aristocrats, wishes to play a political role in society.

In spite of the steps Herzen had taken in defining a new type of superfluous man, his portrayal of Bel'tov is remarkably similar to that of Pushkin and Lermontov, in that Bel'tov's inability to act is blamed not on society, but on Bel'tov himself. Bel'tov's isolation from society and his escape into a world of books and ideas are blamed for his inability to adapt to life. Herzen analyses the figure as a sociological type. Moreover, he casts his superfluous man character in terms that match his discussions in articles, which bring to mind the German philosopher Friedrich Schelling's *Naturphilosophie*. Thus just as human beings are cut off from nature, Bel'tov is cut off from society as a whole.

Herzen's novel, though hardly a literary masterpiece, is essential to a study of the superfluous man. By casting his superfluous man in ideological terms, he nudged the tradition in directions that were soon followed by Dostoevsky and Tolstoy. He therefore played a key role in the history of the superfluous man.

Also key to the tradition are the novels of Ivan Turgenev, a contemporary of Dostoevsky, Tolstoy, and Herzen. Like Bel'tov, the eponymous hero of Turgenev's

Rudin lives in the world of abstract ideas. He is the social outcast who, because of his nonconformity, cannot live a normal life. He uses his idealism as an excuse to dodge responsibility to other human beings. In the process he causes unhappiness and pain to those who are close to him. A lonely wanderer, Rudin sacrifices his life on the barricades in Paris in 1848. Even in death he remains an outsider. The French insurgents incorrectly identify him as a Pole. In contrast, a conformist figure, Lezhnev, is shown to be happy and successful in human relations and in life.

Whereas Rudin fits into the tradition of social misfits, the superfluous men who inhabit Turgenev's other novels are metaphysical outsiders who do not fit into the cycle of nature. *The Diary of a Superfluous Man*, the short novel that, as we know, bears responsibility for popularization of the term 'superfluous man', serves as a case in point. In his diary, the main character Chulkaturin writes, 'Nature, obviously, did not count on my arriving and consequently, treated me like an unexpected and uninvited guest.' In fact, in social terms, Chulkaturin does not differ from those who, like the prince, Bazmenkov, surround him. He feels superfluous, but the only evidence he presents, his loss of Liza, his loved one, to another man, is merely a case of loss in love, not a case of true superfluity. Chulkaturin is superfluous because he has made himself so. He feels cut off from nature as a whole. He even quotes a Pushkin poem, 'Whether I wander along noisy streets' ('Brozhu li ia vdol' ulits shumnykh'), that confirms these feelings of the human being's aloneness and the cyclical quality of nature. Chulkaturin recalls fond childhood memories of feeling at one with nature and, at death, yearns to recapture this state. Even his diary entries demonstrate his lack of oneness with the cycles of nature, for the entries, from March to April, document the time during which nature moves towards spring, towards the awakening of new life, whereas Chulkaturin's comments make it obvious that he is in the dying phase of his own life. In this portrayal of the superfluous man, nature, rather than society, is triumphant.

In Turgenev's *Fathers and Sons*, the nonconformist is treated as social misfit, outsider to nature's cycle, and rebel against God's order. *Fathers and Sons* reflects the historical realities of its age. The novel is often interpreted as a fictional representation of the clash between the generation of fathers, men of the 1840s, liberals, for evolution; and the generation of sons, men of the 1860s, radicals, for revolution. Analyses of the novel have often concentrated on its socio-political dimensions or its aesthetic qualities. Depending on critics' political leanings, arguments have been made that the main character, the nihilist Bazarov, is drawn positively or negatively. (One of the best essays ever written on this aspect of *Fathers and Sons* is Isaiah Berlin's 'Fathers and Children' in his book *Russian Thinkers*, 1978.) Critics who have wanted to wrest the novel from political interpretations have insisted on Turgenev's concentration on art itself.

Yet what we notice is that the real victors in the novel are those characters from each generation – Nikolai Kirsanov; his son Arkadii; and Arkadii's love, Katia – who submit to the natural unfolding of life. The losers from each generation – Nikolai Kirsanov's brother Pavel; Bazarov; and Odintsova, the woman he loves – are those who do not conform to the natural order. Turgenev emphasizes Bazarov's superfluity by drawing him alone, structurally and sociologically. Turgenev makes him a member of the emerging *raznochintsy* (Russian intellectuals not of noble birth) middle class, neither aristocrat nor lower class. As a nihilist, Bazarov rebels against the established order. Turgenev emphasizes Bazarov's isolation. Even at the beginning of the novel, he is made to sit alone in a coach, while his friend Arkadii and Arkadii's father sit together in a carriage. He is often shown arriving or departing. In addition, almost all the other characters, with the exception of Bazarov and Pavel Kirsanov, ideological opponents, belong somewhere and are paired. By the end of the novel, we are left with Bazarov alone and Pavel Kirsanov alone, each having refused to let life flow naturally. Arkadii, unlike Bazarov, has understood that people should accept the forces of life and death. Implicit in Turgenev is the belief that submission to life is a virtue. The issue, therefore, is not only fathers versus sons, but submission versus rebellion. Those who do not belong are condemned, and those who do, thrive.

Goncharov's novel *Oblomov* is about a landowner of the old generation who is so lazy that it takes him approximately one-third of the book to get out of bed. In contrast Oblomov's childhood friend Shtolts, half German and half Russian in origin, believes in action, progress, and new ideas. Turgenev's Bazarov, with his new ideas, was superfluous because he did not fit into the life of the country gentry. Oblomov, with his old ideas of the country gentry, does not fit into the life of the new society. We see an example, in *Oblomov*, almost of superfluity in reverse, in comparison with some of the works examined in this essay. Bel'tov, Turgenev's Rudin and Bazarov, and Chatsky do not fit into society because of their *new* ideas. Oblomov is almost a parody of this because he has *no* ideas. He wants to be left alone to contemplate the life of a bygone era, to live in dreams of the idyllic past. Like other superfluous men, Oblomov does not fit into conventional society. Since he does not want to go forward or to be active or to rush around, he is the social deviant. What Goncharov has done here is to abstract Oblomov's personal problem to the level of old Russia's not fitting into new Russia. Oblomov wants to halt the passage of time. He refuses to leave his house or his bed. He runs away from actions that would lead him to maturity. Rather than marrying Ol'ga, the woman he loves, he buries himself in the protective coating of his dressing gown. Oblomov would prefer to keep life as it was when he was a child. As with other superfluous men, Oblomov is condemned. He chooses as a wife not Ol'ga, his love, but another relic of the past, Agaf'ia Matveevna. The problem is that the past has no part in the present. Those who do not fit into the present are condemned, defeated by change. Shtolts, on the other hand, can change and adapt to life in the new Russia. He accomplishes good, keeping his own estate and Oblomov's in working order. He is not scared by an adult love relationship and wins Ol'ga's hand.

Dostoevsky and Tolstoy built upon the tradition of the superfluous man by casting their depictions in ideological terms. For Dostoevsky, superfluity is represented as the Russian intelligentsia being cut off from the 'people' (*narod*). Those who belong to the intelligentsia, who deviate from the norms of the simple people, are attacked as incomplete, warped, in some other way chastised. Those who are invested with the characteristics of the people are praised.

In the Pushkin speech that Dostoevsky gave near the end of his life, he declared that the Russian intelligentsia were cut off from the 'soil' (*pochva*). Pushkin was, for Dostoevsky, important in allowing Russian society to be resurrected if it were to form a close bond with the 'people's truth'. Dostoevsky sees this in Pushkin's Tat'iana, for she embodies the Russian soul, whereas Europeanized characters like Onegin do not.

These ideas reflect Dostoevsky's ideology of 'concept of the soil' (*pochvennichestvo*) which, during the 1860s, he set forth on the pages of *Vremia* and *Epokha*, political-literary journals that he co-edited and to which he contributed. Dostoevsky, with his *pochvennichestvo*, wanted to synthesize the Westernizer and Slavophile approaches to Russian culture. He believed that the reforms of Peter the Great had been correct, but that Russians should not blindly worship the west. He maintained that the virtues of Russia, its religion, and particular identity were important, but that the westernizing reforms of Peter the Great should not be rejected out of hand. The westernized heroes in Dostoevsky's fiction, therefore, have to take a journey through doubt and rational thought in order to come to an acceptance of Russian spiritual values.

In the early 1860s the 'concept of the soil' supported the political reforms introduced by Tsar Alexander II. Dostoevsky, for a variety of reasons, then lost his confidence in the capacity of political reform to change society. The reforms of Alexander II had not been far-reaching enough. Russian radicals began to use terrorist tactics rather than just discussing new ideas. Dostoevsky's visit to western Europe in 1862–3 convinced him that adherence to rational laws alone would not change people. Instead he concluded that change was possible only by the irrational, spontaneous spiritual love of one human being for another.

Ideological depictions of the superfluous man, wedded to his own particular ideology of 'concept of the soil' are typical of Dostoevsky's fictional works. In the case of *Notes from Underground* (*Zapiski iz podpol'ia*, 1864), the consequence of the underground man's adoption of European forms is his utter paralysis, his inability to cope with reality. For example, the underground man says that the groans of an educated man differ from those of others in that they are the moans of a man '"who has cut himself off from the soil and the people", as the saying goes today'. The underground man lives in books and daydreams and therefore cannot deal with life. Juxtaposed to him is Liza, from Riga, but with Russian parents. She acts spontaneously, naturally, with compassion. *Notes from Underground* fictionally reproduces the tenets of 'the concept of the soil'. The man who is plagued by the rational, abstract ideas of the West does not fit into Russia. The Russian intelligentsia is a misfit, is morally ill, does not fit into the real authentic Russia of the simple people, with their irrational Christian spontaneous love of one human being for another. The underground man is an ideological nonconformist. He is diseased because he is distorted by westernized artificial thinking. He is even from the westernized city of St Petersburg, 'the most premeditated and artificial city' in the world.

Crime and Punishment (*Prestuplenie i nakazanie*) tells the story of Raskol'nikov, whose very name comes from the Russian word for 'schism'. He is split off from himself and from Russian spiritual values because he has the disease of the western ideas of egoism and self-interest. Dostoevsky transforms his diseased protagonist, superfluous to the life-affirming forces of Russia, into a criminal, into a murderer. Joseph Frank, in his *Dostoevsky: The Miraculous Years, 1865–1871* (1995), explains that in *Crime and Punishment* Dostoevsky is showing the literal dead end of the ideas of the Russian radicals of the 1860s. In contrast to Raskol'nikov, Russian Orthodox Christianity infuses the life of Sonia Marmeladova, whose example leads Raskol'nikov to abandon the ideas of western individualism and adopt those of Russian Christianity.

Here too, then, we see the influence of Dostoevsky's 'concept of the soil' as he paints the picture of his superfluous man, Raskol'nikov, superfluous to Russian society and values, and to human society. We see Sonia's natural spiritual love as she submits unquestioningly to God.

Dostoevsky's other major works also present portrayals of superfluous men. In *The Devils* or *The Possessed* (*Besy*), Dostoevsky concludes that it is not just St Petersburg, but Russia itself that is crippled because it has lost its attachment to the values of the people. Dostoevsky sets his novel in the provinces. He documents the way in which characters are 'possessed' by west European ideas and therefore cut off from their native roots. Westernized Russia itself is superfluous. Byronic Stavrogin, radical Petr Verkhovensky, and Stepan Verkhovensky, a man of the 1840s, have lost their way. By the end of the novel, Stepan Verkhovensky literally returns to the earth, through his understanding of the lessons of Christianity.

Prince Myshkin, the main character of *The Idiot* (*Idiot*, 1868), is drawn by Dostoevsky as the positively good individual, who, because of his goodness, is superfluous to the everyday world of corruption. A society filled with suspicion cannot accept the pure person. Myshkin even states: 'I am superfluous in society'. Myshkin is the outcast because, in his meekness, honesty, and Christ-like manner, he defies the mores of conventional society.

Dostoevsky's final novel, *The Brothers Karamazov* (*Brat'ia Karamazovy*, 1881), outlines two paths open to people. One is marked by western rational thought, isolation, individualism, egoism, and literal or spiritual death. This is the path followed by Ivan Karamazov, who questions the very structure of God's universe. Ivan is uprooted from the Russian soil. His thought, Dostoevsky points out, leads to a world in which 'everything is permitted'. The other path is followed by his brother, Alesha, who ultimately does not rebel against God's order, who accepts the world as it is, who conforms to God's community. His path is marked by unconditional love and by an 'everyone is responsible for everyone else' approach to life. Dostoevsky points out that spiritual outcasts, superfluous men like Ivan or the bible-questioning, France-worshipping Smerdiakov, will literally or figuratively die. On the other hand, those who conform to God's law, like Alesha or his spiritual father, Father Zosima, or, by the end of the novel, Kolia Krasotkin, will yield more links to other people, in the unending chain of everyone being linked to everyone.

Tolstoy is not usually considered as a creator of superfluous men, yet in *War and Peace* and *Anna Karenina* we see the same kind of configuration of ideological conformists and nonconformists as we do in Dostoevsky's works. For Tolstoy, in *War and Peace*, the superfluous people are those who do not conform to or who rebel against the laws of history. In *The Brothers Karamazov*, Dostoevsky's heroes conformed to God's laws. The idea of superfluity was linked to religious factors. In *War and Peace*, Tolstoy also connects superfluity with a theory of history, rather than just with a religious doctrine. Those who suffer disaster are those who try to defy, who refuse to conform to the flow of, the laws of history. Tolstoy points out that Napoleon, in believing that history can be made by the will of one individual, is wrong. He wants to control what cannot be controlled. He fails to understand that it is necessary to submit to the laws of history because history is made of the wills of many individuals. Russia's General Kutuzov was a hero, in Tolstoy's eyes, because he knew that there are no heroes. He understood that history consists of the interrelationship of many factors.

Characters other than historical figures are portrayed according to the same dichotomy. Andrei is abstract, cerebral, intellectual, and admires Napoleon. Intellect comes between him and life. He is superfluous to life because he wants to control it. Pierre learns to accept things as they are, through the lessons of Platon Karataev, a simple Russian peasant who teaches him about the connection to God's designs for the universe. In this novel, Tolstoy praises those who conform and who submit to historical destiny. Submission to historical destiny is connected to religion.

In *Anna Karenina*, Tolstoy shows us that conformity to life is praiseworthy if it is attached to genuine religious faith. Levin discovers, by mowing hay with peasants, that the meaning of life is life itself. Anna Karenina, like Levin, acts spontaneously. She is condemned because, as a married woman, she has dared to transgress God's laws by having an affair with a man who is not her husband. Tolstoy even describes Anna as 'superfluous' in the nursery. In fact she is superfluous because she has refused to conform to God's laws. Levin deviates from the norms of high society, but he holds true to the path of God's laws.

In the novels of Dostoevsky and Tolstoy, the further away the characters are from the soil and from the religious beliefs that grow there, the more problems are created. If characters remain close to the Russian soil, they can discern the importance of submitting to the order of things. Levin tills the earth. A simple Russian peasant reveals the meaning of life to him. Platon Karataev plays a similar role with Pierre. Dostoevsky's Sonia Marmeladova and Alesha Karamazov are in harmony with Russian Christianity. Anna Karenina, Stavrogin, Petr Verkhovensky, Ivan Karamazov, and the underground man rebel against God's order. Andrei fails to submit to the laws of history. All of these characters are superfluous because they are nonconformists to some metaphysical order.

In Russian literature of the turn of the century, a direct dealing with the theme of the superfluous man is abandoned. In some of Chekhov's works, though, we see the familiar pattern of society's rejection of the person who thinks differently. One example is in the story *Ward Six* (*Palata No. 6*), whose protagonist, Andrei Ragin, is deemed mad because he finds the inmate of a mental institution more interesting to talk to than the boring people in society at large. Most of Chekhov's works deal with superfluity in a different way, though. For many of Chekhov's characters, people feel superfluous and isolated not because they are different, but because they are human. In previous depictions of the superfluous man, with the exception of Turgenev's Chulkaturin, characters felt like misfits because there was an objective difference between them and their environment. With Chekhov's misfits, there is a sense of the universality of isolation. One such case is the story entitled *The Superfluous Man* (*Lishnii chelovek*), where the main character feels superfluous to his wife's circle of friends.

With the Soviet period, and with the advent of socialist realism in the 1930s, it might be argued that the theme of the superfluous man disappeared. After all, writers were urged to depict positive heroes helping to build socialism. Furthermore, one can, I believe, paradoxically, discern ways in which portrayals of superfluous heroes in the mainstream works of the nineteenth century made their presence felt in the literature of the new Soviet state. First of all, there were those works by fellow traveller writers like Iurii Olesha, which depicted people who could not fit into the new structures of Soviet life. Olesha's *Envy* (*Zavist'*, 1927), follows the adventures of two men, Kavalerov and Ivan Babichev, who cannot adapt to the new life. This pattern is vaguely reminiscent of Oblomov, who did not want to keep pace with the rhythms of change. (Kavalerov, however, would like to participate, but he is incapable of conforming.) Juxtaposed to Kavalerov is Andrei Babichev, who participates fully in the new society. Olesha does not take sides, for he shows both the flaws of those who conform and those who do not.

Second, there were works that directly urged the building of the new Soviet state. Fedor Gladkov's novel *Cement* (*Tsement*, 1925), a prototype of the Soviet industrial novel, shows the importance of adhering to the collective, of adhering to the Soviet system. Gleb comes home from the front, and his wife Dasha shows that working towards the future of communism is more important than expressing personal feelings to particular individuals. Sacrificing oneself to the masses is more important than living one's personal life. Gleb learns that his intimate relationship with his wife is to be subordinated to their common goal of building socialism. By the end of the novel, Gleb learns to shed his personal concerns in the name of the common goal of the workers' building of the new society. Often, in these novels, the outsider becomes the insider. The heroes become actively involved with socialism.

Paradoxically, this tradition had deep affinities with that of the nineteenth-century superfluous man. The person who is different is cast as a villain. The one who conforms is the hero. Accordingly the works of Soviet socialist realism, with their heroes of the Soviet system and their villains rebelling against the system, are tied, in terms of the approach to the conformist and the nonconformist, to the main line of Russian literature of the nineteenth century.

In a 1988 interview in a French literary magazine, Andrei Bitov was asked about his views on the superfluous man today. He explained that the superfluous man tradition still exists, but that it has changed since the nineteenth century. Nineteenth-century conceptions of the superfluous man, explained Bitov, located him within a particular social context. Now, Bitov continued, it makes sense to view the superfluous man within a global context. Bitov asked, 'To what end does Man exist, to what extent is he indispensable (or useless) in relation to his environment, to the system that governs life?' ('Bitov: l'énergie de l'erreur', *Magazine littéraire*, March 1988).

Bitov's novel, *The Monkey Link* (*Ozhidanie obez'ian*), published in 1995, addresses the same question he posed in the interview of the purpose of the human being: 'Is the human being superfluous to nature?' What is the relationship of the human being to other biological species? What is the role of human beings *vis-à-vis* other human beings? To this day, the superfluous man tradition continues to live.

FURTHER READING

Chances, Ellen. *Conformity's Children: An Approach to the Superfluous Man in Russian Literature*, Columbus, Ohio: Slavica, 1978.

Clardy, Jesse and Clardy, Betty. *The Superfluous Man in Russian Letters*, Lanham, Maryland: University Press of America, 1980.

Gifford, Henry. *The Hero of His Time: A Theme in Russian Literature*, London: Edward Arnold; New York: Longmans Green, 1950.

Jackson, Robert Louis. *Dostoevsky's Underground Man in Russian Literature*, The Hague: Mouton, 1958.

Rogers, T.F. *'Superfluous Men' and the Post-Stalin 'Thaw': the Alienated Hero in Soviet Prose during the Decade 1953–1963*, The Hague: Mouton, 1972.

Seeley, Frank F. *From the Heyday of the Superfluous Man to Chekhov*, Nottingham: Astra Press, 1994.

11

NINETEENTH-CENTURY RUSSIAN THOUGHT AND LITERATURE

DEREK OFFORD

In the rich corpus of nineteenth-century Russian belles-lettres it is hard always to establish a clear boundary between essays in thought (within which further boundaries between the aesthetic, moral, religious, social, political and other spheres may also be blurred) and works of fiction. Such writings as Herzen's cycles of *Letters from France and Italy* (*Pis'ma iz Frantsii i Italii*, first published in book form in 1855) and *From the Other Shore* (*S togo berega*, first published in German in 1850) or Dostoevsky's *Winter Notes on Summer Impressions* (*Zimnie zametki o letnikh vpechatleniiakh*, 1863) function on one level as essays in social or political thought or reflections on cultural identity and national destiny. And yet they are themselves literary artefacts, exemplars of the genre of the travel sketch. Similarly, in *My Past and Thoughts* (*Byloe i dumy*, 1861–7) Herzen leaves both an intellectual history of his generation and a carefully crafted example of the personal memoir. At the same time the classical Russian novel, although a supremely polished art form, may operate as a sort of intellectual history too. For example, Turgenev's novels – as distinct from his novellas, according to Turgenev's own definition of the two genres – may be seen as providing a history of the development of the consciousness of the educated Russian during the middle decades of the century from idealistic but ineffectual 'superfluous man' (*lishnii chelovek*) to disaffected rationalist and revolutionary. The novel could also function as a polemical contribution to contemporary intellectual life. Thus in the reign of Alexander II (ruled 1855–81), there developed as distinct sub-groups of the novelistic genre both works extolling the militant younger generation, such as Sleptsov's *Hard Times* (*Trudnoe vremia*, 1865), and the so-called antinihilist novel, in which certain writers (for instance, Pisemsky and Leskov) took issue with contemporary radical thought.

In any case the two bodies of work, thought and fiction, were interdependent and mutually enriching. Literary critics, such as Belinsky and Dobroliubov, or religious, social and political thinkers, such as Chaadaev and Chernyshevsky, exercised profound influence on the views of their contemporaries, including writers of fiction, and often conveyed their ideas through discussion of works of fiction. Conversely, when thinkers failed to exercise influence it was sometimes because their purview seemed too narrowly literary. This was the case with Druzhinin, a talented critic of the middle decades of the century, who insisted on treating a work of art as a thing in itself with no broader, extra-aesthetic implications that interested him. The novelists, for their part, often took up and developed themes addressed by contemporary thinkers, as did Dostoevsky in *Crime and Punishment*

(*Prestuplenie i nakazanie*, 1866), which carries certain contemporary radical ideas to what Dostoevsky sees as their logical conclusion. Writers who ignored the demand for topical content of civic import and subscribed to the doctrine of art for art's sake, like the poet Fet, risked marginalization. Often the examination of a subject by a thinker complements one or more literary studies of the same subject. Chaadaev's *Philosophical Letter* (first published in French in 1836 as *Lettre philosophique*) and Pushkin's *Eugene Onegin* (*Evgenii Onegin*, written in the period 1823–31) illustrate the point. Thinkers themselves resorted at times to overtly fictional genres in order to convey their ideas, as did Ivan Kireevsky in a fragmentary work of utopian literature, *Island* (*Ostrov*, 1838), Herzen in *Who is to blame?* (*Kto vinovat?*, 1845–6), and Chernyshevsky in *What is to be Done?* (*Chto delat'?*, 1863).

It is not surprising, in view of this interdependence, that the rhythms of thought and fiction were often in harmony. For example, the flowering of classical literature in the 1830s and 40s coincided with the unfolding of debate about the nation's destiny. On the other hand the period 1848–55, known as the 'dismal seven years', when governmental fear that the revolutionary disturbances of 1848 in western Europe would spread to Russia provoked particularly severe official repression, was notable by contrast for the dearth of both major works of imaginative literature and thought. In the period immediately following the Crimean War (1853–6) and the accession of the more liberal Alexander II to the throne, work in both fields was again profuse and rich.

It is the fluid boundary between nineteenth-century Russian thought and imaginative literature, the bearing which the thought has on that literature, and the interplay between them, that this chapter will survey.

It may be rewarding as a first step to consider briefly the oneness of Russian thought and imaginative literature in the eighteenth century, at the very beginning of the modern period of Russian culture, when writers were already starting to address topical issues. The earliest Russian users of western literary genres tended to see their writings as part of a general civic service or endeavour. From the Petrine epoch on, many Russian writers – Prokopovich, Kantemir, Fonvizin, Derzhavin, Radishchev and, to a lesser extent, Lomonosov and Sumarokov – held government office or were close to court or sought to influence state policy or the heir to the throne or even the succession. It was therefore natural that they should take a keen interest in social and political matters and directly address or at least obliquely touch upon a large number of interrelated subjects of topical significance: the immensity of Russia and her natural wealth; military prowess and imperial conquest; the reception of western culture and values; education and upbringing; relations between husbands and wives and between parents and children; the rights and obligations of the nobility; the lot of the peasantry and the domestic serf; the outlook and conduct of the clergy; life and conduct at court; the abuse of power by the *vel'mozha* or grandee; official corruption; and – perhaps most daringly – the nature of tyrants and the qualities of the virtuous ruler.

The tradition of engagement with topical issues that had been begun in the eighteenth century was continued by the nineteenth-century intelligentsia, particularly after 1825 when government no longer commanded the respect of the embryonic public opinion articulated by the small – and at that time mainly noble – educated class. The corpus of thought which that intelligentsia produced, and which was to inform the literature of the classical period, may be divided into a number of interrelated fields and paid particular attention to certain quite clearly definable questions. It contained a wealth of literary criticism, which examined among other things the nature of beauty and inspiration, the relation of art to reality, the function of art, and the mission of the writer and critic. Writings on social questions, often seen through the prism of imaginative literature, literary criticism and literary history, explored the role of the intelligentsia itself, the nature of the common people or *narod*, and the relationship between the intelligentsia and the *narod*. Examination of political questions tended to be less explicit but often, insofar as censorship allowed, touched upon serfdom and urban poverty and on the nature of autocracy and its perniciousness or suitability in Russian conditions. Essays in what might be best described as moral philosophy included evaluations of Russian and Western mores and enquiries on the themes of egoism and altruism, duty, service and self-sacrifice. There were discussions of a theological nature into the relationship between rational knowledge and faith and the differences between Orthodoxy and the western forms of Christianity, and at the same time speculation on the extent of the jurisdiction of scientific method, its implications for religious faith, and the similarities and dissimilarities between science and history. In the field of history itself thinkers reflected on the principles that might underlie historical development, on the existence or lack of pattern in history, on chance and necessity, the role of Providence and great individuals, and the role of the state in Russian history. Almost invariably Russian thinkers were also – perhaps above all – preoccupied with the problem of the historical destiny of individual nations, the relationships between nations, and in particular the relationship of 'Russia' to 'the West' (though these two concepts, it should be noted, reached beyond geopolitical entities).

Turning from these broad, general considerations to a chronological account of the way in which the concerns of Russian thinkers impinge upon and find expression in classical Russian literature, we should perhaps dwell first on Chaadaev's *Philosophical Letter*, written in 1829. This letter was the first of a series of eight but the only one published in Chaadaev's lifetime. Chaadaev, who had imbibed the ideas of French Catholic thinkers of the early nineteenth century during a prolonged stay in western Europe in the 1820s, believes nations and societies derive their character from the religious ideas that prevail in them. He shares the Romantic view of the Middle Ages as a period when the notions of duty, justice, law and order that give unity and continuity to Western civilization were established and when the individual personality began to assert itself. It is Russia's profound misfortune, Chaadaev argues, that she remained outside the religious, moral and social development of the Renaissance, with the result that educated Russians find themselves without history, stable values or moral foundations for their existence. In a spiritual sense the educated Russian is a rootless traveller, more nomadic than the shifting tribesmen who inhabit Russia's Asiatic borderlands. This problem of individual identity, role and purpose also exists on a national scale, for nations 'are just as much moral beings as individuals are'. Russia herself, an immense geographical space between the Bering Straits and the Oder, seems to Chaadaev to be suspended as a civilization between Asia and Europe. The fact that Chaadaev chose to write his letter in French not only reminds us of the curious fact that a foreign language was freely chosen as a vehicle for social intercourse among the Russian nobility in the late eighteenth and early nineteenth centuries but also, at a deeper level, serves to illustrate Chaadaev's thesis about the lack of a substantial native culture in Russia.

Chaadaev's *Letter* expresses the loss of purpose experienced by the patriotic Russian nobleman, with his residual sense of a duty to serve, in the increasingly bureaucratic Russian state. It also reflects the nobleman's despondency at the lack of opportunity for concrete political change in the aftermath of the Decembrist Revolt of 1825. It will also readily be seen that the malaise Chaadaev describes is essentially the same as that which afflicts the itinerant 'superfluous man' who features so prominently in classical Russian literature from the 1820s and who is represented, in that decade, by Onegin in Pushkin's novel in verse and, at a later date, by Pechorin in Lermontov's *A Hero of Our Time* (*Geroi nashego vremeni*, 1840). Mutually acquainted, Chaadaev and Pushkin both portray a man who lacks guiding principle and moral compass, is out of harmony with his society and cannot settle or find a satisfying mission in it.

In the course of the 1830s, Russians increasingly imbibed German philosophy and literature, studied in German universities and, as Turgenev put it when writing about his own youth, plunged into the 'German sea'. Inspired in particular by the young nobleman Stankevich, they avidly devoured the works of Schelling and, especially, Hegel until, as Herzen recalled, the overused tomes disintegrated. The intoxication with German Romantic culture – which is foreshadowed in the poetic references to separation, sorrow, '*a certain something* and *a misty faraway*' by Onegin's friend and victim, Lensky, who has studied in Göttingen – provided solace from the harshness of Russian social and political reality. It gave rise to opaque abstractions on the transcendental nature of art and the Absolute Idea, admiration of the Schillerian 'noble soul' (*die schöne Seele*), and a cult of chivalrous friendship. This unpractical otherworldly idealism, with its exaltation of heart over mind, is embodied in a further incarnation of the 'superfluous man', the eponymous hero of Turgenev's first novel *Rudin*, set in the late 1830s or early 1840s though written in 1855–6 at a time of change when the character of the Nicolaevan age seemed in retrospect more clearly definable. Although Onegin's world-weariness and cynicism are supplanted in Rudin by ardent attachment to apparently altruistic ideals, nevertheless Rudin, like Pushkin's protagonist, is at heart egoistic and incapable of lasting attachments or dedication to a practical cause. He is conceived by Turgenev and perceived by Turgenev's contemporaries as typifying the form which the rootless educated Russian has assumed a decade after Onegin's time.

The enthusiasm for western culture among the Russian educated class naturally precipitated debate about the relationship of that culture to Russian culture and the degree to which western culture could or should be accommodated in Russia. Consideration of these questions was in any case encouraged by the growth of interest within Western thought and literature in national distinctiveness and in the relative contribution of different peoples to the development of human civilization. This interest, which emanated from Germany in the late eighteenth century, found expression in the early nineteenth century among many European peoples in a curiosity in their language, history, literature, music and customs, everything that gives a people its specific cultural identity. Thus the question broached by Chaadaev in 1829 unfolds into a broad debate that continues to colour intellectual life for the rest of the century – and arguably still colours Russian intellectual life today – as to the actual national identity of Russia and the attitude it should adopt in relation to other nations. The Slavophiles and Westernizers, as the opposing camps in this debate came to be known (the appellations were rather jocular, gibes invented by their opponents), were broad churches within which there were various shades of belief. Both groups, particularly the Westernizers, tended to define themselves in relation to their adversaries.

The Slavophiles – notably Khomiakov, Ivan Kireevsky, Konstantin Aksakov – believed Russia possessed a distinct national identity which was not only worth preserving but provided a defence against the rationalism, materialism, individualism and collapse of faith that they believed were undermining the West. They abhorred Peter the Great as the ruler who had supposedly set Russia on a western path and looked back nostalgically to an imagined pre-Petrine golden age. They favoured Moscow – the ancient capital, associated from the fourteenth century with the development of a new Russian Orthodox state as the Tartar yoke was thrown off – over St Petersburg, Russia's window on to the pernicious West: the capital founded by Peter in 1703 and built in response to imperial diktat by western architects in an alien style on inhospitable marshland where no township had previously stood. Khomiakov argued that Russian civilization was informed by a different principle (a principle of inner freedom, which he termed 'Iranian') from that which informed Western societies (the 'Kushite' principle, a principle of compulsion). This inner freedom supposedly found expression in the Orthodox Church, which unlike the Catholic Church had not been tainted by the secular world of learning and politics and which cultivated an all-inclusive *sobornost'*, or conciliarism, and resisted organization into a hierarchy like that dominated by the Pope. As for the Russian common people, the *narod*, they remained uncorrupted by the westernization that had infected the nobility. Indifferent to worldly goods and private property, the *narod* manifested a truly Christian leaning towards the life of the spirit. Uninterested in practical secular matters, they willingly conceded political authority to the autocrat. Their capacity for brotherly love was exhibited in the institution of the commune, the *mir* or *obshchina*, which periodically partitioned the land at the disposal of the peasant community according to the changing needs of the families within it. The Slavophiles' interest in the distinctiveness of their own culture found expression in some philological research of dubious scholarly value by Konstantin Aksakov, in the same man's habit – a source of some amusement to his contemporaries – of attiring himself in national costume, and in the collection of Russian folk songs by Petr Kireevsky, brother of Ivan.

The opposing westernist camp included the historian Granovsky, who held a chair at Moscow University in the 1840s; Annenkov, author of travel notes on France and Italy and of valuable literary memoirs as well as of less distinguished literary criticism; Botkin, a wealthy merchant, another ardent traveller, author of a notable travelogue on Spain in the late 1840s; and Turgenev, whose literary career began in the mid-40s. Perhaps Westernism's most brilliant representative was Herzen, who in his essays of the 1840s on science and nature tried to reconcile Hegelian philosophy and French socialism. In 1847 Herzen emigrated to the West with his family and in further cycles of letters on life in western Europe shortly before, during and after the revolutions of 1848 he defended individual liberty in the face of all coercive systems, both political and ideological. However, more influential than any of these men on the intellectual life of his age was the literary critic Belinsky, 'furious Vissarion' as he was known on account of his fierce engagement with moral and social issues as well as literary ones. In the course of his journalistic career, which lasted from 1834 to his death in 1848 at the age of thirty-seven, Belinsky succumbed to numerous intellectual enthusiasms, or more accurately passions: from Schellingian transcendental idealism and a 'recon-ciliation with reality' in all its grimness, inspired by Hegel, to fanatical espousal of utopian socialism and even a measure of respect for the bourgeoisie. What remained constant in Belinsky's writing, though, was a passionate concern for the state of Russian literature and a view of it as a civilizing force, in the absence of other outlets for free expression.

Although individual Westernizers were personally close to Slavophiles in the early 1840s and certainly shared the Slavophiles' deep love of Russia, it was their antipathy to Slavophilism that united them more than anything else. The Westernizers viewed Slavophilism as a defence of an antiquated way of life and medieval superstition. They equated it with repudiation of the scientific and social benefits which western European countries, for all their inequalities and social problems, had brought about and with stubborn resistance to progress, which Belinsky discussed in a review of the state of Russian literature in 1847. With their extensive knowledge of the German states, France, England, Italy and other countries, derived both from their reading and from the travels that several of them had made, the Westernizers believed that Russia needed to learn and borrow – judiciously – from the more advanced members of that same European family of nations to which she herself belonged.

The stirrings of debate about the national destiny are evident in the famous final passage of Part I of Gogol''s *Dead Souls* (*Mertvye dushi*, 1842), where the nefarious Chichikov's *troika*, speeding away from the provincial town from which

Chichikov has to flee, is transformed into an image of Russia, hurtling towards an enigmatic destiny as other nations stand aside. Gogol' himself, although championed by Westernizers as a writer who revealed the social and moral squalor of Russian reality with great power, was personally closer to the conservative nationalist camp and was eventually berated by Belinsky, in the latter's famous *Letter to Gogol* (1847, seen by contemporaries as the testament of the dying critic), for the reactionary views he had expressed in his *Selected Passages from Correspondence with Friends* (*Vybrannye mesta iz perepiski s druz'iami*, 1847). The debate about national identity finds an echo in Turgenev's second novel, *A Nest of Gentry* (*Dvorianskoe gnezdo*, published in 1859 but set in the early 1840s), where the hero Lavretsky struggles to reconcile the disparate parts of his upbringing and in which Turgenev offers a portrait of a superficial Westernizing official in the Ministry of the Interior in the character of Panshin. The debate also informs the literature of the 1840s and 1850s in an implicit way, inasmuch as concerns widely expressed in that literature – for example, compassion for the poor and oppressed in both town and country; respect for the individual personality and a sense of the dignity of the individual; interest in the life and culture of western societies, as expressed in a rich travel literature – reflect civilized values of western provenance which shine brightly in the gloom of Nicolaevan Russia.

Within the Westernizers' camp differences that were eventually to become significant began to develop at an early stage. Already in the 1840s some Westernizers took up more or less extreme positions. Belinsky, in 1841, declared himself prepared to countenance revolutionary violence in order to achieve social justice, defending the wave of terror unleashed by the French Jacobins in 1793–4. Herzen, impressed by the work of the German left-wing Hegelian Feuerbach, whose *Essence of Christianity* (1841) had a major impact in Russia in the 1840s, embraced a materialist outlook. Moreover, as soon as he arrived in western Europe in 1847 as a political refugee, Herzen set about indicting the bourgeoisie, the regnant class in the France and England to which he came, as egoistic, oppressive and morally bankrupt. At the same time he began to preach a Russian socialism which envisaged the Russian peasant, whose collective spirit was manifested in the commune, as the bearer of values that would underpin a new civilization as the 'old world' destroyed itself. A further member of the westernist circles of the early 1840s, Bakunin, embarked on a life of political rebellion that led him to various European barricades in 1848 and subsequently, after imprisonment in the Peter and Paul Fortress in St Petersburg and exile to and escape from Siberia, to renewed emigration in England, Italy and Switzerland, where in the 1860s and 70s he was to play a leading role in the international anarchist movement. On the other hand, more moderate men among the Westernizers (Granovsky, Botkin, Annenkov) resisted complete rejection of religious belief, maintained that the bourgeoisie, for all its faults, had proved a partly positive social force in the West, and in general counselled moderation. They argued for evolution, that is to say gradual change that would not destroy what was valuable in the existing society along with what they deplored, rather than revolution which would sweep away everything.

The cracks apparent in the westernist camp in the 1840s developed into a major fissure in the period after the Crimean War and the death of Nicholas I (1855), when the new tsar, Alexander II, encouraged discussion of the emancipation of the serfs and oversaw the reform itself in 1861. Censorship was relaxed and journalism and literature again flourished. The more radical variant of Westernism was now articulated by militant younger men of lower social origin than the so-called 'men of the 40s'. These 'men of the 60s', led by Chernyshevsky and Dobroliubov (both sons of the lower 'white', or non-monastic, clergy), venerated natural science and invoked its authority. They prized it both as a practical tool for the material improvement of society and as the source of a method – entailing observation, measurement, experimentation, deduction, formulation of laws – that could be applied to human problems in such fields as sociology, psychology, criminology and even ethics and aesthetics as well as to natural phenomena within such disciplines as physics, chemistry and biology. Armed with this tool they launched a wide-ranging attack on what they saw as prevailing values. In aesthetics they rejected the view of art as capable of transcending reality and assigned to it the more menial role of reproducing reality. They argued that art should not be viewed as an end in itself but as a means to an end, which in their own place and time was civic or social. They preached a rigid determinism, according to which one's path in life and even one's everyday actions were dictated not by free will but by physiological or environmental factors. Seen in this light, crime was a product of adverse social conditions and would be almost entirely eliminated when causes such as hunger and poverty were removed. The 'men of the 60s' subscribed to a utilitarian ethics, according to which humans pursued pleasure and sought to avoid pain and were motivated solely by self-interest. Their belief that humans did not really exhibit altruism or compassion was consistent with their atheism, which was based on the thought of Feuerbach and the so-called 'vulgar materialists' Büchner, Moleschott and Vogt. That is to say, they denied the existence of spirit and held that matter is the only substance. Their egoism they reconciled with socialism by arguing that since humans were rational as well as selfish it was possible to persuade them that their own best interest lay in co-operation with their fellows. The interests of the individual were overridden in their minds by those of the larger group or social class – thus in Russia, the peasantry had priority over the nobility – or by the interests of the nation as a whole.

The rebellion initiated in the 1850s by Chernyshevsky and Dobroliubov was continued after Dobroliubov's death in 1861 and Chernyshevsky's arrest in 1862 by Pisarev, who himself died at the age of only twenty-seven in 1868. Pisarev echoed Chernyshevsky's philosophical materialism and shared his reverence for science. He also pressed Chernyshevsky's rejection of art as an end in itself and his demand for utility in art to the limit: for example, he avowed that he would rather be a shoemaker than a Raphael and wrote an article on the 'destruction of aesthetics'. He 'went further' than Chernyshevsky and Dobroliubov, as Dostoevsky once put it, both by virtue of the vehemence of his iconoclasm and by exalting the individual liberated from the constraints of convention and tradition. He did not flinch from the conclusion that that individual, recognizing no authority outside himself, spiritual or political, enjoyed extraordinary power and the freedom to exercise it as he chose, for ends that might be socially destructive or even criminal as well as for socially useful purposes or in the service of charity. It is Pisarev, more than any other Russian thinker, who is associated with 'nihilism', the term coined by Turgenev to denote the moral rebellion of the radical intelligentsia.

Numerous issues examined in Russian literature in the age of Alexander II – for example, tension between the generations; class conflict; attitudes to art and science; the fate of the superfluous man and the emergence of a new positive type of hero; the role of the common people in Russian history; the role of women in Russian society – have their roots in, or are entangled with, the debates agitating Russian thinkers in the post-Crimean period.

The classic fictional exposition of the debate between the older moderate Westernizers and the younger militant ones is Turgenev's masterpiece *Fathers and Children* (or 'Sons': *Ottsy i deti*, 1862), with its portrait of the 'nihilist' Bazarov (whom Pisarev, in two famous essays, took as an example of the 'realist' to be emulated). Bazarov and Arkadii Kirsanov, who is at first his disciple, reject art as a vehicle for pursuit of beauty, a pursuit which they see as a dangerous form of self-indulgence. Accordingly they plan to introduce Arkadii's gentle father, Nikolai, to Büchner's *Force and Matter* (1855) as an alternative to Pushkin's poetry, which they notice him reading. Nature, beloved by the older generation as a beautiful object of contemplation and mysteriously entwined with their emotional lives, is for Bazarov 'not a temple but a workshop' in which the scientist – such as himself, a medical student – can conduct experiments that have practical utility. People Bazarov regards – in the first half of the novel, at any rate – not as individualized beings with a legitimate inner world of their own but as representatives of a type: he compares them to trees in a wood which interest a botanist not on account of their idiosyncrasies but only insofar as they offer material on which to base generalizations. In endowing Bazarov with a capacity for the inexplicable romantic feeling whose existence his ideology seems to preclude, Turgenev transmutes contemporary polemic into a timeless artistic comment on the human condition. Nevertheless it is the stuff of contemporary polemic from which the novel is fabricated. Moreover, with its underlying antagonism between the nobility, represented by the two generations of the Kirsanov family, and the *raznochintsy*, represented by Bazarov, it lays bare the element of class conflict in the struggle between the 'men of the 40s' and the 'men of the 60s'.

Turgenev's novel touches upon a further question that again reverberates between thought and literature in the post-Crimean period, namely the study of the nature of the typical educated Russian of the epoch. All of Turgenev's first four novels reflect a movement, or an aspiration, over the period 1840–60, away from the ineffectual 'superfluous man' of noble origin and towards the more practical 'positive hero' of lower social origin, the *raznochinets*, who is capable of achieving the goals he sets himself. The comparison of these two types, the 'superfluous man' and the 'positive hero', was one to which Turgenev himself gave much thought. In his essay *Hamlet and Don Quixote* (1860) he addressed it with reference to Shakespeare's and Cervantes' characters on an axis running from egoism to altruism. Hamlet is an attractive but ultimately ineffectual hero dogged by introspection ('reflection' as the Russians put it). Since he lives only for himself, he is unable ever fully to give himself to anyone or any cause. Don Quixote, on the other hand, lives entirely for something outside himself and is therefore capable of self-sacrifice. The subject has political implications, which are taken up by Dobroliubov in his famous essays of 1859–60 on Goncharov's *Oblomov* (1859) and Turgenev's *On the Eve* (*Nakanune*, published 1860 but set in 1853–4), in which the radical critic associates the 'superfluous man' with the ineffectual liberal, full of fine phrases but disinclined to disturb the status quo. These implications are further developed by Chernyshevsky in his novel *What is to be Done?* Chernyshevsky offers a cast of positive heroes, the 'new people', led by the proto-revolutionary Rakhmetov, the 'salt of the salt of the earth', who applies a clinical rationalism to all problems and strengthens himself mentally and physically for the coming battles by depriving himself of luxuries – except cigars – and lying from time to time on a bed of nails.

The extent to which the conception of the 'positive hero' represents a description of what actually obtained in contemporary reality, on the one hand, or a prescription as to what thinkers and writers thought it desirable to find, on the other, is problematical, as is the more general question as to the extent to which literature was shaped by or itself helped to shape reality. The fact that Insarov, the hero of Turgenev's third novel, *On the Eve*, is not a Russian but a Bulgarian preparing to help to liberate his country from Turkish rule is suggestive of the unavailability as yet of this type in Russian reality. Moreover, Bazarov in *Fathers and Children*, it will be noted, not only dies before fulfilling any ambition but was also conceived by Turgenev, as he once put it, as standing only 'on the threshold of the future'.

Alongside ideological tension, conflict of generations and classes, and eager anticipation of the appearance of the 'positive hero', thinkers in the post-Crimean period show growing interest in the nature and welfare of the popular masses. This interest combines with the new aesthetics propounded by Chernyshevsky and others, with its demand for an art faithfully reproducing reality and serving the cause of social justice, to stimulate many works of literature (by, for instance, Nikolai Uspensky, Levitov and Sleptsov in the 1860s and Zasodimsky and Zlatovratsky in the next decade) in which the common people were depicted, generally in a sympathetic light. Thinkers also champion the emancipation of women, advocating their emergence as complete social equals of men with the same rights to education, with freedom of choice in marriage and with similar opportunities for socially useful activity. The most energetic and single-minded spokesman for this cause in the immediate post-Crimean period is perhaps M.L. (or M.I.) Mikhailov. However, again it is Chernyshevsky who most famously argued the case, in his novel *What is to be Done?*. Chernyshevsky's heroine Vera Pavlovna escapes with the help of Lopukhov from the tyranny of her family, chooses a new partner, Lopukhov's friend Kirsanov, and establishes a utopian social unit, a successful female co-operative of seamstresses.

The moral rebellion of the 1860s, and the revolutionary ferment of the late 60s and the 1870s to which it gave rise, found expression in the writing of Dostoevsky. Indeed nowhere is the boundary between thought and art more difficult to define than in Dostoevsky's work and it is doubtful whether Dostoevsky himself conceived of a distinction of this sort. For one thing Dostoevsky, as *de facto* editor of the journals *Vremia* (*Time*, 1861–3) and *Epokha* (*Epoch*, 1864–5), participated directly in the polemical journalism of the early 1860s and then again, intermittently, through his *Diary of a Writer* (*Dnevnik pisatelia*) in the period 1873–81. Together with Grigor'ev, an exponent of 'organic criticism' who saw artists as an expression of the inner life of their people, Dostoevsky was a leading representative of *pochvennichestvo* or 'native-soil conservatism', a variant of romantic conservative nationalism close to Slavophilism. The *pochvenniki* dreamed of reconciliation between the westernized educated class, who had been steered away from national roots by the 'Petrine reform', and the Russian common people, who preserved their Orthodox faith. Both Grigor'ev and Dostoevsky formulated a dichotomy, which pervades Dostoevsky's fiction, between predatory and meek types, whom we might identify within these thinkers' schemes of things with western peoples and Russians respectively.

It is true that Dostoevsky's novels, as multifaceted works of art, stand above any single ideological position and in any event they often state a powerful case for a position which Dostoevsky is unlikely personally to have endorsed. And yet the questions agitating the Russian intelligentsia – aesthetic, ethical, spiritual, social and political, and ultimately the question of national identity and mission – are assimilated in his fiction. For example, his *Notes from Underground* (*Zapiski iz podpol'ia*, 1864) takes an irrationalist standpoint to ridicule the blithe Chernyshevskian view of humans as reasonable beings capable of devising a perfect society and to challenge the Victorian notion of progress. In *Crime and Punishment* Chernyshevsky's rational egoism and Pisarev's legitimization of the superman, utopian schemes, the contemporary loss of faith and denial of altruism are all subjected to withering scrutiny. Again, in Dostoevsky's third major novel, *The Devils* (*Besy*, 1871–2), both the liberal Westernism of the 1840s and early Russian socialism as represented by Nechaev, with its cynical Machiavellian tactics, are presented as portending, indeed liable to precipitate, an apocalypse. In *The Brothers Karamazov* (*Brat'ia Karamazovy*, 1880) – set, it should be noted, in the 1860s, the age of moral and incipient political revolt – the murder of old Fedor Karamazov and the enquiry into the legal and moral responsibility for it of his sons unfolds into the broadest disquisition on the disintegration of the Russian family, the relationship between the spiritual and secular domains represented by Church and state respectively, the distinctions between Orthodox Russia and the West, and overarching questions about faith and justice, human and divine. What for Dostoevsky was no less important than these questions, or even separable from them, the novels also passionately uphold the integrity of art and speak of a person's spiritual need for the beauty it embodies against the prevailing utilitarianism of the radical intelligentsia.

Tolstoy's major novels, *War and Peace* (*Voina i mir*, 1865–9) and *Anna Karenina* (1875–7), are less closely related to the topical concerns of the Russian intelligentsia of the time when they were written than are any of Dostoevsky's novels. Towards the end of the 1870s, however, Tolstoy himself underwent a spiritual crisis that made him repudiate his former way of life and the art he had hitherto produced. This crisis found expression in his *Confession* (*Ispoved'*, 1879–81) and gave rise to various tracts in which he himself made a contribution to Russian political thought, or rather apolitical thought inasmuch as the doctrine Tolstoy puts forward is a form of anarchism. His last novel, *Resurrection* (*Voskresenie*, 1899), clearly discloses the many objects of Tolstoy's condemnation in this period: the coercive apparatus of the state, that is to say its army, its penal system and judicial practices and institutions, which are not at all concerned with human justice but uphold existing inequalities and sanction abuses; the rituals and hypocrisies of the Church, which has departed radically from the simple and holy teachings of Christ, exemplified by the Sermon on the Mount; the institution of private property, the greed of the privileged classes and the plight of the underprivileged and the oppressed. No longer, in this case, is the Russian novelist fashioning the reality around him, including the polemics that swirl within that reality, into a work of art that incorporates topical ideas within a plausible living world of timeless appeal. Rather Tolstoy has crossed the boundary into mere advocacy of his single viewpoint, or at least he teeters on that boundary.

With the assassination of Alexander II by terrorists of the party The People's Will in 1881 the optimism and millenarian expectations of the Russian intelligentsia gave way to pessimism and acceptance of 'small deeds', that is to say concentration on fulfilment of modest ambitions. Chekhov's stories and plays reflect the despondent mood of the *fin de siècle*. In any case the golden age of Russian culture came naturally to an end with the death of Dostoevsky in 1881 and Turgenev in 1883 and with Tolstoy's spiritual crisis. Russian thought now became more sharply polarized. At the radical end of the political spectrum, Populists and Marxists – represented by Plekhanov and, later, Lenin – engaged in debate on the history of and prospects for capitalism in Russia. At the conservative end of the spectrum several thinkers, such as Danilevsky, Pobedonostsev and Leont'ev, who continued to stress the distinctiveness of Russia's civilization and the importance of protecting it from contemporary western influences, expressed reactionary views more boldly than their romantic conservative predecessors had done. At the same time the bond that had existed between literature and thought throughout the classical period was somewhat weakened. Admittedly, thinkers continued in the late nineteenth and early twentieth centuries to address literary questions and writers continued to touch upon issues of social, political or broad national significance. Thus Plekhanov discussed aesthetics from the Marxist standpoint and applied Marxism as a tool for the examination of literature, whilst Gor'ky evinced pity for the lower classes and wrote in a way that appealed to the swelling revolutionary ranks. And yet the greatest creative writer of the turn of the century, Chekhov, eschewed political involvement and did not directly engage in his stories and plays with the issues agitating contemporary political thinkers. As for the poetic movements of the last years of the nineteenth century and the early years of the twentieth, they tended to give precedence to metaphysical and religious concerns over social and political ones. Perhaps it was not until the Soviet period that imaginative literature again engaged with social and political issues as intensely as it had in the period 1825–81. Then, from the 1920s, topicality once more became overt in works conforming to the dictates of the official doctrine of socialist realism, while even writers who sought to evade the party's injunctions, such as Zamiatin, Bulgakov, Pasternak and Solzhenitsyn, raised questions which in the totalitarian state inevitably assumed political significance.

FURTHER READING

Berlin, Isaiah. *Russian Thinkers*, London: Hogarth Press, 1978.

Dowler, Wayne. *Dostoevsky, Grigor'ev and Native-Soil Conservatism*, Toronto and London: Toronto University Press, 1982.

Edie, James M., Scanlan, James P. and Zeldin, Mary-Barbara (eds) *Russian Philosophy*, 3 vols., Chicago: Quadrangle Books, 1965.

Kelly, Aileen M. *Toward Another Shore: Russian Thinkers between Necessity and Chance*, New Haven and London: Yale University Press, 1998.

Lampert, Eugene. *Sons against Fathers: Studies in Russian Radicalism and Revolution*, Oxford: Clarendon Press, 1965.

—— *Studies in Rebellion*, London: Routledge and Kegan Paul, 1957.

Leatherbarrow, W.J. and Offord, Derek (eds and trans.) *A Documentary History of Russian Thought: From the Enlightenment to Marxism*, Ann Arbor: Ardis, 1987.

Martinsen, Deborah (ed.) *Literary Journals in Imperial Russia*, Cambridge: Cambridge University Press, 1997.

Moser, Charles A. *Antinihilism in the Russian Novel of the 1860's*, The Hague: Mouton, 1964.

—— *Esthetics as Nightmare: Russian Literary Theory, 1855–1870*, Princeton: Princeton University Press, 1989.

Offord, Derek. *Portraits of Early Russian Liberals: A Study of the Thought of T. N. Granovsky, V. P. Botkin, P. V. Annenkov, A. V. Druzhinin and K. D. Kavelin*, Cambridge: Cambridge University Press, 1985.

Schapiro, Leonard. *Rationalism and Nationalism in Russian Nineteenth-Century Political Thought*, New Haven and London: Yale University Press, 1967.

Terras, Victor. *Belinskij and Russian Literary Criticism: The Heritage of Organic Aesthetics*, Madison: University of Wisconsin Press, 1974.

Walicki, Andrzej. *A History of Russian Thought from the Enlightenment to Marxism*, trans. Hilda Andrews-Rusiecka, Oxford: Clarendon Press, 1980.

—— *The Slavophile Controversy: History of a Conservative Utopia in Nineteenth-Century Russian Thought*, Oxford: Clarendon Press, 1975.

12

THE SILVER AGE: SYMBOLISM AND POST-SYMBOLISM

MICHAEL BASKER

The term 'Silver Age' has been much used in recent years, alongside or in preference to the overlapping concept of 'Modernism', to characterize the period of exceptional literary activity which reached its peak in Russia in the first decade and a half of the twentieth century. Neither name, in the Russian context, is very clearly defined; both have the advantage of potential breadth of reference. 'Modernism', it could be said, inherently connotes artistic innovation, and implies the continuity between pre-revolutionary trends and the avant-garde experimentation sustained through the first decade or so of Soviet power. Reference to a 'Silver Age' would seem instead to accentuate a perpetuation or restitution of previous tradition – primarily, of course, of the putative 'Golden Age' of Pushkin and his pleiad. The phrase has overtones of nostalgia patently inapplicable to artistic developments in Bolshevik Russia, and readily evokes an exquisite, crepuscular epoch, eclipsed by the Revolution of 1917. Though Omry Ronen has argued vigorously that the metallurgical metaphor, with its connotations of Latin poetry, is an ill-conceived fallacy, the term has been adopted here as a convenient shorthand, already too familiar to fall into disuse.

The period in question has its beginnings in the early 1890s, following the period of relative literary stagnation after the deaths of Dostoevsky (1881) and Turgenev (1883), and Tolstoy's religious conversion and renunciation of his previous writing. One significant point of origin is Dmitrii Merezhkovsky's 'On the Reasons for the Decline and on New Trends in Contemporary Russian Literature' ('O prichinakh upadka i o novykh techeniiakh v sovremennoi russkoi literature'), published in book form in 1893, but delivered as two lectures in December 1892, a year marked also by the publication of the same author's *Symbols: Songs and Poems* (*Simvoly: Pesni i poemy*), and by the poetic debuts of Zinaida Hippius (Gippius) and Fedor Sologub in the journal *Severnyi Vestnik*. By 1894, with the appearance of the first two slender issues of Valerii Briusov's *Russian Symbolists* (*Russkie Simvolisty*), Briusov's first meeting with Konstantin Bal'mont, and publication of the latter's *Under a Northern Sky* (*Pod severnym nebom*), Merezhkovsky's 'new trends' were definitively under way. At the other end of the temporal scale, the beginning of the Silver Age's lingering end – like that of its approximate if incongruous coeval, Nicholas II – can be related with hindsight to the outbreak of war in 1914; but its passing was dramatically signalled only after the turmoil of Revolution and bloody Civil War had drawn to an overt close, by the premature deaths of Aleksandr Blok and Nikolai Gumilev in the same month of August 1921. Many of the surviving members of the pre-war intelligentsia were to emigrate over the following year, and it was left to a new generation of young writers to establish Soviet literature. It might equally be argued, however, that the suicide of Vladimir Maiakovsky in 1930 marked the final demise of Russian Modernism. Isolated individuals of course continued to write after the vestiges of a communal literary era had vanished, while the last great representatives of the Silver Age, Pasternak and Akhmatova, survived in Soviet Russia until the 1960s.

The movement which dominated Silver Age literature was Symbolism and, like its counterparts elsewhere in Europe, this found its quintessential embodiment in poetry. With the rarest of exceptions – the prose-writer Aleksei Remizov, or the idiosyncratic Vasilii Rozanov, at the intersection between literature, journalism and philosophical discourse – the creation of poetry was the common denominator which linked together each of the major Symbolists, and set them apart from realist contemporaries: Bunin (whose poems are peripheral to his main output), Chekhov, Gor'ky, Kuprin, Veresaev, Zaitsev and a host of lesser writers, many of whom, such as Serafimovich, Sergeev-Tsensky, Skitalets and Teleshov, were at least temporarily associated with Gor'ky's *Znanie* publishing venture (1903–13). Though all these were influenced to a greater or lesser degree by the intellectual trends and literary experimentation of the Symbolist camp, they concentrated throughout the period on recognizably traditional, representational prose fiction. Such figures as Leonid Andreev and later Artsybashev, whose themes and techniques place them between modernists and critical-realists, were also fundamentally prose- (and drama-) orientated. So too were the immensely popular authors of novels on female sexuality and emancipation: Nagrodskaia, Verbitskaia and, for a narrower audience, Viacheslav Ivanov's wife, Zinov'eva-Annibal.

The Russian Symbolists set great store by their strongly developed individualism, sophistication and even eccentricity, and never regarded themselves as a formally constituted literary school. They accordingly resist easy definition as a coherent group. They were, however, united in their rejection of the positivism, materialism and social utilitarianism of the preceding era, and their writings were significantly shaped by a common indebtedness to Nietzsche (whose *The Birth of Tragedy* [*Die Geburt der Tragödie*] was more important to some than *Thus Spoke Zarathustra* [*Also sprach Zarathustra*]), to Baudelaire and the *poètes maudits*, to Dante, and such European authors of more recent times as Poe, Maeterlinck, Huysmans and Wilde. Among Russian predecessors, they drew particular inspiration from their reappraisals of Pushkin and Lermontov, Fet, Tiutchev and Dostoevsky.

Literary historians frequently distinguish between a 'first generation' of Symbolists, who made their mark in the 1890s – principally Bal'mont, Briusov, Hippius, Merezhkovsky, and Sologub, along with such others as Aleksandr Dobroliubov, Lokhvitskaia, and N.M. Minsky (who had changed tack in the mid-1880s after producing civic poetry in the 1870s, and whose formative influence on his younger contemporaries is greater than is generally acknowledged); and a 'second generation', comprising Blok, Andrei Bely, Ivanov, and perhaps the transitional figure of Ivan Konevskoy (d. 1901), whose literary activity began around 1900. It was a particular feature of the second group that, albeit in differing ways, each was significantly influenced by the poet-philosopher Vladimir Solov'ev (Blok was attracted primarily to Solov'ev's poetry and its cult of the Eternal Feminine as embodiment of love; Bely, like Ivanov, turned also to the philosophical and theological works, and was more inclined to emphasize the apocalyptic aspect of the same seminal concept). Another common critical convention, which defines the first generation of Symbolists as 'decadents' or 'aesthetes' and the second as 'mystics', should nevertheless be treated with caution. Mystical tendencies abound in the writings of the former, just as elements of decadence – morbid despair, self-disgust, an enervating pursuit of the perverse and bizarre in anticipation of the impending doom of self and civilization – often figure in the creative writing of the latter. All, however, might have broadly subscribed to views propounded by Briusov – the most systematic organizer and propagandist among the Symbolists, as well as their most moderate and rational theorist – in an article under the quintessentially Symbolist title of 'The Keys to the Mysteries' ('Kliuchi tain').

Drawing explicitly on Schopenhauer, Briusov regarded art as both a method and an act of cognition, a way of 'comprehending the world through other, non-rational means'. It was also the highest and perhaps the most complex activity of the human spirit: uniquely valuable, in that the three-dimensional realm of reason and science, the empirical reality accessible through the five senses, was a lie, a 'pale-blue prison' (Fet) of which the conscious mind is at best dimly aware. Its confining walls could nevertheless be penetrated in certain moments of ecstasy, of supra-sensual intuition which afford insight into the hidden essence beyond the outer husk of phenomena. To record these moments of visionary perception was the task of art. Artistic inspiration, in other words, was equated with the intuition of a superior truth. Art represented the 'half-opened doors of Eternity', akin to 'what in other realms is known as revelation'; and the 'modern' (i.e. Symbolist) artist, who dedicates his life to unremitting, self-sacrificial pursuit of the experiences fundamental to his art, unencumbered by the obfuscating mis-construction of its purpose which had hampered many predecessors, was an élite, chosen figure: a 'thaumaturge', secret initiate, priest, magus or seer.

Briusov's essay further conveyed an awed optimism, not untypical of the Symbolists, at the power of art to serve humanity. It was a terrible but liberating 'dynamite' with the unique potential finally to illumine the fundamental questions of being. A negative corollary, however, is that the Symbolist artistic project was per se a response to crisis: in Briusov's formulation, essentially spiritual and intel-lectual, elsewhere evidently emotional, moral, political and social besides. Especially characteristic are the lost confidence in traditional religious faith which his expectation of art implies, and the metaphysical dualism which both regards the material world as inferior to some 'other', inner or transcendent, Ideal realm (ill-defined and uncertainly, even inconsistently located as it may in this case be), and arguably betrays a continued yearning for religious or quasi-religious belief. Symbolism in general, that is, stemmed from a neo-Romantic rejection of earthly reality as illusion, chaotic disorder, fragmentation or sham; and sought to penetrate instead to a greater, overarching principle, truth or reality beyond: to progress, in Viacheslav Ivanov's much-quoted formulation, from things real to things more real (*a realibus ad realiora*). In its literary practice, this aspiration was perhaps most frequently realized in the pursuit, as often implicit or subliminal as explicit, of an all-embracing harmony or unity (re-unification): between, say, body and soul, flesh and spirit, external-empirical appearance and internal-esoteric core; also, for example, between East and West, Christian and pagan, artist and people, man and cosmos, world and Godhead. The terms of the Symbolists' beloved polarities were mutable and mutually reflective (singularity was ultimately inherent in multiplicity: All in all). There were also, of course, endless gradations of mood, from febrile anticipation of an imminent synthetic resolution, capable of transfiguring the essence of existence, to hopeless, passive or spitefully vengeful despair at seemingly irredeemable duality and entrapment in the condition of a fallen mortality.

Because of its sceptical mistrust of external surroundings, and the elusiveness of worlds beyond, the inevitable focus of most Symbolist writing was the world within: it sought, as Briusov had stated in an earlier essay 'On Art' ('O iskusstve' [*sic*]), to 'lay bare the soul of the artist, to give expression to its concealed essence'. In poetry, the dominant mode was therefore the lyric. Its inherent subjectivity was developed to unprecedented extremes, well evidenced, for example, by the solipsism of Sologub or the obsessive, almost literally day-by-day charting of intimate inner experience in the voluminous 'lyric diary' from which Blok's *Verses about the Beautiful Lady* (*Stikhi o Prekrasnoi Dame*) were composed. The lyric self might equally be projected as tormented neurasthenic or vigorously confident, protean genius – Bal'mont effectively transmuted his poetic persona from former to latter when he embarked on *Burning Buildings* (*Goriashchie zdaniia*) and *Let us be Like the Sun* (*Budem kak solntse*), collections which firmly established him as the most popular poet of the day – but an underlying conviction in the unrepeatable uniqueness and validity of individual psychical experience rarely wavered. In an era contemporaneous with the emergence of analytical psychology, lyric poets revealed a persistent fascination with the unfathomable depths and irrational contrarieties of the self, and a quasi-narcissistic attunement to the dark stirrings and complex impulses within. This was typically manifest through a cultivation of exceptional mental and moral states – the transport of prayer, repentance or creative inspiration, of madness, intoxication, anguish or passion. A particularly rich focus of attention were the often elusive condition and content of dream, and the uncertain relation between 'dream' and 'reality'.

More generally, it could be said, Symbolist poetry was preoccupied with 'strangeness': with the exotic, the original, the enigmatic and inexplicable; Briusov's unusual 'moment' (*mig*) of heightened intensity, however achieved; anything that promised a departure from the deadening ordinariness of everyday reality, the grotesque flatness and pallid vacuity of which also became a recurrent topic. Other characteristic themes, frequently intertwined, were the mystic and the erotic (Georgii Chulkov's observation that a 'refined eroticism' was the main theme of Sologub was no less applicable to Briusov or Chulkov's closest associates, Blok and Ivanov); the occult, esoteric, and demonic; the impetus for transcendence of moral taboos and boundaries; the apocalyptically-coloured landscape or sunset or starscape; the unreality and/or infernality of the contemporary city. Myth-ological, religious and cultural-historical subjects, familiar, obscure and sometimes invented, were widely treated, less in their own, objective right than as a mask or symbolic correlative of lyric experience; and the most humdrum of experiences – a ride on a tram, a fleeting glance on a street, a chance encounter in a restaurant – were elevated to heightened (symbolic) significance by the use of archetypal imagery. The most famous examples are the various hypostases of the Eternal Feminine: positive, in the mutable guises of Blok's Beautiful Lady, or Bely's Woman Clothed in the Sun; negative, as Blok's Stranger, Sologub's evil sorceress, and innumerable sibyls, sirens, empresses, Cleopatras, Liliths and lasciviously seductive Eves.

In slightly more formal terms, it could be said that it was the main endeavour of Symbolist poetry to suggest rather than to state outright, to intimate more than it could logically say. Tiutchev's assertion that 'the uttered thought is a lie' was widely accepted; Ivanov, in his article 'The Behests of Symbolism' ('Zavety simvolizma'), characteristically defined the task of poetry as 'the creation of an incantatory magic of rhythmic speech, mediating between man and the world of divine essences'. The thematic cult of 'strangeness', in other words, had its counterpart in the cultivation of a linguistic and stylistic strangeness; and formidable technical inventiveness was devoted to the goal of irrational (supra-rational) communication. Ivanov, who regarded Symbolist poetry as a dim recollection of the ancient sacred language of priests and sorcerers, went further than others in his elaboration of a unique vocabulary and syntax, a paradoxically neologistic archaism, laden with Slavonic roots and heavy, monosyllabic con-sonantal clusters. Other Symbolists shared a resonating lexicon of the intangible, with a penchant for capitalized abstracts (Abyss, Dawn, Azure, Dream, Secret, etc.), pluralization of the inherently singular (Distances, Infinities), compound epithets, neologistic negative prefixes and abstract suffixes (of the type *bezglagol'nost'* – 'wordlessness' – etc.), particularly involving the abstracting sub-stantivization of adjectives (*bezlunnost'*, *luchezarnost'*, etc.). In combination with a more general inclination toward the lexically elevated, arcane or occasionally impenetrable (an example might be sonorous proper names, the implicit private resonance of which remains undisclosed), this contributed to the implication of an imposing but deliberately elusive (unfathomable) significance, further supported by illogicalities of phrase and syntax: tautologies, and such phraseological devices for the enigmatic rapprochement of the rationally incompatible as oxymoron and catachresis. Comparable disruptions of empirical possibility with regard to causality and an uncertainty of spatial and temporal location also contributed to the mysterious suggestiveness of lyric setting and 'plot'.

Above all, Symbolism relied on 'musicality' to supplement or supplant rational discourse, and thereby convey 'the depths of the spirit' (Bely). This naturally entailed a pronounced attention to all forms of sound orchestration or alliterative effect – taken to notorious extremes in the precedence of sound over sense in many poems by Bal'mont, perhaps most subtly exemplified, in conjunction with other forms of parallelism and repetition – of rhythm, word (including anaphora), phrase, syntax, image and structure – in the splendid incantatory magic of Blok at his best. Paronomastic exploitation of implied semantic affinities between words juxtaposed through acoustic similarity, was notably less favoured than by the subsequent generation of Mandel'shtam, Khlebnikov and Tsvetaeva; but the more purely musical, non-verbal pursuit of new, expressive effect led the Symbolists to a revolutionary expansion of the resources of Russian versification. Most obvious was the extension in range of the traditional syllabo-tonic metres (the long lines of Briusov and Bal'mont), experimentation with antique metres and logaoedic verse (Ivanov), and the development of the *dol'nik* (Blok, Hippius; the onward progression toward purely accentual verse was completed by the Futurists). Bely anticipated Maiakovsky in his graphic fragmentation of the verse-line; and there was a great expansion in the treatment of rhyme: in the search for new, rare and exotic rhymes; attention to rhyme-enrichment and such special effects as internal and compound rhyme; above all in an unprecedented development and canonization of the various types of approximate rhyme. A striving toward indissoluble identity between form of expression and meaning, implicit in many of the Symbolists' techniques, found striking embodiment in a number of iconographic poems (Blok, Hippius, Sologub).

For all its effectiveness as a vehicle for the expression of Symbolist preoccupations, the lyric nevertheless had obvious limitations in scope. Apart from early endeavours by Merezhkovsky or Minsky, the longer verse narratives which had been integral to Romanticism were a comparative rarity, of marginal importance during the heyday of Symbolism before the First World War. The most notable longer work of the period, Blok's *Retribution* (*Vozmezdie*), was symptomatically unfinished. The quest for larger structures found more typical manifestation in an innovatory concentration on the poetics of the lyric cycle and, beyond that, on the conception of the collection of verse (*sbornik*) as an integral whole. Briusov's *Urbi et Orbi* (1903) was a significant landmark in this respect. Such developments were in keeping with the preference at other levels of composition for impressionistic, inner linkages rather than rigorous sequentiality. Paradoxically, however, the notion of linear plot (or 'path') re-emerges in the most 'macrocosmic' organization of a single lyric output, Blok's concept of the three volumes of his verse as a 'trilogy of incarnation' (*trilogiia vochelovecheniia*).

The principles and preoccupations of Symbolist verse were closely reflected in other aspects of their prolifically broad-ranging literary output. The *Symphonies* which launched Andrei Bely's variegated career (particularly the first published 'Second', the 'Dramatic' – a 'random extract of the real and immense symphony' he claimed to live through in 1901) well encapsulated an impetus toward transcendence of traditional generic boundaries which, as another means of approach to an all-embracing, ideal oneness, often motivated their persistent aesthetic questing and spirit of generic experimentation. Bely strove here to amalgamate words with music in a highly mannered, poeticized prose, used, as his foreword put it, 'to express a series of moods, linked by a primary mood or harmony, with divisions into parts, fragments and verses (musical phrases)'. The latter aim readily recalls the lyric cycle; but it is notable that with remarkably little modification a comparable verbal texture and 'musical' devices of composition (leitmotival, contrapuntal, rhythmic, acoustic; the apparent predominance as constructional principles of rhythm, euphony, even the symbolic value of reiterated sound-clusters over action) determined the unique, powerfully influential linguistic and stylistic impact achievement of his major novels.

The outstanding Symbolist contributions to the Russian novel were Sologub's *The Little* [or *Petty*] *Demon* (*Melkii bes*), and Bely's *Silver Dove* (*Serebryanyi golub'*) and *Petersburg* (*Peterburg*). Significantly, each portrays a world of demonic dissolution and chaos, and the failure of (chaotically?) competing Christian, Dionysian and, to varying degrees, aesthetic and esoteric systems of belief to afford restorative transcendence or transfigurative cure. Each operates with multiple planes of signification and uncertain narrative voice(s) (multifaceted narrative structure), is densely permeated with literary allusion, and, at base, transmutes (or sublimates, given the persistent fixation with pathological states) powerful subjective-autobiographical experiences. *The Little Demon* centres on the escalating paranoia of the provincial schoolteacher Peredonov, whose sickness acquires universal resonance. Bely's novels, conceived as the first parts of an unfinished trilogy (more overarching synthetic structure), reflect the increasing political concerns of Symbolism – and especially the second generation's preoccupation with divisions of national and human community – after the events of 1905. *The Silver Dove* depicts eschatologically inclined peasant sectarians and a disorientated intelligentsia in the depths of Russia. *Petersburg* pursues the concern with national identity and the clash between dark, anarchic East (Mongolism) and cultured rationalistic West, in an ultimately bathetic suspense tale of revolutionary terrorism (anticipatory of apocalyptic explosion) and parricide, using unsettlingly interchangeable characters in the resonantly symbolic location of Russia's most 'cerebral', unreal city.

Although toward the end of his career, in *The Snake-Charmer* (*Zaklinatel'nitsa zmei*), Sologub turned toward greater realism, both he and Bely produced other novels of note, especially their 'next', radically experimental works, respectively *The Created Legend* (*Tvorimaia legenda*) and *Kotik Letaev*. Merezhkovsky, the most prolific Symbolist novelist, tended, however, to be somewhat ponderously over-schematic in his interpretation of historical subjects in the antithetical terms suggested by the title of his ambitious first trilogy, *Christ and Antichrist* (*Khristos i Antikhrist*, comprising novels on the outwardly improbable triumvirate of Julian the Apostate, Leonardo da Vinci, and Peter the Great). More readable was Briusov's *The Fiery Angel* (*Ognennyi Angel*), a splendidly researched fictionalization of private experience in a tale of witchcraft and occultism in sixteenth-century Germany; while Hippius, as in her dramas, favoured sardonic treatment of contemporary revolutionary and (pseudo-) religious pretensions in two novels (another incomplete trilogy) to which she turned only in the 1910s. Short stories, exhibiting elements of the stylistic and thematic 'strangeness' which typified Symbolist verse, were elegantly crafted, with in some cases indefatigable regularity, by virtually all major and many secondary representatives of the movement. Blok and Ivanov, the exceptions in neglecting prose fiction, turned their hand to verse drama. Ivanov's two tragedies on Greek classical themes embodied his cherished concepts of myth, spiritual ascent and the transcendence of individuation through universal community. Briusov and Inokentii Annensky countered with polemically divergent dramatic reworkings of classical myth. Blok cultivated the non-realist 'lyric drama', taken up by Sologub and authors of the next generation (Kuzmin, Gumilev, Tsvetaeva). His first such work, *The Puppet Show* (*Balaganchik*), directed for Komissarzhevskaia by Meierkhol'd, was a milestone in Russian theatre; but like each of his plays it might be considered subsidiary to the grand poetic project to which, thematically, it is indissolubly related.

Without exception, the major Symbolists were also prolific critics and essayists (Bely alone published over 200 articles and reviews from 1903–10). Apart from the conscious approach to their art of which it gives evidence, this activity was of particular significance on several counts. While Bal'mont, for instance, favoured subjective, impressionist criticism, Briusov and successors such as Gumilev, Kuzmin and Khodasevich, cultivated concise, well-written poetry reviews based on formal, aesthetic rather than political or ideological criteria. Many of their incisive perceptions still retain their value. Together with pioneering investigations of versification and other aspects of poetic technique – at various study groups and discussion circles, typical of the era, as well as in publications by Briusov and Bely – they paved the way for the emergence of the Russian Formalists (themselves closely associated with modernist poets of the 1910s). In their repudiation of civic-minded utilitarianism, the Symbolists also provided radical and enduringly influential reassessments of their literary predecessors, writing most voluminously on Dostoevsky, Tolstoy (seers of the spirit and flesh, in Merezhkovsky's famous formulation), Gogol' and the poetry of their compatriots, but extensively also on many foreign authors. Their activity in this last respect might be coupled with their staggering range as translators of poetry in enriching the general level of Russian cultural awareness. Bal'mont, unjustly calumnied as an indiscriminate translator from twenty-two languages, produced many fine renditions of foreign verse; and his voracious activity was amply supplemented by Sologub, Ivanov, Briusov and others. Briusov's enlightenment project also found idiosyncratic embodiment in his *Dreams of Humanity* (*Sny chelovechestva*), an endeavour to offer examples of poetry of all peoples and times, translated or, in the absence of models, inventively reconstructed. Finally, the second generation left copious, erudite, often demanding studies on the nature and metaphysical roots of art, on civilisation, myth, human and national culture, history, and religious consciousness.

Although, in the early days, the Symbolists tended to publish together and were united by the hostility of readers and critics, there were always tensions between them: between, say, Moscow and Petersburg factions; between Briusov and the Merezhkovskys (Dmitrii and his wife, Zinaida Hippius), or later between Briusov and Ivanov for influence over younger artists who inevitably themselves became enmeshed in the frenzied network of jealous personal associations; or between Blok and Bely, or Briusov and Bely, in 'erotic triangles' powerfully coloured by mystical or occult apprehensions. While such collisions became the stuff of their art, the Symbolists also clashed as to the precise nature of art, the degree of its autonomy and its role in cultural and religious life. In 1910, Blok, Bely, Briusov and Ivanov engaged in a mutual polemics on the subject (with asides from the Merezhkovskys' camp and younger writers including Gumilev and Gorodetsky), generally referred to as the 'crisis of Symbolism'. Though this did not signify the end of Symbolist writing, it confirmed a parting of ways among the leading figures, who, having reached maturity, their reputations assured, in most cases having already produced their definitive work, were no longer inclined to function in concert. The way was opened for younger writers to form fresh associations and take new directions.

Foremost among the emergent post-Symbolist groups, even more thoroughly concentrated on poetry than their predecessors, were the Acmeists and Futurists (labels notwithstanding, it could reasonably be argued that these in fact constituted a 'third generation' of Symbolists). There was also, for instance, a substantial number of peasant poets, most notable among them Sergei Esenin and Nikolai Kliuev. Esenin, the most traditional, uncomplicated and broadly appealing of the modernists, drew heavily on Blok, Bely, and Afanas'ev's studies of Slavic ethnography to develop a rural myth of cosmic harmony, never recaptured as he projected himself through a series of masks, including as poet-prophet, 'tender hooligan' and 'last poet' of a village succumbing to industrialization, toward terminal alienation and suicide. Kliuev expressed a profound religious concern with national identity through a challenging combination of Orthodox and sectarian traditions, elements of pantheistic paganism, eroticism and mysticism, in an ornate language laden with obscure dialectisms and archaisms; his greatest achievement were his long poems, particularly his mythologization of the desecration of Russia by the evil barbarism of revolution in *The Burned Ruins* (*Pogorel'shchina*).

Mention should also be made here of Annensky, Maksimilian Voloshin and Mikhail Kuzmin, three considerable writers who emerged during the 1900s and occupy distinctively individual positions, intermediate between the second-generation Symbolists (whose religious mysticism they did not espouse), and the new groupings of the 1910s. Annensky, an important influence on both Acmeists and Futurists, treated muted but tormenting spiritual disquiet, alienation and unbelief through virtuoso linguistic and polysemantic constructions, with an emphasis on psychological analysis and grotesque irony. Voloshin, who described himself as a 'neo-realist', was a philosophical poet, at his best in long historio-sophical poems and cycles. Kuzmin, as versatile and prolific as any of the Symbolists, established a reputation with his novel, *Wings* (*Kryl'ia*), and first book of verse, *Nets* (*Seti*), as an amoral aesthete whose homoerotic themes and hedonistic delight in earthly trifles were elaborated with gracefully stylised elegance. He nevertheless proved an author of considerable profundity and originality, who developed a densely metaphoric poetics, structured primarily on an ostensible flux of emotional and intellectual association. This was masterfully embodied in his last published collection, *The Trout Breaks the Ice* (*Forel' razbivaet led*). Some lesser poets of the same years, such as Lozinsky or Komarovsky, similarly resist classification according to literary school.

The small Acmeist group included three major poets, Gumilev, Anna Akhmatova, and Osip Mandel'shtam, among its six original members. Gumilev, the main organizer and theoretician, did not reject Symbolism outright in the manifesto he published in January 1913, but described it as intemperately one-sided in its sterile pursuit of the 'unknown' (the *nepoznavaemoe*: that which was by definition unknowable). Acmeism would concentrate instead on 'this earth', with man firmly at its centre, and accordingly valued exact meaning over romantic vagueness and immoderate hyperbole. Whereas Symbolism sought cognition of the beyond, Acmeism in other words occupied itself with definition of the immediate: of the (complex, multi-faceted) individual in the total context, spatial, temporal, historical, physical and metaphysical, of the 'reality' (or world or God-given universe) in which he or she finds themselves. Though the practice of the movement's major exponents naturally overlapped, for Akhmatova in particular this meant an emphasis on human psychology, on the subtly detailed nuances of acutely observed, fundamentally 'ordinary' emotion, in the immensely popular poems of frustrated love with which she began her career. A striking contrast to the metaphysical intuitions of the extraordinary in Blok's Symbolist love poetry was underscored stylistically. Akhmatova instead cultivated restraint, epigrammatic concision, and the objectification of first person experience through the maintenance of ironic distance between poetic voice and lyric persona. Similar qualities informed the gradual switch of emphasis from interpersonal relations to the definition of relations between the private individual and history which was to become her great theme.

Gumilev began with dream and the imagination, focusing on inner experience as a path not to the beyond but to personal growth. Much taken at first with the primitive, exotic and archaic, his later interests were more tangibly cultural and historical, and he used the prism of different religious and philosophical traditions as an approach to the ultimate spiritual questions of self, God and the End which Acmeism naturally recognized as a fundamental part of man's existence. Mandel'shtam's chief focus was the location of the individual in relation to human culture, regarded not as a linear past but an endlessly renewable continuum: this was accessible through the creation and reception of art, and afforded triumphant transcendence of the meaninglessness of 'unconnected' solitude. The artist was in these contexts not élitist poet-seer but ordinary mortal and dedicated craftsman, and the clear-sighted vision and sense of responsibility to which (s)he had access led Gumilev to contend that Acmeism was more fully rounded and spiritually mature than Symbolism, the artistic legacy of which it sought to absorb and develop in a complex, organic poetics. This was initially illustrated, by both Mandel'shtam and Gumilev, with reference to their ideal of the 'difficult equilibrium' of the Gothic cathedral: a solidly earthbound object, constructed by man as a lasting monument to his God; not merely, as in Symbolism, an intrinsically unimportant backdrop to mystical experience, but an entity richly multi-faceted in its associations (spiritual, cultural, aesthetic, esoteric, physiological, etc.), each stone, like the words in a well-executed poem, in fully-weighted, intricate relation to all others.

Futurism was a much broader movement (a recent Russian anthology includes over fifty poets), and its history – of repeated groupings, regroupings and subdivisions – is correspondingly involved. At its centre were the so-called Cubo-Futurists, whose strident anti-aestheticism was famously encapsulated in the title of their collectively signed manifesto, 'A Slap in the Face of Public Taste' ('Poshchechina obshchestvennomu vkusu', 1912). At least notionally connected also by their urbanism (negative or positive) and primitivism, it was, however, the focus on experimentation with language that fundamentally united these poets in contradistinction to Symbolist metaphysics or Acmeist cultural constructs. Maiakovsky, in such memorable works as *Cloud in Trousers* (*Oblako v shtanakh*), *Backbone-Flute* (*Fleita-pozvonochnik*) and *Man* (*Chelovek*), exhibits an extra-ordinary originality in rhyme, rhythmic dynamism, and the use of concrete, realized metaphor, extending the conventional lyric situations of rejection in love to the length of full-blown narrative poems. The lyric sense of pain is compounded into a literally manic-obsessive intensity, with bouts of megalomaniac self-sufficiency alternating with infantile vulnerability, a sense of inferiority, or persecution by God, time and the entire world order; and the linguistic resources are comparably hyperbolic: a self-consciously virtuoso display of verbal and metrical ingenuity, stridently vulgar, subversive of proprieties, self-mockingly comic or grotesque, is the disturbingly incongruous vehicle for this unmistakable emotional pain.

Velimir Khlebnikov, the other major poet among the Cubo-Futurists, is more difficult, more concerned with experimentation as such, as his broad legacy of (often textologically chaotic) short poems and verse fragments, thirty long poems, dramas, prose fiction, mathematical, philological and historical researches, and idiosyncratic 'supertales' (*sverkhpovesti*) might suggest. He took a magical and esoteric view of language, delving into the past – world-historical and primitive, especially Slavic prehistorical – to discover the laws of time and project a utopian future in which a 'universal language' might transcend human discord. His rhythms, imagery and composition were built on startling shifts from the familiar, on baffling mixes of heterogeneous linguistic elements, including his own sometimes impenetrable neologisms, and dense, multifarious allusions. His poetry is nevertheless often extraordinarily suggestive, and sometimes profoundly beautiful. His root-based concern with a transrational language (*zaum'*) was self proclamatorially exploited by Aleksei Kruchenykh, whose arbitrary, 'expressive' sound-sequences, based on phonetic analogies and rhythm rather than Khlebnikovian morphology, were an ephemeral sensation and logical dead-end, destructive of meaning. A further bizarre Futurist experiment, as much visual as verbal, were the 'ferro-concrete' poems of the poet–aviator Vasilii Kamensky; while a milder endeavour to achieve fresh poetic directions through the renewal of lexico-semantically based poetic technique was enough also to associate with Futurism the 'Centrifuge' group, including Aseev, Bobrov and, with an exceptional interest in natural process, the young Boris Pasternak. An extravagant poeticization of the lexical stock of bourgeois-consumerist vulgarity, combined with a strong, innovative rhythmic sense, likewise confirm the much-maligned 'Ego-Futurist', Igor' Severianin, as a legitimate member of the broader movement.

Unlike in the West, the First World War did not have a substantial impact on Russian literature. There was much third-rate patriotic verse, rather less unremarkable short fiction, and occasional pacifist poetry by Acmeists and Futurists. It is doubtless significant that the army was essentially peasant, and established writers, with the notable exception of Gumilev, generally avoided active combat. The revolutions of 1917, by contrast, altered the entire complexion of Russian literature. Though a few writers, like the Merezhkovskys, deplored Bolshevism from the outset and emigrated as early as 1919, most were prepared, at least for a while, to see what course events would take. The most immediate literary reaction to the upheavals of 1917 was a spate of longer poems – a notable shift, therefore, from lyric to epic – by Esenin, Bely, Kliuev and, most notably, Blok's *The Twelve* (*Dvenadtsat'*). All in their different ways were looking for a revolution of the spirit to complement the political cataclysm (a yearning frequently echoed by their compatriots), and they became briefly associated with Ivanov-Razumnik's 'Scythianism', an affirmation of Russia's primitive-chaotic Asiatic identity. Blok famously lost his inspiration thereafter. His ideals once more unrealized, he felt unable to 'breathe', and died in 1921. Of the other Symbolists, Bely remained the most prolific. After emigrating briefly from 1921–3, he devoted substantial efforts to a new trilogy of 'Moscow' novels (1926–34) and – following the retrospective reconstruction of the Silver Age in his important narrative poem of 1921 *The First Encounter* (*Pervoe svidanie*) – produced copious memoirs, including another imposing trilogy. (The genre of memoirs commemorating the Silver Age became widespread: it was cultivated in Russia by secondary figures such as Piast, Benedikt Livshits and Chulkov; and from the geographical as well as temporal distance of emigration, by major and minor figures alike: Marina Tsvetaeva, Vladislav Khodasevich and Georgii Ivanov, as well as Berberova, Makovsky, Odoevtseva and many others.) Briusov's late excursion into 'scientific poetry', or after major sonnet cycles of 1919–24, Viacheslav Ivanov's *Roman Diary* (*Rimskii dnevnik*) of 1944, were other Symbolist works of intrinsic interest; but these poets were to die in relative obscurity and neglect: Briusov and Sologub in somewhat harrowing conditions at home; Bal'mont and Ivanov abroad.

The younger generation had a more difficult time. The poetry of the Acmeists gained immeasurably in profundity as they saw the 'world culture' which they championed become threatened by chaos and systematically dismantled by the state. After Gumilev's execution on insubstantial charges as he reached a new level of creative power, and an anguished period of poetic silence during the 1920s, Mandel'shtam, too, sacrificed his life for persisting in the 1930s with the great, unpublishable poetry of his Moscow and Voronezh Notebooks. Akhmatova devoted what her first biographer, Amanda Haight, aptly described as her grim life of 'poetic pilgrimage' to preserving the memory and culture of those who disappeared around her, and in her masterpiece, *Poem without a Hero* (*Poema bez geroia*), revisited the Silver Age with nostalgia and strict moral censure. Esenin, a perpetual misfit, (apparently) killed himself in 1925; other peasant poets, Kliuev, Klychkov and Oreshin, perished in the Terror. The Futurists, by contrast, were more congenial and sympathetic to the new order. Yet Khlebnikov died in poverty in 1922; Maiakovsky struggled between ardent, selfless devotion to the political cause and continuing private pain, and with the exception of *About This* (*Pro eto*) produced little to rival the freshness and vigour of before. The same applied to many of his lesser colleagues, who published prolifically through the 1920s, flirted with notions of an artistic dictatorship of the avant garde, of mass-participation and mass-consumption art, and the social commission; and strongly influenced the next period of Soviet verse. A notable offshoot of Futurism were the Imaginists, formed in 1919, who rejected the Futurists' political involvement and vaguely proclaimed the image rather than the word as the centre of their own anti-aesthetic programme. Shershenevich and Mariengof, as well as Esenin at his most experimental, produced worthwhile verse under the programme's aegis.

Though revolution had brought a new upsurge of ephemeral poetic groups and a large-scale output of thematically monotonous proletarian poetry, technically heavily indebted to Symbolism, there was a clear shift of literary emphasis by the early 1920s. The legacy of the Silver Age – and primarily of Bely – was now best embodied in the prose of Vaginov, Babel', Pil'niak, Zamiatin, and later Olesha, to some extent in the Serapion Brotherhood, and even in less talented, more politically orthodox writers such as Gladkov. Its last substantial reflection in Russia might be considered the absurdist writings of Kharms or Vvedensky. In emigration, the neo-classical manner of the Acmeists was predominant, and was put to new, poignantly moving purpose by Adamovich and, above all, Georgii Ivanov.

Two other poets who defy classification were otherwise the Silver Age's last and most striking representatives abroad. Khodasevich drew idiosyncratically on Symbolism, Acmeism and even Futurism to give voice to his horror at the misery and banality of life, arguably inspired by a sense of Gnostic exile, in precise, disciplined, ironic verse. His despair was translated into poetic silence some ten years before his death. Marina Tsvetaeva combined brilliant linguistic invention, distantly reminiscent of Futurism, and a penchant for classical and cultural mythologemes occasionally reminiscent of Acmeism, in a uniquely passionate, profoundly idiosyncratic, romantic articulation of poetic values and personal drama. Like so many of her literary generation, she died an unnatural death in cruel circumstances, driven to suicide in 1941, two years after returning to Russia.

FURTHER READING

Clowes, Edith. *The Revolution of Moral Consciousness: Nietzsche in Russian Literature, 1890–1914*, De Kalb, Illinois: Northern Illinois University Press, 1988.

Doherty, Justin. *The Acmeist Movement in Russian Poetry: Culture and the Word*, Oxford: Clarendon Press; New York: Oxford University Press, 1995.

Donchin, Georgette. *The Influence of French Symbolism on Russian Poetry*, The Hague: Mouton, 1958.

Elsworth, John (ed.) *The Silver Age in Russian Literature*, London: Macmillan; New York: St Martin's Press, 1992.

Gibian, George and Tjalsma, H.W. (eds) *Russian Modernism: Culture and the Avant-Garde, 1900–1930*, Ithaca: Cornell University Press, 1976.

Hutchings, Stephen C. *Russian Modernism: The Transfiguration of the Everyday*, Cambridge: Cambridge University Press, 1997.

Lawton, Anna (ed.) *Russian Futurism Through Its Manifestoes, 1912–1928*, Ithaca: Cornell University Press, 1988.

Markov, Vladimir. *Russian Futurism: A History*, Berkeley: University of California Press, 1968.

Markov, Vladimir. *Russian Imagism, 1919–1924*, 2 vols., Giessen: Wilhelm Schmitz, 1980.

McMillin, Arnold (ed.) *Symbolism and After: Essays on Russian Poetry in Honour of Georgette Donchin*, London: Bristol Classical Press, 1992.

Peterson, Ronald E. (ed.) *The Russian Symbolists: An Anthology of Critical and Theoretical Writings*, Ann Arbor: Ardis, 1986.

Polonsky, Rachel. *English Literature and the Russian Aesthetic Renaissance*, Cambridge: Cambridge University Press, 1998.

Proffer, Carl R. and Proffer, Ellendea (eds) *The Silver Age of Russian Culture: An Anthology*, Ann Arbor: Ardis, 1975.

Proffer, Ellendea and Proffer, Carl R. (eds) *The Ardis Anthology of Russian Futurism*, Ann Arbor: Ardis, 1980.

Pyman, Avril. *A History of Russian Symbolism*, Cambridge and New York: Cambridge University Press, 1994.

Rabinowitz, Stanley (ed. and trans.) *The Noise of Change: Russian Literature and the Critics* (1891–1917), Ann Arbor: Ardis, 1986.

Richardson, William *'Zolotoe Runo' and Russian Modernism, 1905–1910*, Ann Arbor: Ardis, 1986.

Ronen, Omry. *The Fallacy of the Silver Age in Twentieth-Century Russian Literature*, Amsterdam: Harwood Academic Publishers, 1997.

Williams, Robert C. *Artists in Revolution: Portraits of the Russian Avant-Garde, 1905–1925*, Bloomington: Indiana University Press, 1977.

13

WOMEN'S WRITING IN RUSSIA

CATRIONA KELLY

Russian women have been writing, in the broadest sense, if not producing literature, for many centuries. Female signatures have been found on some of the earliest documents in the Russian language yet discovered – the letters written on birchbark by inhabitants of Novgorod in the eleventh, twelfth, and thirteenth centuries. Another 'private' genre of writing practised by women (though much more rarely) was autobiography. But the ecclesiastical and political nature of much pre-Petrine writing (sermons, hagiography, chronicles) meant that women were largely excluded from the public tradition, and that the named 'bookmen' (*knizhniki*) of the medieval period included no women whatever.

The exclusion of women from public *pis'mennost'* (writing) in medieval times delayed their entry into the literary world, once that had been established in Russia. It was not until the second half of the eighteenth century that women began contributing to the secular, westernized, tradition of literature as such – that is, writing as more than purely functional communication – which had then been established in Russia for about a hundred years. However, from the 1750s various factors combined positively to encourage women's participation in literature. The importation of western treatises of moral education and good breeding, such as François Fénelon's *Instruction for the Education of a Daughter* (*De L'Éducation des filles*) of 1687, meant that reading was now accepted as an important part of young women's intellectual development. The curriculum of Catherine's model school for 'young noblewomen', Smol'nyi Institute, included western and Russian literary classics, and the cultivation of the women in Catherine's court was to be remarked on by foreign visitors during the late eighteenth century.

Accordingly, in the late eighteenth and early nineteenth centuries a number of women, mostly well-educated aristocrats, did indeed begin contributing to the development of Russian letters. Several of them were the sisters, daughters or wives of male writers. Ekaterina Sumarokova (1746–97) was the daughter of the poet and playwright Aleksandr Sumarokov; Elizaveta Kheraskova (*c*.1740–1809) and Ekaterina Urusova (1747–*c*.1817) the wife and cousin respectively of Mikhail Kheraskov, author of the epic *Rossiiada*. The connections of these and comparable women, such as the Svin'ina sisters and Mar'ia Sushkova (1752–1803), facilitated their entrée to literary journals, some of which, for example *A Pleasant and Instructive Manner of Passing the Time* (*Priiatnoe i poleznoe preprovozhdenie vremeni*), and Nikolai Karamzin's *Aonidy*, published a number of original texts and translations by women, in keeping with the Sentimentalist cult of the 'fair sex' as the arbiters of virtue and taste.

Though some late eighteenth- and early nineteenth-century women poets were no more than dilettante rhymesters, some, for example Urusova and Kheraskova, and later Aleksandra Murzina and Aleksandra Magnitskaia (active in the 1790s), Mar'ia Pospelova (1780–1805) and Anna Volkova (1781–1834), were genuinely talented individuals, the best of whose work displays intelligence, wit, and technical facility. The most determined, the most prolific, as well as probably the most talented was Anna Bunina (1774–1829), the first woman writer to live by her pen. Though lacking the social advantages of Urusova and Kheraskova, Bunina by sustained effort turned herself into an erudite Neoclassical poet, the author of epics as well as lyric verse, whose work includes some of the earliest genuinely autobiographical poetry by Russian writers of either gender. Another remarkable figure was the short-lived, but prodigious Elisaveta Kul'man (1808–25), who had a command of classical languages as well as several modern ones, and who was the author of interesting Neoclassical verse, including a tribute to the Greek poet Corinna, much of it written in unrhymed 'Pindaric' stanzas.

Besides poetry, women writers produced didactic drama (Elizaveta Titova as well as the late eighteenth century's most famous woman writer, Catherine II), and fiction. A good deal of the latter was feeble indeed, consisting of sprawlingly-plotted novels and didactic contes; typical was the work of Mariia Izvekova (1790s–1830), author, among other works, of *Milena, or A Rare Example of Magnanimity* (*Milena, ili redkii primer velikodushiia*, 1806), whose titles bespeak their sentimental and moralistic content. However, Russian nationals writing in French also produced some more distinguished works, notably Julie (or Juliane) de Krüdener's *Valérie* (1803), famous in its day throughout Europe.

The rise of Pushkinian Romanticism in the 1820s had contradictory effects on women's writing. The new understanding of 'genius' as an extraordinary individual talent, rather than the individual guiding spirit of every human being, led to questioning of whether a woman could be a 'genius'. In his review of Mariia Zhukova's first collection of stories in 1838, Belinsky argued that women were by nature unfitted for the composition of great imaginative works. Such arguments inhibited the writing of romantic poetry by women; only when Romanticism had become a marginal trend, in the 1840s, when the hegemony of realism began, could the notion of 'genius' be appropriated by women. Karolina Pavlova (1807–93), the outstanding poet of the 1840s and 1850s, made full use of her new opportunities in poems such as 'Life Calls Us' ('Zovet nas zhizn'', 1846) and 'Three Souls' ('Tri dushi', 1845) and also in the remarkable prose and verse tale *A Double Life* (*Dvoinaia zhizn'*, 1848), reminiscent of Christina Rossetti's *Maud* (also written in the late 1840s, though not published until 1897). However, in the 1820s and 1830s, a good deal of women's poetry consisted of melodious but not very original confessions of love, static meditations on nature, and other kinds of salon verse. Yet some writers, such as Nadezhda Teplova (1814–48), were able to manipulate salon stereotypes in order to produce more distinguished work, which questioned the notion that women's primary task was to inspire men, and included self-conscious evocations of the act of writing.

The correlate of the idea that women were naturally limited in imaginative sweep was the notion that they were particularly fitted for the composition of prose. The years after 1820, therefore, led to an upsurge of prose writing by women. From the late 1830s in particular, writers such as Elena Gan (1814–42), Evdokiia Rostopchina (1812–58), and Mariia Zhukova (1804–55) used the 'marginal hero' conventions of the romantic 'society tale' in order to articulate resentment about the unequal status of women in Russian society – a fiercely held feeling since the late eighteenth century – in a way that was less abstract and schematic than before, and which gave closer attention to the fates of women from outside the metropolitan aristocracy. The rise of prose also fostered the development of an interesting tradition among women poets that one could describe as 'prose in verse'. Poets such as Iuliia Zhadovskaia (1824–83) and Rostopchina, again, wrote first-person confessional poetry that employed obvious masks, and (in the case of Rostopchina's *An Unknown Romance* [*Neizvestnyi roman*]) adopted a narrative frame such as was used in the romantic novella, in order to distance and ironize the sentiments expressed.

After the emigration of Karolina Pavlova from Russia in 1853, poetry went into a decline lasting nearly four decades. Though genres such as 'prose in verse' (see above), political poetry (the minor poet Anna Barykova [1839–93] was the author of some fine satires), and religious verse (whose main exponent was the prolific Elizaveta Shakhova [1822–99]) saw some activity, the years between 1850 and 1890 were very much the 'age of prose' for women writers, and of politically committed prose at that.

In the early 1840s, Russian radicals, following in the wake of French Utopian socialism, had begun taking an interest in the 'woman question'. The domination by these radicals of the 'thick journals', literary and political monthlies, the key forums for political debate, meant that issues such as education for women and the liberation of wives and daughters from the shackles of male domination in the family began to play an even greater role in women's writing than before. With few exceptions, women tended to express their views on the 'woman question' in literature and reviews rather than in essays, which gave much of their work a strong didactic bent. Perhaps the most popular type of narrative in the 1850s and 1860s was a 'provincial tale', in which an unmarried young girl from a middling country gentry background struggles against the restricted future conventional expectation has in mind for her, sometimes with the help of a sympathetic man who lends her books and counsel. In one of the most striking of such tales, *The Schoolgirl* (*Pansionerka*, 1861), by Nadezhda Khvoshchinskaia (1824–89), the heroine, Lelen'ka, is successful in her fight against intellectual fossilization. Repudiating both the old-fashioned education offered at her school, the minor civil servant chosen as a husband for her by her appalling mother, she departs to celibacy and a life of self-sufficient labour in St Petersburg. Not all narratives offered such stirring models of self-betterment: in some, such as *A Woman's Lot* (*Zhenskaia dolia*, 1862) by Avdot'ia Panaeva (1819–93) or *Polly's Story* (*Istoriia Poli*, 1866), and *Another Broken Heart* (*Eshche razbitoe serdtse*, 1862) by Sof'ia Soboleva

(1840–84), the weight of convention proves too strong for rebellion to be successful. But the association of education and work with liberation was seldom questioned, and, following the canons of didactic prose established in the eighteenth century, the heroine was usually directly contrasted with her negative counter-image, a frivolous and coquettish sister or friend relentlessly pursuing the conventional feminine reward – marriage to a single man of good fortune. Overwhelmingly, it was young unmarried women, rather than middle-aged ones with family responsibilities, that interested women writers, though in the work of Evgeniia Tur (1815–92), such as *Antonina* (1851), the problems of maternity were sometimes considered as well.

Besides such narratives of women's liberation, women writers of the day also produced some outstanding pieces of regional prose (especially notable here were Nadezhda Sokhanskaia [1823–84], also the author of a superb confessional autobiography, and Aleksandra Kobiakova [1823–92], writer of interesting stories about provincial merchant women). The tradition of adopting masculine pseudonyms espoused by many writers in the 1850s and 1860s also allowed women, if they wanted, to raise their voices in the debate about topical questions that had nothing to do with the 'woman question' as such, including serf emancipation (Sof'ia Khvoshchinskaia [1828–65] in her *A Domestic Idyll of Olden Times* [*Domashniaia idilliia ne nashego vremeni*], 1863), and monasticism (Anna Korvin-Krukovskaia [1843–87] in her *Mikhail*, 1864).

The development from the 1860s of women's liberation groups organized by women did not have a strong direct impact on women's writing, though some of the realist writers of the 1890s, such as Ol'ga Shapir (1850–1916), were feminist activists, and others, such as Ekaterina Letkova (1856–1937), sympathetic to at least some of its aims. However, participants in the women's movement rarely figured in the writings of these or of other women authors. Much more significant as a force in women's fiction was Populism, whose effects began to be felt from the late 1870s: the 'positive heroines' of didactic narratives were now often women of peasant or working-class stock, with neurotic upper- or middle-class ladies sometimes acting as foils. One of the earliest examples of the new trend was the story *The Turkish Soldier's Wife* (*Akhmetkina zhena*, 1881) by Valentina Dmitrieva (1859–1947), of peasant origin herself. In the 1890s, Sof'ia Smirnova (1852–1921), Iuliia Iakovleva, pseudonymously 'Bezrodnaia' (1858–1910), and Anastasiia Verbitskaia (1861–1928), besides Shapir and Letkova, were all to produce interesting examples of such stories about working women, downtrodden or resilient. Now that employment opportunities had expanded, stories about professional women were another popular genre; the fact that women's employment often remained low-status and unfulfilling was confronted, for example, in Letkova's story *The Holiday* (*Otdykh*, 1896), in which an unfulfilled white-collar worker puts an end to her life during a river cruise. The prevalence of suicide, murder, and other extreme events often gave work by women naturalists (as with their male contemporaries) a melodramatic coloration, which was also observable in the many narratives in which questions of sexual liberation were explored. A key text of the 1890s was Mariia Krestovskaia's anti-*Kreutzer Sonata* novel *The Actress* (*Artistka*, 1891), which showed a heroine torn between fulfilment as an artist and as a sexual being. The novel was the forerunner to such notorious early twentieth-century bestsellers as Verbitskaia's *The Keys to Happiness* (*Kliuchi schast'ia*, 1909–13) and *The Anger of Dionysus* (*Gnev Dionisa*, 1910) by Evdokiia Nagrodskaia (1866–1930).

Another vehicle for debates on professionalism, if less often on sexuality, in the 1880s and 1890s was the memoir. Some women who had achieved outstanding success in their professions, such as Sof'ia Kovalevskaia, pioneering woman mathematician (1850–91), left memoirs of their lives which, while not explicitly 'feminist' in orientation, were all the same remarkable works of female self-assertion.

An entirely contrary trend in the 1890s was represented by the incipient Decadent movement in Russia. Like her male counterpart, the Decadent heroine jettisoned the Russian intelligentsia's treasured ideals of self-sacrifice to the collective good in favour of self-fulfilment, often of a sexually hedonistic kind. Mariia Bashkirtseva, a budding painter whose diary was posthumously published in 1887, three years after her death at the age of twenty-six, became famous all over Europe. Translated from the original French into Russian in 1892, the diary had an enormous impact on at least two generations of Russian women; those influenced or inspired by it included the young Marina Tsvetaeva. Echoes of Bashkirtseva's neurotic self-aggrandisement can also be heard in the powerful verse of Mirra Lokhvitskaia (1869–1905), who expressed a bold sexuality new to Russian women's poetry. But the towering woman writer of Russian decadence was Zinaida Hippius (1869–1945), whose artful and disturbing poetry of moral transgression pioneered the liberating androgyny that was to become fashionable among most early twentieth-century women poets. Posing now as an egotistical man, now as a demonic woman, Hippius was also one of the first woman poets to exploit Russian Symbolism's new interest, after 1900, in specifically feminine prophetic voices – the oracle, the soothsayer, the wise woman. Besides poetry, she was the author of interesting, often distinctly Gothic, stories, and of perhaps the first major dramatic works by a Russian woman writer. *The Red Poppy* (*Makov tsvet*, 1908) and *The Green Ring* (*Zelenoe kol'tso*, 1914, staged by Meierkhol'd in 1915) are powerful evocations of the claustrophobic atmosphere in the early twentieth-century Russian intelligentsia, in which armed uprisings, intellectual disputation, and romantic outpouring alike prove futile and redundant, and fond hopes in the capacity of the 'younger generation' to jettison the past are the only consolation for disillusioned observers in their middle years.

Hippius was the first swallow of what was to prove a remarkable summer for women writers. Between 1900 and 1920, countless women took up the pen as poets, prosaists, memoirists, and occasionally dramatists. The Symbolist cult of the 'eternal feminine' could pose dangers in that it supposed the 'feminine' to exist for the delight or edification of a contemplating male. But the more intelligent women writers, such as Adelaida Gertsyk (1874–1925), Liubov' Stolitsa (1884–1934),

Poliksena Solov'eva (1867–1924), and Liudmila Vil'kina (pseudonym of Izabella Vil'ken, 1873–1920), were fully aware of the threats, and wore their 'eternal feminine' masks ironically and self-consciously. Women's capacity for ironic distance was enhanced by the so-called 'crisis of Symbolism' (1910–13), in which young representatives of would-be post-Symbolist schools attacked what had by then become the literary establishment for the stereotypicality of its themes and the poverty of its stylistic apparatus. Though women poets were relatively poorly represented in the various Futurist movements, some (for example Elena Guro, 1877–1913) were encouraged by the new taste for primitivism in poetry and painting to publish work in an original vein of childish naivety (see particularly *The Little Camels of the Sky* [*Nebesnye verbliuzhata*] 1914.) Among the Acmeists, emphasis on the centrality of (judiciously aestheticized) everyday experience led to a revival of 'prose in verse', of which Anna Akhmatova soon proved an out- standingly talented practitioner. Whatever the passing fashions in types of prose and theme, the new emphasis everywhere on 'the word as such' (*slovo kak takovoe*) was helpful to women poets, whose historical weakness, as a group, had been the all too artless outpouring of feeling. A particularly impressive example of a poet who benefited from the new emphasis on 'the word as such' was Sofiia Parnok (1885–1933).

The new stress on the importance of craftsmanship was not without significance in the quite different tradition of realist prose, where writers such as Liubov' Gurevich (1866–1940), Lidiia Avilova (1864–1943), and Varvara Tsekhovskaia (writing as 'Ol'nem', 1872–1941) worked with more innovative techniques than their predecessors, such as stream-of-consciousness and mixed perspective. In the early stories of Ol'ga Forsh (1873–1961), populist subjects appeared to radically novel effect through the employment of material from folklore and folk-beliefs (*Hunting the Fire-Bird* [*Za zhar-ptitsei*] 1910). But perhaps the most original writer was Lidiia Zinov'eva-Annibal (1866–1907), whose extraordinary short-story cycle, *The Tragic Menagerie* (*Tragicheskii zverinets*, 1907), the first-person narrative of a coldly observant, calculating, and self-indulgent adolescent girl, suggests that the author might have developed, had she lived, into one of Russia's foremost modernist writers.

For various reasons, the Bolshevik Revolution in 1917, while by no means stifling women writers' activities, did not always nurture the promising traditions that had developed in the three decades before its occurrence. The 'bourgeois feminist' movement – an insulting catch-all term used to denote all the various non-socialist groupings, ignoring considerable differences between these – was one casualty of the Bolsheviks' action against oppositional political groupings of all kinds. The women's liberation agenda was set according to the Bolsheviks' own programme of legal and economic reform and political consciousness-raising. Responsibility for the latter was assigned in particular to the women's section of the Party, which was founded in 1919 and came to be known as the *Zhenotdel*. Its determined organizers, unlike their feminist predecessors, made themselves felt in fiction as well as in life; one of them was, for example, given a leading role in a 1927 production novel, *The Saw Mill* (*Lesozavod*), by Anna Karavaeva (1893–1979). The 'new woman', a socially and sexually emancipated individual in sympathy with revolutionary ideals, if not invariably a Party official, also figured widely, most famously in *Love of Worker Bees* (*Liubov' pchel trudovykh*, 1923), a collection of short stories by Aleksandra Kollontai (1872–1952), Commissar for Social Welfare from 1917 to 1922 and politically the most powerful woman writer in Russian history, with the exception of Catherine II. Like pre-revolutionary realism, the new fiction of women's liberation was often openly didactic, and the 'new woman' had her negative counterpart in the 'backward' bourgeois or peasant woman, hostile to communist ideology and self-servingly attached to her children, husband, lover, personal appearance, religious beliefs, or other such reprehensible object. No wonder that the more adventurous writers, such as Lidiia Seifullina (1889–1954), often preferred to adopt a masculine viewpoint in their work.

After 1930, when Stalin declared the 'woman question' solved, and closed down the *Zhenotdel*, its activists disappeared from fiction, but the 'new woman' continued to be a popular figure until the mid-1930s, when increasing disapproval of extramarital intercourse and other such 'promiscuous' behaviour meant that fiction, like ideology, began to place a new emphasis on women's duties as wives and mothers. In the late 1930s and the 1940s, the main characters of factory-and-collective-farm novels by writers such as Karavaeva, Antonina Koptiaeva (b. 1909), Galina Nikolaeva (real name Volianskaia, 1911–63), and Vera Panova (1905–73) were often women in full-time employment and taking an active role in Party business who nonetheless managed to work the 'second shift' of domestic duties smilingly and uncomplainingly. Though equality of women continued to be proclaimed as a Soviet achievement, the new emphasis on rigidly defined gender roles in the home now made the proclamations ring hollow. Wartime propaganda and fiction briefly revived a feistier kind of heroine (for example, the partisan fighter Zoia Kosmodemianskaia), but in a manner that made clear the enormity and 'unfemininity' of such behaviour. Ironically, one of the most important texts produced by a woman in the post-revolutionary period, and published in 1930–31 just before the imposition of socialist realism, was the autobiographical trilogy, *The Little Caftan* (*Kaftanchik*), *The Polack* (*Liakh*), and *The Break* (*Otryv*) by Vera Gedroits (1876–1932). So far from observing traditional boundaries in these books, Gedroits, who wrote using the male first name Sergei, suggested that conventional sex denominations might be wholly illusory (after her brother's death, the heroine, Vera, 'becomes' Sergei). The trilogy, which the publisher's reviewer, the writer Konstantin Fedin, compared to Pasternak's autobiographical writing, is one of the outstanding achievements in women's prose writing of any period.

In poetry, cultural centralization had still more unfortunate effects. During the early 1920s, a certain limited pluralism was in evidence, with 'bourgeois' writers such as Anna Akhmatova or Sofiia Parnok, or, before her emigration, Marina Tsvetaeva (1892–1941), as well as many less prominent figures, able to publish their work with hindrance, either in Russia or abroad. But attacks on such poetry as 'backward' were frequent (for example, in Trotsky's *Literature and Revolution*

[*Literatura i revoliutsiia*] of 1923). Furthermore, the new order did not generate any significant tradition of revolutionary poetry by women. With rare exceptions, such as Anna Barkova's *Woman* (*Zhenshchina*, 1922), a collection of poems about revolutionary female types whose callow romanticism later embarrassed a Barkova grown wise and cynical about revolutionary blood-letting, women made no contributions to the development of proletarian poetry. And Mariia Shkapskaia (1891–1952), while committed to the revolutionary cause from the start, produced, in her poetry, fierce critiques of Civil War violence, rather than comfortable endorsements of Bolshevik policy; in *Reality* (*Iav'*, 1923), for example, she offers a representation of a political execution that only external evidence (the place and date of composition) indicates must be a White atrocity, rather than a Red one. All this, as well as women's under-representation in key organizations such as RAPP (Association of Proletarian Writers), meant that women poets were particularly vulnerable after cultural centralization began. Akhmatova, Parnok, Anna Radlova (1891–1949), Elizaveta Polonskaia (real name Movshezon, 1890–1969), Mariia Shkapskaia, and Anna Barkova represent only the better-known instances of talented poets who stopped publishing, and in some cases writing, poetry in the late 1920s. The pity was the greater in that officially-published poetry by women was generally undistinguished in formal and intellectual terms. In the 1930s, poets such as Ol'ga Berggol'ts (1910–1975) and Margarita Aliger (1915–92) published some energetic, if rather inchoate, poems about the life of the 'new woman'. However, their efforts were quickly overtaken by the policy changes of the mid-1930s, which made motherhood the proper subject of poetry as much as prose. Though the war allowed some women poets (Vera Inber [1890–1972], as well as Ol'ga Berggol'ts) respite from the duty to represent heroines of monolithic socialist virtue, the effect of cultural centralization was to push most serious women's poetry underground. Even talented poets, such as Vera Zviagintseva (1894–1972), published mostly mediocre verse in the Stalin period.

Most of the better work by Soviet women poets came from the 'internal emigration': it was done by writers such as Akhmatova, Barkova, Parnok, Mariia Petrovykh (1908–79), and Elena Tager (1895–1964), writing without hope of immediate publication. During the late 1920s and early 1930s, Parnok produced some of her best poems, including some unique celebrations of lesbian love. In the 1930s, 1940s, and early 1950s, some remarkable poetry was composed in prison camps by incarcerated writers, including Tager and Barkova; a selection later appeared in the series Prisoner Poets of the Gulag ('Poety – uzniki Gulaga'), put out by the Vozvrashchenie organization in Moscow. Literary distinction was also achieved by many of the poets living in actual, physical, emigration from Russia, in Paris, Berlin, Helsinki, and other centres of the Russian diaspora. Undoubtedly the pivotal figure was Marina Tsvetaeva, the best of whose work, including superb narrative poems and plays as well as lyric verse, dates from her early years in emigration, 1921–6. But there were also a number of other talented women poets in the diaspora, among them Raisa Blokh (1899–1943), Vera Bulich (1898–1954), Sofiia Pregel' (1902–72), Alla Golovina (1909–87), and Anna

Prismanova (1892–1960), all of whom produced well-crafted and original verse that eschewed the tendency, rather marked among other émigrées, to offer more or less well-composed reassortments of Akhmatovian themes and images. In prose, émigrées were less remarkable by force of numbers but two writers in particular did interesting work. Teffi (1872–1952), a very popular humourist before the Revolution, lost some of her light-heartedness in emigration, and embarked on a series of poignant, satirical, and sometimes bitter portraits of life in exile that are among the most interesting prose produced in the Russian diaspora. Nina Berberova (1901–93), while at most a mediocre poet, was a talented prose writer whose work includes elegant novellas of émigré society and an accomplished autobiography, *The Italics Are Mine* (*Kursiv moi*, 1969). Less distinguished in literary terms were the autobiographies of Irina Odoevtseva (real name Iraida Geinike, 1895–1990), *On the Banks of the Neva* (*Na beregakh Nevy*, 1967) and *On the Banks of the Seine* (*Na beregakh Seny*, 1983), which, however, offer striking impressions of literary life during the first years of Soviet rule in the Paris emigration.

Given the peculiar restrictions that socialist realism had imposed on women writers, there was a certain historical justice in the fact that several of them played a prominent part in de-Stalinizing the Writers' Union after 1953. At the Union's second Congress in 1954, Ol'ga Forsh acted as symbolic figurehead, while Ol'ga Berggol'ts made a memorable speech denouncing the pompous inhumanity of Soviet literature. Women also made notable contributions to the recovery of history that began with Khrushchev's assaults on Stalin's crimes at the twentieth Party Congress in 1956. Two central works were Evgeniia Ginzburg's *Krutoi marshrut* (translated into English as *Journey into the Whirlwind* and *Within the Whirlwind*) and Nadezhda Mandel'shtam's *Vospominaniia* (translated into English as *Hope Against Hope* and *Hope Abandoned*), both written in the early 1960s, which circulated widely in manuscript prior to their publication in the west (the first volumes came out in 1967 and 1970 respectively). These were followed by Lidiia Chukovskaia's justly famous diary-biography *The Akahmatova Journals* (*Zapiski ob Anne Akhmatovoi*, 1976–80). All these works appeared for the first time in their author's native country during the late 1980s, when Mikhail Gorbachev's policy of glasnost also gave opportunities to previously unpublished women memoirists. A 1989 collection edited by S. Vilensky, *The Pain Lasts* (*Dodnes' tiagoteet*), contained accounts, many very powerful, by more than thirty women of life in Stalin's camps. During the 1980s and 1990s, women who spent the Stalin years in more fortunate circumstances, such as Raisa Orlova and Elena Bonner, have offered striking chronicles of growing up under the leader's rule, while Larisa Vasil'eva's popular biography *The Kremlin Wives* (*Kremlevskie zheny*, 1992), was both a luridly readable bestseller and a pioneer in a genre new to Russian literary culture.

Though by no means all women writers wholeheartedly welcomed de-Stalinization (the veteran Marietta Shaginian [1888–1982] being among those who urged caution), women writers were notable participants in the revival of critical realism that was ushered in by the Thaw. Khrushchev's announcement in 1956 that discrimination against women was still a problem was crucial, since it allowed the 'woman question' to be posed once more. Issues such as women's struggles at work, and especially their need to work the 'double shift' as housekeepers and carers, were explored by writers such as Irina Grekova (pseudonym of Elena Ventsel', b. 1907), Maiia Ganina (b. 1927), and Natal'ia Baranskaia (b. 1908). Baranskaia's *A Week Like Any Other* (*Nedelia kak nedelia*), a refreshingly honest account of an ordinary working mother's week, created a furore when first published in 1969. Critical realism remained a central genre for women writers into the 1980s, though some, particularly Liudmila Petrushevskaia (b. 1938), became more ambitious in their formal approach. Petrushevskaia, also a major playwright, made extensive use of internal monologue in her fiction, and in stories such as *The Time: Night* (*Vremia noch'*, 1992), employed devices such as the 'found text' in a way that clouded the transparency, and problematized the accessibility to which women's realism has so often pretended. The realism of the 1960s and 1970s had sometimes expressed nostalgia for the 'traditional' femininity supposedly 'destroyed' by communist rule, but here too Petrushevskaia was an innovator, suggesting – for example in *Our Crowd* (*Svoi krug*, 1988) – that women's much-celebrated role as carers for others often turns them into downtrodden drudges, self-serving manipulators, or bullies. Another interesting and innovative realist was Nina Katerli (b. 1934), who made free use of fantasy in works such as *The Monster* (*Chudovishche*, 1983); *Polina* (1984) has attracted a good deal of interest among western feminists because of its imaginative revision of the Soviet ideal of maternity. Katerli was also the author of stimulating essays, including a dramatic account of her indictment for libel by right-wing nationalists.

The forty years since 1956 also witnessed a tremendous renaissance in women's poetry, in which the rediscovery of Akhmatova's work was a significant moment. Though Akhmatova's commemoration of the Great Terror, *Requiem* (*Rekviem*) written 1935–43, remained unacceptable to Soviet officialdom until 1987, the cycle, like the memoirs of Ginzburg or Mandel'shtam, was circulated privately before being published in the West in 1963. *Requiem* apart, a good number of Akhmatova's lyric poems did see the light of day in the late 1950s and early 1960s, most significantly in the substantial collection *The Flight of Time* (*Beg vremeni*, 1965). Contemporaneously, Marina Tsvetaeva's poetry also started reaching the Soviet public for the first time; a landmark was the publication of a critical edition of her work, *Lyric and Narrative Poems* (*Stikhotvoreniia i poemy*) in 1965. The reappearance of these two 'ancestors' strengthened the emerging talents of such young poets as Bella Akhmadulina (b. 1937), Novella Matveeva (b. 1934), and Iunna Morits (b. 1937), who all later established themselves as major writers. In the 1960s and especially the 1970s and 1980s, women's poetry has been a significant and recognized force in Russian literature, with such outstanding 1970s debutantes as Elena Shvarts (b. 1948) and Ol'ga Sedakova (b. 1949) joined by promising younger writers such as Mariia Avvakumova and the religious poet Oles'ia Nikolaeva (b. 1955).

On the whole, post-Thaw poets were more adventurous, in technical terms, than their contemporaries working in prose; they were also more attracted to metaphysical dimensions of reality. However, the 1980s saw a revival of such 'poetic' directions in prose too. As with anti-realism in 1980s Russian prose generally, the silencing of the early twentieth-century avant-garde sometimes led to a curious conservatism in more recent experimental writing. The controversial work of Valeriia Narbikova (b. 1958), for example, had much in common with the writing of Gertrude Stein. The ornamentalist prose of Tat'iana Tolstaia (b. 1951) looked to Nabokov and Bunin, the short stories of Nina Sadur (b. 1950) to Daniil Kharms. Compared with some of their western counterparts, such as Angela Carter, Monique Wittig, Louise Erdrich, Candia McWilliam, or Toni Morrison, and indeed with some Russian women poets, some younger-generation Russian women prosaists seemed more promising in their intentions than in their achievements. However, the prose writers were in no sense weighed down by their influences, and there is no doubt that Sadur, Tolstaia or Narbikova, along with 'hyper-realists' such as Svetlana Vasilenko (b. 1956) and Larisa Vaneeva (b. 1953), produced some of the most innovative work coming out of Russia after 1988.

The 1990s saw women writers, like their male colleagues, struggling with the effects of the commercialization of the book market. It became common for poets, playwrights and authors of prose fiction alike to complain that their audience had 'vanished' and that the Russian public was now as indifferent to literature as its counterpart in western countries. But some were able to exploit the new demand for popular fiction that opened up at this time. Notably successful in this was Aleksandra Marinina (the pseudonym of Marina Alekseeva, a lieutenant colonel in the Russian police force, and former employee of the Moscow Juridical Institute). Marinina published her first detective novel in 1995. By 1997, she was one of the two best-selling writers in Russia, and in the late 1990s, several stories featuring her heroine, Anastasiia Kamenskaia of 38 Petrovka (the headquarters of Moscow Police), were serialized on Russian television.

Marinina's work was firmly grounded in the post-Soviet world: her subsidiary characters generally held new professions (advertising agents, stylists, scientists running their own businesses), and her plots often read like morality dramas (for instance, in *Death has a Bright Face* [*U smerti – svetlyi lik*], young women lured to Cyprus on the promise of wealth and glamour found themselves expected to work in a massage parlour in order to pay their way). This topicality stood out against a marked move away from social relevance in most non-mass-market women's writing of the era, though there were some exceptions, for example a fine elegy for Galina Starovoitova by Bella Akhmadulina; or a bitter epigram on a fashionable fur-wearing vegetarian by Ella Krylova: 'Butchers are executioners! she cried / But a whole cemetery of squirrels died / to make the furs she draped around her sides' (*Znamia* no. 1, 1999). Perhaps, too, the ubiquity of extremely abstract religious poetry could be seen as at some level a refraction of the real world, given the expansion of ostentatious church-going that Ol'ga Sedakova, a believer since childhood, satirized in her poem *Rain* (*Dozhd'*, 1998): 'Now the people who said there was no God / are lighting candles in churches, / ordering masses for the dead, / shunning those of other faiths'. But in prose, fictionalized memoir and anti-realist genres such as the fable and folk-tale prevailed (the two types of narrative came together in Svetlana Bychenko's short tale about the Second War, *The Return* [*Vozvrashchenie*, in *Novyi mir* no. 7, 1999], in which a child is sure that the menfolk of the village have been spirited away by a sinister accordionist, and is vindicated when the men return on the day she vandalizes his accordion). Indicative of the increasing marginality of documentary prose was the fact that even Liudmila Petrushevskaia began making unexpected excursions into verse. *Karamzin: a Village Diary* (*Karamzin: derevenskii dnevnik*, 2000) was a chronicle of post-Soviet rural life that emphasized whimsical detail rather than social realia ('Oksa has a rug / over her bed / she sewed it herself / and it says SINATORIUM'). *Po, Li Bo and Cui: Tongue-Twisters for Theatre Schools* (*Po, Li Bo i Kui: Skorogovorki dlia teatral'nykh uchilishch*, 1999: limited edition of 500 copies) was a neo-Futurist collection of tiny nonsense poems ('Li, Li Bo and Lili / (or in full, Lilith) / sailed down the Po / in a skiff owned by Li Bo . . .'), illustrated by the author's own vigorous line drawings. The danger was that, in demonstrating proud defiance of commercial pressures, women also tended to marginalize themselves in terms of the respectable literary market too (as represented, say, by literary prizes or translation requests from western publishers). However, one writer who successfully occupied the middle ground of taste was Liudmila Ulitskaia (b. 1943), the author of lively, accessible family chronicles: *Sonia* was shortlisted for the Booker Russian Novel Prize in 1993, and several of Ulitskaia's narratives had, by 2000, made their way into western languages.

This short survey of Russian women's writing has done no more than mention the best-known names, all of them producing 'literature' in the most conventional sense. It should be noted, though, that women writers have also made notable contributions to various para-literary or non-literary genres for writing. As in other countries, children's writing has attracted numerous talents: after the Revolution, these included writers who might have had trouble placing their work under the new system, such as the poets Elizaveta Dmitrieva (better known under her pseudonym Cherubina de Gabriak) and Elizaveta Polonskaia. Women have worked with distinction as literary critics (Mariia Tsebrikova, Liubov' Gurevich, Alla Latynina, Natal'ia Ivanova), as literary historians (Lidiia Ginzburg, Emma Gershtein), as journalists (Evgeniia Tur, Anna Volkova, Tat'iana Bogdanovich, Mariia Shkapskaia), as biographers (Lidiia Chukovskaia), as cultural theorists (Ol'ga Freidenberg), and as film scenarists (Natal'ia Riazantseva, Mariia Khmelik). All of these are areas urgently requiring the detailed consideration that has now begun to be given to women's prose, poetry and autobiography, which, until the early 1980s, themselves attracted little serious study, whether in Russia or abroad.

FURTHER READING

Andrew, Joe (ed.) *Russian Women's Shorter Fiction: An Anthology, 1835–1860*, Oxford: Clarendon Press; New York: Oxford University Press, 1996.

Barker, Adele M. (ed.) *Consuming Russia: Popular Culture, Sex, and Society since Gorbachev*, Durham, North Carolina: Duke University Press, 1999.

Clyman, Toby W. and Greene, Diana (eds) *Women Writers in Russian Literature*, Westport, Connecticut: Greenwood Press, 1994.

Goscilo, Helena (ed.) *Balancing Acts: Contemporary Stories by Russian Women*, Bloomington: Indiana University Press, 1989.

—— (ed.) *Lives in Transit: A Collection of Recent Russian Women's Writing*, Dana Point, California: Ardis, 1995.

—— *Dehexing Sex: Russian Womenhood During and After Glasnost*, Ann Arbor: University of Michigan Press, 1996.

Goscilo, Helena and Holmgren, Beth (eds) *Russia: Women: Culture*, Bloomington: Indiana University Press, 1996.

Kagal, Ayesha and Perova, Natasha. (eds) *Present Imperfect: Stories by Russian Women*, Oxford and Boulder, Colorado: Westview Press, 1996.

Kalina, E.I. (ed.) *Soviet Women Writing: Fifteen Short Stories*, New York: Abbeville Press, 1990; London: John Murray, 1991.

Kelly, Catriona (ed.) *An Anthology of Russian Women's Writing, 1777–1992*, Oxford and New York: Oxford University Press, 1994.

—— *A History of Russian Women's Writing, 1820–1992*, Oxford and New York: Clarendon Press, 1994.

Ledkovsky, Marina, Rosenthal, Charlotte, and Zirin, Mary. *Dictionary of Russian Women Writers*, Westport, Connecticut: Greenwood Press, 1994.

McLaughlin, Sigrid (ed. and trans.) *The Image of Women in Contemporary Soviet Fiction: Selected Stories from the USSR*, New York: St Martin's Press; London: Macmillan, 1989.

Pachmuss, Temira (ed. and trans.) *Women Writers in Russian Modernism*, Urbana: University of Illinois Press, 1978.

Rosslyn, Wendy. *Anna Bunina, 1774–1829, and the Origins of Women's Poetry in Russia*, Lewiston: Edwin Mellen, 1997.

Tomei, Christine D. (ed.) *Russian Women Writers*, 2 vols., New York: Garland, 1999.

14

RUSSIAN LITERARY THEORY: FROM THE FORMALISTS TO LOTMAN

MICHAEL O'TOOLE

Literary theory in Russia was not the exclusive concern of literary theorists and critics. Just as in England writers as varied as Alexander Pope, T.S. Eliot, and David Lodge have theorized about literary form and language, about the place of literature in culture and in relation to the other arts, so in Russia Mikhail Lomonosov in the eighteenth century, Aleksandr Pushkin and Lev Tolstoy in the nineteenth, and Andrei Bely, Vladimir Maiakovsky, and Boris Pasternak in the twentieth century made not only radical experiments with form in poetry and prose fiction, but also original and significant theoretical statements.

The main focus of this essay is on the Russian Formalist critics of the 1910s and 1920s and their contemporaries Mikhail Bakhtin (1895–1975) and Vladimir Propp (1895–1970), and the leaders of the Tartu semiotics school in the 1960s to 1980s who have also had a major influence on literary theory outside Russia. Here again, however, theory was not divorced from the practice of writing. Two of the leading Formalists, Viktor Shklovsky (1893–1984) and Iurii Tynianov (1894–1943), wrote fascinating novels and biographies, while Shklovsky and Osip Brik (1888–1945) experimented with film scenarios and scripts.

The material of which literary works are made is, ultimately, language, so it is no accident that the two young organizations that united to form the Russian Formalists in 1914 were the Moscow Linguistic Circle and the St Petersburg-based Society for Poetic Language (OPOIAZ). Shklovsky, one of the founders of OPOIAZ, insisted that the first object of literary study should be form: 'The literary work is pure form, it is neither thing, nor material, but a relationship of materials.' This kind of statement fitted in, of course, with the materialist philosophy of the early Soviet period. However, the Formalist theorists were at odds with what they regarded as the 'naive sociologizing' of the typical Marxist critics of the 1920s, who only looked to literature for reflections of the social structure and manners of its age. This conflict with the hardline Marxists led to the enforced demise of the Formalist movement.

In the early Formalist pronouncements, however, the main enemy was traditional literary history, criticism, and teaching. Roman Jakobson (1896–1982) contrasted its faults with the approach of a true science of literature in 1921 in a typically picturesque way:

> The subject of literary science is not literature, but literariness, i.e. that which makes a given work a literary work. Up till now, however, historians of literature have

mostly behaved like the police who, when they want to arrest someone, take in everyone and everything found in the apartment and even chance passers-by. Historians of literature have in the same way felt the need to take in everything – everyday life, psychology, politics, philosophy. Instead of a science of literature we have fetched up with a conglomeration of cottage industries.

The keys to the new literary science were system and function. Every literary text involves choices from systems of possible options that are typical of the genre to which that text belongs: a narrative has a plot structure (complication–crisis–denouement) which is typical of a certain kind of story or novel; it has typical characters (heroes, villains, helpers, witnesses) and characteristic settings for the action. All of these are chosen, like ingredients in a recipe, from the available systems of plot-structure, character-type, and setting-frame that the writer's literary culture makes available. Similarly, a lyric poem creates a particular 'I–you' relationship and a particular sound structure with selections from systems of grammar, imagery, metre, rhythm, rhyme, assonance, alliteration, and so on. But the scientific aspect of literary form does not stop with these systems of choice. They do not operate in isolation from each other in the work. Each chosen element has a function within the whole; it interacts with the other elements to produce a complex play of forces and meanings. Take something as simple as a rhyme in a poem: at first glance – or hearing – it merely sets up a sound echo with the final word or phrase in a preceding line. But the rhyming words are different, they mean different things, they may belong to different grammatical categories, and the context of both grammar and meaning of the lines in which they occur is quite different. The rhyme may also point outwards from the poem to other poems, 'intertextually', or may even be a kind of comment by the poet on himself, on the nature of poetry, or on his readers. It may have all these functions at once and interact with other functioning elements such as metre, the interplay of grammatical and metrical units, or may highlight a clash of imagery.

Peter Steiner, an American commentator, has instructively highlighted and compared what he calls 'the three metaphors of Russian Formalism': the machine, the organism, and the system. Certain Formalists were mainly preoccupied with the components of a literary work and their articulation, like cogs in a machine; others saw a literary work as having more in common with a living organism, each organ, each cell, each nerve functioning in a complex and self-balancing interaction that guaranteed life to the organism; others focused on the notion of the individual work as a system of choices and interactions, and even on the whole of literature as a complex, self-balancing system, whose very evolution could be described in systemic terms. Steiner chooses to see these three metaphors as distinguishing different phases of Formalism dominated in turn by different theorists. But the scientific nature of the enterprise stressed by Shklovsky and Jakobson involved all three metaphors from the start.

The first article of Formalist theory by Viktor Shklovsky, 'The Resurrection of the Word' ('Voskreshenie slova'), was published in 1914. His complex notion was much discussed in the following decade. In the first place 'the word' – language – is the very material from which literature is constructed; theories of literature must resurrect an interest in this material. Second, language is different in a literary text from other contexts; one important definition of 'literariness' is that the literary text rescues words from the stale, clichéd usage of everyday discourses, reanimates their meaning, makes their form palpable. But this was not just a technical matter for Shklovsky; it becomes an ethical issue. One reason why we should take literature very seriously indeed is that it refreshes and renews our vision of reality; it resurrects not just 'the word', but *the world*:

> As they become habitual, actions are automatized . . . This is a process ideally typified by algebra, where objects are replaced by symbols . . . through this algebraic mode of thinking we grasp things by counting them and measuring them; we do not see them, but merely recognize them by their primary features. The thing rushes past us, prepacked, as it were; we know that it is there by the space that it takes up, but we see only its surface. This kind of perception shrivels a thing up, first of all in the way we perceive it, but later this affects the way we handle it too . . . life goes to waste as it is turned into nothingness. Automatization corrodes things, clothing, furniture, one's wife and one's fear of war . . . and so that a sense of life may be restored, that things may be felt, so that stones may be made stony, there exists what we call art.

Shklovsky called the main literary device for this kind of renewal of our vision 'making strange'. This is sometimes translated by the more technical-sounding words 'defamiliarization' or 'de-automatization', that is, opposing the process of automatization described in Shklovsky's quotation. But 'making strange' is a better term. Lev Tolstoy, reputedly one of the world's great 'realist' writers, has everyday social customs observed through the eyes of a naive character, and they are 'made strange' for us too: all the charades and pretences involved in an opera or a church service are unmasked by the innocent gaze – and, of course, by the innocent language – of a child or an uneducated person. The most extreme example of this device occurs in Tolstoy's story *Strider* (*Kholstomer*), which is told from the point of view of a horse. The behaviour of people with each other and towards animals – indeed, the whole concept of private property – is subjected to the ruthlessly naive gaze of the horse.

Shklovsky shows, however, that this trick is not confined to literary fiction, because he sees it as one of the key mechanisms of the erotic riddle where locks and keys or rings and marlinspikes provide the metaphors for female and male sexual organs and their interplay. This move on Shklovsky's part to link the use of a device in complex literary genres with its use in simple and even 'disreputable' folk genres is characteristic of the Formalists' lively thinking across established categories and of their desire to shake up categorized thinking about the institution of literature. It is reminiscent of the anecdote told by the great Russian film director and theorist Sergei Eisenstein (1898–1948), who was a contemporary and friend of the Formalists, about how an erotic folk-tale (about a fox – a vixen – getting trapped and raped by a hare) gave him the inspiration for the turning-point in his great historico-political recreation of the defeat of the Teutonic Knights in *Aleksandr Nevsky* (1938).

All of the Formalists were keen to loosen the boundaries between the literature that is officially sanctioned and taught in school and the other forms of discourse, like the joke, the riddle, the proverb, the folk-tale, which are typical creative forms of non-literate people's culture. To this extent they were in tune with the aspirations of the Russian Revolution and the subsequent drive for the re-evaluation of popular culture with which they coincided. On the other hand, much of their work was aimed at elucidating exactly what is 'literariness' and involved contrasting speech in literature with speech in 'everyday genres', such as news reports, scientific papers or official announcements. One of the determinative devices of the literary text, Shklovsky claimed, was its tendency to 'lay bare the device', and this too became a Formalist slogan. A novel like *Don Quixote* or *Tristram Shandy* does not stop at 'making strange' the worlds of medieval knights or married couples – it shows off the devices that make this defamiliarization possible: in *Tristram Shandy* Laurence Sterne drags out trivial actions, constantly interrupts the progress of the narrative, shifts chapters around, mixes rows of asterisks or drawings with verbal text, and, moreover, shows off in doing so.

For the Formalists this had both psychological and ethical implications. They were not convinced by Herbert Spencer's widely popular notion that art works psychologically, according to the principle of greatest efficiency with least effort. On the contrary, Shklovsky asserted, art works deliberately through 'form made difficult'; our perceptions are deliberately 'slowed down' through a whole variety of technical ploys: in narrative, the normal order of events may be inverted, or digressions introduced; in poetry, sequences of sounds may be deliberately hard to pronounce, or fresh images or startling rhymes or puns or grammatical distortions may force us to stop and read again or reflect. Only the 'automatized' forms of everyday speech flow seamlessly and aim to achieve the most with the least effort. Ethically, this deliberate 'putting the brakes on' perception is part of the 'resurrection of the word' and the revival of moral awareness.

Most of Shklovsky's programmatic and memorable theoretical pronouncements related to literary prose. We should note, however, that most of the other Russian Formalists between 1917 and 1929 were equally interested in poetry and prose: Boris Eikhenbaum (1886–1959) wrote on 'Verse Melody' and the poetry of Anna Akhmatova as well as on the prose of Gogol' and Tolstoy; Boris Tomashevsky (1890–1957)'s book *On Verse* (*O stikhe*, 1929), was as significant as his *Theory of Literature* (*Teoriia literatury*, 1925), which dealt mainly with narrative; Iurii Tynianov explored the relationship between systems and functions equally thoroughly in his books *The Problem of Verse Language* (*Problema stikhotvornogo iazyka*, 1924), and *Gogol' and Dostoevsky. Towards a Theory of Parody* (*Gogol' i Dostoevskii. K teorii parodii,* 1921). The three other most prominent theorists of the heyday of Russian Formalism, Roman Jakobson, Osip Brik, and Viktor Zhirmunsky (1891–1971), wrote almost exclusively about poetry. In many ways all of these writers opened up areas of poetic theory and analysis that have been explored in depth outside Russia relatively recently. Yet their work is hardly known outside circles of Russian specialists. The reasons are fairly obvious: the argument is untranslatable. In order to illustrate patterns of word-choice, rhythm, stress, sound patterning and so on in Russian poetry you have to use the Russian words and patterns. The only satisfactory way to translate Osip Brik's concepts of 'Sound Repetitions' from Pushkin and Lermontov, for instance, would be to rewrite his paper in terms of comparable patterns in two comparable English poets, say, Byron and Coleridge. But none of the poetic devices is isolated; they interact in different ways linguistically in the two languages, and culturally in the two poetic traditions. Even the fact that most educated Russian readers know their greatest poets by heart, while the English do not, makes a difference to the way the theory is taken up.

The lack of awareness outside Russia of the high quality of the Formalists' theories and analyses of poetry (except, at second-hand, through Victor Erlich's excellent book *Russian Formalism: History, Doctrine*, first published in 1955) has reduced appreciation of just how scientific their 'science of literature' could be. There is something so intense about short poetic forms like the verse lyric that it becomes much easier to show the choices that are being made from the systems of metre, rhythm, verse structure, rhyme, alliteration, assonance, enjambment, grammatical units, and so on, than is the case with the larger and more diffuse forms of the novel and short story or dramatic genres. Jakobson was able to show that Pushkin's most famous two-stanza poem 'I Loved You Once' ('Ia vas liubil') achieves its emotional power from the interplay of grammatical structures with rhythm and sound patterning and depends hardly at all on imagery, which for most earlier critics had been the touchstone of lyric poetry. Moreover, the function of each choice – say, a rhyme or a change of rhythm – in the overall texture of a poem is also more easily determined than the function of analogous choices – a pair of characters who are foils for each other or a change of setting – in a novel.

Ia vas liubil: liubov' eshche, byt' mozhet
V dushe moei ugasla ne sovsem;
No pust' ona vas bol'she ne trevozhit;
Ia ne khochu pechalit' vas nichem.

Ia vas liubil bezmolvno, beznadezhno,
To robost'iu, to revnost'iu tomim;
Ia vas liubil tak iskrenno, tak nezhno,
Kak dai vam Bog liubimoi byt' drugim.

I loved you: it may be that love has not completely died in my soul; but let it not trouble you any more; I do not wish to sadden you in any way.

I loved you silently, hopelessly, tormented now by diffidence and now by jealousy; I loved you so truly, so tenderly as God may grant you to be loved by another.

(prose translation by Dimitri Obolensky)

It was mainly in relation to poetry that the Formalists evolved many of their most significant ideas and methods of analysis. One key idea was the concept of 'foregrounding': a literary text foregrounds particular features, while others keep the 'automatized' functions they have in ordinary language. Thus, 'making strange' is one variety of foregrounding. An obvious example in verse would be the pairs of matching adverbs or instrumentals in successive lines of the second stanza of Pushkin's poem: *bezmolvno – beznadezhno* (silently – hopelessly), *to robost'iu – to revnost'iu* (now by diffidence – now by jealousy), *tak iskrenno – tak nezhno* (so truly – so tenderly). We note that these not only relate to each other in both meaning and grammatical form, but each has a marker of its match at the beginning: *bez-, to-, tak*. This is a heavy degree of foregrounding of parallelism: we tend not to utter such heart-felt pairs of words in everyday language. Part of its function, however, is to set up a kind of automatism within the stanza (Jakobson compared the rhythms involved to heartbeats) which is shattered by the shock of the direct appeal on behalf of the beloved in the last line, where the grammar is much more complex and difficult to process ('form made difficult') and the only parallel is the implied one between *drugim* (another) and the poet.

There was a further dimension to foregrounding, however, which emerged quite early in the writings of Jakobson, Eikhenbaum, and Tynianov, and that was the concept of the dominant, which has implications for all literary theories that involve close study of the text. In 1927 Iurii Tynianov wrote:

> The work is a system of correlated factors. Correlation of each factor with the others is its *function* in relation to the whole system. It is quite clear that every literary system is formed not by the peaceful interaction of all the factors, but by the supremacy, the foregrounding, of one factor (or group) that functionally subjugates and colours the rest. This factor bears the name that has already become established in Russian scholarly works of the *dominant* . . .

Tynianov went so far as to claim that this complex functioning of the dominant was the defining characteristic of literature: 'Since a system is not a free interplay of equal elements but presupposes the foregrounding of one group of elements ("a dominant") and the deformation of others, a work becomes literature and acquires its literary function through just this dominant.' The implications of this assertion were developed a decade later by Jan Mukařovský of the Prague School of Structuralism and in the 1970s by Zholkovsky and Shcheglov, whose work will be mentioned later. In a non-Slavonic context they have contributed to 'systemic-functional' approaches to literary stylistics.

Linked to the untranslatability of theoretical writing about poetry mentioned earlier is the fact that the first translation of 'Formalist' writing to reach English-speaking readers was Vladimir Propp's *Morphology of the Folktale* (*Morfologiia skazki*), originally published in 1928 and published in English translation in the United States in 1958. Propp was an anthropologist who did not belong to the Formalist movement, yet he pioneered the 'morphological' method of analysing the structure of a narrative genre by assigning a consistent set of 'functions' to stages of the plots of a large range of Russian folk-tales. The value of this work was immediately recognized in a lengthy review by Claude Lévi-Strauss, the influential French structural anthropologist, and the fame and influence of Propp's work in the West was assured. Theories of literary characters as 'actants' whose roles relate to their designated plot-functions were developed by French Structuralists such as Roland Barthes, Claude Bremond, and A-J. Greimas. 'Proppian' analyses have flourished in literary and semiotic courses in universities worldwide and have been tested on such diverse texts as 'Little Red Riding Hood' and Alfred Hitchcock's film *North by North-West.*

The other Russian contemporary of the Formalists, who did not count himself a Formalist but who has had a major influence on literary scholarship, cultural studies, and film studies in our own time, was Mikhail Bakhtin. His early work on Dostoevsky and the long tradition of 'dialogic' discourse in the novel broke new ground in Russia when it was published in 1929; in France, when it was recognized and developed by Julia Kristeva in the late 1960s; and in the English-speaking world, when it finally appeared in translation, along with many of Bakhtin's other writings, in the 1970s and 1980s. According to Bakhtin and his close colleague, Voloshinov, every utterance, all speech used in natural contexts, is 'dialogic', that is, it presupposes the point of view and possible reactions of a listener. In much of the early Dostoevsky this 'dialogism' becomes an obsession as the paranoid heroes of *Poor Folk* (*Bednye liudi*) or *The Double* (*Dvoinik*) constantly speak 'glancing over their shoulder' at possible contradictions or criticisms. But Bakhtin goes further. He claims that Dostoevsky is unique among nineteenth-century novelists in making this dialogism a constructional principle: not only do all his characters speak dialogically, but the narrator himself is dialogic and never resolves the conflict represented by the competing voices of his characters. Bakhtin's concept led to certain other important ideas such as intertextuality (the dialogic relations between one literary text and other implied texts) and the chronotope (the way in which time and space are often collapsed into a single frame in the modern novel). Bakhtin himself developed these concepts in some depth in his later writings and they have been explored by a wide range of literary theorists and analysts since they were first published in English in 1981.

With the concept of 'carnival' Bakhtin projected the notion of dialogue from the 'micro-level' of the speech situation (in novels and in discourse in general) to the 'macro-level' of the socio-political arena. In an extended analysis of the writings of Rabelais, Bakhtin argued that the medieval carnival, with its buffoonery, inversions of norms, and generally 'scandalous' character and language, was the 'dialogic' response of the lower classes to the secure ideology and monologic pronouncements of those in power. Since the appearance in English of *Rabelais and His World* in 1968 this concept has had a major influence on theories of literature, film, theatrical performance, cultural studies, and sociology.

One of Bakhtin's closest colleagues, Pavel Medvedev, published what purported to be a major critique of Russian Formalist theory in 1928, *Formal'nyi metod v literaturovedenii* (published in English in 1978 as *The Formal Method in Literary*

Scholarship). This came at the end of a decade in the new Soviet Union in which life got progressively more difficult for Shklovsky and his colleagues. The early years following the Revolution of 1917 had opened up exciting prospects for writers, artists, filmmakers, and even literary theorists, with the new regime's drive for universal education, for experimentation with new structures in art and literature as well as in society and politics, its concern for the common man (hence Formalist interest in folk literature), and its cult of the machine (reflected in the Formalist preoccupation with 'devices' and 'mechanisms'). But by the mid-1920s education was becoming social engineering, experimentation was giving way to extreme conventionalism, respect for the common man had become the 'dictatorship of the proletariat', and the state under Stalin was turning itself into a machine that would crush all free thought and all opposition.

Russian intellectual life, even in times of trouble – perhaps particularly in times of trouble – has always involved lively and combative exchanges. The debates between the Formalists and their sympathizers and the sociologically-minded ultra-Marxist critics raged on the pages of the many new literary journals, in committees of writers and scholars, and on the platforms of public meetings, but the tide gradually turned against the Formalists. Shklovsky, who in 1927 had called an article *V zashchitu sotsiologicheskogo metoda* (*In Defence of the Sociological Method*) (arguing for a synthesis of formal analysis and social interpretation), by 1930 had capitulated with *Pamiatnik nauchnoi oshibke* (*A Monument to Scientific Error*). The other Formalists did not take recantation this far, but they all steered away from theory and busied themselves with traditional and unchallenging scholarly activity such as editing or writing biographies and memoirs. In any case, apart from the personal attacks on individual theorists and the group, the possibilities for publishing either original theory or original poetry and prose were dwindling as the doctrine of socialist realism was enforced. Only Roman Jakobson, who had moved to Prague in 1921, was able to continue his wide-ranging theorizing and became a founding member of the Prague School of Structuralists, who continued many of the best initiatives of the Russian Formalist theorists – until they too were driven out or underground by another totalitarian regime, that of Hitler.

Medvedev, then, published his detailed account of Formalist theory at precisely the time when the cultural powers-that-be required a critique and rebuttal of such lively and innovative thinking. But Russians under authoritarian rulers often resort to the 'Aesopian' ploy of dressing up a positive account as if it were a fierce critique, and Medvedev's readers would have learned from his book a great deal about the virtues of the 'formal method', as well as some of its extremes and vices. Even this publicity was, however, short-lived, because by the early 1930s all mention of the Formalists (and the literary and artistic movements of Futurism, Acmeism, Constructivism, Suprematism, and so on) was banned: they were not even history.

A revival of interest in Russian Formalism and the work of Bakhtin, Voloshinov, Propp and the other theorists of the 1920s began in the 1960s under the philistine but more benign, regime of Nikita Khrushchev. It may have been helped by Victor Erlich's monumental treatise and the appearance of translations in the West of

Propp, Shklovsky, Eikhenbaum, Tomashevsky and – eventually – Bakhtin and Medvedev. In 1967 two young literary theorists in Moscow, Aleksandr Zholkovsky and Iurii Shcheglov, published a paper from the Tartu Summer School on Sign Systems entitled – in true Aesopian style – 'From the Prehistory of Soviet Work on Structural Poetics'. This was an appreciation of the pioneering work of the Formalists and an appeal for the resurrection of some of their principles and methods. In the 1970s these same scholars pioneered their own 'generative model' of the literary text that developed further several key aspects of Formalist theory. They called it a 'Theme <Expressiveness Devices> Text Model' and it involved postulating an underlying theme for a work – which might be as short as a maxim or as long as a novel – and then generating the ultimate text through successive stages of elaboration. The 'devices' (a very Shklovskian word) were such general psychological-textual mechanisms as parallelism, contrast, augmentation, concretization, and so on (mechanisms recognized also by the Formalists). The model involved a very coherent and consistent engagement with the details of the literary text and was tested on drama (Molière) and film (Eisenstein), as well as on poetry and prose forms of literature. The authors both emigrated to North America in the late 1970s, however, and their method was not adopted by other Russian theorists. It tended to get lost in the welter of 'post-structuralist' theorizing that by this time was the dominant mode in the West.

It is instructive that the 'centre' for the revival of Russian structural poetics and semiotics from the late 1960s to the early 1990s was Tartu, a small city in Estonia on the Baltic periphery of the Soviet Union. Established academics and officialdom alike mistrusted or feared 'theory', so it was only tolerated in isolated departments of literature and discreetly organized and published summer schools. However, the interest generated worldwide by the Tartu group and its regular collections of 'Papers on Sign Systems' made a mockery of their marginalization in Russian scholarship – indeed, it showed up the inadequacy of most of the mainstream literary scholarship going on in the Soviet Union during this period, which was reminiscent of the 'conglomeration of cottage industries' criticized by Jakobson back in 1921.

The central organizing genius of this group was Iurii Lotman (1922–93), who held the Chair of Russian Literature at Tartu University. He not only organized and published the summer schools with a dedicated group of colleagues, but himself wrote and published a series of books and articles that were widely read and used in courses on literary theory in the west. The best-known of these were *The Structure of the Artistic Text* of 1970 (*Struktura khudozhestvennogo teksta*) and *Analysis of the Poetic Text* (*Analiz poeticheskogo teksta*, 1972), which extended many of the concepts and methods of the Formalists and Prague School Structuralists. At the same time, Lotman and his closest colleagues were evolving theories of cultural semiotics that explored far beyond the boundaries of officially recognized literature and pioneered recent movements in cultural studies and critical ethnography. In Moscow Boris Uspensky, a senior and active member of the Tartu group, explored in his 1970 book *A Poetics of Composition* (*Poetika kompozitsii*) not only the play with point-of-view in literary and other verbal texts, but its significance in the analysis of pictorial texts such as medieval Russian icons.

With Lotman's untimely death in 1993, much of the drive has gone out of the Tartu School, and in most countries the precise formal study of the literary text has given way to the looser, more contextual, more intuitive approaches of Marxist, feminist, psychoanalytical, and cultural theorizing. Politically, too, the times have been changing in Russia. The openness made possible by Gorbachev's policy of glasnost made it possible for all intellectual movements to be heard. But Russian literary theory has generally thrived in conditions of isolation and intellectual overheating. The economic plight of many intellectuals and writers in Russia, coupled with a new freedom to travel, has led many of the most original and best-known theorists to live and work abroad where their work has to take its chances in the over-stocked 'open market' of ideas and approaches. The intense and open-minded theorizing about literature and the other arts that flourished so paradoxically in the 'closed society' of Soviet communism in the 1920s and 1970s may succumb to the chill winds of 'economic rationalism'. It is to be hoped that the achievements of Russian literary theory will be kept alive by students of Russian literature until it is ready for rediscovery and development at some time in the twenty-first century.

FURTHER READING

Bakhtin, M.M. *The Dialogic Imagination: Four Essay*, ed. Michael Holquist, Austin: University of Texas Press, 1981.

Bakhtin, Mikail. *Problems of Dostoevsky's Poetics*, ed. and trans. Caryl Emerson, Minneapolis: University of Minnesota Press, 1984.

Bakhtin, M.M. / Medvedev, P.N. *The Formal Method in Literary Scholarship: A Critical Introduction to Sociological Poetics*, trans. Albert J. Wehrle, Baltimore and London: Johns Hopkins University Press, 1978; Cambridge, Massachusetts: Harvard University Press, 1985.

Erlich, Victor. *Russian Formalism: History, Doctrine*, 1955; revised edn, The Hague: Mouton, 1965; New Haven: Yale University Press, 1981.

Jackson, Robert Louis and Rudy, Stephen (eds) *Russian Formalism: A Retrospective Glance*, New Haven: Yale Center for Humanities and Area Studies, 1985.

Jakobson, Roman. *Language in Literature*, eds Krystyna Pomorska and Stephen Rudy, Cambridge, Massachusetts: The Belknap Press, 1987.

Lemon, Lee T. and Reis, Marion J. (eds) *Russian Formalist Criticism: Four Essays*, Lincoln: University of Nebraska Press, 1965.

Lotman, Yury. *Analysis of the Poetic Text*, ed. and trans. D. Barton Johnson, Ann Arbor: Ardis, 1976.

Lotman, Jurij. *The Structure of the Artistic Text*, trans. Ronald Vroon, Ann Arbor: University of Michigan, 1977.

Lotman, Yuri M. *Universe of the Mind: A Semiotic Theory of Culture*, trans. Ann Shukman, London: I.B. Tauris, 1990.

Lotman, Ju. M. and Uspenskij, B.A. *The Semiotics of Russian Culture*, ed. Ann Shukman, Ann Arbor: University of Michigan, 1984.

Matejka, Ladislav, and Pomorska, Krystyna (eds) *Readings in Russian Poetics: Formalist and Structuralist Views*, Ann Arbor: University of Michigan, 1978.

Russian Poetics in Translation, Colchester: University of Essex and RPT Publications, Oxford, 1975–83 [a valuable occasional series of translated materials].

Shcheglov, Yury and Zholkovsky, Alexander. *Poetics of Expressiveness: A Theory and Applications*, Amsterdam: John Benjamins, 1987.

Shklovsky, Viktor. *Theory of Prose*, trans. Benjamin Sher, Elmwood Park, Illinois: Dalkey Archive Press, 1990.

Steiner, Peter. *Russian Formalism: A Metapoetics*, Ithaca: Cornell University Press, 1984.

Tynianov, Yuri. *The Problem of Verse Language*, trans. Michael Sosa and Brent Harvey, Ann Arbor: Ardis, 1981.

Uspensky, Boris. *A Poetics of Composition: The Structure of the Artistic text and Typology of a Compositional Form*, trans. Valentina Zavarin and Susan Wittig, Berkeley: University of California Press, 1973; 1983.

Voloshinov, V.N. *Marxism and the Philosophy of Language*, trans. Ladislaw Matejka and I.R. Titunik, New York: Seminar Press, 1973; Cambridge, Massachusetts: Harvard University Press, 1986.

Zholkovsky, Alexander. *Themes and Texts: Toward a Poetics of Expressiveness*, Ithaca and London: Cornell University Press, 1984.

15
SOCIALIST REALISM IN SOVIET LITERATURE

KATERINA CLARK

Socialist realism was the official literary 'method' or 'theory' of Soviet literature virtually until the break-up of the Union in 1991. After Stalin died, however, in 1953, writers began to dismantle the tradition, pushing the limits of the possible. This process continued until, by the last decade or so of Soviet rule, most literary practice had strayed a long way from what, in the 1930s and 1940s, might have been accepted as socialist realism. Yet, at the same time, the conventions of socialist realism had become so ingrained as habits of composition that in the first decades of the post-Stalin period even dissident writers rarely broke out of its formal, as distinct from ideological, mould (the legacy of socialist realism can be found, for example, in the early novels of Solzhenitsyn). This essay, however, will discuss socialist realism only in its most classical, Stalinist version and will not treat the successive layers of complexity that accrued to the tradition in the post-Stalin years.

Not all Soviet literature is socialist realist. Not even all Stalinist, non-dissident literature is socialist realist. When discussing Soviet literature, one has to draw a distinction between at least three categories of works: those that exemplify socialist realism, those that are read as non- or anti-Soviet but which happen to have been published in the Soviet Union, and a third category, those that are representative of Soviet literature but not specifically socialist realist. Many in the latter category are (or were) even officially promoted (in, for example, the Writers' Union's 'Golden List' of around a hundred classics of Soviet literature).

Socialist realism as such did not exist until the Bolshevik Revolution of 1917 was almost fifteen years old, or more precisely until after a decree as promulgated in April 1932 abolishing all independent writers' organizations and forming the single Union of Soviet Writers. The term itself was not presented to the Soviet public until 17 May 1932, in a speech made by Gronsky, the president of the new Writers' Union's Organizational Committee (legend has it that the term 'socialist realism' had been thought of by Stalin in a meeting in Maksim Gor'ky's study).

Having coined the term, those in power in Soviet literature had to decide what it meant. Gor'ky (the First Secretary of the Writers' Union) and other authoritative figures began to clarify this in articles and speeches of 1932–4 and the First Plenum of the Organizational Committee, held in October 1932, was devoted to the topic. It was not, however, until August 1934, when the First Congress of the Writers' Union was held, that socialist realism acquired a canonical formulation in two keynote addresses to the Congress, one by Gor'ky, and the other by Andrei

Zhdanov, the chief representative of the Party's Central Committee. Thereafter, these two speeches functioned as *the* canonical source for the definition, together with Lenin's 1905 article 'Party Organization and Party Literature' and Gor'ky's articles in the book *On Literature* (*O literature*), published in 1933 (and in later redactions of the same book).

These sources identify a number of features that socialist realism should contain. Many of the stipulations are in effect taboos which, in that they have been fairly rigorously enforced over the decades, have ensured that socialist realism has, both aesthetically and thematically, been a conservative and even somewhat puritanical literature. For example, writers were enjoined to expunge from their work any trace of bald 'physiologism' (read mention of sex and other such bodily functions). They were also to avoid all approaches and language that might not be accessible to the masses. This injunction has meant that socialist realism is not highbrow, but lowbrow, or at best middlebrow. Effectively, it also put an end to the literary experimentalism and modernist trends that had flowered in the 1920s.

The language to be used in socialist realism was circumscribed. There were to be no sub-standard locutions, no dialecticisms, no scatology, and no abstruse or long-winded expressions – let alone the neologisms and trans-sense language that had been favoured by the Russian avant-garde. In consequence, most socialist realist writers used only a somewhat *comme il faut* version of standard Russian, resulting often in stilted dialogue (this was one of the trends that was reversed in the post-Stalin era, starting from the late 1950s).

Other proscriptions were more ideological in nature. For example, there was to be no 'obscurantism' – no infusion of religious or mystical sentiment, no positive account of the occult. Needless to say, a socialist realist work was *not* to espouse the views of any political group that rivalled the Bolsheviks, whether of the left or of the right. Instead, literature was to serve the ideological position and policies of the Bolshevik Party, and in so doing should be 'optimistic' and forward-looking (that is, it should intimate the great and glorious future).

These ideological prescriptions were contained in the doctrine of mandatory *partiinost'*, the cornerstone or *sine qua non* of socialist realism. *Partiinost'* – a term that is generally and somewhat barbarously translated into English as 'party-mindedness' – is, then, ostensibly a quality inherent in a socialist realist work. It might be more accurately described, however, as a code word signalling the radical reconception of the role of the writer that is so central to socialist realism. If, before, the writer (and this was largely true even of the politically committed writer) saw himself as an original creator of texts, once socialist realism was instituted his role became much more instrumental, as is implicit in Zhdanov's famous character-ization of the Soviet writer (in his speech to the First Writers' Congress) as an 'engineer of human souls'. Literature was now viewed in a utilitarian way (even more so than before) in terms of how it might 'engineer' certain habits of thinking in the populace. Indeed, the writer was seen as rather like a trained professional, working for the government, who was to implement certain assignments or elaborate certain themes that were given to him either explicitly or implicitly (in either case, often through official speeches, articles in *Pravda*, and so on). Even then, he was not to fulfil these assignments in a freehanded way. The socialist realist writer did not really have autonomy over his own texts, which would often be rewritten several times before publication; sometimes he reworked them himself under prompting; sometimes another writer reworked them, and at other times it might be an editor at the publishing house. Such rewritings could at times be without the author's knowledge or permission.

The many injunctions contained in the official speeches to the First Congress of the Writers' Union and other authoritative sources, which determined the ultimate shape of socialist realism, do not fully define the heart of the tradition or establish its unique qualities. This is even true of the doctrine of mandatory *partiinost'* which, though it signals a purely service role for the writer, does not, after all, specify much about the kind of writing he will produce. The injunctions to the writer found in the canonical sources for socialist realism set out the parameters in which he was to operate, but provide only sketchy guidelines for what was to become a highly conventionalized literary tradition. The socialist realist writer was, in practice, not just to be politically correct; as an 'engineer of human souls', he was expected to adhere to a particular code of construction.

The principal function of the Soviet socialist realist writer was to provide legitimizing myths for the state, to 'show the country its heroes'. In consequence, the second cornerstone of socialist realism, together with *partiinost'*, was the 'positive hero', an emblematic figure whose biography was to function as a model for readers to emulate. Thus socialist realism is a version of heroic biography. Small wonder the novel, the most popular biographical genre of the modern period, became the central genre of socialist realism. The heroic conventions that were established in the socialist realist novel were used to a greater or lesser extent in most other literary genres, and in other media, such as film.

The particular conventions that define the socialist realist tradition were themselves established by exemplars. Ever since 1932, when the Writers' Union was formed and socialist realism was declared the sole method appropriate for literature, most official pronouncements on literature, and especially the addresses that opened every Writers' Congress, contained a short list of exemplars to guide the writers in their future work. Each new version of the list contained at its core the official classics of socialist realism, plus a few recently published works. No two lists were exactly the same, and those recently published works added to a given list were often omitted in subsequent lists. There is, however, a core of novels that were cited with sufficient regularity to be considered a canon. They include: Dmitrii Furmanov's *Chapaev* (1923); Aleksandr Fadeev's *The Rout* (*Razgrom*, 1927) and *The Young Guard* (*Molodaia gvardiia*) originally published in 1946, but the rewritten redaction of 1951 is the canon text; Fedor Gladkov's *Cement* (*Tsement*, 1925); Maksim Gor'ky's *The Life of Klim Samgin* (*Zhizn' Klima Samgina*, written 1925–36); Iurii Krymov's *The Tanker Derbent* (*Tanker 'Derbent'*, 1937–38); Nikolai Ostrovsky's *How the Steel Was Tempered* (*Kak zakalialas' stal'*, 1934); Aleksandr Serafimovich's *The Iron Flood* (*Zheleznyi potok*, 1924); Mikhail

Sholokhov's *Quiet Flows the Don* (*Tikhii Don*, 1928–40) and *Virgin Soil Upturned* (*Podniataia tselina*, 1932–60).

These canonical works have been a crucial factor in determining the shape of all socialist realist works, but particularly of the novel. There was a good deal of external stimulus for following these exemplars besides the mere fact that they were advanced by authoritative voices. In the early 1930s, a literary institute was set up to train writers to follow the models. A preferential scale of royalty payments and other attractions such as dachas and visits to Houses of Creativity in idyllic locations were dangled before the writer as positive inducements to follow the developing official traditions of the Soviet novel. In other words, when authoritative voices cried out 'Give us more heroes like X [the hero of some model novel]', the cry did not fall on entirely deaf ears.

As a result, the business of writing novels soon became comparable to the procedure followed by medieval icon painters. Just as the icon painter looked to an 'original' to find the correct angle for a given saint's hands, the correct colours for a given theme, and so on, the Soviet writer could copy the gestures, facial expressions, actions, and symbols used in texts already pronounced canonical.

The Soviet writer did not merely copy isolated tropes, characters, and incidents from the exemplars. He organized the entire plot structure of his novel on the basis of patterns present in them. From the mid-1930s on, most novels were *de facto* written to a single masterplot that itself represents a synthesis of the plots of several model novels (primarily Gor'ky's *Mother* [*Mat'*, 1907] and Gladkov's *Cement*).

This shaping of the plot does not, however, account for everything in a given socialist realist novel. Despite the frequent western charge that these novels are clichéd and repetitive, it is not true that every novel is nothing more than the reworking of a single formula. In any given novel one must distinguish between, on the one hand, its overarching plot or macrostructure and, on the other, the microstructures, the smaller units that are threaded together by this shaping formula – the digressions, sub-plots, and so on. If a novel is looked at in terms of these smaller units, much of it will be found to be somewhat journalistic and topical; it may, for instance, be geared to praising a recent Soviet achievement or to broadcasting or rationalizing a new decree.

The overarching plot of a given novel is not tied, as are these smaller units, to the particular point in time when it was written (such as to celebrating a recent decree that may be revoked subsequently). If its plot were stripped of all references to a particular time or place, or to a particular theme of the novel, it could be distilled to a highly generalized essence. The abstract version of a given novel's plot is the element that is, in effect, shaped by the masterplot.

Not all Soviet novels follow the masterplot. Not even all novels in the canon follow it completely. One will note, for example, that many of the canonical exemplars were published in the 1920s, or even earlier (like Gor'ky's *Mother*), namely, before socialist realism *per se* existed. They may from a post-1932 standpoint, however, be seen as embryonically socialist realist. In practice, once socialist realism had been instituted, aspects of earlier works that did not become conventional for socialist realism, or perhaps were even proscribed in canonical formulations of it, either became, as it were, 'non-aspects' in that they were totally ignored in the criticism, or they were written out in subsequent redactions (one example of this can be found in the first, 1925 redaction of Gladkov's *Cement*, in which an apparently positive character, Badin, is a rapist!). More remarkably, one of the official classics of Soviet literature, Sholokhov's *Quiet Flows the Don*, shows only occasional traces of the masterplot, and primarily in connection with lesser characters. Statistically, however, a detectable (though hypothetical) masterplot has been followed to a greater or lesser degree in the overwhelming majority of Soviet novels from the 1930s and 1940s. Its status as a defining trait of socialist realism does not depend on the actual percentage of novels patterned on it, for the masterplot is not random or arbitrary; it illustrates major tenets of Marxism-Leninism.

The use of a formulaic plot suggests that socialist realism might be compared with other varieties of popular formulaic literature, such as detective stories and serial romances. Such comparisons have their limits, however, because the socialist realist novel is not intended to be 'mere entertainment'. From at least 1932–4, the time when the canon was instituted, its main function was to serve as the repository of official state myths. It had a mandatory allegorical function in that the biography of its hero was expected to stand in for the great myths of national identity.

Stalinist political culture centred on two major, and interrelated, myths of national identity, the myth (or master metaphor) of the 'Great Family', and the myth of Moscow. The Great Family of Stalinist myth is essentially the Stalinist state. As a 'family', it is contrasted with the 'little', or nuclear, family to which individuals are expected to pay allegiance only to the extent that this nuclear family is itself subordinated to the interests of the Great Family (should any conflict between the two arise, the family that is 'greater' must take priority). The Great Family, unlike the nuclear family, contains in effect only two categories of kin, both generally masculine. There are 'fathers', who are primarily represented as strong, determined leaders who are enlightened politically. Their worthy 'sons' are exemplary citizens, or citizens of extraordinary potential, whose exploits mark them out from the others but who are as yet limited in their ability to assume leadership roles (to become 'fathers') by an immaturity that is of course political, but is commonly represented in literature, film, and other cultural products reinforcing the status quo as an almost boyish hotheadedness, an impulsiveness or tendency to act on their own initiative and not be sufficiently guided by the Party.

The identification between developmental and political immaturity in the 'sons' is facilitated by the fact that their impetuousness is represented as a form of *stikhiinost'*. *Stikhiinost'*, which would be translated literally as 'elementalness' since its root *stikhiia* means 'the elements', can be used for a wide range of arbitrary, wilful or headstrong behaviour but is at the same time a technical term in Marxism for 'spontaneity'. 'Spontaneity', in one of the most abstract versions of the overall Marxist model for historical progress, is locked in dialectical conflict with political consciousness or *soznatel'nost'*.

In effect, the socialist realist novel is a kind of *Bildungsroman* with the *Bildung*, or formation of character, having more to do with public values than individual development. In the myth of the Great Family, the model 'son's' spontaneity must be tempered under the guidance of an exemplary, highly conscious 'father' before he can gain that status for himself. Each novel is structured as a story of how a particular model 'son' (the positive hero) progresses over time as his spontaneity is tempered under the guidance of a highly conscious 'father'. Towards the end of the novel, in a highly charged moment, the hero's attainment of mastery is recognized in a sort of ritual of initiation that enables him to cross over to the status of a 'father'. Generally, what this initiation amounts to is a conversation, conducted with a particular aura, between the 'son' and his moral/ political mentor, his 'father', who may, in addition to his homily, hand him a Party or Komsomol card as a form of passing on the baton. In some instances, this conversation is the last testament of a loyal communist before a heroic death (whether in revolutionary battle, or because he has ruined his own health in his tireless work for the cause).

This event (the initiation), or series of events (of encounters between the 'son' and his 'father') in the individual life of the hero represents the broader processes taking place in society at large. The general plot, with its emphasis on the succession by a more robust 'son' to the status of his 'father' who is most often shown as spent and in decline (or about to be posted elsewhere so that the son literally succeeds him in the local hierarchy), affirms that the country is progressing in a series of ever greater passages or revolutionary leaps to that end moment when it will attain a state of fully achieved communism. This moment (the initiation) is also one when the dialectical conflict between the (politically) conscious and those whose political consciousness is as yet inchoate and undisciplined, will be resolved. Then, all will be conscious politically without sacrificing spontaneity completely, and all will have attained an extra-personal identity, having jettisoned their narrow, counterproductive, self-centred identities.

In a typical socialist realist novel this general process unfolds at a deep structural level and is manifested largely only in the encounters between 'father' and 'son' which, in the interests of maintaining an elevated tone for such moments, are infrequent but crucial. At the surface level, the hero is otherwise shown to progress, to mature, as he undergoes all sorts of trials and tackles insurmountable obstacles, thus enhancing his stature as a true hero. Most socialist realist novels are structured around the task the hero is to perform in the public sphere (such as raise the yield of grain in the collective farm, build a bridge or a power station, exceed the plan's figures for his factory's output, or drive the enemy out of a particular town), the obstacles confronting the hero are often from the natural world. For example, as he tries to build a power station in his district, he may find the project threatened by a flood. Even more frequently, the obstacles in fact come from within the world of the hero's bureaucratic administration, or from military life, but are represented *as if* from the natural world. This is particularly the case for representing the enemies (national or class) who may be described as beasts or vipers, or as advancing like a firestorm or a flow of molten lava.

In presenting the hero principally with natural or natural-like obstacles, writers were effectively realizing the metaphor that is at the base of *stikhiinost'*. As, in a given work, the hero learns to control the 'elemental' that is without, as he shows his mastery over it, this signifies his mastery of *political* consciousness. Alternatively, he may have to learn to master the seething passions within, a process that is *de facto* conflated with political mastery.

When the positive hero crosses over to a higher order of consciousness, when he makes his 'great leap forward', this affirms that the country under the present leadership is on its proper course towards communism. The novel is both a primer for the Soviet Everyman to follow and a repository of myths of maintenance for the Soviet status quo.

This parabolic structure of the socialist realist novel is enabled by a common convention followed by the majority of Stalinist novels: the novel is set not in Moscow or Leningrad, but in a provincial locale. This locale, the novel's micro-cosm, is generally depicted as a relatively hermetic unit situated a considerable distance from these major cities. The novels that *are* set in Moscow or Leningrad are generally set in a particular factory or city district. The isolated, provincial locale that is the setting of most socialist realist novels functions as a 'typical' place, a microcosm in which one may see to scale the general processes taking place in society. But the microcosm is, as befits its location, more backward both politically and economically than Moscow, that higher point of orientation for all the novel's characters.

Thus the myth of Moscow was also an integral element in the socialist-realist tradition. This myth was not, however, generated only within literature and film. At more or less the same time as the doctrine of socialist realism was established, a central preoccupation of the leadership was a project for the reconstruction of the city of Moscow to make it an exemplum of the socialist city. Moscow, as capital of a highly centralized society, was to be an enhanced space, ahead of its time physically as the leaders were politically. Hence, in socialist realism the provincial setting of a given work functioned as a periphery, contrasted as such with the 'centre' that was Moscow.

Thus the positive hero progresses both through time (in a ritual of maturation) and through place. In so doing, he bridges the gap between 'the periphery' and 'Moscow', and he narrows the gap between ordinary citizens (those of the 'periphery') and the country's élite.

Thus the 'son' figure in a socialist realist novel, or in other words the protagonist, is both ordinary and extraordinary. For most of the novel, he appears as one of the most politically committed and inspiring representatives of the Soviet Everyman. Like most ordinary human beings, he is impulsive and subject to the passions. However, he is generally distinguished from the other characters by brimming with greater energy and initiative. Thus he can be more appealing as a model for the reader to emulate than the 'father' figure who is much more perfect, disciplined, and austere than his 'son' and generally appears in the novel much less (it is, after all, more difficult to organize a readable, or particularly suspenseful, novel around a model figure).

This dual identity in the positive hero (ordinary/extraordinary) is a characteristic of socialist realism. Zhdanov, in his speech to the First Writers' Congress, called for the new Soviet literature to combine 'the most matter-of-fact, everyday reality and the most heroic prospects'. As if in response, novels kept oscillating between 'realistic' representation and a hyperbolically heroic world where heroes perform seemingly impossible feats. Moreover, the transition between ordinary and extraordinary is often quite unmotivated.

The lack of motivation for shifts in mode is not problematical within the system of socialist realism because each of the major characters in a given work is not really a character *per se*, so much as he (sometimes it is a she) is a sub-function of his moral/political role ('son' or 'father'). Indeed, the positive heroes are marked as having that special status by a cluster of iconic traits and epithets that indicate symbolically their moral/political identity or, in other words, their function as a positive form of 'consciousness' or 'spontaneity' incarnate. 'Consciousness', for example, is indicated by such epithets as 'calm', 'determined', 'austere', and 'stern'. Another cluster of clichéd epithets and attributes indicate the position that each of the two positive characters occupies on the life cycle. Regardless of their respective ages, a character whose function is that of a 'son' must be youthful and full of vigour, and a 'father' figure decidedly older (possibly with a bent back or heavily lined face that reveals how much he has sacrificed himself for the cause). These small details effectively functioned as a code. Indeed, it was partly in these tiny details that, over time, one saw development in the socialist realist tradition.

Each novel was written in a context affected by change, controversy, and even the author's own position. All these factors bore upon how the code was deployed in an individual work and had the power to change its meanings. New meanings could come from within the system of signs by the slightest rearrangement, emphasis, or shading of the standard signs and sequences. Such changes may be scarcely perceptible to an outsider not schooled in the tradition, but they would be striking to most Soviet readers.

The patterns outlined here emerged in the 1930s. However, they remained generally applicable in the 1940s because of the cultural conservatism that characterized that decade. Even though the 1930s saw the worst purges of Soviet history, the 1940s enjoy the reputation of being the worst period of Soviet cultural history, known as the Zhdanov era. The era therefore took its name from Andrei Zhdanov, who had delivered one of the keynote speeches to the First Writers' Congress and who, in 1946, delivered a lecture on the journals *Zvezda* and *Leningrad* (directed also against the writers Anna Akhmatova and Mikhail Zoshchenko). This barrage, together with other speeches and newspaper attacks that appeared in its wake, signalled the end of hopes of liberalization, and a return to rigid adherence to the socialist-realist canon (which had been less strictly enforced during the war years). Consequently, there was less modification of the socialist-realist code during that period than one might otherwise have expected. However, given the stress on adherence to the conventions of socialist realism, writers, in their anxiety to prove their dedication, tended to overdo their obeisance to the masterplot. Most of its standard functions do not just occur, but are proliferated throughout a given novel. For example, a typical novel of the 1940s has not just one mentor figure as its main character, but many. Functions lost their logic and their ideological purpose in the novel's overall design and became yet another pattern of whorls in some superabundant decoration.

The two functions used with greatest extravagance in 1940s novels were the mentor's 'last testament' and the scene in which he symbolically 'passes the baton' to the hero. Most novels do not rest with one such scene, but contrive to introduce at least two or three. Perhaps the novel that outdoes them all in this respect is the 1951 rewritten, canonical version of Valentin Kataev's *For the Power of the Soviets* (*Za vlast' sovetov*), whose protagonist, Pet'ia, receives so many 'batons' from older, Party and partisan stalwarts (many of them entrusted as they are dying, or even posthumously) that one begins to suspect his primary function is to receive batons.

The effect of such superabundance in 1940s novels is not to reinforce the masterplot but rather to undermine it. The result is the main weakness of these novels – incongruity. Indeed, in novels published after Zhdanov's 'signal' lecture the mode was tilted so far away from the 'realistic' in favour of the 'romantic' (the glossy or larger-than-life) that even before Stalin died (as early as 1951) critics began to complain that there was too much 'varnishing of reality' (*lakirovka deistvitel'nosti*), a charge that was heard more loudly and insistently once Stalin had died in 1953.

After Stalin's death, there was a return to more realistic, less bombastic – or simply improbable – depiction of Soviet reality. Yet one should not assume that writers were merely 'strait-jacketed' in the Stalin years, mere 'afflati' of the official position. After all, many of them were serious intellectuals. Since the clichés of socialist realism effectively formed a code, they could be used not only to establish a given writer's political loyalty, but to hint at meanings that he might not be able to make explicit.

If a Soviet writer wanted to be sure his novel would be published, he had to use the proper language (epithets, catch phrases, stock images, and so on) and syntax (to order the events of the novel in accordance with the *de facto* masterplot). To do so was effectively a ritual act of affirmation of loyalty to the state. Once the writer had accomplished this, his novel could be called 'party-minded'. But he had room for *some* play in the ideas these standard features expressed because of the variety of potential meanings for each of the clichés. The system of signs was, simultaneously, the components of a ritual of affirmation and a surrogate for the Aesopian language to which writers resorted in tsarist times when they wanted to outwit censors. Thus, paradoxically, the very rigidity of socialist realism's formations permitted freer expression than would have been possible (given the watchful eye of the censor) if the novel had been less formulaic.

FURTHER READING

Brown, Edward J. *The Proletarian Episode in Russian Literature, 1928–1932*, New York: Columbia University Press, 1953.

Chung, Hilary, and Falchikov, Michael (eds) *In the Party Spirit: Socialist Realism and Literary Practice in the Soviet Union, East Germany and China*, Amsterdam and Atlanta: Rodopi, 1996.

Clark, Katerina. *The Soviet Novel: History as Ritual*, Chicago: University of Chicago Press, 1981; 2nd edn, 1985; 3rd edn Bloomington: Indiana University Press, 2000.

Dobrenko, Evgeny. *The Making of the State Reader: Social and Aesthetic Contexts of the Reception of Soviet Literature*, trans. Jesse M. Savage, Stanford: Stanford University Press, 1997.

Gutkin, Irina. *The Cultural Origins of the Socialist Realist Aesthetic, 1890–1934*, Evanston, Illinois: Northwestern University Press, 1999.

James, C. Vaughan. *Soviet Socialist Realism: Origins and Theory*, London: Macmillan; New York: St Martin's Press, 1973.

Luker, Nicholas (ed.) *From Furmanov to Sholokhov: An Anthology of the Classics of Socialist Realism*, Ann Arbor: Ardis, 1988.

Scott, H.G. (ed.) *Soviet Writers' Congress 1934: The Debate on Socialist Realism and Modernism in the Soviet Union*, London: Lawrence and Wishart, 1977 (first published 1935).

Tertz, Abram [Andrei Siniavsky]. *On Socialist Realism*, trans. George Dennis, New York: Pantheon, 1961; with *The Trial Begins*, New York: Vintage, 1965; Berkeley: University of California Press, 1982.

16

EXPERIMENT AND EMIGRATION: RUSSIAN LITERATURE, 1917–1953

BORIS LANIN

In the first few years after the 1917 October Revolution, more than three million Russians were beyond the rapidly diminishing geographical borders of the Russian Empire. There were those who were simply swept along by the wind of the proletarian revolution, but in the main the exodus comprised the intelligentsia and the officer class – the potential readership of the literature of the Russian emigration. Thus a new mass readership came spontaneously into being, with an abundance of writers and works on which to feast. The diaspora contained representatives of the most diverse styles and trends: among the realists were Ivan Bunin, Aleksei Tolstoy, and Ivan Shmelev; the modernists included Andrei Bely (temporarily) and Aleksei Remizov, and were later joined by Evgenii Zamiatin; the Symbolists were represented by Konstantin Bal'mont, Dmitrii Merezhkovsky, Zinaida Hippius, and Viacheslav Ivanov – the latter subsequently becoming head of the Vatican library in Rome; of the Acmeists there were Georgii Ivanov and Nikolai Otsup; the Futurist contingent comprised Igor' Severianin and David Burliuk; others included the writers of popular fiction Ivan Nazhivin and Mikhail Artsybashev, and important figures such as Leonid Andreev, Irina Odoevtseva, Boris Zaitsev, Aleksandr Kuprin, and many other lesser names. In emigration they shared the general politicization of their environment, a nostalgia for a vanished world, and the desire to come to a new understanding of their sharply altered literary status. Many of them considered it their duty to combine their literary pursuits with political engagement by exposing the vices of the Soviet regime and continually drawing world attention to what they saw as its evils. Among these artistically weak, but publicistically powerful, works can be included Ivan Bunin's *The Cursed Days* (*Okaiannye dni*, 1935), Ivan Shmelev's *The Sun of the Dead* (*Solntse mertvykh*, 1926), Aleksei Remizov's *Russia in the Whirlwind* (*Vzvikhrennaia Rus'*, 1927), and Mikhail Osorgin's *Quiet Street* (*Sivtsev Vrazhek*, 1928).

The political views of many writers had hardened even before they left Russia. If Vladimir Maiakovsky welcomed the Revolution and embraced it, then writers in the opposing camp rejected it utterly. Examples of anti-Bolshevik activities include Aleksandr Kuprin as editor of General Iudenich's army newspaper *Prinevskii krai*, Gleb Struve's editorship of the Rostov newspaper *Velikaia Rossiia*, and Ivan Bunin and Academician Kondakov as editors of the Odessa newspaper *Iuzhnoe slovo*. Others, such as Roman Gul', Antonii Ladinsky, and Ivan Lukash, actively took part in the Civil War on the side of the Whites.

If literary life in Russia was characterized by creeping censorship and the closure of privately owned publishing houses during the 1920s, then the picture in emigration was different. In Europe, China, and the United States many new publishing outlets, newspapers, and journals emerged. One hundred and thirty Russian newspapers were published in 1920, the next year 250, and in 1922 more than 350. The most popular of these were the Paris-based *Poslednie novosti* (1920–40); and *Obshchee delo* and *Vozrozhdenie* (1925–40), *Rul'* (1920–31), *Segodnia* and *Za svobodu*, which operated, respectively, from Berlin, Riga, and Warsaw. The leading literary journals included *Griadushchaia Rossiia* (Paris), *Russkaia mysl'* (Sofia–Prague–Paris, 1921–7), edited by P.B. Struve, *Volia Rossii* (Prague), and the famous *Sovremennye zapiski* (Paris, 1920–40). In 1942, with the second wave of Russian emigration, *Novyi zhurnal* began to be published in New York. Important publishing houses were set up in Paris and Berlin. In Berlin Z.I. Grzhebin and I.V. Gessen established outlets, and others worthy of mention are Mysl' and Petropolis. In Paris the publishers Russkaia zemlia, Sovremennye zapiski, and Vozrozhdenie were founded. Elsewhere Bibliofil in Revel, Russkaia biblioteka in Belgrade, Severnye ogni in Stockholm, Gramatu draugs in Riga, Plamia in Prague, Rossiia-Bolgariia in Sofia, and many others contributed to what was a vibrant and active literary community.

The years 1921–3 saw Berlin as the capital of Russian emigration, uniting both Soviet writers and émigrés. It was in Berlin that the journals *Russkaia kniga* (after 1922 it became *Novaia russkaia kniga*), and Andrei Bely's *Epopeia* were published, as well as *Beseda*, founded by Gor'ky and orientated towards Soviet Russia even though it was banned there. The literary situation in Berlin was unique because émigrés were published side by side with Soviet writers, so-called fellow-travellers. Some writers who were resident in Berlin at this time decided to return to Soviet Russia, including Bely, Gor'ky, Aleksei Tolstoy, Ivan Sokolov-Mikitov, Viktor Shklovsky, and Il'ia Erenburg.

Berlin was not, however, the only centre of Russian émigré literary activity. The printing presses in Paris and then New York were also busy. The poet Igor' Severianin lived out the rest of his days in Estonia. The Riga-based newspaper *Segodnia* was read throughout the Baltic republics and Poland. The publishing house Salamandra produced the daily newspaper *Slovo* and the illustrated journal *Perezvony* (1925–9), whose literary section was run by Boris Zaitsev. *Perezvony* was responsible for publishing works by Bunin, Shmelev, Konstantin Bal'mont, Teffi, Mark Aldanov, and Georgii Adamovich.

In Warsaw the Taverna poetov was run by Professor A.L. Bem, before he left for Prague (he was arrested and executed there in 1945 by the Red Army). In Harbin the journal *Rubezh* flourished between 1927 and 1945. Its most frequent contributor was the notable poet Arsenii Nesmelov, who was to die in prison after his return to the USSR. Shanghai was the birthplace of the journal *Russkie zapiski* (1937–9), as well as *Shankhaiskaia zaria*, *Slovo*, *Novyi put'*, *Russkii avangard*, *Russkoe znamia*, *Emigrantskaia mysl'*, *Putevoi znak*, *Svet*, *Dal'nevostochnyi vestnik*, several daily and weekly newspapers, and some publishing houses.

Nashe znanie, based in Tientsin, published the crude anti-communist novels of N.N. Breshko-Breshkovsky: *King of the Machine-Guns* (*Korol' pulemetov*), *Beneath the Cloak of Satan* (*Pod plashchom satany*), and *Europe Aroused* (*Vzdyblennaia Evropa*). A.I. Serebriakov's publishing house in Tientsin established some sort of record by producing Ivan Nazhivin's *Collected Works* in forty volumes.

Yugoslavia became first and foremost the military centre of Russian emigration, although Belgrade was the home of the newspaper *Novoe vremia*, founded by M.A. Suvorin, son of the eminent Russian journalist and publisher. The Yugoslav king gave funds to émigré writers, and the publishing house Russkaia biblioteka was attached to the Serbian Academy of Sciences. Belgrade also hosted in September 1928 the first (and last) Congress of Writers and Journalists. Among those who took part were Aleksandr Kuprin, Dmitrii Merezhkovsky, Zinaida Hippius, Vasilii Nemirovich-Danchenko (the brother of Vladimir, founder of the Moscow Arts Theatre), and Boris Zaitsev.

One of the most important centres was Prague, the home of the satirist and journalist Arkadii Averchenko until his death in 1925. There existed here a Union of Russian Writers and Journalists, and literary discussions and soirées were organized around readings of works by Bunin, Vladimir Nabokov, and Mikhail Osorgin. The Free Russian University held seminars on literature, including modern literature.

When the cream of Russian philosophy was expelled from Russia in 1922, and with the consequent pressure exerted by the Soviet regime towards its intellectuals, the atmosphere in Berlin changed for the worse. No longer was dialogue and co-operation between Soviet and émigré writers possible. The capital of the first wave of the Russian emigration switched to Paris, which in the early 1920s was already the home of Aldanov, Bal'mont, Bunin, Hippius, Teffi, Dmitrii Merezhkovsky, and others.

Sovremennye zapiski emerged as the leading journal of the emigration. One of its editors was I.I. Bunakov-Fondaminsky, whose organizational capabilities attracted some of the leading lights of the emigration. It was also largely thanks to Bunakov-Fondaminsky that, despite straitened circumstances, seventy issues in all were published. Bunakov-Fondaminsky maintained close relations with Hippius and Merezhkovsky, whom he had known before the Revolution, Aleksei Tolstoy and his wife Nataliia Krandievskaia, Bunin, and Nabokov. Aleksei Tolstoy published the first (and best) version of his novel *Road to Calvary* (*Khozhdenie po mukam*) in *Sovremennye zapiski* (1920–21).

Bunakov-Fondaminsky also founded, together with Fedor Stepun and Georgii Fedotov, the journal *Novyi grad* (1931–9). As a Jew, Bunakov-Fondaminsky was sent to a concentration camp in the aftermath of the Nazi occupation of France. He was killed in 1942 in Auschwitz. *Sovremennye zapiski* was closed down on the eve of the Nazi invasion of France in 1940. In its time it had published such leading lights as Andrei Bely, Maksimilian Voloshin, Zamiatin, Remizov, Bunin, Gaito Gazdanov, Vladislav Khodasevich, Marina Tsvetaeva, Boris Poplavsky, and many others.

In ideological terms the political life of the emigration revolved around the Socialist Revolutionaries. In 1921 the collection *Changing Landmarks* (*Smena vekh*), edited by Iu.V. Kliuchnikov, S.S. Luk'ianov, and N.V. Ustrialov, put forward the idea of accommodation with the Bolsheviks, and from this idea the newspaper *Nakanune* was born. Together with the Berlin journal *Novaia russkaia kniga*, it published works by both émigré and Soviet writers. The literary section of *Nakanune* was edited by Count Aleksei Tolstoy, and was so popular in the Soviet Union that works written by Moscow authors were sent to Berlin via the diplomatic bag! Soviet writers who were published here included Konstantin Fedin, Sergei Esenin, Valentin Kataev, and Mikhail Bulgakov. Unfortunately, the real nature of the Soviet regime became clear later to the leaders of the *smenovekhovtsy* (the 'Changing Landmarks' group of émigré intellectuals, seeking rapprochement with the USSR), for on their return to Soviet Russia many of them were repressed.

Another trend that flirted with Bolshevism was Eurasianism. It emphasized Russia's links with Asia and the East, and saw Russia's geographical position between Europe and Asia as a 'third path' of development. Leading representatives were the philosophers Nikolai Trubetskoi and Georgii Florovsky. Between 1926 and 1928 the Eurasian journal *Versty*, edited by D.P. Sviatopolk-Mirsky, P.P. Suvchinsky, and S.Ia. Efron, was published in Paris. The ideas of Eurasianism even found reflection in Soviet literature, in the work of Boris Pil'niak and Vsevolod Ivanov. The leaders of the Eurasian movement met with representatives of the Soviet leadership, including General Tukhachevsky, unaware that they were being set up as part of a political intrigue. The Eurasian movement was later destroyed through the machinations of the NKVD.

If the Eurasians and the *smenovekhovtsy*, and the writers who supported them, advocated some rapprochement with the Bolsheviks, then the followers of the 'white idea' categorically rejected any such compromise. Through their Paris-based newspaper *Vozrozhdenie*, edited from 1925 to 1927 by P.B. Struve, the white movement developed a coherent anti-communist programme and a whole political ideology.

The literary section of *Vozrozhdenie* was edited by Vladislav Khodasevich. One of its central figures was Ivan Bunin, since 1920 one of the spiritual leaders of the White movement, and the chairman of the Union of Russian Writers and Journalists. The Russian literary emigration gained the recognition it craved in 1933, when Bunin became the first Russian to win the Nobel Prize for Literature.

A place where writers could meet was the social centre 'Pravoslavnoe delo' (Orthodox Cause) in Paris, founded by Elizaveta Skobtseva, née Pilenko (Kuz'mina-Karavaeva by her first marriage), otherwise known as Mat' Mariia. Her two-volume book on the lives of the saints, entitled *Harvest of the Spirit* (*Zhatva dukha*), came out in 1927, and her *Poems* (*Stikhi*) was published in 1937. She died in the Nazi concentration camp at Ravensbrück in 1945, and her posthumous collection *Poems* (*Stikhotvoreniia*) came out in 1947.

Any real literary process is impossible to envisage without the interaction of different generations of writers. The younger generation of émigré writers was disenchanted with the liberal ideas of their fathers, as a result of which two organizations were established. Molodaia Rossiia (Young Russia) accommodated both monarchists and National Bolsheviks-cum-Fascists, and in 1934 called itself the 'second Soviet Party' in far-left opposition to the Bolsheviks. They worked with the journal *Novyi grad*, founded by Bunakov-Fondaminsky, Stepun, and Fedotov. During the War 'Molodaia Rossiia' fought against the Nazis. A far more durable organization was the National Labour Union, which has survived to this day. Basing its ideology on the philosophy of Sergei Levitsky and Roman Redlikh, the Union saw Soviet totalitarianism in the same light as that later described by George Orwell in his novel *1984*. In 1946 the Posev publishing house was set up, its name deliberately symbolic (i.e. sowing the seeds of enlightenment). Posev published books by both the first and subsequent waves of emigration. It also still runs two journals: *Posev*, which is inclined to social and political debate; and *Grani*, which is more of a literary journal. *Grani* was the first émigré journal permitted by the Soviet government to gain subscribers on the territory of the USSR, in 1988. Today its editorial offices are situated in Russia, in the town of Ramenskoe, near Moscow.

The younger generation of émigrés in Paris gathered around Vladislav Khodasevich and Georgii Adamovich. Indeed, these elder statesmen played the same role in the emigration that Zamiatin played in Soviet Russia in the early 1920s, and which was later taken up by Gor'ky. Finally, many young writers of the emigration were associated with the Russian Christian Movement Abroad, which also included such luminaries as the philosophers Father Sergei Bulgakov and Nikolai Berdiaev, and the literary scholar Konstantin Mochul'sky.

The emigration's fidelity to the traditions of classical Russian literature became not just a protest against their profanation in the Soviet literary process – suffice it to mention here the numerous comparisons of Aleksandr Fadeev with Lev Tolstoy – but also a separate theme. Full-length studies of the Russian classical heritage include, apart from those by Berdiaev, Bunin's *Tolstoy's Liberation* (*Osvobozhdenie Tolstogo*, 1937), and his unfinished *About Chekhov* (*O Chekhove*), published in 1955; Boris Zaitsev's *The Life of Turgenev* (*Zhizn' Turgeneva*, 1932), *Zhukovsky* (1954), and *Chekhov* (1954); Khodasevich's novel *Derzhavin* (1931), and his critical works *Pushkin's Poetic Economy* (*Poeticheskoe khoziaistvo Pushkina*, 1924) and *On Pushkin* (*O Pushkine*, 1937).

One of the features of émigré literature that made it distinct from Soviet literature was the unfettered evolution of its religious motifs. One of the most prominent Orthodox writers in the diaspora was Boris Zaitsev, who developed the religious themes already evident in his *oeuvre* in such works as *The Life of St Sergius of Radonezh* (*Prepodobnyi Sergii Radonezhskii*, 1926), *Strange Journey* (*Strannoe puteshestvie*, 1924), *Athos* (*Afon*, 1928), and *Valaam* (1936). The same themes are evident in his secular writings, such as his four-volume autobiographical *Gleb's Journey* (*Puteshestvie Gleba*, 1937–53).

Ivan Shmelev moved from anti-Bolshevik tirades in the 1920s to books infused with religious feeling. These include *Pilgrimage* (*Bogomol'e*, 1935), *The Summer of Our Lord* (*Leto Gospodne*, 1933–48), and *Heavenly Ways* (*Puti nebesnye*, 1937–48).

The literature of the Russian emigration retained its links with the literary past, but was inwardly free, under no pressure from State diktat, and did not have to look nervously over its shoulder for the censor or the secret police. In this, of course, it is markedly different from the literature of the Soviet Union, which depended on the arbitrary whim of the censor and which was subject to editorial interference. Soviet writers *en masse* willingly compromised themselves, and submitted to self-censorship in their artistic and philosophical reflections. Only a handful (Anna Akhmatova, Osip Mandel'shtam, Evgenii Zamiatin, and a few others) were able to distance themselves from the approaching totalitarian onslaught. For those outside the country, inner freedom was perhaps the only compensation for being torn from their land and their roots.

The first wave of the literary emigration was formed during the Civil War, but its numbers continued to increase in subsequent years. One of the most important prose writers of the twentieth century, Evgenii Zamiatin, was among the growing number of later émigrés. Zamiatin's run-in with the Bolshevik authorities was occasioned by his novel *We* (*My*), written in 1920. It is typically anti-utopian in form, with its heretical lone hero who stands in opposition to the regime. In the 1920s and 1930s Zamiatin was no dissident wanting fundamentally to change the structures of power (all the more so as these structures had not yet taken shape in the form in which we know them today). Above all he was concerned with questions of the writer's freedom to create. His 1921 article 'I Fear' ('Ia boius' ') was prophetic in this respect, for in it he asserted that 'Russian literature has but one future – its past'. Zamiatin's own subsequent career in his native land was to be ample proof of that.

Zamiatin wrote to Stalin requesting permission to emigrate (although on reading the letter one could be forgiven for thinking that he actually demanded permission to emigrate). In November 1931 Zamiatin left Russia, and never returned. He was accompanied to the railway station by another 'heretic', Mikhail Bulgakov, who was to remain in Russia. Zamiatin remained a Soviet citizen to the end of his days, and at international conferences he spoke as the representative of the Soviet delegation.

In emigration Zamiatin developed his career in other areas, for instance in writing screenplays (notably for Jean Renoir's adaptation of Gor'ky's *The Lower Depths* [*Na dne*] as *Les Bas-fonds*) and literary criticism. He published articles on Soviet literature in *Novyi zhurnal* and the French journal *Marianne*, and in 1931 gave a lecture in Prague on the contemporary Russian theatre. His most important publications in his émigré period, though, remain works of fiction. His novel *Scourge of God* (*Bich bozhii*), about Attila the Hun, was written between 1928 and 1935, and a collection of miscellaneous writings appeared in New York in 1955. Other notable works by Zamiatin include *Miracles* (*Chudesa*) and *Russia* (*Rus'*), which are reminiscent of works by Nikolai Leskov, Aleksei Remizov, and Anatole France. However, although Remizov, despite the vagaries of his chosen subject, expressed himself to the point of self-parody, Zamiatin in *Miracles* remains ironically detached, even erotic, and rejects the possibility of returning to the past.

Zamiatin had much in common with the Formalists in his emphasis on the importance of style and composition, rhythm and syntax. It is therefore not fortuitous that it was Viktor Shklovsky, the last surviving Formalist, who campaigned for Zamiatin's publication in the Soviet Union in the early 1980s. Like the Formalists, Zamiatin spoke of the art of discourse, and for him a poetic work was something akin to a musical composition or an architectural monument constructed from words. His views on the poetic and narrative technique of Boris Pil'niak echo the Formalist thesis of making reality 'strange' (*ostranenie*) in a literary work. (Both Pil'niak and Zamiatin were subjected to harsh ideologically-based persecution in 1929.) In his 1920 lecture 'On Language' ('O iazyke') Zamiatin announced that a writer must create his own language, with its own laws and its own lexis. The lexis must be wide-ranging, from dialect to archaisms to terms from contemporary science. The narrative must be built around a meticulous selection of images. In 'Behind the Scenes' ('Zakulisy') Zamiatin also said that the writer must forget about the technical side of writing to allow his characters to take on their own life within his consciousness.

Zamiatin's lectures laid the groundwork for the emergence of other literary groupings in the 1920s, in particular the Serapion Brothers. This group contained many young writers, such as Vsevolod Ivanov, Nikolai Tikhonov, Konstantin Fedin, Mikhail Zoshchenko, Nikolai Nikitin, Mikhail Slonimsky, Veniamin Kaverin, Lev Lunts, the critic I. Gruzdev, and others. The theoretician and unofficial leader of the Serapion Brothers was the brilliant Lev Lunts, who died at the tragically young age of twenty-three. He wrote the manifesto 'Why Are We Serapion Brothers?' ('Pochemu my Serapionovy brat'ia?', 1922), and the article 'Ideology and Publicistic Literature' ('Ob ideologii i publitsistike', 1923). On 27 February 1922 the Communist Party Central Committee decided to support the Serapionovy brat'ia publishing house on condition that the members of the group did not publish in other 'reactionary' publications.

The Serapion Brothers regarded Zamiatin as their literary 'uncle'. The subsequent erasing of his name from the literary annals naturally produced a distorted picture of the nature of the post-revolutionary literary process. Zamiatin was indefatigable and transformed the House of Art, where he delivered his lectures, into something of a literary academy. The writer and artist Iurii Annenkov notes that it was impossible to calculate the number of lectures Zamiatin gave to his class, all accompanied by readings from the works of the Serapion Brothers and informed discussion of them.

Another leading figure of the 1920s who refused to buckle before the onslaught of left-wing criticism and state coercion was Mikhail Bulgakov. Real debate that would be impossible in the succeeding decades raged around his 1926 play *The Days of the Turbins* (*Dni Turbinykh*) and the novel on which it was based, *The White Guard* (*Belaia gvardiia*, 1925). After clashes with the censor, Bulgakov wrote his celebrated 'Letter to the Soviet Government' ('Pis'mo sovetskomu pravitel'stvu'), in which he asserted it as his duty as a writer to fight censorship in all its forms. It was in this spirit that he wrote the plays *The Crimson Island* (*Bagrovyi ostrov*), *Flight* (*Beg*), and *The Last Days (Pushkin)* (*Poslednie dni*), the dystopian novella *The Fatal Eggs* (*Rokovye iaitsa*), and the prose work *The Life of Monsieur de Molière* (*Zhizn' gospodina de Mol'era*). Nevertheless, Bulgakov gained some ideological insurance by writing the pro-Stalin play *Batum*. Having survived the terrible years of the 1930s, Bulgakov died in 1940 of sclerosis of the kidneys.

Among the most important names in Russian literature of the 1920s and 1930s were Andrei Platonov and Boris Pil'niak. Platonov depicted Marxism as a new religion, totalitarianism as the destruction of culture, machinery, and technology as the new symbols of life. Pil'niak, on the other hand, saw the Revolution as an elemental upsurge of energy. Pil'niak began work on his novel *The Naked Year* (*Golyi god*) in the summer of 1917, and completed it on 25 December 1920. He realized that the Revolution was history being made before his very eyes, and he tried to convey the colossal scale of events in his novel. Thus the image of the storm, with its elemental fury, plays a vital role. The novel is episodic in structure, built around a montage of conflicting themes that express the author's basic idea of post-revolutionary Russia as torn asunder and worn down by life's redundant details.

The publication in 1926 of *Tale of the Unextinguished Moon* (*Povest' nepogashennoi luny*), based on the death of the legendary military commander Mikhail Frunze after an unnecessary operation that Stalin forced him to have, brought Pil'niak to the attention of the secret police. His novel *Mahogany* (*Krasnoe derevo*), which he himself called his 'harshest anti-Soviet work', was published abroad in 1929, and Pil'niak, alongside Zamiatin, was subjected to bitter attacks. Among those demanding their exclusion from the Writers' Federation were Valentin Kataev, Efim Zozulia, Eduard Bagritsky, and Mikhail Kol'tsov.

Pil'niak wrote the essay 'Che-Che-O' with Andrei Platonov in 1928. Further works include *The Volga Falls to the Caspian Sea* (*Volga vpadaet v Kaspiiskoe more*), an attempt to obey the 'social command' of literature, *The Ripening of Fruit* (*Sozrevanie plodov*) and *OK: An American Novel* (*O'kei: Amerikanskii roman*). Even this latter, a favourite of Stalin's, was not enough to save him from arrest in 1937 and execution in 1938. Despite his posthumous rehabilitation in 1956, it was only in 1976 that the first book edition of his works appeared.

Leonid Dobychin (1896–1936) wrote very little: two volumes of short stories and the short novel *The City of N* (*Gorod En*). Dobychin's experimentalism was not understood by his contemporaries, as it adhered neither to the dictates of socialist realism nor imitated the ornamental prose of Pil'niak and Zamiatin, and he remained on the periphery of Russian literary life. *The City of N* runs counter to the ideological tendentiousness of much Russian literature of the time, with its world of phantasmagoria and travesty in which nothing has a name. Dobychin was accused by the Leningrad Writers' Union of Formalism and naturalism, as a consequence of which he disappeared. His body was fished out of the Neva several months later.

One of the most important developments in the emigration was Maksim Gor'ky's departure from Russia in 1921. This act may have been occasioned by the increasing clampdown on the literary intelligentsia, but may also owe something to the fact that he was not elected head of the Writers' Union in either the Moscow or Petrograd branches. Instead, Boris Zaitsev was elected head of the Moscow branch, and his deputies were Mikhail Osorgin and Nikolai Berdiaev. It is now obvious that after the Revolution, and after his anti-Leninist *Untimely Thoughts* (*Nesvoevremennye mysli*, 1918), the quality of his literary output declined. In these years Gor'ky wrote the cycle *Through Russia* (*Po Rusi*), the plays *Somov and Others* (*Somov i drugie*, written 1930–1), *Yegor Bulychov and Others* (*Egor' Bulychov i drugie*, written 1931), *Dostigaev and Others* (*Dostigaev i drugie*, 1934), and the novels *The Artamonov Business* (*Delo Artamonovykh*, 1925) and *The Life of Klim Samgin* (*Zhizn' Klima Samgina*, 1925–36). After he returned permanently to Russia in 1933 he was declared the 'founder of socialist realism'.

The Life of Klim Samgin is an important work, embracing Russian history over four decades. But his rewriting of *Vassa Zheleznova* in 1935, his protracted work on *Klim Samgin* and its artificial ending all speak of the creative crisis brought about by Gor'ky's absolute capitulation to Stalinism. He not only worked with the tyrant, but also supported him with both his own moral authority and his writings, in which he disparaged the intelligentsia and glorified the dictatorship of the proletariat. To the young writers who looked to him as their mentor he affirmed that a writer was first and foremost 'the eyes, ears, and voice of his class'.

Gor'ky's attitude towards the reality around him continues to arouse controversy. He justified the Solovki concentration camp after his trip there in 1929, as well as the White Sea canal constructed entirely by Gulag slave labour, and even the regime's repression of its political opponents (the Industrial Party, for instance). He furthermore shut his eyes to the brutality of collectivization, which led to tens of millions starving to death. Also, aspects of his life in emigration have yet to be clarified. For instance, was Gor'ky or his milieu involved in NKVD operations, or was Gor'ky's residence in the West used as a cover for Soviet espionage activities? Was Gor'ky involved in exporting and selling Russian cultural artefacts in order to buy grain for the Soviet Union to offset the calamitous consequences of collectivization? To what extent did the regime subsidize his various newspapers and journals, and encourage his acquaintance with those Western writers and journalists it deemed tolerable?

A particular genre in the literature of this time, especially in emigration, was autobiography. There were a number of works devoted to the nostalgia of childhood in the 'golden age', where the child's view of the world is complemented by that of the adult author/narrator. Among such works are Bunin's *The Life of Arsen'ev* (*Zhizn' Arsen'eva*, 1930–9); Gor'ky's trilogy *My Childhood* (*Detstvo*), *My Apprenticeship* (*V liudiakh*), and *My Universities* (*Moi universitety*), 1913–23; Zaitsev's *Gleb's Journey*, 1937–53; Kuprin's *The Junkers* (*Iunkera*, 1928–32); Aleksei Tolstoy's *Nikita's Childhood* (*Detstvo Nikity*, 1945); and Ivan Shmelev's *The Summer of Our Lord*, 1933–48 and *Pilgrimage*, 1935.

There were some writers whose talent blossomed in the emigration. Among these were Roman Gul', writer of prose, memoirs and screenplays, literary scholar and publisher, and one of the most colourful figures in Russian literature of the twentieth century. He fought on the side of the Whites during the Civil War, and began writing his first book, *Campaign of Ice* (*Ledianoi pokhod*), in a German camp for displaced persons. An extract appeared in V.B. Stankevich's Berlin-based journal *Zhizn'* in 1920, and the book as a whole was published in 1921. Gul''s own experience of emigration and the stories of other émigrés formed the basis of three further books: *A Life on Good Luck* (*Zhizn'na fuksa*, 1927), *The Dispersed Community* (*V rasseianii sushchie*, 1923), and *Whites on Black* (*Belye po Chernomu*, 1928).

In 1929 Gul''s novel *General BO*, subsequently renamed *Azef*, appeared. Its main characters are the *agent provocateur* Azef and the terrorist B. Savinkov (in 1949 Albert Camus was to base his play *Les Justes* on this novel). This was followed by the novel *The Scythian* (*Skif*), which Gul' called a 'historical chronicle', whose main characters are Tsar Nicholas I and the anarchist Mikhail Bakunin. In 1932 his book *Tukhachevsky. The Red Marshal* (*Tukhachevskii. Krasnyi marshal*) was published in Berlin, and remains one of Gul''s best psychological studies. This was followed a year later by *The Red Marshals. Voroshilov, Budenny, Bliukher, Kotovsky* (*Krasnye marshaly. Voroshilov, Budennyi, Bliukher, Kotovskii*).

In *General BO* Gul' is interested in Russian terrorism as a struggle for power. His 1936 book *Dzerzhinsky* (*Menzhinsky, Peters, Latsis, Iagoda*) discusses those Bolsheviks in whose hands terror became a weapon of power, and shows the history of communist terror beginning in 1918.

Gul' miraculously survived a twenty-one-day incarceration in a Nazi concentration camp in 1933. He was profoundly affected by the refined tortures inflicted on the camp's inmates, although he himself was not tortured, and wrote about it in his book *Orianenburg. What I Saw in One of Hitler's Concentration Camps*, (*Orianenburg. Chto ia videl v gitlerovskom kontsentratsionnom lagere*, 1937). After the war Gul' helped many displaced Soviet people in western Europe, setting up the democratic group Rossiiskoe narodnoe dvizhenie and publishing the journal *Narodnaia pravda* in 1948. In 1950 he moved to New York, where he continued to publish *Narodnaia pravda* for another two years. He then became involved with *Novyi zhurnal*, conceived by its founders Mark Aldanov and M. Tsetlin as a successor to *Sovremennye zapiski*, and he edited it until his death in 1986. Gul' published the book *Odvukon'* (*Relay Rider*) in 1973, followed by *Odvukon'* 2 in 1982. He wrote about his own life at least three times: in *The Chestnut-Coloured Steed* (*Kon' ryzhii*, 1952), *My Biography* (*Moia biografiia*, 1986), and the three-volume *I Carried Russia Away With Me. An Apologia for the Emigration* (*Ia unes Rossiiu. Apologiia emigratsii*, 1981–4). This trilogy became one of the most important and authoritative works on the history of twentieth-century Russian literature in both Soviet and émigré letters.

Vladimir Nabokov was born on 23 April 1899 (he was actually born on 22 April, but, after 1900, his birthday became the 23 April), and thus liked to boast that he was born on the same day as Shakespeare, and a century after Pushkin. His first literary efforts were published under the pseudonym V. Sirin. In emigration since 1919, he graduated from Trinity College, Cambridge in 1922. His first works of the 1920s, *Mary* (*Mashen'ka*); *King, Queen, Knave* (*Korol', dama, valet*); and *The Defence* (*Zashchita Luzhina*) were all marked by their stylistic virtuosity as well as their adherence to the Russian classical tradition. Whereas the official literature of socialist realism emphasized 'reality', Nabokov gave free rein to the play of myth, parody, and imagination.

One of the main themes of his 1932 novel, *Glory* (*Podvig*), was Russia itself, as it was to be in his autobiographical *Speak Memory* (*Drugie berega*) more than twenty years later. The theme of *Invitation to a Beheading* (*Priglashenie na kazn'*, 1935–6), is the separation of body and soul, as in Zamiatin's *We*. He continued his stylistic experimentation in his 1937 novel *The Gift* (*Dar*), with its ferocious parody of Nikolai Chernyshevsky. Nabokov also wrote a number of plays, the most famous of which is the 1938 *The Waltz Invention* (*Izobretenie Val'sa*).

Nabokov left Europe for the United States in 1940, after which time his literary language became English. His novels *Bend Sinister* (1947), *Lolita* (1955), and *Pnin* (1957) were written during his stay in America. In 1959 he returned to Europe, where he wrote *Pale Fire* (1962) and *Look at the Harlequins!* (1974), as well as translating Pushkin's *Evgenii Onegin*. He died in Switzerland on 2 July 1977.

It was in emigration that the talent of Mark Aldanov flourished. Aldanov was already approaching middle age when he developed a taste for the historical novel. There followed *Saint Helena, Little Island* (*Sviataia Elena, malen'kii ostrov*, 1923), the tetralogy *The Ninth Thermidor* (*Deviatoe termidora*, 1923), *The Devil's Bridge* (*Chortov Most*, 1925), and *The Conspiracy* (*Zagovor*, 1927). Aldanov's approach to history was fundamentally at odds with that of the prevailing Soviet class-based ethos, as he aimed to explore the inner life of his dramatis personae, and shows the close interaction of the individual and his time. Among his other novels are those about the Russian Revolution and its roots: *Before the Deluge* (*Istoki*), *The Key* (*Kliuch*), *The Escape* (*Begstvo*), and *The Cave* (*Peshchera*).

A word should be reserved for the poet Aleksandr Vertinsky, the first and most important of the Russian balladeers. He left Russia in November 1920, returning to the Soviet Union in the winter of 1943. He was enormously popular in Russia, and gave rise to a whole new generation of bards that includes Bulat Okudzhava, Aleksandr Galich, and Vladimir Vysotsky.

The year 1941 placed the first Russian emigration in a dilemma: should they support the Nazis fighting communism, or should they stand by the beloved motherland? On 22 June 1941, the day after the German invasion, Dmitrii Merezhkovsky spoke on the radio of his support for the Nazis. Many émigrés, especially those who had been in the military, were ready to take up arms against the Soviet Union, seeing the German attack as tantamount to the destruction of the communist regime. One of the commanders of General Vlasov's Russian

Liberation Army was the ageing Cossack leader Petr Krasnov, the author of more than twenty novels. He was handed over to the Red Army after his surrender to the Allies, and in 1945 was hanged with piano wire in the Lubianka prison.

Other literary émigrés, however, fought against the Germans, including Gaito Gazdanov, Zinaida Shakhovskaia, and Georgii Adamovich. Many others who did not fight, even the vehement anti-Bolshevik Bunin, supported the Red Army.

The New York-based *Novoe russkoe slovo* became the main literary outlet of what had now become two waves of emigration. The new literature of emigration brought with it experience of the camps, and differed from the literature of the first wave both in terms of style and theme. Notable works include Nikolai Narokov's *The Chains of Fear* (*Mnimye velichiny*, 1952), Sergei Maksimov's *Denis Bushuev* (1949), the novels of Leonid Rzhevsky (editor of the journal *Grani*), and the poetry of Ivan Elagin from the early 1950s until his death in 1987.

With the onset of glasnost in 1987 all the various strands of Russian literature – Soviet literature, socialist realism, the literature of the emigration, *tamizdat* and *samizdat* – came together, enabling the whole of twentieth-century Russian literature to be studied as an integrated whole, regardless of where a particular writer lived. Nevertheless, if in the Soviet Union émigré literature was always regarded as self-enclosed and inward-looking, émigrés themselves always emphasized the unity of Russian literature. The words of the critic Vladimir Weidlé here are characteristic: 'There were Stalin and Lenin Prizes, there was Soviet rubbish, but on our side there was also rubbish. But there did not exist two literatures, there has always been only one Russian literature in the twentieth century.'

translated by David Gillespie

FURTHER READING

Gerenstein, Grigori (ed.) *The Terrible News: Russian Stories from the Years Following the Revolution*, London: Black Spring Press, 1990.

Gillespie, David. *The Twentieth-Century Russian Novel: An Introduction*, Oxford: Berg, 1996.

Luker, Nicholas (ed.) *After the Watershed: Russian Prose, 1917–1927: Selected Essays*, Nottingham: Astra Press, 1996.

Maguire, Robert A. *Red Virgin Soil: Soviet Literature in the 1920's*, Princeton: Princeton University Press, 1968; Evanston, Illinois: Northwestern University Press, 2000.

Nilsson, Nils Åke (ed.) *Art, Society, Revolution: Russia, 1917–1921*, Stockholm: Almqvist & Wiksell, 1979.

Proffer, Carl R., Proffer, Ellendea, Meyer, Ronald and Szporluk, Mary Ann (eds) *Russian Literature of the Twenties: An Anthology*, Ann Arbor: Ardis, 1987.

Roberts, Graham. *The Last Soviet Avant-Garde: OBERIU – Fact, Fiction, Metafiction*, Cambridge and New York: Cambridge University Press, 1997.

Shepherd, David. *Beyond Metafiction: Self-Consciousness in Soviet Literature*, Oxford: Clarendon Press; New York: Oxford University Press, 1992.

Struve, Gleb. *Russian Literature Under Lenin and Stalin, 1917–1953*, Norman: University of Oklahoma Press, 1971.

Thomson, Boris. *The Premature Revolution: Russian Literature and Society, 1917–1946*, London: Weidenfeld and Nicolson, 1972.

Thomson, Boris. *Lot's Wife and the Venus of Milo: Conflicting Attitudes to the Cultural Heritage of Modern Russia*, Cambridge and New York: Cambridge University Press, 1978.

17

RUSSIAN POETRY SINCE 1945

G. S. SMITH

The period from the end of World War Two to the present may be divided into four segments according to the political factors that shaped the creative lives of most Russian authors then active: late Stalinism (1945–53); post-Stalinism (1953–68); the decline of Soviet power (1968–91); and the post-Soviet period. The first was the most barren in the entire history of modern Russian literature. The second and third witnessed a flowering of poetry that continued into the fourth. If one poet has to be chosen as pre-eminent during this half century, then that poet must inevitably be Joseph [Iosif] Brodsky (1940–96), the most outstanding individual among an exceptionally talented generation born in Russia between 1935 and 1941. These writers came to consciousness just in time for de-Stalinization, and eventually faced the same hard choices as their intellectual grandfathers: to stay in Russia and participate, to stay and try not to participate, or to leave. Brodsky gave his first public reading in Leningrad in February 1960, was arrested and sent into internal exile in 1965, and left Russia for the USA in 1972, never to return. His mature work, all of which had been published abroad, was first made available to the general readership in Russia in 1987, the year he was awarded the Nobel Prize. As these landmarks suggest, Brodsky did not attain his pre-eminence because he exemplified, in life or art, the principal characteristics that the majority of his immediate predecessors and contemporaries shared.

An account of these characteristics may begin with the fact that on 1 March 1986 the Union of Soviet Writers had 9,561 members. Of these (the ratio of men to women among them was about seven to one), no less than 3,466 were registered as poets. In every issue of the dozen or so central monthly journals at the forefront of current literary publishing in Russia at the time – a situation that has continued into the post-Soviet period, but to a lesser extent following the thinning out of state subsidies – there would be at least one substantial batch of poems. These poems would regularly be consolidated into selected works, and then reappear in the collections that were afforded to right-thinking persons, and perhaps also in anthologies. The existence of this Party-controlled, state-sponsored, and carefully censored body of writing, whose level of public exposure had very little directly to do with literary merit or public taste, formed the most distinctive characteristic of Russian poetry for the forty years following 1945. In no other society has the attempt been made to organize poetry in quite so systematic a way as in the USSR since the introduction of the Stalinist cultural system in the early 1930s.

Despite the constant trouble they experienced with it, the Party and state authorities to the end remained committed to funding the production of poetry, and they did so in such a way that the authors they recognized could enjoy a prosperous, privileged, and prestigious career. The inevitable result was that this career attracted people who would not normally have anything to do with poetry as it has usually been understood and practised in other modern societies. Instead, the people who became Soviet poets would in other societies probably have been involved in some aspect of the entertainment business, but perhaps most likely of all in advertising, where copywriting, which is essentially what the official 'creative method' of socialist realism mandated, is recognized and rewarded in honestly commercial terms. In return for their support, the Soviet authorities, not surprisingly, reserved the right to direct the activities of the people they subsidized. At the same time, conspiring to maintain their claim to centrality and authority was part of these people's own mechanism of corporate self-preservation and self-promotion. Conniving with the system was not necessarily more corrupting than opposing it; writing in opposition to the official system was not necessarily a liberating activity, but one which often brought with it demoralization and even its own kind of servitude.

To deduce from the Soviet authorities' privileging of what they deemed to be poetry an indication of its importance commensurate with and comparable to its status in more open societies is a profound misapprehension. It is still sometimes argued that in Russia, at least until 1991, poetry was more important than in most other parts of the world. Russian poets, it is often said, functioned as the conscience of the nation, articulating its deepest beliefs and fears, doubts and joys, and sometimes even in Christ-like fashion suffering unto death for the sins of others that they took upon themselves. These notions are justified in part. Up until about 1980 poets – like other dissident individuals – were indeed thought of as important enough to be worth persecuting in Russia, though in nothing like as severe a fashion as had been the case before 1941. Some poets were indeed worshipped as saints and martyrs. Books of poetry were indeed published in the USSR in editions of a size that to the western mind was inconceivable, unless – as would be more appropriate – they are thought of in terms of the sales of popular music, say, rather than 'serious' poetry.

To achieve recognition as a poet in the USSR it was necessary to gain access to a career ladder that by 1945 had been firmly put in place by those professionally concerned with literature. Evgenii Evtushenko's *Precocious Autobiography* (*Avtobiografiia*), published in English in 1963, gives an account of this process from the point of view of a talented and ambitious person who enjoyed one of the most important initial advantages – being born a man – but lacked another of them, the luck to have been born and brought up in either Moscow or Petersburg. The aspiring poet in Soviet Russia would be spotted, usually by a schoolteacher or a family member and – provided there were no signs of excessively unconventional traits that could result in political unreliability – would be encouraged by being directed into a poetry workshop of the kind that was attached to all the principal economic and educational enterprises in the country.

The fundamental official view was that Soviet citizens with verbal talent could and should be professionally trained to serve the state, like for example gymnasts, chess players, dancers, and musicians. Partly as a result of this institutionalization and the guild mentality it fostered, but mainly by willing consensus rather than through extraneous pressure on the part of the official system, expectations regarding technical competence in Russian poetry have remained on the whole demanding in a traditionally sanctioned sort of way. At the end of the twentieth century a verbal text was still felt by Russians to be worthy of consideration as a serious poem only if it exhibited at least a minimal degree of formal articulation in respect of such features as metre and rhyme. The training offered by the official system should not be thought of as necessarily a course in conformity. Some of the workshops concerned were led at various times by poets of considerable talent and genuine disinterested dedication. Inevitably, though, most of these workshops provided an opportunity for has-beens to find a nominally poetry-related focus for their life and to foster disciples – quite apart from being an ideal arena for sexual harassment.

Most persons who became outstanding poets rather than rank-and-file journeymen under the Soviet system, though, seem to have advanced themselves largely outside the official system of nurture by making contact with a guru – 'drinking vodka with geniuses', as this process was formulated by Iunna Morits (b. 1937), an excellent woman poet who boasted of refusing to take part in it. The guru would offer patronage, most vitally in the form of eventual recommendation for publication in a Moscow or Leningrad journal. Among these gurus were Anna Akhmatova (1889–1966) and Boris Pasternak (1890–1960) towards the end of their lives, in Leningrad and Moscow respectively, but there were many others less legendary. For the rank and file, the decisive step forward from amateur workshop towards professional inclusion was enrolment at the Gorky Institute in Moscow, the university-level institution set up in 1933 under the aegis of the Union of Writers to train professional literary cadres. With seeming inevitability, though, the most talented individuals either failed the course there or avoided embarking on it. Whatever the initial stages might have been, after making a sufficient show of promise and reliability the aspiring poet would eventually need to secure, one way or another, enough senior sponsorship to get into the Union of Soviet Writers, and thus be launched as a professional.

There was a relatively liberal period of admission to the Union in the post-Stalinist period, but after the Siniavsky-Daniel' trial in 1966 and the scandal connected with the expulsion of Solzhenitsyn in 1969, it became much more difficult to break in, and the Union acquired the authentic gerontocratic aspect of the period of decline. Once inside the Union, a poet was secure for life, with access to perks that were beyond the aspirations of ordinary members of the population: foreign travel, privileged health care, holidays at exclusive institutions. It was not necessary to go on writing original poetry, and many did not; the Union member could make a comfortable living by teaching, making public appearances, reviewing other people's work either for publication or in confidence for the authorities, and most frequently of all by translating into Russian poetry originally written in one of the minority languages of the USSR. In order to make a decent living as a translator of poetry it was not necessary to know the foreign language or languages concerned; specialists were normally hired to provide literal versions from which the recognized Russian poet would work up a passable version.

An official canon of poets was constructed by the Union bureaucracy and by loyal critics and academics, and their work was promoted in textbooks for schools and universities, the broadcasting media, and the recording industry, all of which operated under monopoly rules. The most tangible expression of the canon was the 'Poet's Library'('Biblioteka Poeta') series, which was launched in 1933 and then relaunched in 1954 and 1985 with the appropriate adjustments; a demonstratively post-Soviet 'New Poet's Library' ('Novaia Biblioteka Poeta') took over in 1995. From 1945 the canon was headed by Aleksandr Tvardovsky (1910–71), who, after making his name with the epic *Vasilii Terkin*, the greatest work in verse to come out of World War Two, attained higher political office than any Russian poet since Derzhavin and was also an influential editor. Tvardovsky was rivalled in official esteem in the post-war years only by Mikhail Isakovsky (1900–73), Aleksandr Prokof'ev (1900–71), and Nikolai Tikhonov (1896–1979). The reputations of these former titans collapsed with the Soviet system, together with those of an army of their less eminent colleagues. The homespun doggerel of which Isakovsky and Prokof'ev were the recognized masters was also produced, for example, by such as Nikolai Rylenkov (1909–69), B.A. Ruch'ev (1913–73), and S.V. Vikulov (b. 1922). Another body of folk-style poets specialized in an especially lucrative genre of Soviet verse, lyrics for 'mass songs': the most prominent among them were Nikolai Dorizo (b. 1923), Sergei Ostrovoy (b. 1911), Lev Oshanin (1912–97), and Konstantin Vanshenkin (b. 1925), the last two being particularly able stylists.

Alongside these journeymen was ranged what was often referred to as the 'middle generation' of poets whose youth coincided with World War Two and who originally became specialists in the patriotic lyric, especially in its military aspect, another staple of the Soviet canon. They included: Sergei Narovchatov (1919–81), who rose higher in the official hierarchy than any other writer of his generation; Boris Slutsky (1919–86); Sergei Orlov (1921–77); Semen Gudzenko (1922–53); Aleksandr Mezhirov (b. 1923); Nikolai Panchenko (b. 1924); Nikolai Starshinov (1924–98), and Evgenii Vinokurov (1925–93). With the exception of Narovchatov, these men were genuine poets whose testimony, however well-laundered, to the tribulations of their times will endure at least as long as their generation – and in the case of Slutsky, as we shall see, will certainly live on past it. In addition to this poetry on public themes there was a continuing tradition of the more personal, philosophical lyric, which was kept alive by some older poets, very different from each other, whose creative energy, despite all odds, survived the Stalin years: Leonid Martynov (1905–80), Arsenii Tarkovsky (1907–89), Semen Lipkin (b. 1911), and the most accomplished poet of this kind from the 'middle' generation, David Samoilov (1920–90). Among the poets of the next generation, Vladimir Sokolov (1928–97) endured as a low-key bard of quiet nostalgia; his more volatile contemporary on the left, Vladimir Kornilov (b. 1928), came to grief as a dissident in the 1970s, but survived to become the Job of the post-Soviet period.

In the post-Stalin period a group of poets came along who demonstratively addressed the newly permitted public and private themes, and also showed some interest in formal experimentation: Evgenii Evtushenko (b. 1933), Robert Rozhdestvensky (1932–94), and Andrei Voznesensky (b. 1933). These civic poets of the Khrushchev Thaw enlivened the scene as performance artists and helped verse attain its maximum public resonance in the middle 1960s, but they were born just too soon for their own good, and found their reputations rapidly impugned by younger colleagues less willing and able to promote themselves within official guidelines. There were also some genuine poets of the post-Stalin period whose views were sometimes embarrassingly to the right of the standard Party line, an approximate equivalent of the more famous 'village prose' writers: among them were Nikolai Rubtsov (1936–71), and the immensely gifted but indecorous Iurii Kuznetsov (b. 1941).

By the time the Soviet system began to break down irretrievably in the mid-1980s, the official canon had been expanded to admit, in some cases after many years of calculated denigration, some older poets whose stature reflected other merits besides political reliability. The most prestigious individuals among them, who managed despite everything to preserve their talent and integrity into middle and even old age, were Anna Akhmatova, Boris Pasternak, Nikolai Zabolotsky (1903–58), Leonid Martynov (1905–80), and Iaroslav Smeliakov (1913–72). Akhmatova and Pasternak survived to become the last living embodiments of pre-revolutionary high culture. Among other things they were explicit Orthodox believers and as such an immense inspiration to their juniors; sovietization, it turned out, was not inevitable. Inevitably, religious faith eventually became the most frequently exploited new theme in post-Soviet poetry, with women poets especially to the fore, notably Olesia Nikolaeva (b. 1955).

The canonical poets of the USSR created a huge body of verse in response to the shifting requirements of Party policy. Some of it promoted widely shared myths such as the superiority of Russian spirituality and humanism over Western commercialism and materialism, and the moral superiority of women over men; the bulk of it celebrated mandatory subjects that only Party zealots could believe in, such as love for Lenin, the world-beating economic achievements of the Soviet people, brotherly love between the various peoples of the USSR, and popular devotion to the Party itself. In their analyses of this material, the critics sometimes mentioned more specifically literary but essentially uncontroversial matters such as the relative significance of poetry and prose at any given time, the prominence within poetry of the long poem as opposed to the lyric, and the characteristics of the poets concerned in terms of a public versus a private stance, an opposition sometimes expressed in terms of 'loud' versus 'quiet'. But they never went in for analysis that prioritized form rather than content; 'formalism', which essentially meant focusing attention on the medium rather than the message, was anathema in both practice and criticism.

Official opinion in the USSR took a normative idea of literary language and enforced this norm through censorship. In developing their canon, the official critics and academics expressed themselves in language as formulaic and circumlocutory as that of the texts they discussed. After the post-Stalin galvanization of the 1960s public discourse soon relapsed into the wooden bureaucratese characteristic of the front page of *Pravda*, and especially as exemplified in the speeches of the leaders. Revulsion for this language and the lies it proclaimed was shared by all real writers, official and dissident alike, and the determination to reject and discredit it was the fundamental driving force of practically all the genuine poetry of the period.

The most effective such subversion from the linguistic point of view came in the songs of Aleksandr Galich (1919–77), with their juxtapositioning of official slogans with vivid colloquial speech and the lost language of common humanity. All Russian poets active since the 1950s, both official and dissident, seem to view the principal stylistic development of their time as a continuing expansion into colloquialism. Some of them think this process has gone too far and needs to be reversed, perhaps to recover the (somewhat hollow) high seriousness of earlier times, while others think that colloquialization has not gone far enough. Liberation from the constraints represented by stylistic censorship, which curtailed both high and low registers, has been the most important literary change since 1991, and this is another important respect in which Joseph Brodsky had shown the way long before.

The official system brought about a degradation both of literature itself and the way it was studied in Russia during the decline of Soviet power. The policy-makers succeeded in their task of levelling. The requirement for accessibility produced banality; stylistic controls produced blandness; the suppression of specific comment on all vital matters public and private made literary texts (and comment on them) ritualistic, sanitized, and abstract; and the mandatory prescription of certain stock themes made the subject matter parochial. Censorship had isolated Soviet literature from international cultural developments since the mid-1920s, and the incestuous provinciality of the 1970s was a fitting monument to fifty years of literary control.

One paradoxical manifestation of the provinciality of Russian poetry is the long-standing division between Moscow and Petersburg, which cuts across the division into official and unofficial. The contrast between them in the history of Russian culture has long been familiar: European versus Asiatic, classicism versus Romanticism, artificial versus natural, imposed versus organic, the rationalism of Petersburg and the emotional rebelliousness of Moscow. Both Petersburg and Moscow think of themselves as capital cities, and amazingly for a country of its size, in Russian poetry there is no significant extra-metropolitan tradition, no first-rank literature based in the provinces of the kind there is in Britain and the USA. There is also a remarkable degree of mutual ignorance between the literary worlds of the two major cities; there has not even been much physical movement between them. Several important poets have started out in the provinces, but they have had to move in to make anything of themselves; and they have moved to Moscow, not Leningrad. The two most significant exceptions since 1945 have been

Boris Chichibabin (1923–94), who apart from a spell in the Gulag stayed in Kharkov, and more recently Svetlana Kekova (b. 1951), who has remained in Saratov.

During the decline of Soviet power there was a frequently voiced official consensus that no individual of indisputably major, generation-defining talent had emerged to replace Tvardovsky. Meanwhile, there was an unsayable private consensus, among critics and even more strongly among poets, that Joseph Brodsky, the ultimate nonconformist, was such a talent. He was by no means alone in his nonconformism. From the very beginning of Soviet power, not all people who thought of themselves as poets were willing to pay the price of entering the official system and prospering within it. There were many compromises, and many alternative stances at various points on the spectrum between acceptance and rejection. The fundamental fact of the matter was that outside the official system it was not possible to make a living from being a poet. It was illegal in the USSR not to be in registered employment, and membership of the Union of Soviet Writers took care of this requirement. As for the outsiders, during the 1970s and 1980s the male unofficial poet usually held a menial job, night watchman or boilerman being particularly favoured. Also, parents, spouses, and relatives shouldered the burden of economic support for 'kitchen culture', as the underground scene was sometimes called. More often than not, wives and mothers kept husbands and sons going; inside the official system they were amply rewarded for their care and nurture, while outside it they consoled themselves with notions of service to a higher cause than material reality. The image of the saintly wife and mother as constructed by the miscreant, self-indulgent husband and son, and the social reality it reflects, is the most important respect in which official and unofficial Russian literature remained absolutely at one.

Outside the official system, informal associations of poets came together at various times, with a greater or lesser degree of stability. These groups, however heterogeneous may have been the individuals who composed them, provided a fundamental sense of collective identity for the people concerned. They were the primary generators of the samizdat or self-publishing culture that was such an important feature of the poetry scene inside Russia when dissent took root during the 1960s and 1970s, and which commonly referred to itself as the 'underground'; it contained a vociferous internal constituency on the left that called itself the 'avant-garde'. From the early 1960s samizdat began to be published abroad, with or without the consent of the authors concerned. By the mid-1980s, there were about fifty poets writing in the USSR but publishing abroad on a regular basis; sanctions were taken against them with different degrees of severity at different times.

One crucial technological development in the form of the private tape recorder arrived in Russia in the late 1950s and was soon being used to 'publish' poetry in a way that obviated the censorship and other ideological controls. Three poets in particular exploited this medium, creating texts that they sang to their own guitar accompaniment. Bulat Okudzhava (1924–97) was the pioneer, and for many years he uniquely combined official respectability with underground and foreign 'publication' of dissident works; he survived to become the grand old man of Russian literature in his last years. Aleksandr Galich, one of Russia's greatest satirists, was thrown out of the country in 1974. The prodigiously talented Vladimir Vysotsky (1938–80) made his living as an actor; his songs, which he never saw in print, made him the most genuinely popular poet in his own lifetime that Russia has ever known. Ordinary people were not bothered by the question of whether Vysotsky was or was not a 'real poet', but the intelligentsia and the Soviet establishment were.

The poets born in the early 1930s who fully entered official literature during the 1960s soon forfeited their credibility as nonconformists; it was clear beyond all doubt by 1968 that the official monopolies and privileges were not going to be seriously loosened, much less abandoned. The major poets born between 1935 and 1940 tended to find some para-literary niche for themselves. Poets born after 1940, though, with Brodsky in the van, increasingly rejected the official path in favour of nonconformism. But many of those involved realized to their growing mortification as the Soviet system ground on that their writing was degenerating into increasingly childish epatage and all-pervasive irony. One of the best underground poets, Aleksandr Soprovsky (1953–90), pointed out in 1980 that irony is productive only where it proceeds from a position of strength; meanwhile, underground irony was based on disillusion, and brought with it a loss of responsibility and a good deal of bohemian self-destructiveness. As they lived on into middle age, the non-publishing poets who stayed in Russia, who had no memory of 'normal cultural conditions', became an increasingly pitiful brotherhood; their exclusion from the literary mainstream was the most regrettable triumph of the official system. Four stalwarts of successive waves of underground poets who had a saving sense of the absurd, though, were Igor' Kholin (1920–2000), Vsevolod Nekrasov (b. 1934), Lev Rubinshtein (b. 1947), and Timur Kibirov (b. 1956); they also had wickedly acute eyes and ears.

The poets of the 1935–41 generation who seemed to survive best inside Russia were those who at least had a toe-hold in the official literary system, but deliberately kept away from the limelight and the attendant obligations and compromises. Among them, the most prominent has been the phenominally productive Aleksandr Kushner (b. 1936), whose smooth lyrics somewhat self-consciously epitomize the Petersburg tradition. Two much more rugged and profound poets who remained on the sidelines of the official scene until the times changed were Evgenii Rein (b. 1936) and Oleg Chukhontsev (b. 1938); their stoical autobiographical lyrics do honour to the historically aware male consciousness of their generation. Their female equivalent in some ways has been Bella Akhmadulina (b. 1937). Some other non-publishing poets of the first rank survived in Russia completely outside the public literary system, prominent among them the Leningraders Vladimir Ufliand (b. 1936), Mikhail Eremin (b. 1936), and Viktor Krivulin (1944–2001). From the next generation came the best woman poet of post-war Leningrad, Elena Shvarts (b. 1949), and her Moscow contemporary Ol'ga Sedakova (b. 1948). In

Moscow there were also the tragically short-lived Soprovsky, and the most robust intellect and delicate stylist of his group, Sergei Gandlevsky (b. 1949). One startling exception among the poets of his generation is Ivan Zhdanov (b. 1948), who somehow managed to publish a book of uncompromisingly surreal, a-Soviet lyrics in 1982. But led by Brodsky, poets either emigrated or were exiled. The next senior after Galich was Naum Korzhavin (b. 1924), followed by Natal'ia Gorbanevskaia (b. 1936) and Dmitrii Bobyshev (b. 1936). Lev Losev (b. 1937) started writing his supremely witty lyrics only after leaving Russia. Among the younger émigrés were two former informal group-mates of Soprovsky and Gandlevsky, Aleksei Tsvetkov (b.1947) and Bakhyt Kenzheev (b. 1950); and also the most important religious poet of this generation, Iurii Kublanovsky (b. 1947).

The work of these poets started to appear substantially in the USSR in 1987, and in the course of the next decade they all returned, at least in print. Before this, though, the published record was not ossified, by any means. Texts that had once been canonical were constantly being discredited, and in some cases excluded more severely than intentionally unorthodox works. The vast body of panegyric poetry dedicated to Stalin forms the biggest single element of this corpus; because of this material it was inconceivable after 1956 to print genuine collected editions of the classic official poets of the Stalin period. After 1991 the same thing has happened to panegyric poetry about Lenin and other canonical Soviet subjects. In addition to the published or sometime-published record, there was a body of manuscript texts whose extent could only be guessed at before 1985. The relationship between what was actually being written and the published record, especially inside the country, was oblique. There was no possibility for the broad Russian readership inside the country to make informed objective judgements about what was actually going on.

A significant number of major Russian poets went into emigration soon after the revolutions and Civil War. The death in 1958 of Georgii Ivanov, the last of them and arguably the most important Russian poet in the world during the last thirty years of his life, would be as good a reason to date the end of a literary era as any other; his terminal and best creative phase happened to coincide with Boris Pasternak's return to writing original poetry after a long concentration on translation. After World War Two the surviving émigrés of Ivanov's generation (he was born in 1894) were joined by a smaller and on the whole culturally less well-favoured group of émigrés, but they included two major poets, Ivan Elagin (1918–87) and Nikolai Morshen (b. 1918), both of whom have much in common with the 'middle generation' of Soviet poets. Igor' Chinnov (1909–96) went into emigration as a child and had published very little before 1945, but he blossomed into a lyric poet of consistently high quality from then until his death. By the mid-1980s, when the Union of Soviet Writers counted up its three and a half thousand poets, about 130 others were living and regularly publishing poetry outside the country, and from about 1975 to the fall of the USSR their work was much more significant in terms of literary quality than the new poetry being published in Russia.

Despite the abundance of this new poetry, there can be no doubt that since 1945, and perhaps long before that, dead poets have been admired and read more than living ones. In this respect, of course, Russia is no exception in the modern world. But radically different situations existed inside and outside the country before about 1986; before this date, writers and scholars of the Russian emigration and their western colleagues laboured to publish those poets who were blacklisted in the USSR. In the sixty years before 1991, adequate editions of the following front-rank modern Russian poets were available only outside Russia: Anna Akhmatova, Andrei Bely (1880–1934), Zinaida Gippius (1869–1945), Nikolai Gumilev (1886–1921), Georgii Ivanov, Viacheslav Ivanov (1866–1949), Daniil Kharms (1905–42), Vladislav Khodasevich (1886–1939), Nikolai Kliuev (1884–1937), Mikhail Kuzmin (1875–1936), Osip Mandel'shtam (1891–1938), Sofiia Parnok (1885–1933), Boris Pasternak, Marina Tsvetaeva (1892–1941), Aleksandr Vvedensky (1904–41), and Maksimilian Voloshin (1878–1932). To this list could be added a substantial number of reprinted works that were originally published in Russia but were subsequently anathematized.

Hardly any of these poets were absolute unpersons before the Gorbachev reforms. Their work was mentioned in academic Soviet histories of literature during the Brezhnev period; such publications as the annual Poetry Day anthologies, which began in 1956, constantly nibbled at the official realm of oblivion. But before 1986 a writer usually had at least to die inside the USSR to stand a chance of rehabilitation; Marina Tsvetaeva was one such. The partial return to the Soviet readership of these figures had begun in the later 1960s. The first substantial volume of Tsvetaeva's poetry, heavily censored, appeared in Russia in 1965. A selected Mandel'shtam appeared in 1973, but it was 1987 before his later work was published for mass circulation in Russia. The importance of the renewed presence of these poets for those born in the 1930s and 1940s cannot be over-estimated. During the last five years of Soviet power, the émigrés who never returned, such as Khodasevich and Viacheslav Ivanov, also began to be redeemed.

More remarkable in some ways than the restitutions of poets previously considered anti-Soviet have been the revelations of repressed texts by the former official élite. Even Aleksandr Tvardovsky and Mikhail Isakovsky, it turned out, wrote poetry they could not publish under Soviet conditions. The same was true of the less highly esteemed Ol'ga Berggol'ts (1910–75). The most remarkable of all these cases is that of Boris Slutsky, who during his lifetime was thought of as a sound but rather stodgy official poet of the middle generation. His unpublished legacy, which amounted to more than half his total lifetime's work, was the biggest revelation of the Gorbachev period; he now stands as the most important poet who lived his life in Soviet Russia, a pitiless and plain-spoken chronicler of the public and private history of the Russian people during the Communist era.

The restoration to the metropolitan audience of texts that were previously suppressed or published abroad has been the most important development in Russian poetry since 1985. The backlog was about made up by the end of the 1990s, and Russian poets, critics, and readers began to face a gigantic task of redefinition and re-evaluation, taking into account the mass of hitherto inaccessible texts, and trying not to let it completely overshadow the new work that living poets were trying to bring out in the new conditions. The epitome of the effort to write and promote 'just poetry' (rather than poetry as substitute politics or anything else) is Russia's first journal specifically devoted to the publication and discussion of poetry, *Arion*, which began to appear in 1994 under the editorship of Aleksei Alekhin and has set new standards for dignified, inclusive, aesthetics-led decorum. The venerable ex-Soviet journal *Znamia* has played a similar role since the critic Sergei Chuprinin took over as editor-in-chief in 1989. Two poets who have emerged from these pages as indisputably first-rank figures are Tat'iana Bek (b. 1949) and Tat'iana Shcherbina (b. 1954).

The period since about 1956, as we have seen, has benefited from the substantial contributions of three generations of poets, some of them posthumously. The two previous great flowerings of Russian poetry, which took place *c*. 1810–40 and 1895–1925, were made by relatively small and sociologically homogeneous groups of Russian poets who worked and lived in close communication with each other in Moscow and St Petersburg, for the most part able to go abroad and return at will, and attuned to contemporary literary developments outside Russia. The period since 1945 has been characterized by the existence of a major tradition outside the metropolitan territory, which consciously opposed what was going on there. There is also a profound difference between the three periods of flowering in terms of the relationship between poetry and other literary genres. The Golden Age was the culmination of a century-long period of apprenticeship in Russian poetry, and none of the recognized masterpieces of Russian prose fiction was created before 1830. The Silver Age saw a resurgence of poetry into a leading position after the long domination of prose fiction. In the period since 1956, poetry revived alongside prose, and it is not at all clear which of the two has been the more important. Also, the resurgence of poetry since 1956 coincided with the domination of the visual and rise of the electronic media in Russia and elsewhere, placing written texts in a marginalizing context that did not exist before. In the last analysis, the first two great flowerings may be understood mainly as culturally-led processes whereby Russian poetry caught up with, assimilated, and went on to develop in its own particular way the recent legacy of western European literary culture: French and German Romanticism in the first, French and German Symbolism and Parnassianism in the second. In the third flowering, Russian poetry has mainly been concerned with restoring and building upon its own past. At the same time, Brodsky's work was nurtured belatedly on the principal cultural tradition from which Russia had been artificially isolated: Anglo-American modernism. His enthusiasm for this lost heritage overcame the spirit of aridity that informed the heritage itself; it remains to be seen whether his successors, in the new conditions of freedom, will be able to maintain the commitment that sustained him – a commitment to the supreme value of high verbal culture, which had been venerated by the intelligentsia in Russia since Pushkin's time.

FURTHER READING

Kates, J. (ed.) *In the Grip of Strange Thoughts: Russian Poetry in a New Era*, Newcastle: Bloodaxe Books, 1999.

Loseff, Lev, and Polukhina, Valentina (eds) *Joseph Brodsky: The Art of a Poem*, Houndmills: Macmillan Press, 1999.

Lowe, David. *Russian Writing since 1953: A Critical Survey*, New York: Ungar, 1987.

Polukhina, Valentina. *Brodsky through the Eyes of his Contemporaries*, Houndmills: Macmillan Press, 1992.

Sandler, Stephanie (ed.) *Rereading Russian Poetry*, New Haven and London: Yale University Press, 1999.

Slutsky, Boris. *Things that Happened*. Edited, translated, and with an introduction and commentaries by G.S. Smith, Moscow, Birmingham, and Chicago: Glas Publishers, 1999.

Smith, Gerald S. *Songs to Seven Strings: Russian Guitar Poetry and Soviet "Mass Song"*, Bloomington: Indiana University Press, 1984.

Smith, Gerald S. (ed. and trans.) *Contemporary Russian Poetry: A Bilingual Anthology*, Bloomington: Indiana University Press, 1993.

Weissbort, Daniel (ed.) *Post-War Russian Poetry*, Harmondsworth: Penguin, 1974.

Yevtushenko, Yevgeny, Todd, Albert C. and Hayward, Max (eds) *Twentieth Century Russian Poetry: Silver and Steel: An Anthology*, London: Fourth Estate, 1993.

18

POST-REVOLUTIONARY
RUSSIAN THEATRE

BIRGIT BEUMERS

FROM THE REVOLUTION TO SOCIALIST REALISM

The Bolshevik Revolution had an enormous impact on cultural life in general, but particularly on the theatre, which was quickly perceived as a possible tool for 'agitation' among the masses and the propagation of socialist ideas. Many theatre directors supported the Revolution, and were themselves supported in turn by the People's Commissar for Enlightenment, Anatolii Lunacharsky. Vsevolod Meierkhol'd (1874–1940), who had staged rather grandiose pre-revolutionary productions at the Aleksandrinsky Theatre in St Petersburg, immediately dedicated his art to the Revolution, and from 1918–21 he was in charge of the Moscow Theatre Section of the Commissariat. During this time, commonly known as the 'Theatrical October', he demanded a complete break with theatrical traditions: the theatre should become exclusively a tool for state and Party propaganda. Along with the young directors Sergei Eisenstein, Nikolai Evreinov and Nikolai Okhlopkov, Meierkhol'd favoured mass spectacles, such as Evreinov's *Storming of the Winter Palace* (*Vziatie zimnego dvortsa*), performed on 7 November 1920 for 100,000 spectators with 8,000 participants commanded by the director with the help of a field phone. A celebration of the Revolution, the spectacle underlined at the same time a theatricalization of life (based on real events), and a politicization of art. Both directors and playwrights sought to politicize themes and theatricalize form in the years immediately after the Revolution. Vladimir Maiakovsky's *Mystery Bouffe* (*Misteriia-Buff*, 1918 and 1921), was the first 'Soviet' play, specifically written in compliance with these demands. While thematically showing the triumph of the proletariat, Maiakovsky commented in the prologue of the play on the need to break down the fourth wall and openly attacked the verisimilitude of Stanislavsky's realism.

While Stanislavsky had aimed at creating an illusion of reality on stage, and wished the theatre to mirror reality, Meierkhol'd perceived the function of theatre as that of a magnifying glass, which would enhance certain fragments or episodes of reality. Meierkhol'd therefore restructured plays into fragments and episodes which would rouse the audience rationally rather than (as in Stanislavsky's method) emotionally. The sets were constructivist in style, the costumes resembled factory wear, and leaflets were distributed to the audience as if at a political meeting; all these features were designed to bring art closer to the worker. Meierkhol'd perceived theatre as having a social function; he went out to factories to perform plays, and closely monitored audience response in order to heighten the comical and agitational elements in his productions. Calling for the collaboration of all aesthetic disciplines, he aspired towards a synthesis of the arts. He worked with renowned artists such as Liubov' Popova, Aleksandr Rodchenko, Varvara Stepanova in his constructivist productions of *Dawns* (*Zori*, 1920), *The Magnanimous Cuckold* (*Velikodushnyi rogonosets*, 1922) and *Tarelkin's Death* (*Smert' Tarelkina*, 1922). Meierkhol'd's use of placards for locations serves to stylize rather than to create reality on stage, and documentary evidence and cinematic devices such as screens, slogans and projections enhanced parallels to real life, making the spectator aware of being in a theatre which sought to 'agitate'. His actors trained in biomechanics, so that movements on stage would be choreographed and paced, rather than motivated by psychological identification. Words were less important than the body language, characters became types, lacking in psychological depth: his was a theatre of demonstration rather than of identification and experience.

Despite his political engagement for the revolutionary cause, Meierkhol'd came under attack from Proletcult, an organization deprecating professionalism in the arts, and claiming that only workers should be creative in the artistic realm. Although this claim was not endorsed officially – in fact, Lenin defied its proponent Kerzhentsev by arguing that high standards must be maintained in culture and Lunacharsky called for a 'return to Ostrovsky' and his critical realism – it was realism which would be favoured over formal innovation in the late 1920s. The prevalence of realism is obvious from the dramatic writing of the 1920s, and its treatment of the revolution and civil war. Initially, recent history was presented in foreign settings as in Sergei Tret'iakov's *Roar, China!* (*Rychi, Kitai!*) and *Are You Listening, Moscow?!* (*Slyshish', Moskva?!*), the latter set in Germany; later it was set in Russia, as for example in Vishnevsky's *Optimistic Tragedy* (*Optimisticheskaia tragediia*). Such writing lent itself to the purposes of propaganda of the official 'historical truth' and was therefore supple enough to fit within the parameters of Socialist Realism, such as the plays of Bill'-Belotserkovsky, Boris Lavrenev, Lidiia Seifullina, Aleksandr Afinogenov, Nikolai Pogodin and others. Konstantin Trenev's *Liubov' Iarovaia* is a play whose eponymous heroine denounces her husband to the Reds; it enjoyed great success at the Maly Theatre in 1926. Vsevolod Ivanov's *Armoured Train 14–69* (*Bronepoezd 14–69*), in which a Red officer is so devoted to the cause of the Revolution that he seizes a train of Whites which is about to leave the country, was staged at the Moscow Arts Theatre (MKhAT) in 1927. Both productions were hailed by the realists.

Satire was prominent as a genre in the 1920s, inspired largely by the incongruencies of life during the New Economic Policy (NEP), introduced by Lenin in 1921. Bulgakov's *Zoya's Apartment* (*Zoikina kvartira*) and Erdman's *The Mandate* (*Mandat*) and *The Suicide* (*Samoubiitsa*) are as scathing towards NEP as are Maiakovsky's later plays, written specifically for Meierkhol'd's theatre, *The Bathhouse* (*Bania*) and *The Bedbug* (*Klop*). Censorship, exercised by the Central Repertoire Board (*Glavrepertkom*), established in 1922, prevented this genre from flourishing. Satirical and grotesque elements informed the productions at the Vakhtangov Theatre, which had developed a style of fantastic realism for which Bulgakov's *Zoya's Apartment* with its dream sequences provided ideal material. Evgenii Vakhtangov (1883–1922), one of Stanislavsky's favourite pupils, had led the Third Studio at the MKhAT, which in 1926 became the Vakhtangov Theatre. Vakhtangov reconciled the formal innovations of Meierkhol'd with the psychological depth of Stanislavsky, while emphasizing the need for an imaginative reading of the text (rather than an obsession with the word, or a restructuring of the text into episodes) and enhancing the grotesque element of reality which came as a result of his preoccupation with the theme of death. His approach is best captured in his 1922 production of *Princess Turandot*. Vakhtangov died prematurely, leaving no direct successor, although his tradition was continued at the theatre by Ruben Simonov (1899–1968), and inspired the work of Aleksei Popov (1892–1961).

Aleksandr Tairov (1885–1950) founded and headed the Kamerny Theatre (1914–49). Tairov remained unpolitical after the Revolution, drawing on the classical heritage of Western and Eastern theatre. He relied heavily on the actor to 'master his instrument' – to control voice, gesture, movement – yet without turning him into an acrobat as Meierkhol'd did. His productions were choreographed and depended on rhythm set by musical scores, while formally relying on the expressivity of the gesture (mime). In order to allow for more movement in space, he used constructivist sets and collaborated with leading artists and designers (Aleksandra Ekster, the Stenberg Brothers). His Soviet masterpiece was his production of Vishnevsky's *Optimistic Tragedy* in 1933, based on the Kronstadt rebellion, in which he underlined the dialectic forces of life and death, harmony and chaos.

The purges of the late 1930s had a tragic and devastating effect on the diversity of artistic expression: Mikhail Chekhov had emigrated, and the Second Studio of the MKhAT, founded by him, was closed in 1936; Nikolai Okhlopkov was removed from the Realistic Theatre (which was merged with the Kamerny) in 1937; the playwright Sergei Tret'iakov was arrested and shot in 1939; Meierkhol'd's theatre was closed in 1938, and Meierkhol'd was arrested and shot in 1940; his actress wife Zinaida Raikh was murdered in the same year. From the pantheon of Russian directors of the twentieth century Tairov alone survived, but he was removed from the Kamerny Theatre in 1949, a late victim of the 'cultural policies' of Andrei Zhdanov (*Zhdanovshchina*). Stanislavsky's theory was canonized in 1938 (following his death), and the psychological realism of the Moscow Arts Theatre, which had been elevated to an Academic Theatre, was the only tolerated style. However, Stanislavsky left no successor at the Moscow Arts Theatre; it was headed for almost thirty years by groups of actors and directors who preserved the productions largely in their original shape, and turned what was an innovative theatre at the turn of the century into a museum piece.

Socialist realism dominated dramatic writing during the 1930s. Aleksei Arbuzov's *Tania* (1938) is archetypal: when she gets married Tania leaves medical school for her husband's sake, but he sees in this act a lack of devotion to socialism, and eventually leaves her for another woman who takes part in the transformation of society. Tania undergoes a change, and realizes her potential as doctor before she can find happiness. The theme of transformation (or elimination) of those who do not work for social goals made this play comply with socialist realism, while it is structurally overloaded with coincidences and seems contrived. However, the characters are portrayed as psychologically convincing. Arbuzov would make a more important contribution to theatre and drama in a different way, though. In 1938, together with the director Valentin Pluchek, he set up a studio for young actors and dramatists, with whom he worked in a 'joint stock' method on a socialist theme, the construction of the city of Komsomolsk on the Amur. However, the play *City of the Dawn* (*Gorod na zare*, 1941) was published under his name with no reference to its collaborators. The studio's activities came to a halt with the war. After Zhdanov's return to Moscow in 1946 the arts suffered from his attempt to tighten control in the cultural sector. The 'theory' of conflictless drama postulated that socialist-realist drama cannot contain a conflict (other than between good and better or good and perfect). This led to a total stagnation in dramatic writing – conflict being the most vital ingredient in a dramatic structure – and consequently to a crisis in the theatre arts, in the absence of good contemporary drama and the conforming of theatres to the model of the MKhAT.

THE THAW AND AFTER

The Thaw remedied this crisis. Initially, an editorial in *Pravda* on 7 April 1952 attacked the drama-without-conflict theory and called for playwrights to express the truth and to strike against any negative aspects of Soviet life, thereby enabling dramatists to write again. Second, the theatre arts were affected directly when an editorial in *Kommunist* in 1955 favoured diversity and deprecated the levelling and uniformity in the arts. The rehabilitation of Meierkhol'd led to a revival of some of his productions, and the Stanislavsky system which had dominated Soviet theatre was challenged by Boris Zakhava and Ruben Simonov, who called for a synthesis of the acting methods of emotional experience (*perezhivanie*) and representation (*predstavlenie*).

Under the Soviet regime theatre had functioned as a tool for propaganda and a platform for ideological debate. As such, the theatre was subjected to Party and state control. The immediate responsibility for theatres lay with the Moscow City Council which controlled the repertoire, allocated budgets, gave preliminary consent to each new play for its inclusion into the repertoire and a final consent to the stage production in the form of a licence. In 1953 *Glavrepertkom* was abolished in order to introduce decentralization so that the expanding media system could be covered; matters relating to theatre were henceforth referred to the newly formed USSR Ministry of Culture. It received its directives both from the Council of Ministers and from the Central Committee of the Communist Party.

The Thaw bore upon the theatre in a variety of ways: first, a new generation of playwrights emerged with Leonid Zorin, Viktor Rozov, Aleksandr Shtein and others. Second, young and promising directors were appointed to head prestigious theatres: Mariia Knebel, a pupil of Mikhail Chekhov, was appointed to the Central Children's Theatre in Moscow. Meierkhol'd's pupil Nikolai Okhlopkov was put in charge of the Maiakovsky Theatre, while Valentin Pluchek was appointed to head the Satire Theatre. Most significant for the future were the appointments of Georgii Tovstonogov to the Bolshoi Drama Theatre (BDT) in Leningrad; Anatolii Efros to the Lenin Komsomol Theatre, Moscow; and Iurii Liubimov to the Taganka Theatre of Drama and Comedy, Moscow. Third, for the first time in many years, new theatres were founded, such as the Sovremennik (Contemporary) in Moscow, headed by Oleg Efremov.

The plays of Viktor Rozov (b. 1913) provided the impulse for young directors to explore further the psychological realism of Stanislavsky. Rozov's plays focus on 'young boys', children on the way to adulthood, and therefore appealed to a theatre which wanted to create a hero with whom both actor and audience could easily identify psychologically. His plays became the main source for the repertoire of Anatolii Efros and Oleg Efremov. In Rozov's *In Search of Joy* (*V poiskakh radosti*, 1957), the hero demolishes a piece of furniture, symbol of the petty bourgeoisie, with his father's sabre; the gesture accompanying this act became symbolic for the break with tradition. The Sovremennik started as a studio from the MKhAT School under Efremov, opening in 1957 with Rozov's *Alive Forever* (*Vechno zhivye*). Efremov had begun acting at a time when monumental realism was receding. He did not aim at outward verisimilitude, and consciously combined a stylized, abstract set with an authentic way of life (the everyday realism of 'kitchen drama'). For Efremov psychological realism did not require that the actor's personality should merge with the character's. Apart from Rozov's dramatic writing, other new playwrights also found their way onto the stage of the Sovremennik, such as Aleksandr Volodin, who criticized in his plays the interference of personal motives with the achievement of higher social goals, exposing the negative aspects which were obstacles on the road to communism. Efremov was often criticized for including too many contemporary plays in the repertoire. The Sovremennik also staged historical plays, such as Zorin's *The Decembrists* (*Dekabristy*), Aleksandr Svobodin's *Narodovol'tsy* and Mikhail Shatrov's *The Bolsheviks* (*Bol'sheviki*), a trilogy investigating the psychological motivation of revolutionary figures from the Decembrist Uprising to the Bolshevik Revolution. Efremov left the Sovremennik to become Chief Artistic Director at the MKhAT in 1970. There, he successfully introduced a generation of young dramatists into the repertoire, such as Aleksandr Gelman and Mikhail Roshchin, whose plays dealt with the inner conflicts of contemporary men resulting from work. In his often controversial productions Efremov investigated work ethics in relation to the individual conscience. He was also the first director to stage successfully the plays of Aleksandr Vampilov. When the theatre had to move to its new building on the Tverskoi Boulevard, the bond with the audience, so vital for Efremov's approach, was broken, and MKhAT ossified.

Anatolii Efros had gained most of his experience working on contemporary drama, and at the Theatre of the Lenin Komsomol he continued staging plays by Rozov, Arbuzov and Eduard Radzinsky. He developed a repertoire almost entirely based on contemporary drama. In Rozov's *On the Day of the Wedding* (*V den' svad'by*, 1964), the revolt of the heroine against her marriage out of duty was represented formally by her breaking free from the set, which consisted of tables and chairs arranged for a wedding party. Efros started to work with the concept of 'psycho-physics', where movement has the function of making inner psychological changes visible. Radzinsky's *104 Pages about Love* (*104 stranitsy pro liubov'*, 1964), opposing the rationalism (of the 'Scientific-Technological Revolution') to emotional behaviour, and explicitly talking about sexual relationships, met many objections from the censoring body. Radzinsky's *A Film is Being Shot* (*Snimaetsia kino*, 1965), was equally criticized for outspoken sexuality, taboo on the Soviet stage. Arbuzov's *The Promise* or *My Poor Marat* (*Moi bednyi Marat*, 1965), about a woman choosing her husband out of duty rather than love (she marries him after he has been injured during the Leningrad blockade) saw love triumph at the end. Objections were made to Efros's concern with failure rather than success. Most controversial were Efros's interpretations of two classics: Chekhov's *The Seagull* in 1966 and *The Three Sisters* in 1967. Both productions were condemned as an unorthodox interpretation of Chekhov in terms of 'lack of communication', perceiving Chekhov as a predecessor of the Western theatre of the absurd (with no equivalent in the Soviet Union, since a socialist society knew no absurdity). Efros was removed from the Lenin Komsomol Theatre and transferred to an inferior post at the Malaya Bronnaya Theatre where he worked mainly on classical drama, enhancing the tragic dimensions in comic texts (such as Gogol''s *The Marriage*). Efros developed his method of structural analysis for the exploration of character psychology and his concept of the necessity for the psychological motivation of movement on stage, 'psycho-physics'. Efros perfected his method of structural analysis for a clear-cut image of character and externalization of psychological motivation while teaching at the Theatre Institute (GITIS).

In 1956, Georgii Tovstonogov (1913–89) was appointed Chief Artistic Director of the BDT in Leningrad. Tovstonogov merged the approaches of Stanislavsky and Meierkhol'd, mixed stylization with authenticity, and combined figurativeness with psychological analysis. Tovstonogov's was an actor's theatre in which the director did not impose an idea on the actor, but had a concept of the production as a whole. Tovstonogov's use of theatrical devices was balanced, because purposeful. His productions showed a harmony between historical and contemporary meaning, between the objective and the subjective, the historical and the personal, which created an ambivalent meaning. Tovstonogov's repertoire included contemporary plays by Volodin and Rozov, Gelman and Radzinsky; the classics of Gor'ky and Chekhov; prose adaptations of Sholokhov, Tolstoy and Dostoevsky. A remarkable production of this decade was the adaptation of Tolstoy's *Strider – The Story of a Horse* (*Kholstomer*, 1975). The set was made of sack-cloth, which was draped around the stage. The costumes were made of the same material, and the actors playing horses wore leather straps around their head and body as a harness, thus imprisoning the body. Tovstonogov used cinematic devices, such as the reading by a disembodied voice of an essay by Tolstoy. Similarly, he maintained the narrative stance through the voice of an actor who assumed the narrator-function for the dream sequences. Tovstonogov interpreted the condition of the horse as a tragic metaphor for human life, creating at the same time an allegory for the deformation of nature by claiming it as human property. His concern rested with the universal and the general rather than with explicit social criticism, and thus Tovstonogov was not a controversial figure in Soviet theatre.

The opposite is true for the *enfant terrible*, Iurii Liubimov (b. 1917). Liubimov had noticed the dangerous uniformity in Soviet theatre and abhorred the use of make-up, costume and decorative props. With his acting class he staged in 1963 Brecht's *The Good Person of Szechwan* in which he successfully came to terms with the Brechtian epic theatre. Liubimov was subsequently put in charge of the Taganka Theatre. *The Good Person* was set on a bare stage; posters decorated the sides, panels indicated locations; songs were used for comment and a musical rhythm set the pace of the production; choreographed movement replaced verbal action. These elements, drawn from Brecht and Meierkhol'd, characterized Liubimov's style of the 1960s, and the message of the production – the individual must be in solidarity with the people to be successful in his actions – enhanced the strong socio-political stance of the theatre. The range of theatrical devices was fully explored in the initial years, but especially vividly in *Ten Days that Shook the World* (1965), based on John Reed's account of the Revolution. Liubimov drew heavily on the devices of circus, shadow play, folk theatre, agitational theatre and documentary theatre to create a revolutionary spectacle. The integration of the audience into the festive revolutionary atmosphere served to deprive history of its magnificence and private life of its seclusion. Like many other directors, Liubimov staged prose adaptations and poetic montages to establish a repertoire in the absence of genuinely good drama. Liubimov's theatre therefore is an 'author's theatre' (*avtorskii teatr*): the director composes or adapts texts and imposes his personal interpretation on the production. In Liubimov's theatre, the actor is an executor of the director's will. A perfect symbiosis between director and designer was reached when Liubimov collaborated with David Borovsky who only worked with natural material and authentic objects, an approach which ideally matched Liubimov's concept that there should be nothing 'false' on stage. A preoccupation with image and form dominated Liubimov's approach to the theatre. A central metaphor concentrated the contents of the literary material in a formal image.

Censorship interfered heavily with the creation of new repertoires in the late 1960s when during the XXIII Party Congress in 1966, several critical and controversial productions were banned: Aleksandr Tvardovsky's *Terkin in the Other World* (*Terkin na tom svete*); Radzinsky's *A Film is Being Shot*. Efros was dismissed for 'ideological shortcomings' in 1967. Cultural policy continued along a reactionary line in the 1970s, and theatre repertoires turned stale. The XXV Party Congress of 1976 promoted the 'production theme' in drama, compelling playwrights to show the hero at work. Since such plays were not very attractive, the theatres instead proceeded to adapt prose works. However, a new generation of directors (not necessarily young, though) started to emerge on two fronts in the late 1970s: on the 'small stages' which opened under the auspices of the established theatres for experimental work, allowing also for a more intimate contact with the audience; and in some new appointments, like those of Mark Zakharov to the Theatre of the Lenin Komsomol in Moscow and of Lev Dodin to the Maly Drama Theatre in Leningrad.

GLASNOST CONQUERS THE STAGE

Mark Zakharov (b. 1933) came to the Theatre of the Lenin Komsomol in 1973 and developed a wide-ranging repertoire, including musical productions, political documentaries, contemporary plays, and classics given a modern interpretation. He had been catching the spirit of the time, attracting young audiences with productions such as the rock-opera *Perchance* (*Iunona i Avos'*) by Voznesensky and Rybnikov (1981). Zakharov created a reputation for himself through his political engagement in the early days of *perestroika*, when he was among the first to support the course of reform, challenging in his articles bureuacratic interference in the theatrical process. In his subsequent productions, he tackled historical issues with a hitherto unknown openness. Mikhail Shatrov's *The Dictatorship of Conscience* (*Diktatura sovesti*, staged 1985) for the first time mentions figures such as Bukharin and Trotsky, who had been blotted out of Soviet history books; it marks the turning point in repertoire politics under Gorbachev.

Lev Dodin (b. 1945) formed a fine repertoire at the Maly Drama Theatre (Leningrad), following his appointment there as artistic director in 1983. His interest mainly lies in the adaptation of prose works for the stage. He gained worldwide recognition with his trilogy based on Fedor Abramov's 'village prose', *The House* (*Dom*, 1980) and *Brothers and Sisters* (*Brat'ia i sestry*) Parts 1 and 2, 1985. The latter text tackles the devastating effects of the purges on the life of a village community in northern Russia. It was the combination of the subject matter (the opening of formerly closed pages of Soviet history which would become a particularly popular theme in glasnost) and a congenial aesthetic presentation of this epic on stage which has made this production legendary. Dodin followed up the themes that had become fashionable under glasnost in his production of Aleksandr Galin's play *Stars in the Morning Sky* (*Zvezdy na utrennom nebe*, 1987), which deals with the evacuation of prostitutes from Moscow during the 1980 Olympics in order to represent a 'clean' city to foreign visitors.

After the collapse of the Soviet Union, Dodin continued to work on adaptations from prose fiction. He mounted Dostoevsky's *The Devils* (*Besy*, 1991), turning it into a series of episodes without preserving narrative coherence. Dodin adapted contemporary texts, such as *Gaudeamus* (1990) based on Sergei Kaledin's *The Humble Cemetry* (*Smirennoe kladbishche*) and *Claustrophobia* (1994) based on texts by Vladimir Sorokin, Liudmila Ulitskaia and Mark Kharitonov. His productions of Chekhov's *The Cherry Orchard* (1995) and *Ivanov*, as *Play without a title* (*P'esa bez nazvaniia*, 1998), reflect his strong visual orientation, while they also underscore a desire for a technically versatile set (that for *Ivanov* contains a pool in which the characters bathe). Dodin's talent is well deployed in individual episodes, while the overall composition remains unfocused. His production of Platonov's *Chevengur* (1999) highlights Dodin's talent for creating powerful, static images within a highly technical set, while the actors' faces are gradually effaced. Dodin's style is much formed by Liubimov: like Liubimov, he aims at the creation of a central metaphor through the set; his sense of rhythm and light very much echo those from the early Taganka productions; his emphasis is always on the ensemble rather than the individual actor. In terms of his contribution to world theatre Dodin may be overrated. His international success reflects a reliance on visual and illustrative modes as contributions to a universally comprehensible theatrical language.

By the end of the Soviet period the great directors of the 1960s and 1970s had disappeared from the stage: Liubimov returned from exile, but had lost touch with the reality of the new Russia; Anatolii Efros and Georgii Tovstonogov had died, leaving no successors. Most of the directors who emerged with *perestroika* are pupils of theatre theorists rather than of practitioners, and many contemporary directors teach at the State Theatre Institute RATI (GITIS).

Petr Fomcnko (b. 1932) had worked in Moscow during the 1960s and, following the banning of several productions in 1968, such as *Tarelkin's Death*, he moved to the Comedy Theatre in Leningrad. It was not until the 1980s that he returned to Moscow to become a teacher at GITIS. His work as a pedagogue and later in the Workshop Theatre set up with his students testifies to his outstanding contribution to theatre, in the training of an entire generation of first-class actors. Fomenko himself continues to direct in established theatres, such as the Vakhtangov, where he staged Ostrovsky's *Guilty without Guilt* (*Bez viny vinovatye*). This production is not set on the stage: the first act takes place in the foyer and the second in the buffet, so as to remove the action from the theatrical environment, thus underlining the human element in the fate of the main characters of a play which is itself set in a theatrical context. Fomenko's strength is his work with the actor, while he captures the core of each scene in wonderful images.

Anatolii Vasil'ev (commonly spelt 'Vasiliev', b. 1942), a pupil of Mariia Knebel', revived the Stanislavsky Theatre artistically when he joined it in 1977. Vasiliev uses the actor like wax in his hands, creating a psychologically and physically real character on stage. His production of Viktor Slavkin's *A Young Man's Grown-Up Daughter* (*Vzroslaia doch' molodogo cheloveka*, 1979) was spectacular because of its use of jazz music, condemned in the 1950s and 60s as decadent. The play is about the meeting of old university friends, now in their forties, who were once jazz fans and *stiliagi* ('Teddy boys'). Two levels of time are contrasted: the present of the 1970s; and the past of the 1950s, expressed through jazz music. On the small stage of the Taganka Theatre, Vasiliev rehearsed for several years Slavkin's next play, *Cerceau*, premièred in 1985 and acclaimed as a landmark in Soviet theatre history. The forty-year old 'Rooster' invites some colleagues, neighbours and accidental acquaintances for a dacha weekend. Everybody leads their own lives without revealing their true feelings. After a series of excursions into the past, the tragic isolation of each person becomes apparent, and yet they are incapable of sharing more of their lives with each other. In 1987 Vasiliev set up his own theatre, the School of Dramatic Art, with the ensemble of *Cerceau* and his pupils from GITIS. For a while he experimented with improvisation within rigid textual structures in the plays of Pirandello, before withdrawing into experimental work in search of a new theatrical form. His work in the 1990s differs from his earlier work and is discussed below.

After 1986 Russian theatre benefited greatly from Gorbachev's reforms. The theatres actively supported the course of openness (glasnost) and organizational reform (*perestroika*) with great determination. The reforms affected mainly the organization of theatres and their management, initiating a gradual transition of theatres to partly state-funded, but financially and administratively largely independent cultural organizations. Theatre's function, to educate the masses and to raise political awareness, was initially exploited by Gorbachev, who replaced hard-liners in key positions in the cultural sector of state and Party and encouraged a process of liberalization in the arts; through this he hoped to instil support for his reforms.

An experiment allowing theatres to run their own budgets proved beneficial to the studio theatres. They were able to obtain official status and claim subsidy from the local authorities; consequently, their number grew rapidly. The studios enjoyed enormous popularity during the initial Gorbachev years, almost outdoing the established theatres. From 1991 new conditions of management were introduced by law: funds for the running of theatres were created and alternative sources of financing (sponsoring, partial lease of the premises) were encouraged, while the subsidies for staff salaries remained fixed. Apart from theatres receiving municipal or federal subsidies, private theatres could be set up also. A contract system was introduced whereby only essential staff would be kept on the payroll. Nevertheless, some large, established theatres found it rather difficult to compete with the studios in popularity, and several theatres with particularly large troupes split: the Moscow Arts Theatre split in 1987 into the Chekhov-MKhAT, headed by Oleg Efremov, and the Gorky-MKhAT led by Tat'iana Doronina. The Taganka theatre broke up into the 'Comradeship of Taganka Actors' under Gubenko (new stage) and the 'Taganka Theatre' (old stage) under Liubimov. The Ermolova Centre split off from the Ermolova Theatre; both share one venue.

After the collapse of the Soviet system, independent and commercial projects, banking on star names rather than artistic quality to draw in audiences, became increasingly popular. The number of studio theatres dropped again, those surviving being largely those that had existed before 1986. However, these have made a powerful impact on the Russian theatre scene, reviving the notion of collective responsibility and restored intimacy with the audience, as opposed to the unconvincing psychologism of the Arts Theatre style in a huge auditorium.

During the early Gorbachev years the repertoires included a number of old, formerly banned productions, and plays both of the Western theatre of the absurd, and of the Russian OBERIU writers (Daniil Kharms, Aleksandr Vvedensky). Absurd and non-representational plays had been prohibited by censorship, with the long-term effect that Soviet theatre suffered throughout the century from a lack of an absurd tradition, both in dramatic writing and in theatre practice. A multitude of plays and adaptations of Western and émigré playwrights and authors appeared on the playbills. New plays were quickly absorbed into the repertoire, although most were written by already established dramatists, such as Liudmila Razumovskaia, Nina Sadur, Liudmila Petrushevskaia and Aleksandr Galin. In the 1990s Sadur and Petrushevskaia largely withdrew into prose fiction.

THE POST-SOVIET SCENE

After a long period dominated by a concern with political and historical documentalism (as evidenced by the plays of Vladimir Gubarev, Mikhail Shatrov, Aleksei Kazantsev, and Eduard Radzinsky), a new generation of playwrights has revitalized dramatic writing in Russia. However, it is still rare to find plays by the younger generation in the repertoires. Aleksandr Galin's plays about social issues, Grigorii Gorin's period dramas and Kazantsev's psychological dramas have ranked among the most widely staged plays, yet these dramatists hardly belong to the 'younger generation'. The reluctance to stage unknown playwrights is partly due to a lack of interest in, and inexperience on the part of directors with new dramatic forms, and partly for commercial reasons.

Mariia Arbatova (b. 1957) and Kseniia Dragunskaia (b. 1966) have had their plays staged by various studio theatres. Elena Gremina's plays made their way from studios to the big stage of the Chekhov Moscow Arts Theatre. The plays of Ol'ga Mikhailova (b. 1953) are in the repertoire of the Lenin Komsomol Theatre in Moscow. In addition, a theatre run by the established playwrights Roshchin and Kazantsev, as well as the Debut-Centre in Moscow, are doing their utmost to enable young directors to stage new plays.

Nikolai Koliada (b. 1957) is probably the most prolific playwright of the newer generation, with plays in the repertoires of several large and established Moscow theatres. Roman Viktiuk, one of the most scandalous and therefore best-selling directors in the city, staged two of his plays, *The Catapult* (*Rogatka*), staged 1993, and *Oginski's Polonaise* (*Polonez Oginskogo*, 1994). Viktiuk had established his reputation with a most controversial production of *The Maids* by Jean Genet. In sympathy with Genet's homosexual inclinations, Viktiuk cast men for the parts of the maids and produced a show influenced by dance-theatre, using elaborate choreographic scores. *The Catapult* is about the development of a homosexual relationship between two young men. Beyond the surface of reality lurks a dream world, in which the characters admit their true feelings and acknowledge death. The dream sequences free the characters from the restrictions of the everyday and social reality in which they live by means of displacement into another world. This dream world is beautiful and perfect, and offers a counterbalance to the grim Russian everyday life (*byt*). This juxtaposition of two worlds (reality and dream), which are separate and irreconcilable while one nevertheless enriches the other, forms an underlying principle of Koliada's plays.

Mental worlds, realms of imagination, and recollections of the past have become the main place of action in works such as *City Romance* (*Gorodskoi roman*) by Mikhail Ugarov (b. 1956), staged by Aleksandr Galibin in St Petersburg (1996). Galibin associates the different times of the central character's recollections with different spaces on stage, a technique he has successfully deployed in other productions of contemporary plays, such as *La Fuenf in der Luft* by Aleksei Shipenko (b. 1961). This theme also features in Oleg Bogaev's *Russian Popular Post* (*Russkaia narodnaia pochta*), staged by Kama Ginkas in Moscow (Komnata smekha, 1999: awarded the 'Golden Mask' for best production). Bogaev deals with the obsession of an old man with history, and makes historical figures come alive in the old man's world.

Evgenii Grishkovets (b. 1967) has risen to stardom with his solo-performances of *How I Ate a Dog* (*Kak ia s"el sobaku*, 1998), and *Simultaneously* (*Odnovremenno*, 1999). His episodic plays *Notes of a Russian Traveller* (*Zapiski russkogo puteshestvennika*, 1999), and *Winter* (*Zima*, 2000), were immediately picked up by commercial theatres for production in Moscow – a rare, but promising indication of the quest for new talent. Grishkovets is a performer, director and writer all at once, who parodies Soviet *byt* while drawing on associations and experiences shared with a specifically Russian audience. However, his plays remain episodic, while dramatic structure is lacking.

Olia Mukhina (b. 1970) is a young playwright who has reached popularity with her second play, *Tania-Tania* (1995), followed by *You* (1997), both staged by the Fomenko Workshop Theatre. Mukhina's *Tania-Tania* has a double love triangle involving two Tanias in a plot full of intrigues. The character Tania is married to Ivanov, who is having an affair with the Girl, called Tania. Another pair complicates the triangle, and so does another character, the Boy. However, during the play nothing happens, except for a playful realization of relationships. The characters play a game called 'life', at the expense of others, in this case the feelings of the Girl, who remains alone at the end of the play. In the world of these characters, uncertainty reigns: neither situations nor character names are made clear, and the past is 'created' through discourse. For Mukhina, language is a powerful means for the construction of reality, past and present, and its mystification. There is no longer an objective concrete social reality, but only insecurity, instability, uncertainty. Mukhina's texts are extensively illustrated with photographs, which serve to create an atmosphere and extend dramaturgy beyond its traditional boundaries.

Maksim Kurochkin (b. 1970) is a playwright with huge potential. His plays bear a utopian stamp, displayed well in his *Fighter "Medea"* (*Istrebitel' klassa "Medea"*, 1995). In this play he draws on the ancient myth of revenge, setting the action in an apocalyptic future where a war has eradicated an imagined enemy (here men), but this turns out to have been in vain – all the men are already domesticated and feminized. The movement of the Conceptualists has crossed over into drama and theatre. Experiments with the word, as exemplified in the work of Dmitrii Prigov and Lev Rubinstein, lie at the heart of the plays of Vladimir Sorokin (b. 1955). In *Dismorphomania* he dwells on the degeneration of man in parallel to his gradual linguistic incompetence. *Dostoevsky-trip* displays a postmodernist concern with the deconstruction of classical literature (Dostoevsky's *The Idiot*) by means of character transformation induced by drugs. This ploy enables Sorokin to move freely between literary discourse and vulgar street language.

Many of these new plays do not lend themselves to stage production in a theatre based on psychological realism. They call for different methods of staging and new ways of approaching a fragmented role which lacks psychological development. Therefore, the success of new drama is closely linked to new directions in theatre.

In terms of new directions, Anatolii Vasiliev has re-emerged after ten years of laboratory work and experiment to show his pioneering findings with regard to a new acting method. *Mozart and Salieri. Requiem* (2000) demonstrates the degree of perfection Vasiliev has reached in his search for new theatrical forms, while it also opens the gates for the future of Russian theatrical tradition into the twenty-first century and establishes Vasiliev as the founder of a new theatre, which may be called 'verbal', 'abstract', 'conceptual', 'metaphysical', or 'ritual'. In his theatre work Vasiliev gradually departed from the position of 'theatre as an illusion of reality', in which the actors experience emotionally the role they play. Instead he moved toward a theatre based on improvisation within rigid textual and ludic structures. These enable the actor to stand apart from the text and make its meaning transparent in the distance between actor and character. The emotional content of a character's action has been replaced by the philosophical content of his speeches; instead of the illusion of reality, there stands an abstract, yet stylistically precise architectural space.

Vasiliev's experiment also extends to the manner in which the text is spoken. The word precedes reflection, action or emotion; rather, it causes a response. The text is deprived of the usual intonation in order to destroy the linear, narrative intonation. Instead, the metaphysical quality of the word and its pure meaning are laid bare. The unemotional acting, the playful relationship of the actor to his character and the text, combined with the symbolism of the decorative elements, creates a ritual performance that opens up toward the absolute truth contained in mystery plays.

Vasiliev's theoretical findings have strongly influenced an entire generation of directors, whose concern lies with the text as a surface, as an object of the play (e.g. Klim, Galibin). Similar approaches to the text can also be found in the work of Kama Ginkas, Roman Smirnov, and Grigorii Kozlov. In this new form of theatre the text is no longer enacted or illustrated; it is a surface for a multiplicity of reactions and reflections by actors and director. In the new millennium it would seem that there is a future for new voices both in Russian drama and theatre.

FURTHER READING

Beumers, Birgit. *Yury Lyubimov at the Taganka Theatre: 1964–1994*, Amsterdam: Harwood Academic, 1997.

Glenny, Michael (ed.) *Three Soviet Plays*, Harmondsworth and Baltimore: Penguin, 1966; as *The Golden Age of Soviet Theatre*, Harmondsworth and New York: Penguin, 1981.

Kommissarzhevsky, Victor (ed.) *Nine Modern Soviet Plays*, Moscow: Progress, 1977.

Mikhailova, Alla (ed.) *Classic Soviet Plays*, Moscow: Progress, 1979.

Reeve, Franklin D. (ed. and trans.) *Contemporary Russian Drama*, New York: Pegasus, 1968.

Russell, Robert. *Russian Drama of the Revolutionary Period*, London: Macmillan; Totowa, New Jersey: Barnes and Noble, 1988.

Russell, Robert and Barratt, Andrew (eds) *Russian Theatre in the Age of Modernism*, London: Macmillan; New York: St Martin's Press, 1990.

Segel, Harold B. *Twentieth-Century Russian Drama: From Gorky to the Present*, (revised edn), Baltimore: Johns Hopkins University Press, 1993.

Smeliansky, Anatoly. *The Russian Theatre After Stalin*, trans. Patrick Miles, Cambridge: Cambridge University Press, 1999.

19

THAWS, FREEZES AND WAKES: RUSSIAN LITERATURE, 1953–1991

DAVID GILLESPIE

If the 1930s and 1940s saw the dominance of socialist realism in all areas of Soviet cultural endeavour, the years following Stalin's death saw its inexorable decline and eventual death. Indeed, it was no longer the 'basic method' by as early as 1962, because a plurality of voices and styles had by then fatally subverted its monolithic hold on culture. Still, in the minds of Party ideologues socialist realism remained a valid cultural concept, and even as late as 1984 the Party General Secretary Konstantin Chernenko was calling for writers to return to the 'positive hero' as an inspiration for society. By then, however, such appeals were too late.

After Stalin's death writers did not need long to voice doubts and concerns over the Party's control of literature, and in the 1950s and early 1960s there were several Thaws, with writers at the forefront of liberal enquiry, and Freezes as the Party and its advocates took fright at the increasing demands for intellectual freedom and tolerance being voiced in the media. Thus, the first Thaw of 1953–4 was marked by the publication of critical articles in leading literary 'thick' journals. The period got its name from the title of a fortuitously published novel by Il'ia Erenburg, but it was criticism and publicism that then, just as thirty years later during Gorbachev's Thaw, were the quickest to react to changes in the political environment. Fedor Abramov's 1954 article 'People of the Collectivized Village in Post-War Soviet Literature' ('Liudi kolkhoznoi derevni v poslevoennoi proze') attacked the falsity of literary conventions in the depiction of rural Russia since the war, singling out for special criticism some of the most celebrated socialist realist novels (by Stalin Prize winners Semen Babaevsky and Galina Nikolaeva, among others). Vladimir Pomerantsev's 'On Sincerity in Literature' ('Ob iskrennosti v literature') denied the ideological prerogative of literature, and insisted on the writer's own personal intuition as the true mark of authenticity in a given work. Both articles were mercilessly lambasted in the conservative and Party press. As a consequence of publishing these articles, Aleksandr Tvardovsky was removed as editor-in-chief of *Novyi mir*, replaced by the loyal conservative Konstantin Simonov.

Another Thaw occurred in 1956, marked this time with the appearance of literary works. The publication of Vladimir Dudintsev's novel *Not by Bread Alone* (*Ne khlebom edinym*) and several controversial shorter pieces (most notably by Aleksandr Iashin and Nikolai Zhdanov) in the second volume of the almanac *Literaturnaia Moskva* (*Literary Moscow*) caused some anxiety to diehard literary bureaucrats, and seemed again to signal an easing of the cultural control mechanisms. However, they were again followed by a Freeze in the wake of the suppression of the Hungarian uprising that year. In particular, the campaign of abuse and vilification waged against Boris Pasternak following the publication in Italy in 1957 of *Doctor Zhivago* was a clear sign that the Party still insisted on its control of literature, and would continue to persecute those who chose their own path. Seemingly paradoxically, though, Tvardovsky was reinstated at *Novyi mir* in 1958. Nothing in Soviet literary politics was ever quite what it seemed.

Following the 22nd Party Congress in 1961 came the third Thaw, marked by the removal of Stalin's body from Lenin's Mausoleum and culminating in the publication of works by Aleksandr Solzhenitsyn in 1962–3, especially *One Day in the Life of Ivan Denisovich* (*Odin den' Ivana Denisovicha*) and *Matryona's House* (*Matrenin dvor*). Even in 1962, however, there were signs that the Party was not happy with cultural pluralism. During Khrushchev's unexpected visit to an exhibition of modernist art in the Manezh gallery he verbally abused some artists as sexual deviants and criticized modernism generally as decadent and antithetical to socialist realism. His words came to be seen as Party policy. The trial of the young poet Iosif Brodsky in March 1964 reinforced the idea that the Party was not yet prepared to accept any art that was not subservient to its ideology. With the dismissal of Khrushchev as General Secretary of the Communist Party in October 1964 de-Stalinization was brought to an end, and a tougher, less tolerant cultural policy took hold. Writers, artists, and intellectuals generally were made abundantly aware of this when in 1966 the writers Andrei Siniavsky and Iulii Daniel' were sentenced to seven years' imprisonment for printing their fictional and critical works in the West. In 1968 the writers Aleksandr Ginzburg and Iurii Galanskov were sent to the Gulag for protesting publicly about the Siniavsky-Daniel' trial (Galanskov died there in 1972, at the age of thirty-three).

Nevertheless, the death of Stalin had at least destroyed the monolithic sterility of Soviet literature. Even during the various Freezes, as the Party and its watchdogs struggled to contain new modernist trends, both 'conservative' and 'liberal' writers continued to coexist, albeit often uneasily, and both sides had their official supporters. Indeed, to a large extent culture as a whole became something of a political football, kicked about by both conservatives and liberals as part of a broader agenda. Throughout the 1950s and early 1960s there was debate and discussion, and the emergence of significant talents. Throughout the 1950s, for instance, there appeared a series of semi-fictional sketches (*ocherki*) and short prose pieces by Valentin Ovechkin, Gavriil Troepol'sky, Vladimir Tendriakov, Efim Dorosh, and others criticizing the calamitous state of agriculture and the pathetically low social level of the Russian village, and calling for reform and change. It was also in this period that writers such as Fedor Abramov, Vasilii Shukshin, Vasilii Belov, and Andrei Bitov, to name a few, began writing fiction that was heavily influenced by the spirit of the Thaw. Nevertheless, at the same time the arch-conservative Vsevolod Kochetov was publishing pro-Stalin pieces and anti-liberal tracts, such as *The Brothers Ershov* (*Brat'ia Ershovy*, 1958) and *The Party District Committee Secretary* (*Sekretar' obkoma*, 1961). The ideological battle-lines adopted by writers were reflected also in the stand-off between literary journals, most notably that of the liberal *Novyi mir* and the conservative *Oktiabr'*.

Even under the more ostentatious repression of the Brezhnev years, writers such as those associated with Village Prose continued to push back the borders of the permissible. Indeed, by the time Mikhail Gorbachev came to power in 1985 and embarked on his policy of cultural openness and ideological pluralism, many forbidden topics had, in fact, already been broached, if not fully explored. Moreover, if in 1953 Russian literature was divided into two ideologically opposed camps – that of the Soviet Union and that of the emigration – by 1991 that distinction had all but disappeared. Emigré writers and their works, both those from the first emigration and those still alive, and therefore still regarded as 'hostile', became available in print to the Soviet reading public. After 1986 émigrés were invited to the Soviet Union, meetings between émigrés and Soviet writers and critics were officially encouraged, and public discussion of the culture of the emigration flourished. Even the greatest iconoclast of them all, Aleksandr Solzhenitsyn, was published, including that most damning indictment of the Soviet regime, *The Gulag Archipelago* (*Arkhipelag GULag*).

Let us return, however, to the 1950s, and attempt to penetrate the surface of significant events. To be sure, the death of Stalin seemed to change relatively little. Socialist realism remained the 'basic artistic method', and the vast majority of works published in the 1950s and 1960s conformed to the established model of the 'masterplot'. Even those that strove to pose difficult questions and thereby push back the frontiers of censorship, such as Il'ia Erenburg's *The Thaw* (*Ottepel'*, 1954), Vladimir Dudintsev's *Not by Bread Alone* (*Ne khlebom edinym*), and the controversial pieces in the second volume of *Literaturnaia Moskva*, did not question the legitimacy of Soviet power but merely raised questions of the excesses of Stalin's rule and the moral and spiritual consequences for society.

Indeed, the dominant motif of post-Stalin literature of the 1950s was the 'rediscovery' of simple human values and emotions, and the longing for a new, more humane society. Works that criticized the Stalinist legacy could do little more than reject the heavy-handed ways of the recent past and call for more tolerance and human understanding. Nevertheless, there was a clear shift away from ideology, and a new-found celebration of the little man and the simple pleasures of life. Perhaps nowhere is this better exemplified than in Vladimir Soloukhin's *A Walk in Rural Russia* (*Vladimirskie proselki*, 1958), simultaneously an affirmation of the joys and beauty of the unspoilt Russian countryside well away from the metropolis, and at the same time a triumphant re-discovery of Russia's historical (i.e. pre-revolutionary) past.

The first work that explicitly questioned the rationale of Soviet power was Solzhenitsyn's *One Day in the Life of Ivan Denisovich*, a novella of blistering power that not only laid bare the raw facts of life within the Gulag, but also showed that the Gulag *was* the system. In the building of socialism, the Soviet people were constructing their own prison. The next year saw the publication of Solzhenitsyn's shorter *Matryona's House*, which is at the same time both a damning critique of rural devastation since the collectivization of agriculture in the late 1920s, and an affirmation of the durability of an age-old Russian spirituality and moral goodness. This latter work is generally seen as the inspiration for the Village Prose movement that began in earnest a few years later.

In the Soviet Union culture was, of course, always linked with politics, but whereas under Stalin politics suppressed and perverted the creative impulse, after Stalin culture became the stimulus for critical debate, however muted, that then reinvented itself as public opinion. The anti-Stalinist messages in the poetry of Evgenii Evtushenko in the 1950s and 1960s warned against the dangers of a return to the old totalitarian ways. The guitar poetry of Aleksandr Galich, Bulat Okudzhava, and Vladimir Vysotsky reached a vast audience and inspired a generation of young people with its sheer accessibility and simplicity. The extremely popular plays of Aleksei Arbuzov, Eduard Radzinsky, and Viktor Rozov touched on topical problems of youth alienation and moral and spiritual stagnation, but, because of the official sanction of the theatre, could go no further than slight social criticism.

Perhaps the most important aspect of the cultural regeneration of the 1960s was the rediscovery of the past. A major contribution to this was the publication in instalments in the first half of the decade of Il'ia Erenburg's memoirs under the title *Men, Years, Life (Liudi. Gody. Zhizn'*, 1961–6), which introduced to the younger generation of Soviet intellectuals important names of which they would have had but a faint inkling: Marina Tsvetaeva, Osip Mandel'shtam, Vsevolod Meierkhol'd, Roman Jakobson, Kazimir Malevich, and many others.

It was in this area, as elsewhere, however, that prose fiction led the way. Village Prose emerged as a distinct literary trend that followed on from the socially-minded criticism of agricultural practice and management in the 1950s, and Solzhenitsyn's picture of a holy Russia not yet tainted with materialism and urban culture. Works such as Sergei Zalygin's *On the Irtysh (Na Irtyshe*, 1964), and Vasilii Belov's *Carpenters' Yarns (Plotnitskie rasskazy*, 1968), discussed openly for the first time the excesses and injustices of the collectivization of agriculture, and also created a climate in which issues of historical relevance could no longer be ignored. Collectivization became a popular subject for Village Prose writers, and for Belov, Boris Mozhaev, and Vladimir Soloukhin it became the cornerstone of their work from the 1960s up to the late 1980s. Even establishment figures such as Mikhail Alekseev felt bound to touch on it in such works as *The Brawlers (Drachuny*, 1982).

Village Prose was significant not only for its opening up of an important area of historical enquiry, but also for its discussion of the present. If socialist realism had emphasized man's dominance and conquest of the natural world, Village Prose presented in lyrical, contemplative images man's humility before it. In the 1970s, delight in the natural world became replaced by a concern for it as, in Viktor Astaf'ev's *King Fish (Tsar'-ryba*, 1976) and Valentin Rasputin's *Farewell to Matyora (Proshchanie s Materoi*, 1976), the consequences of Soviet man's attempts to remake the world according to ideological criteria had increasingly alarming implications for his moral, spiritual, and even physical well-being.

The moral state of the nation and the individual was of concern to writers interested in other areas of Soviet life. By far the most popular theme throughout the 1960s and 1970s was World War Two, and, although stalwarts such as Ivan Stadniuk and Aleksandr Chakovsky expressed pro-Stalinist sentiments and glorified the sacrifices made by the Russian people, others, such as Vasil' Bykov and Iurii Bondarev showed that the conflicts and losses of the past have far-reaching consequences for the present. Indeed, Bykov shows a murkier side to the Soviet war effort, depicting cowardice and treachery in *The Ordeal* (*Sotkinov*, 1970), and pointing to falsification and injustice in *The Obelisk* (*Obelisk*, 1972). One of his most powerful works, *The Dead Feel No Pain* (*Mertvym ne bol'no*, 1966), linked these negative features with the Stalinist legacy, and was severely criticized.

Another writer who courted politically-minded criticism was the leading exponent of so-called Urban Prose, Iurii Trifonov. He was concerned above all by the moral dilemmas of the post-war intelligentsia, especially that based in Moscow, revealing that the price for gaining material prosperity and status was moral compromise. In his Moscow stories of 1969–75 he shows weak, vacillating intellectuals who either capitulate to a cynical materialism, or are crushed. In his latter years he became increasingly outspoken, and in *The House on the Embankment* (*Dom na naberezhnoi*, 1976), he drew a bleak picture of the type of mediocrity who prospered under Stalin through the denunciation of others. It was a bitterly ironic portrait, and attracted criticism from the head of the Writers' Union, Georgii Markov. In subsequent works, such as *The Old Man* (*Starik*, 1978), he looked back as far as the Revolution and the Civil War in his search for the loss of contemporary idealism and values, and in the posthumously published *Disappearance* (*Ischeznovenie*, 1987), he showed the destruction of the Old Bolsheviks and their idealism during the Ezhov terror of 1937.

A new phenomenon in Soviet Russian literature was the emergence, from the mid-1960s onwards, of so-called 'women's literature', that is, fiction written by women, about women, and largely for women. With the publication in 1969 of Natal'ia Baranskaia's *A Week Like Any Other* (*Nedelia kak nedelia*), and subsequent novels and novellas by I. Grekova in the 1970s and 1980s, the 'double burden' of the working mother was brought home to the Russian reading public, as were the emotional and social difficulties faced by single mothers, widows, and pensioners. It was an acute social problem and, like the issue of collectivization, became the subject of heated public discussion through the medium of literature. Other important women writers who began to acquire a reputation in these years include Viktoriia Tokareva and Nina Katerli.

By the 1970s Russian literature was in dialogue with itself. Its soul had been profoundly affected by external events, such as the Hungarian uprising of 1956, the fall of Khrushchev in 1964 and the invasion of Czechoslovakia in 1968, and there was within the intelligentsia disillusion with the prospect of liberalization, often bordering on despair. Political repression was mirrored in the cultural arena. Of considerable interest to Sovietologists, but rather less to literary scholars or observers of the Soviet cultural scene, was the award of the prestigious Lenin Prize in 1979 to Leonid Brezhnev, General Secretary of the Communist Party, for his autobiographical trilogy *Little Land* (*Malaia Zemlia*), *Rebirth* (*Vozrozhdenie*) and *Virgin Lands* (*Tselina*), published in print-runs of several million in 1978. All three were near-perfect examples of socialist realism, with stereotyped characters and hidebound plots. Within the Soviet Union there was an escalating tension between writers who struggled against increasing odds to keep alive the spirit of de-Stalinization, and the diehard writers and literary bureaucrats trying to maintain ideological hegemony in the spirit of the Brezhnev trilogy.

Censorship and ideological vigilance became ever more stifling. In 1979 a group of writers, including Andrei Bitov, Evgenii Popov, Fazil' Iskander, and Vasilii Aksenov, attempted to publish an almanac entitled *Metropol'* without the permission of the Writers' Union. The almanac included pieces by Popov, Aksenov, Iuz Aleshkovsky, Vladimir Vysotsky, and Andrei Voznesensky. For their involvement, Aksenov was forced into exile and Popov banned from further publication. However, the controversy surrounding the almanac, like that associated with *Literaturnaia Moskva* two decades earlier, ensured that the authors and editors achieved a degree of renown that would otherwise perhaps have eluded them. The almanac was immediately circulated among interested readers through that most Soviet of institutions, *samizdat*.

In the 1960s and 1970s phenomena that could only have come about in a totalitarian state emerged: *samizdat* and *tamizdat*. By no means confined to artistic literature, *samizdat* ('for the drawer') was the publication and distribution of works that had either been banned from official publication or written with the express intention of not being officially published. Such literary works that circulated across the land in the 1960s and 1970s included all of Solzhenitsyn's writings, Venedikt Erofeev's *Moscow Circles* (*Moskva-Petushki*), Vladimir Voinovich's *The Life and Extraordinary Adventures of Private Ivan Chonkin* (*Zhizn' i neobychainye prikliucheniia soldata Ivana Chonkina*), Georgii Vladimov's *Faithful Ruslan* (*Vernyi Ruslan*), and many others. As a result of appearing in *samizdat*, most works then appeared in editions published in the West, usually the United States or Germany. This was known as *tamizdat*, literally 'books published over there' (i.e. the West). In the case of the guitar poets, another phenomenon emerged. *Magnitizdat* was the recording on a tape-recorder (*magnitofon*) of songs that were then re-recorded and circulated across the land, thus bringing about the vast nationwide popularity of Vysotsky and Okudzhava, from the Baltic to the Pacific ocean.

There was, moreover, a fundamental struggle going on, one that sought to claim the soul of Russian culture. Both the literature of the Soviet Union and the emigration had long vied for the right to be the true legacy of the classical Russian tradition. Certainly, by the mid-1970s, the undoubted greats of the twentieth century were all living abroad: Nabokov, Iosif Brodsky, and Aleksandr Solzhenitsyn. Within a few years Nabokov, the last representative of a lost Russia, was dead, but the ranks of émigrés were being swollen with the 'third wave', representing the flower of the post-war creative intelligentsia: Vasilii Aksenov,

Vladimir Voinovich, Georgii Vladimov, Fridrikh Gorenshtein, Sergei Dovlatov, Aleksandr Zinov'ev, and many others. By the mid-1980s the Russian emigration boasted more genuinely reputable creative talents than the motherland.

One of the key works of Soviet Russian literature of the 1970s was Andrei Bitov's *Pushkin House* (*Pushkinskii dom*, 1978). Although published in Russia only in 1987, the novel explicitly places Nabokov within the Russian literary tradition, and denies that 1917 provided a break in the Russian literary process. The emphasis throughout is on continuity and evolution. Bitov's novel can be seen to have prepared the ground for the re-integration of Soviet and émigré cultures that began under Gorbachev.

The lifting of Party control of culture that accompanied Gorbachev's accession to power in 1985 was both exhilarating for the reading public and shattering for the hold of ideology on the minds, if not the hearts, of the population. Glasnost began rather cautiously, as was to be expected, with the publication in 1986–7 of poems by safely dead, though avowedly anti-Soviet, writers, such as Nikolai Gumilev and Vladislav Khodasevich, Vladimir Nabokov's novels *The Defence* (*Zashchita Luzhina*) and *Mary* (*Mashen'ka*), as well as some of his poetry and literary criticism. There were also major works by writers from the past who had at least been tolerated by the Soviet canon. Among these were the following major works: Mikhail Bulgakov's satirical and subversive *The Heart of a Dog* (*Sobach'e serdtse*), and many other plays and prose works; Andrei Platonov's anti-Utopian, and thus anti-Bolshevik, *The Foundation Pit* (*Kotlovan*) and *Chevengur*; Aleksandr Tvardovsky's childhood lament *By Right of Memory* (*Po pravu pamiati*), which discusses his kulak father's downfall during collectivization; Anna Akhmatova's *Requiem* (*Rekviem*), her great epic poem devoted to, and written on behalf of, all the women who suffered loneliness and loss during the Ezhov Terror of 1936–8; Nikolai Kliuev's epic poem *The Burned Ruins* (*Pogorel'shchina*), a highly original and linguistically-challenging account of the fate of the Russian village after the Revolution.

Another feature was the appearance of previously banned works by writers still living in the Soviet Union. These included Sergei Antonov's *Ravines* (*Ovragi*), an account of collectivization seen from the point of view of the activists who came to enforce it from the town; Bitov's *Pushkin House*; Vladimir Dudintsev's *White Robes* (*Belye odezhdy*), an account of the persecution of Soviet biologists in the late 1940s; and particularly Anatolii Rybakov's *Children of the Arbat* (*Deti Arbata*), concerning the beginnings of the purges and the individuals who took part in them or were affected by them. These works all raised hopes that the current Thaw would not stop at publishing merely a few selected authors and texts, as had been done on previous occasions. Moreover, this Thaw went much further than previous ones in the range of authors either discovered for the first time by Soviet readers, or authors whose work had only been partially known. Thus important writers, both from the emigration and from within the Soviet state, who became known to the Soviet reading public in these years include Leonid Dobychin, Mikhail Osorgin, Gaito Gazdanov, Boris Poplavsky, Georgii Obolduev, Evgenii Chirikov, and Konstantin Vaginov. It did seem that Russian culture would at last become whole.

In 1988–9, though, glasnost assumed a qualitatively different aspect with the publication of Pasternak's *Doctor Zhivago*, and in particular Vasilii Grossman's novels *Life and Fate* (*Zhizn' i sud'ba*) and *Forever Flowing* (*Vse techet*). Grossman's works threw up a fundamental challenge to the whole edifice of Marxism-Leninism. They had offered so devastating a critique that the Soviet Politburo in the early 1960s had declared *Life and Fate* unpublishable for several centuries. It was clear that Soviet literature, if it could adapt and survive at all, would never be the same. Furthermore, 1989 also saw the re-emergence of works by Solzhenitsyn in Soviet print, and, together with works by other former dissidents and exiles, it now seemed distinctly possible that a few years of cultural freedom had fatally undermined an already demoralized and weakened totalitarian system.

Yet alongside the exhilaration of cultural revival there were other emotions stirred up. Nationalism in its various guises had been rearing its head since the 1960s, especially in the works of some of the Village Prose writers, who found a platform in the journal *Nash sovremennik*. The Village Prose writers surviving into the 1980s were now able to indulge their nationalistic tastes to produce controversial works of varying xenophobic and anti-modernist hues in Valentin Rasputin's *The Fire* (*Pozhar*) in 1985, and in 1986 Viktor Astaf'ev's *The Sad Detective* (*Pechal'nyi detektiv*) and Vasilii Belov's *The Best is Yet to Come* (*Vse vperedi*). Belov continued his cycle of novels on collectivization under the general title *The Eves* (*Kanuny*) and *The Crucial Year* (*God velikogo pereloma*), begun in 1972, with further instalments in 1987 and 1989 that became ever more vitriolic and anti-Semitic. On the other hand, the late 1980s saw the publication of both fictional and private writings by the recently deceased Fedor Abramov, especially his short story *The Journey into the Past* (*Poezdka v proshloe*), and by Vladimir Tendriakov, in particular the novel *Shooting at Mirages* (*Pokushenie na mirazhi*). Both had been respected, but hardly eminent, figures from the 1960s and 1970s, but now a thorough reappraisal of their reputations became necessary. They have emerged as free-thinking and courageous individuals whose best work, published only posthumously, exhibits great satirical power, a clear vision of the evils of their environment, but also anguish at being forced to live and work within an iniquitous system.

By the turn of the decade it was obvious that the Soviet state could not survive the monumental upheaval brought about by freedom of expression. Things were changing very quickly, not least the role of the writer and the importance of the written word. The role of the 'thick' journals, for over 150 years the main outlet for cultural production, was also changing. In the early months glasnost was enacted largely by the 'liberal' monthlies: *Novyi mir*, from 1986 edited by Sergei Zalygin; *Ogonek*, edited by Vitalii Korotich; *Druzhba narodov*, edited by Sergei Baruzdin; and *Znamia*, edited by Grigorii Baklanov. Soon, though, other journals not noted for their liberal leanings, such as *Moskva*, *Neva*, and *Oktiabr'* also got in on the act. Initially sales soared as people in their millions rushed to read the latest revelations or long-lost works, and journals competed to publish previously banned pieces by émigrés or other established Soviet figures. However, in a time of worsening economic crisis, amid paper shortages and ever-decreasing resource allocations, some journals found life difficult. Nevertheless, despite straitened circumstances, most survived in one form or another and continued to prosper into the 1990s.

The amazing transformations in Soviet cultural life in the late 1980s had many consequences, most of them positive, but some, as with the resurgent nationalism, giving cause for disquiet. In addition, many new voices also came to be heard, including those of younger writers such as Tat'iana Tolstaia, Sergei Kaledin, and Valeriia Narbikova. More significant were the 'new' voices of older writers who were enabled to express publicly their true selves for the first time. These include Liudmila Petrushevskaia, who had published some short stories and plays in the 'stagnation' years, but among whose major works are *A Modern Family Robinson* (*Novye Robinzony*, 1989), and *Our Crowd* (*Svoi krug*, 1988). Others include Vladimir Makanin, whose first prose works appeared in 1967 but whose most powerful work was published only after glasnost, and Evgenii Popov, who had some short stories published in 1976 and, as a result of his involvement in the *Metropol'* affair, had been unable to publish for six years. He soon brought out two major novels, *The Soul of a Patriot or Various Epistles to Ferfichkin* (*Dusha patriota ili razlichnye poslaniia Ferfichkinu*, 1989) and *The Splendour of Life* (*Prekrasnost' zhizni*, 1990).

The year 1991 was a major turning-point in the history of Russia. Russian culture also underwent a profound and probably irreversible transformation. If we see the struggles of the post-Stalin period as a reflection of the creative desire, on the one hand, to gain freedom of expression and, on the other, the political need to subjugate the creative impulse to the demands of the state, we can also see that the resolution of this battle in favour of the former also brought to an end a particular feature of Russian culture: namely, its civic-mindedness. With the death of a totalitarian society and the birth of a democracy, no longer could the writer see him/herself as the moral guide or teacher of his people, bridging the vast gulf between the rulers and the ruled. Viktor Erofeev announced a 'wake' for Soviet literature in a celebrated article in 1990. Moreover, in the post-industrial age, the Russian writer, just like his western counterpart, now had to compete with varying forms of popular entertainment and information technology for the attention of an increasingly selective and informed reading public. In short, with what is regarded in the West as the 'normalization' of the creative process came the death of Soviet literature, and a severe challenge to the place and role of the writer in an increasingly diversified and pluralistic society.

In 1991 a world and a culture came to an end. Ideology had been defeated. Russian culture was united, the past had been overcome. The struggle, ongoing since 1953, for greater freedom had finally been resolved. The great themes of these decades – the return to nature, memory of the past and the correction of historical injustice, the call to human values – had been played out against a lively, occasionally tumultuous background of literary politics, but had made a great contribution to the overhauling of an oppressive and murderous regime. The last few years of this regime were vitally important but also bewildering, as works from the past appeared alongside works by new writers, as socialist realism vied with modernism and postmodernism, as competing political ideologies made themselves heard through works that purported to be fiction. The overriding motif was that one world was over, but there was not yet another to replace it.

Perhaps the best illustration of this is to be found in the work of the avant-garde writer Vladimir Sorokin (b. 1955), whose two major novels *The Norm* (*Norma*) and *Novel* (*Roman*) were written in the 1980s, though published in full in Russia only in 1994. Sorokin's prose is distinguished by its eagerness to shock, disgust, and appal the reader with its unashamed preoccupation with bodily functions, dismemberment, cannibalism, and all manner of physical and verbal abuse. Sorokin subverts and destroys all symbols of authority, and his satire is particularly ferocious when directed at Lenin, the father of the Soviet state. Even linguistic conventions become mangled beyond recognition, and the language of the totalitarian state tears itself apart so that ultimately it becomes gibberish. Sorokin's prose rips away the falsity and pretence of a society built on lies and violence; but it leaves the reader staring into the abyss with no indication of a way out.

The four decades between the death of Stalin and the death of the Soviet Union proved to be cataclysmic not only for society, but also for its culture. Literature bore the brunt of those upheavals, with arrests, imprisonment, and exile of some writers, and the stagnation of the cultural process in general. Russian literature abroad flourished and developed alongside the hidebound home-grown product, continually enriched by the exiled individuals filling its ranks. In Russia, writers were increasingly drawn into social and political debate on the future of the country. By the late 1980s the contradictions of a freely functioning literary process and the needs of a one-party state had become irreconcilable. Whereas in 1953 an oppressive ideology had dominated literature, by 1991 literature had played a decisive part in its downfall.

FURTHER READING

Aksenov, Vasilii, Bitov, Andrei, Erofeev, Viktor and Popov, Evgenii (eds) *Metropol: A Literary Almanac*, New York: Norton, 1982.

Brown, Deming. *Soviet Russian Literature since Stalin*, Cambridge and New York: Cambridge University Press, 1978.

—— *The Last Years of Soviet Russian Literature: Prose Fiction, 1975–1991*, Cambridge and New York: Cambridge University Press, 1993.

Eshelman, Raoul. *Early Soviet Postmodernism*, Frankfurt: Peter Lang, 1997.

Field, Andrew (ed.) *Pages from Tarusa: New Voices in Russian Writing*, Boston: Little, Brown, 1964; London: Chapman and Hall, 1965.

Frankel, Edith Rogovin. *Novy Mir: A Case Study in the Politics of Literature, 1952–1958*, Cambridge and New York: Cambridge University Press, 1981.

Gibian, George. *Interval of Freedom: Soviet Literature During the Thaw, 1954–1957*, Minneapolis: Minnesota University Press, 1960.

Goscilo, Helena and Lindsey, Byron (eds) *Glasnost: An Anthology of Russian Literature under Gorbachev*, Ann Arbor: Ardis, 1990.

Hosking, Geoffrey. *Beyond Socialist Realism: Soviet Fiction since 'Ivan Denisovich'*, London: Granada; New York: Holmes and Meier, 1980.

Lakshin, Vladimir. *Solzhenitsyn, Tvardovsky and 'Novy Mir'*, ed. and trans. Michael Glenny, Cambridge, Massachusetts: MIT Press, 1980.

Marsh, Rosalind J. *Soviet Fiction since Stalin: Science, Politics and Literature*, London: Croom Helm; Totowa, New Jersey: Barnes and Noble, 1986.

Matich, Olga and Heim, Michael (eds) *Third Wave: Russian Literature in Emigration*, Ann Arbor: Ardis, 1984.

Parthé, Kathleen. *Russian Village Prose: The Radiant Past*, Princeton: Princeton University Press, 1992.

Peterson, Nadya L. *Subversive Imagination: Fantastic Prose and the End of Soviet Literature*, Boulder, Colorado: Westview Press, 1997.

Porter, Robert. *Russia's Alternative Prose*, Oxford: Berg, 1994.

Proffer, Carl and Proffer, Ellendea (eds) *The Barsukov Triangle, The Two-Toned Blond and Other Stories*, Ann Arbor: Ardis, 1984.

Ryan-Hayes, Karen L. *Contemporary Russian Satire: A Genre Study*, Cambridge and New York: Cambridge University Press, 1995.

Shneidman, N.N. *Soviet Literature in the 1980's: Decade of Transition*, Toronto: University of Toronto Press, 1989.

Svirski, Grigori. *A History of Post-War Soviet Writing: The Literature of Moral Opposition*, ed. and trans. Robert Dessaix and Michael Ulman, Ann Arbor: Ardis, 1981.

20

POST-SOVIET RUSSIAN LITERATURE

ALLA LATYNINA AND MARTIN DEWHIRST

The year 1990, often known as Solzhenitsyn Year, since several of the main literary journals were then rushing to get out his remaining prose works in case the literary 'thaw' was succeeded by a new 'freeze', marked the end of both glasnost and of the literary boom that had begun in 1986. The publication of most of the *The Gulag Archipelago* (*Arkhipelag GULag*) in *Novyi mir* in 1989 meant that the official censorship system had finally been overcome, but it simultaneously signified the beginning of a new literary situation, wherein literature would have to exist in conditions of freedom of speech and freedom of the press.

This is what all writers who were in one way or another opposed to the regime had apparently been dreaming of, but few people then realized that official support for socialist realism was the prerequisite not only for 'approved' art and literature but also the precondition for the appearance of such diverse anti-totalitarian works as Vladimir Dudintsev's *White Robes* (*Belye odezhdy*), Anatolii Rybakov's *Children of the Arbat* (*Deti Arbata*), the novels by B. Iampol'sky, Iurii Dombrovsky, Vasilii Grossman, Aleksandr Bek, and others that had led to the literary boom at the beginning of the period of *perestroika*. All these works had been undermining the ideological walls surrounding the aesthetic field of the socialist realist novel, the validity of whose foundations these and other writers denied. When the walls finally collapsed, there was no need for other works of this type. Readers, who had been following the struggle of anti-establishment literature against the system of taboos and 'disapproved-of' themes, language, and forms with the intensity of spectators at a top-rated sporting event, quickly lost interest after it became clear that there were no more officially forbidden subjects or styles of writing.

In 1991 the last remaining 'bastions' were taken. Many people had felt that, because of the all-pervasive 'modesty trope' inherent in Soviet socialist realism, it was more likely that *The Gulag Archipelago* would be printed in Russia than Nabokov's *Lolita*, not to speak of Iuz Aleshkovsky's *Nikolai Nikolaevich*, containing large chunks of 'non-normative' language, and that, if some of the works by Vasilii Aksenov and by Eduard Limonov were passed for publication, then substantial cuts would be required. But in that year it was easy enough – at least in the largest cities of the USSR – to pick up a 'Soviet' edition of Aleshkovsky's novella as well as Limonov's novel *It's Me, Eddie!* (*Eto ia, Edichka!*). It was now the writers (and not the Party or the state) who would have the final say as to the language, as well as the form and content, of their works. There were no longer any words that had to be censored out of all printed matter.

The dividing line between the previous literary period and the present one was drawn by the failed coup attempt in August 1991 and the subsequent economic reforms introduced at the beginning of 1992. There were now virtually no official restrictions on what could be published (other than limitations of the sort found in the most mature liberal democracies), but henceforth the writers had to cope on their own with the vagaries of the chaotic free-for-all of the unregulated post-Soviet market.

One of the key signs of this problem is the critical state of the traditional Russian 'thick' literary monthlies. Subscription rates have not been able to keep up with galloping price rises in general, and the increasing costs of paper, printing, and postage in particular. Entire issues, completely ready to go to press, gather dust at the printers and reach subscribers and sales outlets several months late. The number of copies published and sold has been declining steeply. For instance, in 1990 the journal *Novyi mir* had a print run of 2,660,000, whereas the figure for 1991 (*before* the economic reform and concomitant price increases) was 958,000. This dropped in 1992 to 250,000, in 1993 to 74,000, in 1994 to 53,000 and in 1995 to 25,000 (most copies went to libraries, supported by a project of the Soros Open Society Foundation). Circulation is therefore considerably lower now than in the 'years of stagnation', prior to glasnost, when *Novyi mir* was printed in an edition of some 250,000 to 300,000 copies. (The figure for January 1996 was 30,200, but it had sunk to 20,570 in July. In October 2000 the print-run was 13,300.) This trend is characteristic of all Russian literary magazines. Readers now cannot afford and/or do not want to buy and read 'serious' writing.

There is also a general crisis in the publishing industry. State publishers have been starved of cash, and even contemporary writers who were popular in the *perestroika* period are experiencing difficulties in reprinting their earlier works and publishing their new ones. Most of the new private publishers, having successfully helped to weaken their state-owned competitors, are naturally driven mainly by the logic of commerce and the search for profits to give priority to bestsellers and pot-boilers, for which, as in all other countries, there is a ready market. At the same time, collections of works by authors such as Mikhail Bulgakov, Mikhail Zoshchenko, Andrei Platonov, and Boris Pasternak, émigré Russian writers (and philosophers) and, of course, the classics have proved to be commercially viable, so the more discerning reader has a wider choice than ever before. That, however, is of little comfort for contemporary Russian writers and literary critics unless they are capable of producing works that look as though they will immediately find a ready sale.

There is also a sense of a much more profound crisis than that manifested by the problems of the literary journals and the publishing industry – the widely perceived difficulty of the role and function of literature itself. Russian society no longer focuses on literature as a crucial orientating factor, and many writers, unable to adapt to a situation where they are no longer near the centre of public attention, feel that they are redundant and even that 'high' culture itself is surplus to society's present requirements.

This has produced a new split in the world of the arts, not so much on political grounds (as, during *perestroika*, between supporters and opponents of reforms, between democrats and anti-democrats, monetarists and anti-monetarists), as on aesthetic and to some extent generational grounds. On 4 July 1990, *Literaturnaia gazeta* published an article by Viktor Erofeev called 'A Wake for Soviet Literature' ('Pominki po sovetskoi literature'), which proved to be the start of, and provided the basis for, a long-running discussion. Erofeev declared that all the texts generated by the Soviet system, whether supportive of or hostile to it, were now out-dated and irrelevant; what was needed was a different sort of literature, which did however already exist (and which we are inclined to trace back to Venedikt Erofeev's *Moscow Circles* [*Moskva-Petushki*], dating from 1969). The main features and the demarcation lines of this 'other' literature were extremely difficult to pin down, but it had to be politically uncommitted, devoid of moralizing and preaching, and to go beyond the boundaries of 'ordinary' realism as well as those of socialist realism. A tighter definition of this 'other' or 'new' literature was provided by Mikhail Berg, a theoretician of the artistic 'underground' and editor of the independent St Petersburg periodical *Vestnik novoi literatury*, founded in 1989 and setting its face against the traditional Russian and Soviet 'thick' journals. From the outset the magazine gave priority to three literary movements: religious poetry by Elena Shvarts, Viktor Krivulin, Sergei Stratanovsky, L. Aronzon, A. Shel'vakh, V. Filippov and others (Berg prefers to call this the 'Leningrad School of Poetry'); 'Moscow Conceptualism', with three of its four main pillars (Vsevolod Nekrasov, Dmitrii Prigov, Lev Rubinshtein, but not, so far, Vladimir Sorokin) and their precursors E. Kropivnitsky, Ia. Satunovsky and M. Sokovnin; and the 'new postmodernist prose' by B. Kudriakov, Viktor Erofeev, Evgenii Popov, N. Isaev, S. Korovin *et al.* (see Berg's article in *Znamia*, 1 [1995], 175–6). Berg defines this 'other' or 'new' literature as literature of the end (of the century, of an era, of a system) and as a 'literature without illusions', meaning not only social and political but also 'psychological and metaphysical illusions that result in a rigid attitude to human nature as such'.

Another much-discussed article was Aleksandr Ageev's 'Notes on the Crisis' ('Konspekt o krizise', *Literaturnoe obozrenie*, 3 [1991], 15–21), which insisted that the crisis in Russian literature was deeper and more comprehensive than it initially appeared, that this was linked to literature's claims to provide moral guidance, and that in the future the only books that could expect to gain the reader's attention were those that focused on the sphere of values of the private individual.

In the early 1990s another proposition was put forward, according to which the potential of all existing styles had been exhausted, a fact that would inevitably generate a literature that played with a variety of styles, as is typical of post-modernism. Considering the characteristics of postmodernism to be quotational and other meaningful references to other texts, a heightened degree of intro-spection, a propensity for commenting and self-documentation, a tendency towards syncretism, interweaving, and the fusion of a variety of art forms, V. Kuritsyn asserts – with perhaps more than a touch of irony – that the 'postmodernist consciousness, continuing its decisive and derisive expansion, remains . . . the only aesthetically vital factor in the literary process' (*Novyi mir*, 2 [1992], 225–32).

Despite such attempts to define the issues, the vagueness of concepts like 'new literature', 'other literature', Conceptualism and postmodernism enables proponents of each of them to lay claim to adjacent territories or simply to try to take them over. One of the most talented members of the generation in its forties, Vladimir Sorokin, is claimed as 'one of them' both by the conceptualists and by the postmodernists. His novels *The Hearts of the Four* (*Serdtsa chetyrekh*, 1994), *The Norm* (*Norma*, 1994), and *Novel* (*Roman*, 1994) have delighted those who like his virtuoso game-playing with other styles and his extraordinarily inventive examples of sadism, and disgusted those who are not inclined to think that literature requires detailed descriptions of the consumption of excrement and pus or of how best to dismember corpses. Although writers like Mark Kharitonov, Viacheslav P'etsukh, and the distinctive St Petersburg author A. Melikhov have spoken publicly about postmodernism in very cool terms, that has not prevented some critics from discovering postmodernist elements in their works.

In 1990 and 1991 many critics who until then had written sympathetically about politically committed anti-Soviet belles-lettres switched their attention and preferences to the literary 'underground', which was then confidently coming up to the surface and moving onto the stage of public artistic life. Viktor Erofeev, Evgenii Popov, and others were then continually reminding people of the 1979 *Metropol'* almanac that had caused such a scandal at the time, even though it was intended not as an act of political defiance but as an aesthetic statement indicating that the boundaries of Soviet literature and the official style were not too narrow for the adequate expression of artistic freedom. Yet when, in 1991, this legendary anthology was finally published in Moscow, Pavel Basinsky, a young critic who had been brought up on tales about the importance of the volume that had acquired mythological status, wrote angrily that 'It would have been better if there hadn't been such a text . . . *Metropol'* is of interest only as a myth or as a historical reference work' (*Literaturnaia gazeta*, 19 [1992], 4).

Another point became clear in 1991. This 'new' or 'other' literature had seemed to constitute a single entity, but only because it existed in defiance of an official veto. In conditions of freedom some of its practitioners were perfectly capable of wrangling and bickering with their colleagues in full view of the public. Not long after Viktor Erofeev's article on the end of Soviet literature, Ol'ga Sedakova, a sophisticated and highly cultured underground poet who enjoyed experimenting in a variety of styles, commented that the entire generation of self-proclaimed writers of a supposedly 'new' literature, including Erofeev himself, belonged in actual fact to the 'post-Soviet' school. 'They have inherited the same old aesthetic irresponsibility. . . . It's simply disgusting. They are behaving like the generals of Soviet literature. For me they aren't anything new, they are the tail-end of Soviet literature. Its witches' sabbath' (*Gumanitarnyi fond*, 31 [1991], 3).

At about the same time, the practitioners of this 'different' literature were having to answer questions like 'Different from what?'. From the aesthetics and content of socialist realism? But if there's *no* official literature at all any longer, doesn't that mean a change in the status of 'different' literature?

The theoreticians of conceptual poetry and 'sotsart' (straight-faced parodies of socialist art) commended themselves for 'washing' words and concepts clean of the 'greasy fingers of the state'. The critic Aleksandr Arkhangel'sky said that these 'washermen' had fallen into a trap laid for them by 'official' art, since they could function only as long as it did. If it passed away, no one would understand or care what Igor' Irten'ev was making fun of in his verse (or what Melamid and Komar were sending up in their paintings). By the end of 1992 this was indeed largely the case, which for some members of the former 'underground' was more traumatic and harder to bear than their recent confrontations with the political authorities. The public was no longer interested in the writer's stance *vis-à-vis* the state, and many writers found that they could not operate in conditions of political (but not usually economic) freedom.

In the nineteenth century the critic Vissarion Belinsky introduced the idea of annual surveys of the latest belles-lettres. Between 1986 and 1990 a number of journals tried to carry on this tradition, but in the 1990s, because of the general crisis, this gave way to newspaper questionnaires. At the end of 1991 and the beginning of 1992 several publications, including *Literaturnaia gazeta*, *Nezavisimaia gazeta*, *Moskovskie novosti* and *Ogonek*, attempted to sum up the recent and current literary situation. The prevailing feeling among professionals was one of disappointment, all the harder to bear because of what had proved to be unfounded hopes of a cultural boom once Party tutelage was removed. Moreover, the predominant tone of the experts' forecasts was pessimistic. Lovers of realistic prose complained that contemporary fiction had lost the ability to find any sense or meaning in the current period. Recent supporters of the avant-garde (for example, B. Kuz'minsky) admitted that it had not met their expectations and that it was the least gifted of its practitioners who had become the market leaders and completely adjusted to the new situation. Yesterday's *aficionados* of postmodernism cannot hide their disappointment. Many of them agreed that the squabbles and in-fighting between and within groups and grouplets is having a deleterious impact on literature.

If we take a look at the analogous questionnaires filled in a year later, at the end of 1992, we find that the tone has changed substantially. Apocalyptic prophecies have disappeared. No one writes about the impending demise of Russian literature as a whole, or even of the collapse of literary journals in particular. Instead of gloomy forecasts there is a matter-of-fact recognition of a protracted crisis and a catalogue of successes as well as failures. There is an awareness that the cultural sphere has collapsed into a multitude of subcultures, each of which is more or less self-sufficient. The expectations are guardedly optimistic. What had occurred in 1992 to impart this feeling of hope? Had the literary critics got used to a state of crisis, or had the nadir been passed? An important factor was that not one single well-known literary journal published in Russia had folded; moreover a host of new journals had appeared, ranging from the narrowly professional (*Novoe literaturnoe obozrenie, De visu*) to highbrow culturological (*Apokrif, Mirovoe drevo, Novyi krug, Logos*), and including ephemeral publications like *Chernyi zhurnal, Bezhin lug, Zlatoust, Bogema* and *Zolotoi vek*, the magazine of the Union of Graphomaniacs (and not to be confused with the splendid periodical with the same title published since 1991 by Vladimir Salimon and rather reminiscent of the aesthetic tastes of the Silver Age of Russian culture at the beginning of the twentieth century). Another initiative was the creation of an élitist Moscow–St Petersburg illustrated journal called *Russkaia viza*, which began by publishing the memoirs of Natal'ia Krandievskaia and fiction by Sasha Sokolov and Venedikt Erofeev. Some of the contents of some of these periodicals, as well as of other journals or magazines not listed here, can be regarded as 'the outcome of an epidemic of graphomania', but critics such as Alla Marchenko have a valid point when they state that it would be better to talk about 'the emission of vital energy', regarding the efforts to start up new journals at a time of such difficulties as proof of the inexhaustible literary potency still to be found in the Russian Federation.

In 1992 and 1993 the situation in book publishing was also changing. Whereas in the preceding years contemporary Russian literature appeared almost exclusively in journals, with book publishers concentrating on established works and popular foreign literature, by 1993 there was an increasing interest on the part of book publishers in contemporary Russian literature. Moreover, many Russian 'traditionalist' writers were recovering their self-assurance in the face of the failure of the avant-garde and postmodernism to attract the interest of the post-Soviet Russian readership. The 'alternative' literature mentioned earlier was providing very few new texts worthy of serious discussion, despite all the attempts to stage literary happenings and scandals. In 1992 many critics and writers discussed the harm being done by the much publicized book launches and other noisy public literary events intended to raise the profile and create an image of 'the writer', but in reality turning literature into a game, if not a farce. Equally characteristic of the time was the counter-attack mounted by, among others, Dmitrii Prigov, the maestro of Muscovite Conceptualism, who insisted that the image, gesture, and behaviour pattern of the writer mean no less than his *artistic* image. Disputing this, Ian Probshtein noted ironically that substituting the writer's image for his literary works must be very attractive for those who have few worthwhile texts of their own to offer, although it must be said that Prigov himself has a multitude of texts, individual lines of which have already turned into popular sayings, and one of whose characters, an ultra-loyal Soviet militiaman, has now become part of Russian folklore. Probshtein maintains that the present Russian avant-garde, for all its power of negation and attempts to shock, is derivative and imitative, adding nothing to what had already been done by the avant-garde in the early decades of the twentieth century. In his view, the 'new' avant-garde has failed to respond to the spiritual and creative requirements of the time and is unlikely to bequeath any texts of intrinsic significance to the future (*Literaturnaia gazeta*, 30 April 1993). There were similar assertions about (and occasional acknowledgements of) the low quality of most Russian postmodernist writing. As a result, it was obvious by

1993 that there had not been any aesthetic revolution. The 'new' literature was being published in *Vestnik novoi literatury* and *Labirint* (St Petersburg), *Ekstsentr* (Ekaterinburg), later in the combined *Labirint-Ekstsentr*, and in the newspaper *Gumanitarnyi fond*, but all these publications came out in a small number of copies and seemed to arouse more interest among foreign literary specialists than in Russia (hence the ironic term 'literature for Slavists'). S. Chuprinin also felt by 1993 that the avant-gardists, whether postmodernists, Conceptualists or whatever else, had become academically respectable and *passé*, a striking change in attitude, as he had earlier been one of those who had placed great hopes on the 'new' literature. He named three authors currently working in the 'artistic danger zone' near the front line dividing and linking high culture and mass culture (*Znamia*, 9 [1993], 181–8): Viktor Pelevin, Evgenii Popov, and Anatolii Kurchatkin.

Pelevin's novella *Omon Ra* (*Znamia*, 5 [1992]), a mixture of science fiction and thriller, gloomily and ironically demythologizing the Soviet space programme, was the most striking literary debut of the year. He followed this with another novella, *The Life of Insects* (*Zhizn' nasekomykh*, *Znamia*, 4 [1993]), which, if less original, was no less powerful. Popov's remake of a Turgenev novel, *On the Eve of the Eve* (*Nakanune nakanune*, *Volga*, 4 [1993]), replacing the amiable landowners with squabbling dissidents who can think and talk of nothing but the KGB, shows that a writer associated with Russia's alternative literature from the time of *Metropol'* can still retain Chuprinin's sympathy (Pelevin too is regarded by many as a postmodernist, which shows how fluid are the dividing lines between one school and another). Kurchatkin's *The Guardian* (*Strazhnitsa*, *Znamia*, 5 [1993]), about a woman obsessed by Gorbachev, was lambasted by some sophisticated critics as nothing but kitsch.

There can be no doubt that Chuprinin's attitude was well-founded and widely shared. Most highbrow Russian critics, for instance, were cool and sceptical from the outset towards a work such as Viktor Erofeev's *Russian Beauty* (*Russkaia krasavitsa*). They regarded it more as an illustration of views expressed in his article, 'A Wake for Soviet Literature', and as a game with various artificial literary rules and regulations than as a new word in Russian literature. A number of foreign academic experts, however, were persuaded that Erofeev was a brave innovator who represented the beginning of a new wave in Russian literature.

Vladimir Sorokin is a more complex figure, who began to attract attention in the mid-1980s with his verbal virtuosity, sparkling originality, and bold detonations of ossified literary devices. Sorokin was better known abroad than in Russia until 1992–3, but after he was short-listed for the Booker Prize in 1992 (for *The Hearts of the Four* [*Serdtsa chetyrekh*]) it stopped being politically incorrect to disparage his works, and young as well as older critics were not afraid to 'come out' and state that they found his postmodernist rewriting of and attacks on the Russian classical novel somewhat tedious and dated, no matter that he was an undeniably gifted author.

In 1993 even a traditionalist journal like *Novyi mir* published a postmodernist novel, V. Sharov's *Before and During* (*Do i vo vremia*), in which the author plays with history and literature in an intellectually provocative game. The narrator, a patient in a hospital where experiments are being carried out on his memory, asserts that the ascetic thinker Nikolai Fedorov (1828–1903) – the author of *The Philosophy of the Common Cause* – had an affair with Madame de Staël (1766–1817), which resulted in the birth of their child – Joseph Stalin (1879–1953). This postmodernist phantasmagoria would not have had such an impact if the journal had not printed a letter by two members of its own editorial staff, I. Rodnianskaia and S. Kostyrko, 'Washing Our Dirty Linen in Public' ('Sor iz izby'), containing an extremely strong attack on the novel, which the two editors viewed as a threat to the very existence of Russian literature.

In 1993 it also became apparent that it was no longer possible to use a term that had been very popular in Soviet times, 'the literary process'. Natal'ia Ivanova was one of the first to notice that in the minds of literary critics 'it has been replaced by "the literary situation" or, even more accurately, "the literary landscape" ' (*Znamia*, 9 [1993], 190). It is a landscape that is blurred and fuzzy, sadly lacking in harmony and charm.

The three major Soviet literary monthlies fiercely opposed to the introduction of liberal democracy to Russia, *Nash sovremennik*, *Moskva*, and *Molodaia gvardiia*, are still publishing today. *Nash sovremennik* supports the radical nationalists; *Moskva* favours the 'back-to-the-soil' movement and is seriously interested in the Russian Orthodox Church and Russian religious thought and philosophy; *Molodaia gvardiia* is closer to the (neo)-communists and particularly close to the armed services and the 'military-industrial complex'. Many of the works published in these three journals (for example Aleksandr Prokhanov's *The Last Soldier of the Empire* [*Poslednii soldat imperii*], *Nash sovremennik*, 7–9 [1993] and Iu. Kozlov's *A Geopolitical Romance* [*Geopoliticheskii romans*], *Nash sovremennik*, 11 [1993]) collapse and disintegrate once they are subjected to aesthetic analysis, but it is a pity that most professional critics completely ignore everything published in these periodicals. At least one of the stories published by Valentin Rasputin in *Nash sovremennik*, 8 (1995), for example, is a masterpiece. *V tu zhe zemliu . . . (Into that Selfsame Earth)*, about an elderly woman who has spent her whole life working on the 'great building-sites of communism', who has only a minute pension and a wretched little flat to show for it, and who has to bury her aged mother secretly at night, shows that great literature can still be produced by people regarded by liberals and democrats as having completely unacceptable political views.

It cannot be excluded that, when the development of Russian literature in the early 1990s is seen in historical perspective, a significant place will be given to the prose of other 'nationalist' writers such as Vladimir Lichutin (1993 saw the publication in *Nash sovremennik* [nos. 10–11] of the beginning of his historical novel *The Way of the Cross* [*Krestnyi put'*], which forms part of his trilogy *The Split* [*Raskol*]), Vladimir Krupin, and Leonid Borodin. It is characteristic of this period (1993–5) that works published in 'right-wing' journals were simply not discussed by liberal and democratic critics and journalists. On the other hand, virtually no distinction was made by this time between émigré writers and works produced by authors living in Russia. Whereas the first years of *perestroika* saw the belated publication in Russia of older works by 'third-wave' émigrés, which had already come out abroad, journals in Russia itself since 1991 have been the first publishers of new works by émigrés such as Vasilii Aksenov, Vladimir Voinovich, Iuz Aleshkovsky, Fridrikh Gorenshtein, Georgii Vladimov, and Iurii Miloslavsky. (One should note that Russian émigré publishing houses and periodicals have lost much of their importance in the 1990s. Even though the print-runs of 'metropolitan' magazines and books are now much lower than in the Soviet period, the print-runs of émigré publishing-houses were and are lower still.) Critics based in the Russian Federation have until recently paid perhaps too much attention to, and been too indulgent of, émigré authors, even forgiving Eduard Limonov for his political eccentricity based on the dangerous combination of Bolshevism and Russian nationalism. The concept of 'the émigré writer' has been gradually disappearing, especially as most émigré authors visit Russia regularly, and little attention is devoted to where a writer spends most of his time. Among the most significant works written abroad and (rather than 'but') *first* published in Russia are Gorenshtein's novel *Place* (*Mesto*, 1991); Aksenov's *Moscow Saga* (*Moskovskaia saga*), chapters of which were published in *Iunost'* as early as 1991; Iuz Aleshkovsky's novella *A Ring in a Case* (*Persten' v futliare*), an ironic description of the literary world in the 1980s (*Zvezda*, 7 [1993]); and Sergei Iur'enen's *The Desire to Be a Spaniard* (*Zhelanie byt' ispantsem*), the story of the love of a Moscow student and a young Spanish girl (*Soglasie*, 7 and 8–12 [1993]). All these works were and are being read and analysed on a par with works written in Russia. It was therefore quite logical and no great surprise that the winner of the 1995 Booker Prize for the best piece of Russian prose fiction first published the previous year was a writer who happened to be living abroad, Georgii Vladimov. His novel *The General and His Army* (*General i ego armiia*, Znamia, 4–5 [1994]), about a talented military leader who falls foul of the Stalinist system, was regarded as an outstanding text and a significant literary event by almost all Russian critics, who were not concerned with where the author was when he was writing the novel.

The Russian Booker Prize, established in 1992, has had a positive impact on post-Soviet literature and its readership, and even helped to structuralize the Russian literary world, not least because the prize is awarded to the most deserving text, regardless of the status of its author. The first shortlist of novels and novellas (by Vladimir Makanin, Liudmila Petrushevskaia, Gorenshtein, Sorokin, Aleksandr Ivanchenko, and Mark Kharitonov) was in itself enough to dispel gloom about the 'crisis' of Russian literature in the early 1990s. Only the novel by Sorokin belonged clearly to the category of 'new' or 'other' literature. Ivanchenko's *Monogramma* (*The Monogram, Ural*, 2–4 [1992]), despite its postmodernist devices (such as playing games with Buddhist texts), rests firmly on the realist tradition. So does the winning book, Kharitonov's *Lines of Fate* (*Liny sud'by, ili Sunduchok Miloshevicha*) published in *Druzhba narodov*, 1–2 (1992). This novel also contains postmodernist elements, but is written for the most part in the Russian realist tradition with more than a trace of the Western intellectual novel; the influence of Hermann Hesse and Thomas Mann is especially apparent (the almost unknown Kharitonov had translated both these authors). Having beaten the favourites for the prize, the much better known Makanin, Petrushevskaia, and Gorenshtein, Kharitonov found it much easier to publish his earlier and new fiction, and has thus become an established figure on the Russian literary scene. His 1995 novel, *Return from Nowhere* (*Vozvrashchenie niotkuda*), modernist rather than post-modernist, and set in a mysterious, possibly non-existent, world recalling Nabokov rather than Orwell, has confirmed his reputation as a master.

The 1993 Booker Prize was widely expected to be awarded to Oleg Ermakov for his novel *Sign of the Beast* (*Znak zveria*, Znamia, 6–7 [1992]), about Soviet soldiers serving in the war in Afghanistan in the 1980s, and questioning in the classical Russian tradition the purpose of the loss of life on both sides. However, instead of giving the award to the young writer from Smolensk, the judges chose the novella by Makanin, *Baize-Covered Table with Decanter* (*Stol, pokrytyi suknom i s grafinom poseredine*, Znamia, 1 [1993]). This work – far from Makanin's best – well describes the Kafkaesque surrealism of Soviet life, where an application to go abroad requires a public confession under torture. Makanin is a key figure in contemporary Russian literature, having moved away from his earlier dispassionate, realistic manner to experiment with new forms, such as science fiction (*Escape Hatch* (*Laz*), *The Long Road Ahead* (*Dolog nash put'*), and *The Captive of the Caucasus* (*Kavkazskii plennyi*). This last work, freshly and vividly written, graphically reveals the absurd metaphysics of war by turning the tables on classical Russian fiction set in the Caucasus, and focusing not on a Russian captured by locals but on a local man captured, loved, and murdered by a Russian.

The 1994 Booker Prize was awarded to Bulat Okudzhava for his auto-biographical novel *The Closed Theatre* (*Uprazdnennyi teatr*, Znamia, 9–10 [1993]). This unexpected choice (the focus of attention had been on two much younger writers, Petr Aleshkovsky and Aleksei Slapovsky) can perhaps be explained by the fact that both the style and the content of the work marked a new departure for the popular 70-year-old writer, known hitherto for his more sentimental and romantic songs and his historical novels set in the nineteenth century. The sympathetic portrayal of Okudzhava's relatives and their friends, communists who genuinely, if naively, wanted to 'remake the world' and institute a system of social justice, was a real challenge to the 'political correctness' of the last few years, which required such idealists to be depicted as absurd individuals and objects of mockery.

Apart from the main award, the 'small' Booker Prize (financed by an anonymous British benefactor) is also awarded annually, but each year for a different kind of literary activity. In 1992 this prize, which was split, was awarded to two new journals that had done most, in the opinion of the judges, to promote the development of the new Russian literature. One of the winners, the St Petersburg *Vestnik novoi literatury*, edited by Mikhail Berg, is a journal for aesthetes that sets itself not only against politicized Soviet criteria, but also against realism as the traditionally dominant current in Russian art. The other winner *Solo*, edited by Aleksandr Mikhailov, is aesthetically omnivorous, with traditional prose and poetry intermingled with experimental texts that are intended to shock. *Solo* quickly became a journal for new names in literature, and although it is unprepossessing in appearance and has a very small circulation it makes an important contribution to contemporary literature. In 1993 the 'small' Booker was awarded to the most promising short-story writer, deemed to be Viktor Pelevin, whose collection *The Blue Lantern* (*Sinii fonar'*) also included some of his novellas. Pelevin has perhaps received more critical attention than any other Russian writer of his generation, for he appeals equally to lovers of 'sots-art' (parodies of socialist realism), of the egocentric 'underground', and of Russian postmodernism. Pelevin's prose is dynamic, has a strong story-line, and is accessible to the reader at several levels. There is usually no clear dividing-line between fantasy and reality. In his novella *The Prince of the State Planning Organization* (*Prints Gosplana*) the world of computer games takes over from the real world; virtual reality replaces reality.

In 1994 the 'small' Booker Prize was awarded to the journal published outside Moscow and St Petersburg that had made the greatest contribution to Russian literature in the preceding year. The two strongest contenders were *Ural* (Ekaterinburg) and *Volga* (Saratov), both of which had been, until recently, typical Soviet provincial literary periodicals, but which by the end of the 1980s had used the opportunities presented by glasnost to publish hitherto banned writers and 'difficult' texts, sometimes ahead of their Moscow and Leningrad colleagues. *Ural*, which was showing strong postmodernist inclinations, published members of the 'Ekaterinburg wave' like the aforementioned Aleksandr Ivanchenko (short-listed for the main Booker Prize in 1992 for his novel *The Monogram*). *Volga* regularly printed local authors, especially the extremely prolific Aleksei Slapovsky (short-listed in 1994 for his novel *The First Second Coming* (*Pervoe vtoroe prishestvie*)), but also 'risqué' works by writers living in Moscow, such as Evgenii Popov's postmodernist *On the Eve of the Eve*. *Volga*, which finally won out against *Ural*, demonstrates that not all Russian literary life is concentrated in the two major cities and shows that a magazine published in the provinces does not have to be, in the pejorative sense, provincial. In the following year the 'small' Booker Prize was intended for the most deserving Russian-language literary periodical(s) still being published outside the Russian Federation. The winners were *Rodnik* (Riga, Latvia), which had played a very important role in the early years of *perestroika*, and *Idiot* (Vitebsk, Belarus), a new, small-circulation avant-garde journal, suggesting that Russian 'émigré' literature still has a future.

The Russian Booker Prize has generated a number of other developments. In 1993 St Petersburg writers founded the Peterbooker Award, which required all entries to be submitted anonymously in the hope of avoiding favouritism. The first winner was a literary outsider, a professional mathematician called Aleksandr Melikhov, for his novel *Out of Eden. The Confession of a Jew* (*Izgnanie iz Edema. Ispoved' evreia, Novyi mir*, 1 [1994]). Not only the subject-matter, the problems of national self-identification, but also Melikhov's mastery of language have made this writer an important figure in the literary landscape. This prize was later renamed 'Severnaia Palmira' ('The Palmyra of the North'). The prize can now be awarded for any work of literature or literary criticism first published in St Petersburg (regardless of where the author lives) and/or for publishing activities in that city. The 1995 awards went to the St Petersburg poet Aleksandr Kushner (for his collection *On a Gloomy Star* [*Na sumrachnoi zvezde*]), the prose writer Feliks Roziner, resident in the United States (for his novel *Achilles on the Run* [*Akhill begushchii*], *Neva*, 7–8 [1994]), and to Feliks Lur'e for his documentary account of the life of the nineteenth-century revolutionary Sergei Nechaev.

Whereas this prize has only a symbolic value in financial terms, the 'Anti-Booker Prize' established in 1995 by *Nezavisimaia gazeta* brings the winner one dollar more than does the original Russian Booker Prize. The newspaper felt that the Booker judges (five in all, in office for only one year, each panel being made up of Russians and foreigners) had proved to be unable to appreciate 'new literature'. The first winner of the Anti-Booker Prize was, however, Aleksei Varlamov, for his traditional realistic novella *Birth* (*Rozhdenie*, *Novyi mir*, 7 [1995]), about the struggle of the parents of a seriously ill infant to save his life. This suggests that works deriving from the Russian realist tradition will set the tone for future developments. The answers to a questionnaire published in the last issue of *Literaturnaia gazeta* for 1995 are guardedly optimistic. No one prophesies 'the end of literature', although all admit that the role of literature in Russia is on the wane.

All the above-mentioned trends continued until the end of the century, but whereas at the beginning of the decade Russian literature was still alive and kicking, albeit in crisis, the end of the decade was rather flat. No new big names appeared, internecine literary struggles were half-hearted in nature, no-one went on insisting that traditional prose had had its day, avant-garde techniques began to look musty, and postmodernist omniverousness and corrosive irony no longer wrong-footed the reader but began to look stale and *déjà lu*. Print-runs of the literary journals continued to fall as the 'thick' monthlies began to lose their main function, that of being the best guide to new directions in the world of letters. Ever more writers chose to publish their longer works straight away in book form, as books can now be published within a month or two of submission of the typescript. Thus the long-promised death of Russian literature has not taken place, the gloomier type of predictions has gradually gone out of fashion, and the reanimation of the publishing industry has even prompted a certain optimism about the future. It is clear to all that the place of belles-lettres in Russian society has changed for ever, but the 'literary landscape' is still rather interesting and distinctive. As the critic Andrei Nemzer put it (*Novyi mir*, 1 [2000]), the 1990s was a time of 'individual writers' who worked 'without regard for current fashions and group values'.

Realistic prose, firmly based on the traditions of the Russian classics, had almost been elbowed aside a few years earlier by the *avant-garde* and postmodernism, but in the second half of the decade it made something of a comeback, confidently demonstrating the inexhaustibility of its resources. The public still craves for a 'great Russian writer', and the only person who really fits the bill is still Aleksandr Solzhenitsyn, despite the facts that he doesn't play an active role in 'literary life' and that all his major works have already been published. And for all its merits his most recent output – several two-part short stories and his essays on nineteenth- and twentieth-century writers, which show him to be an attentive and punctilious reader (all published in *Novyi mir*) – doesn't add anything qualitatively new to readers' perceptions of this phenomenal figure. Even his second volume of memoirs, about his life in the West (*Novyi mir*, nos. 9 and 11, 1998 and no. 2, 1999), aroused considerably less interest than its much earlier predecessor, *The Calf and the Oak* (*Bodalsia telenok s dubom*, 1975). Another claimant for the role of 'great Russian writer', Viktor Astaf'ev, won a number of literary awards in the latter part of the 1990s, published a great deal and produced several substantial new works. However, his output is extraordinarily uneven in quality, and on the whole he has been repeating what he had already told us earlier. His main themes are the war, not in its heroic aspects (as in most Soviet literature), but its everyday and repulsive sides, and the post-World War Two period, a time of disappointed hopes and bitter disillusionment – the 1995 and 1996 novellas *The Desperate Desire to Live* (*Tak khochetsia zhit'*) and *Overtones* (*Oberton*), and the novel *The Accursed and the Killed* (*Prokliaty i ubity*), begun in 1992 and not yet completed. Critics were particularly impressed by his novella *The Happy Soldier* (*Veselyi soldat*), in *Novyi mir*, 5–6 [1998]), about a man crippled in the war and then abused and humiliated by his own country, but who still remains a decent and honourable human being.

Another claimant to the title of 'great Russian writer' is Vladimir Makanin, who moved centre-stage in the second half of the 1990s as a, if not the, most important and productive writer. His novel *The Underground, or A Hero of Our Time* (*Undegraund, ili geroi nashego vremeni*) which, rather unusually these days, was first serialized in a journal (*Znamia*, 1–4 [1998]) before coming out as a book, marked a new stage in his development and was dubbed by Andrei Nemzer 'one of the best books of the decade'. The novel's protagonist, a writer who earlier functioned outside the Soviet literary establishment and later operated well away from the dissident and unofficial cultural scene when it was turning into the new establishment, not only lives in the recent and present metaphorical underground but also has links with the traditional Russian underground man as depicted by Lermontov, Dostoevsky and numerous later authors. This novel is a complex and weird mixture of naturalism and the avant-garde with elements of postmodernism. The stinking corridors of a hostel, which has been converted into an anthill of poky flats and where the protagonist lives (he hasn't managed to acquire a place of his own and only looks after someone else's), alcoholism, sex without love, jeering evil-tempered queues, dishonest traders, oafish policemen taking out their impotence on defenceless underdogs – all this is depicted in the greatest naturalistic detail. At the same time the hostel, with its endless corridors, rich and poor inhabitants and luxurious and tasteless apartments, is clearly a metaphor for society as a whole, as is the mental hospital where an artist of genius, the protagonist's brother, is confined after being 'cured' by criminal psychiatrists.

This work was discussed by critics for almost a year, and then two other novellas by Makanin appeared, *The Letter 'A'* (*Bukva 'A'*, *Novyi mir*, 4 [2000]) and *A Successful Story About Love* (*Udavshiisia rasskaz o liubvi*, *Znamia*, 5 [2000]). These works also contain some hints at Russian literary traditions and play with earlier literary models – without, however, jumping on the once fashionable bandwagon to deconstruct earlier authoritative styles; Makanin makes use of authoritative myths in order to give them a new lease of life. At first *The Letter 'A'* clearly resembles 'labour-camp literature' (prisoners, barracks, watery soup, armed guards, the construction of a railway embankment), but as the narrative develops it takes on more and more surrealist features. We have not so much the model of a camp as the camp as a model. The events of the last fifteen years are described with the help of a metaphor: the entire USSR was a concentration camp. During the first tentative years of *perestroika* the prescribed ways of doing things began to break down and then the whole construction collapsed. The inmates fondly imagined that shortly after the watch-towers and guards had been removed an era of prosperity would begin and that once the barbed wire was taken down social peace would automatically ensue. On the contrary, however, internecine battles lead to yet more corpses in the barracks, and the ferocious camp guards can no longer be blamed for that. The novella ends with a disgusting expressionist scene – the entire camp is covered over in excrement by vindictive people driven crazy by the period when 'everything is permitted'. 'It didn't bother them and it didn't pain them that the barbed wire and the posts were their barbed wire and their posts, or that the land was their land. . . . OK, other people, other generations will be living here, but we'll muck it up for them.' This harsh sentence imposed by Makanin on Russian society and the Russian intelligentsia puzzled many readers, because this work, like his other recent novella, is clearly about defeat and moral bankruptcy, the failure of an entire generation which dreamed of freedom but could not liberate itself internally, the failure of the proponents of the new ideology, the leaders of the new Russia.

When we speak of the writers of the older generation who have come into their own in the 1990s we have to give pride of place to Anatolii Azol'sky. Unable to start his literary career in the early 1960s in Tvardovsky's *Novyi mir* because his grotesque novella about the work of a Soviet scientific research institute was rejected 'for censorship reasons', Azol'sky didn't give up and finally managed to publish it a quarter of a century later, in 1987. By then it seemed to many to be dated, a leftover from the 60s, but the author, by now in his sixties and a naval architect by profession, persisted and proved himself to be an original and striking writer, publishing a string of novellas throughout the 1990s about the Soviet period, each time combining a graphic and grotesque picture of a nauseating world with a really gripping plot. One of the literary highlights of 1997 was Azol'sky's polysemantically-titled novel *The Cell* (*Kletka*). The protagonist, a brilliant geneticist who was persecuted under Stalin and still leads an impoverished underground existence, makes an astonishing scientific breakthrough in the pathetic laboratory he has created in his home – he works on the mystery of the DNA helix.

The novel's title thus denotes the hero's area of specialization, but it also alludes to society, the regime and the country which even heroes cannot 'break through' (the title in Russian means 'cage' as well as 'cell'). With its exciting plot, dynamic narrative and unusual characters, this work justly won the Russian Booker Prize in 1997.

Another notable work of the late 1990s is Iurii Davydov's *Bestseller* (*Znamia*, 11–12 [1998]). This well-known historical novelist returns here to one of his favourite heroes, Vladimir Burtsev, who exposed a good many agents provocateurs, including the notorious Azef, about a century ago. But Davydov also writes here about himself and his friends and acquaintances, with plenty of apparently idle chatter and humdrum details of contemporary daily life. Periodically the narrative breaks into rhythmical prose, and the story is interrupted by soul-searching and the philosophizing is tempered by irony. This is a new and unexpected departure for someone with the reputation of being a traditionalist. Here we should make a distinction between a writer's present-day popularity and publishing successes on the one hand and, on the other, his current participation in and contribution to the ongoing movement of literature. Several remarkable authors who set the tone in the Gorbachev period – Andrei Bitov, Vladimir Voinovich, Vasilii Aksenov, Fazil' Iskander and Liudmila Petrushevskaia, to name but some – have published their most recent works (as well as republishing older ones) during the last few years, but it is widely held that not one of them has really said a 'new word'. Yet at the same time less famous writers, such as Evgenii Popov, Mark Kharitonov, Mikhail Kuraev, Anatolii Naiman, Iurii Buida, Liudmila Ulitskaia, Galina Shcherbakova and Tat'iana Tolstaia, have continued to develop and to work productively and successfully, even though they may not have produced a truly seminal work for the end of the millennium.

When we speak of the prose of the 'middle generation' we again find ourselves talking about individual writers, not about groups, trends or movements. Even so, one can divide most middle-aged authors into those who by and large continue the classical tradition (no matter how complex, way-out and weird their texts might be) and those who demonstratively reject this tradition. At the same time it should be added that the space that at the beginning of the 1990s separated those writers who felt that literature should still address questions concerning morality, 'eternal values', 'the dialectics of the soul', etc., and those who preferred to deconstruct such concepts has now narrowed from a gulf to a gap. Postmodernist experiments are now looking less experimental. On the one hand Vladimir Sorokin, Vladimir Sharov and Viktor Pelevin are becoming widely published and even establishmentarian figures, and on the other hand features of postmodernist aesthetics can be found in a multitude of works ranging from highbrow novels through popular fiction to pot-boilers and trash. In 1998 'Ad Marginem' publishers produced a two-volume edition of the complete works of the 'scandalous' Sorokin, but the event passed off quietly and several erstwhile proponents of anything and everything postmodern wrote rather restrained reviews. Dmitrii Bykov, for instance, claimed in *Literaturnaia gazeta* (18 November 1998) that Sorokin was too 'functional' to be a really important writer. Sorokin's 1999 novel *Blue Lard* (*Goluboe salo*) did create something of a scandal, not, however, because it crudely denigrates some of the most venerated Russian writers, such as Akhmatova, Pasternak, Mandel'shtam and Brodsky (Akhmatova literally licks Stalin's boots, Brodsky forces himself to swallow an egg laid by Akhmatova, etc.), but because of the publisher's protests about the unauthorized posting of the text on the Internet and the subsequent polemics on whether the demand to remove the text limited the public's right to freedom of information. The actual content of the novel did not arouse much interest, as the public had become rather tired of postmodernist games with 'alternative histories' (Pelevin, Sharov, Buida, Valerii Zalotukha, etc.), cloning (long ago a feature of SF), and the language of the future (in this case the large Chinese component was found to be heavy-handed and dull). Nonetheless the idea that blue lard, a mysterious substance produced by writers' clones during the creative process, is immune to change, indestructible and capable of changing history was new and unexpected, coming from the pen of a 'gravedigger of literature', as Sorokin is sometimes called.

The idea of the end of literature is a common one in postmodernist writing. In Pelevin's 1999 novel *Babylon* (*Generation P*), which quickly became unprecedentedly popular, the virtual world subsumes reality, as apparently real-life politicians, including the President, are actually 'created' in a TV studio. All the events covered in the news are in fact the product of the work of the scriptwriters and of complicated animational devices. In a way Pelevin's novel suggests that 'virtual' technologies have triumphed not only over literature but also over reality itself, although, paradoxically enough, the very fact of the novel's existence gives the lie to that suggestion. In contemporary Russian literature discourses on construction are much more vigorous and productive than discourses on deconstruction. We should draw the reader's attention at least to the names of a few more 'constructivist' writers, such as Andrei Dmitriev, Irina Polianskaia, Svetlana Vasilenko, Marina Palei and Aleksei Slapovsky, a highly productive writer from Saratov who has already been shortlisted for the Booker Prize more than once – including 1998, for his novel *The Questionnaire* (*Anketa*). That year many pundits rooted for Polianskaia, whose 1997 novel *The Passing of a Shadow* (*Prokhozhdenie teni*) tells of the interrelationships between a girl and a number of blind youths studying at a provincial music college. The narrative is periodically interrupted by flashbacks to the girl's childhood (her father, a scientist who has been incarcerated in Nazi as well as Soviet labour camps, was then working on an atomic project in a prison laboratory), to the drama of her parents' marriage, involving betrayal and self-sacrifice, to deaths and suicides – everything illustrates the tragic essence of the time she has lived through. However, neither Slapovsky nor Polianskaia won the 1998 Booker Prize (for a work first published in 1997), which rather strangely went to Aleksandr Morozov for a 'critical realist' novel in letters that he had written some thirty years earlier.

We should perhaps add a note here about the fate of the Russian Booker Prize, especially as 1998 was the last year in which it existed more or less in its original respectable, independent and disinterested form. Unlike Bookers, which had no obvious commercial stake in Russia, the new sponsor, Smirnoff, was widely perceived as engaging in a very aggressive campaign to increase its share of the Russian market for vodka. The change of sponsor led to other regrettable changes: no more foreigners on the committee, which appointed several not very competent judges, who made some not very wise decisions which were criticized by professionals and which detracted from the reputation of the Prize. The 1999 award went to Mikhail Butov's novel *Liberty* (*Svoboda*), *Novyi mir*, 1–2 (1999), about a writer who feels no nostalgia for the communist past but is no less repelled by the current period of 'primary accumulation'. The judges' choice aroused neither strong criticism nor particular enthusiasm – another sign of the decline of interest in this Prize. This is partly caused by the recent proliferation of other literary awards: the Apollon Grigor'ev, the Solzhenitsyn, the modified and now more conventional Anti-Booker, the State and the President's Prizes (both of which now operate under new procedures), as well as several others which, though smaller, still play an important role in Russian literary life.

In conclusion, it can be claimed that the increasing number of these awards and the growing interest on the part of numerous publishers in contemporary Russian belles-lettres indicate that despite the protracted crisis in which Russia finds itself and the fact that literature is no longer a central feature of Russian life, prose fiction has not completely lost its social or artistic significance, and evidently will never do so.

FURTHER READING

Epstein, Mikhail N. *After the Future: The Paradoxes of Postmodernism and Contemporary Russian Culture*, Amherst: University of Massachusetts Press, 1995.

Epstein, Mikhail, Genis, Alexander and Vladiv-Glover, Slobodanka. *Russian Postmodernism: New Perspectives on Post-Soviet Culture*, ed. and trans. Slobodanka Vladiv-Glover. New York and Oxford: Berghahn Books, 1999.

Glas: New Russian Writing, Moscow, Birmingham and Somerville, Massachusetts, 1991– [journal of literature in translation].

Janecek, Gerald. *Sight and Sound Entwined: Studies of the New Russian Poetry*, New York and Oxford: Berghahn Books, 2000.

Laird, Sally (ed.) *Voices of Russian Literature: Interviews with Ten Contemporary Writers*, Oxford: Oxford University Press, 1999.

Lilly, Ian K. and Mondry, Henrietta (eds) *Russian Literature in Transition*, Nottingham: Astra Press, 1999.

Lipovetsky, Mark. *Russian Postmodernist Fiction: Dialogue with Chaos*, Armonk, New York: M.E. Sharpe, 1999.

Shneidman, N.N. *Russian Literature, 1988–1994: The End of an Era*, Toronto: University of Toronto Press, 1995.

Tait, Arch. 'The Awarding of the Third Russian Booker Prize', *Modern Language Review*, 92/3 (1997), 660–77.

BIBLIOGRAPHY

SELECTED HISTORIES OF RUSSIA AND RUSSIAN CULTURE

Billington, James H. *The Icon and the Axe: An Interpretive History of Russian Culture*, New York: Alfred A. Knopf, 1966; Vintage Books, 1970.

Brown, Archie, Kaser, Michael and Smith, G.S. (eds) *The Cambridge Encyclopedia of Russia and the Former Soviet Union*, 2nd edn, Cambridge: Cambridge University Press, 1994.

Chew, Allen F. *An Atlas of Russian History: Eleven Centuries of Changing Borders*, New Haven: Yale University Press, 1967.

Christian, David. *A History of Russia, Central Asia and Mongolia. Volume I: Inner Eurasia from Prehistory to the Mongol Empire*, Oxford: Blackwell, 1999.

Ellis, Jane. *The Russian Orthodox Church: A Contemporary History*, London: Routledge, 1986.

Figes, Orlando. *A People's Tragedy: A History of the Russian Revolution*, New York: Viking, 1997.

Hosking, Geoffrey. *Russia: People and Empire, 1552–1917*, Cambridge, Mass.: Harvard University Press, 1997; London: Fontana 1998.

Kelly, Catriona, and Shepherd, David (eds) *Constructing Russian Culture in the Age of Revolution: 1881–1940*, Oxford: Oxford University Press, 1998.

—— (eds) *Russian Cultural Studies: An Introduction*, Oxford: Oxford University Press, 1998.

Lieven, Dominic. *Empire: The Russian Empire and its Rivals*, London: John Murray, 2000.

Malia, Martin. *The Soviet Tragedy: A History of Socialism in Russia, 1917–1991*, New York: Free Press, 1994.

Milner-Gulland, Robin, with Nikolai Dejevsky. *Cultural Atlas of Russia and the Former Soviet Union*, Oxford: Phaidon, 1998.

Milner-Gulland, Robin. *The Russians*, Oxford, Blackwell, 1997.

Obolensky, Chloe (with an introduction by Max Hayward). *The Russian Empire: A Portrait in Photographs*, London: Jonathan Cape, 1980.

Raeff, Marc. *Russia Abroad: A Cultural History of the Russian Emigration, 1919–1939*, New York: Oxford University Press, 1990.

Riasanovsky, Nicholas V. *A History of Russia*, 6th edn, New York: Oxford University Press, 1999.

Service, Robert. *The History of Twentieth-Century Russia*, Harmondsworth: Penguin, 1998.

Seton-Watson, Hugh. *The Russian Empire 1801–1917*, Oxford: Clarendon Press, 1967.

Shaw, Denis J.B. *Russia in the Modern World: A New Geography*, Oxford: Blackwell, 1999.

Treadgold, Donald W. *The West in Russia and China: Religious and Secular Thought in Modern Times*, vol. 1: *Russia 1472–1917*, New York and London: Cambridge University Press, 1973.

HISTORIES, GUIDES AND ENCYCLOPEDIAS OF RUSSIAN LITERATURE

Auty, Robert and Obolensky, Dimitri (eds) *An Introduction to Russian Language and Literature, Companion to Russian Studies*, vol. 2, Cambridge and New York: Cambridge University Press, 1977.

Benn, Anna and Bartlett, Rosamund. *Literary Russia: A Guide*, London: Papermac, 1997.

Bristol, Evelyn. *A History of Russian Poetry*, Oxford and New York: Oxford University Press, 1991.

Chudo, Alicia. *And Quiet Flows the Vodka, or When Pushkin Comes to Shove: The Curmudgeon's Guide to Russian Literature and Culture with The Devil's Dictionary of Received Ideas*, Evanston, Illinois: Northwestern University Press, 2000.

Čiževskij, Dmitrij. *History of Nineteenth-Century Russian Literature*, 2 vols., trans. Richard Noel Porter, Nashville: Vanderbilt University Press, 1974.

Cornwell, Neil (ed.) *Reference Guide to Russian Literature*, London and Chicago: Fitzroy Dearborn, 1998.

Kasack, Wolfgang. *A Dictionary of Russian Literature since 1917*, trans. Maria Carlson and Jane T. Hedges, New York: Columbia University Press, 1988.

Leach, Robert, and Borovsky, Victor (eds) *A History of Russian Theatre*, Cambridge: Cambridge University Press, 2000.

Levitt, Marcus C. (ed.) *Early Modern Russian Writers, Late Seventeenth and Eighteenth Centuries*, vol. 150 of the *Dictionary of Literary Biography*, Detroit: Bruccoli Clark Layman/Gale Research, 1995.

Lindstrom, Thaïs S. *A Concise History of Russian Literature*, 2 vols., London: University of London Press; New York: New York University Press, 1966 and 1978.

Lvov-Rogachevsky, L. *A History of Russian Jewish Literature*, ed. and trans. Arthur Levin, Ann Arbor: Ardis, 1979.

Mirsky, D.S. *A History of Russian Literature*, ed. Francis J. Whitfield, New York: Knopf; London: Routledge, 1949; reprinted Evanston, Illinois: Northwestern University Press, 1999.

Moser, Charles (ed.) *The Russian Short Story: A Critical History*, Boston: Twayne, 1986.

—— (ed.) *The Cambridge History of Russian Literature*, Cambridge and New York: Cambridge University Press, 1989; revised edition, 1992.

Peterson, Ronald E. *A History of Russian Symbolism*, Amsterdam: Benjamins, 1993.

Rydel, Christine A. (ed.) *Russian Literature in the Age of Pushkin and Gogol: Prose*, vol. 198 of the *Dictionary of Literary Biography*, Detroit: Bruccoli Clark Layman/Gale Research, 1999.

—— (ed.) *Russian Literature in the Age of Pushkin and Gogol: Poetry and Drama*, vol. 205 of the *Dictionary of Literary Biography*, Detroit: Bruccoli Clark Layman/The Gale Group, 1999.

Stacy, Robert H. *Russian Literary Criticism: A Short History*, Syracuse, New York: Syracuse University Press, 1974.

Terras, Victor (ed.) *Handbook of Russian Literature*, New Haven: Yale University Press, 1985.

—— *A History of Russian Literature*, New Haven: Yale University Press, 1991.

Weber, Harry B. *et al.* (eds) *The Modern Encyclopedia of Russian and Soviet Literature*, Gulf Breeze, Florida: Academic International Press, vols. 1–10, 1977–91; thereafter

Rollberg, Peter *et al.* (eds), *The Modern Encyclopedia of East Slavic, Baltic and Eurasian Literatures*, vols. 11–12, forthcoming.

GENERAL LITERARY STUDIES AND COLLECTIONS

Anderson, Roger, and Debreczeny, Paul (eds) *Russian Narrative and Visual Art: Varieties of Seeing*, Gainesville: University Press of Florida, 1994.

Andrew, Joe (ed.) *The Structural Analysis of Russian Narrative Fiction*, Keele: Essays in Poetics Publications, [1984].

Barta, Peter I., Larmour, David H. and Miller, Paul Allen (eds) *Russian Literature and the Classics*, Amsterdam: Harwood Academic, 1996.

Bethea, David M. *The Shape of Apocalypse in Modern Russian Fiction*, Princeton: Princeton University Press, 1989.

Brodsky, Joseph. *Less than One: Selected Essays*, New York: Farrar, Straus & Giroux; London: Viking, 1986; Harmondsworth: Penguin, 1987.

Brooks, Jeffrey. *When Russia Learned to Read: Literacy and Popular Literature, 1861–1917*, Princeton: Princeton University Press, 1985.

Brostrom, Kenneth N. (ed.) *Russian Literature and American Critics: In Honor of Deming B. Brown*, Ann Arbor: University of Michigan, Department of Slavic Languages and Literatures, 1984.

Field, Andrew (ed.) *The Complection of Russian Literature*, London: Allen Lane; New York: Atheneum, 1971.

Frank, Joseph. *Through the Russian Prism: Essays on Literature and Culture*, Princeton: Princeton University Press, 1990.

Freeborn, Richard (ed.) *Russian Literary Attitudes from Pushkin to Solzhenitsyn*, London: Macmillan; New York: Barnes and Noble, 1976.

—— *The Russian Revolutionary Novel: Turgenev to Pasternak*, Cambridge and New York: Cambridge University Press, 1982.

Freeborn, Richard and Grayson, Jane (eds) *Ideology in Russian Literature*, New York: St Martin's Press; London: Macmillan, 1990.

Garrard, John (ed.) *The Russian Novel from Pushkin to Pasternak*, New Haven: Yale University Press, 1983.

Gasparov, Boris, Hughes, Robert P. and Paperno, Irina (eds) *The Cultural Mythologies of Russian Modernism: From the Golden Age to the Silver Age*, Berkeley: University of California Press, 1992.

—— *Christianity and the Eastern Slavs*, vol. 3 of *Russian Literature in Modern Times*, Berkeley: University of California Press, 1995.

Gasparov, M.L. *A History of European Versification*, trans. G.S. Smith and Marina Tarlinskaja, eds G.S. Smith and Leofranc Holford-Strevens, Oxford: Clarendon Press, 1996.

Heldt, Barbara. *Terrible Perfection: Women and Russian Literature*, Bloomington: Indiana University Press, 1987.

Kelly, Catriona, Makin, Michael and Shepherd, David (eds) *Discontinuous Discourses in Modern Russian Literature*, London: Macmillan; New York: St Martin's Press, 1989.

Kornblatt, Judith Deutsch. *The Cossack Hero in Russian Literature*, Madison: University of Wisconsin Press, 1992.

Mandelker, Amy and Reeder, Roberta. *The Supernatural in Slavic and Baltic Literature: Essays in Honor of Victor Terras*, Columbus, Ohio: Slavica, 1988.

Marsh, Rosalind (ed.) *Gender and Russian Literature: New Perspectives*, Cambridge and New York: Cambridge University Press, 1996.

—— (ed.) *Women and Russian Culture: Projections and Self-Perceptions*, New York and Oxford: Berghahn Books, 1998.

Mathewson, Rufus W., Jr. *The Positive Hero in Russian Literature*, New York: Columbia University Press, 1958; (revised edn) Stanford: Stanford University Press, 1975; Evanston, Illinois: Northwestern University Press, 2000.

McMillin, Arnold (ed.) *From Pushkin to "Palisandriia": Essays on the Russian Novel in Honour of Richard Freeborn*, London: Macmillan; New York: St Martin's Press, 1990.

Mihajlov, Mihajlo. *Russian Themes*, trans. Marija Mihajlov, New York: Farrar, Straus & Giroux; London: Macdonald, 1968.

Morson, Gary Saul (ed.) *Literature and History: Theoretical Problems and Russian Case Studies*, Stanford: Stanford University Press, 1986.

Press, Ian. *Learn Russian*, London: Duckworth, 2000.

Rancour-Lafferrière, Daniel (ed.) *Russian Literature and Psychoanalysis*, Amsterdam and Philadelphia: Benjamins, 1989.

Reyfman, Irina. *Ritualized Violence Russian Style: The Duel in Russian Culture and Literature*, Stanford: Stanford University Press, 1999.

Rosenthal, Bernice Glatzer (ed.) *The Occult in Russian and Soviet Culture*, Ithaca: Cornell University Press, 1997.

Sandler, Stephanie (ed.) *Rereading Russian Poetry*, New Haven: Yale University Press, 1999.

Scherr, Barry. *Russian Poetry: Meter, Rhythm, and Rhyme*, Berkeley: University of California Press, 1986.

Semeka-Pankratov, Elena (ed.) *Studies in Poetics. Commemorative Volume: Krystyna Pomorska (1928–1986)*, Columbus, Ohio: Slavica, 1995.

Wachtel, Andrew Baruch. *The Battle for Childhood: Creation of a Russian Myth*, Stanford: Stanford University Press, 1990.

—— *An Obsession with History: Russian Writers Confront the Past*, Stanford: Stanford University Press, 1994.

Wachtel, Michael. *The Development of Russian Verse: Meter and its Meanings*, Cambridge: Cambridge University Press, 1999.

Weiner, Adam. *By Authors Possessed: The Demonic Novel in Russia*, Evanston, Illinois: Northwestern University Press, 1998.

Wigzell, Faith (ed.) *Russian Writers on Russian Writers*, Oxford: Berg, 1994.

Worrall, Nick. *The Moscow Art Theatre*, London and New York: Routledge, 1996.

Ziolkowski, Margaret. *Hagiography and Modern Russian Literature*, Princeton: Princeton University Press, 1988.

Zholkovsky, Alexander. *Text Counter Text: Rereadings in Russian Literary History*, Stanford: Stanford University Press, 1994.

EIGHTEENTH AND NINETEENTH CENTURIES

Andrew, Joe. *Writers and Society During the Rise of Russian Realism*, London: Macmillan; Atlantic Highlands, New Jersey: Humanities Press, 1980.

—— *Russian Writers and Society in the Second Half of the Nineteenth Century*, London: Macmillan; Atlantic Highlands, New Jersey: Humanities Press, 1982.

—— *Women in Russian Literature, 1780–1863*, London: Macmillan; New York: St Martin's Press, 1988.

—— *Narrative and Desire in Russian Literature, 1822–1849*, London: Macmillan; New York: St Martin's Press, 1993.

Brown, William Edward. *A History of Russian Literature of the Romantic Period*, 4 vols., Ann Arbor: Ardis, 1986.

Cockrell, Roger and Richards, David (eds) *The Voice of a Giant: Essays on Seven Russian Prose Classics*, Exeter: University of Exeter, 1985.

Cornwell, Neil (ed.) *The Society Tale in Russian Literature: From Odoevskii to Tolstoi*, Amsterdam: Rodopi, 1998.

—— *The Gothic-Fantastic in Nineteenth-Century Russian Literature*, Amsterdam: Rodopi, 1999.

Fennell, John (ed.) *Nineteenth-Century Russian Literature: Studies of Ten Russian Writers*, London: Faber; Berkeley: University of California Press, 1973.

Finke, Michael C. *Metapoesis: The Russian Tradition from Pushkin to Chekhov*, Durham, North Carolina: Duke University Press, 1995.

Gutsche, George and Leighton, Lauren G. (eds) *New Perspectives on Nineteenth-Century Russian Prose*, Columbus, Ohio: Slavica, 1982.

Hingley, Ronald. *Russian Writers and Society in the Nineteenth Century* (2nd revised edn) London: Weidenfeld and Nicolson, 1977.

Katz, Michael R. *Dreams and the Unconscious in Nineteenth-Century Russian Fiction*, Hanover, New Hampshire: New England University Press, 1984.

Layton, Susan. *Russian Literature and Empire: Conquest of the Caucasus from Pushkin to Tolstoy*, Cambridge and New York: Cambridge University Press, 1994.

Leighton, Lauren G. *Russian Romanticism*, The Hague: Mouton, 1975.

—— (ed.) *Russian Romantic Criticism: An Anthology*, Westport, Connecticut: Greenwood Press, 1987.

—— *The Esoteric Tradition in Russian Romantic Literature: Decembrism and Freemasonry*, University Park: Pennsylvania State University Press, 1994.

Levitt, Marcus C. *Russian Literary Politics and the Pushkin Celebration of 1880*, Ithaca: Cornell University Press, 1989.

Maegd-Soep, Carolina de. *The Emancipation of Women in Russian Literature and Society*, trans. the author and Jos Coessens, Ghent: Ghent State University, 1978.

Nabokov, Vladimir. *Lectures on Russian Literature*, ed. Fredson Bowers, New York: Harcourt Brace Jovanovich, 1981; London: Weidenfeld and Nicolson, 1982; London: Picador, 1983.

Nilsson, Nils Åke (ed.) *Russian Romanticism: Studies in the Poetic Codes*, Stockholm: Almqvist & Wiksell, 1979.

O'Toole, L. Michael. *Structure, Style and Interpretation in the Russian Short Story*, New Haven: Yale University Press, 1982.

Reid, Robert (ed.) *Problems of Russian Romanticism*, Aldershot, Hampshire, and Brookfield, Vermont: Gower, 1986.

Todd, William Mills III. *The Familiar Letter as a Literary Genre in the Age of Pushkin*, Princeton: Princeton University Press, 1976; Evanston, Illinois: Northwestern University Press, 1999.

—— (ed.) *Literature and Society in Imperial Russia, 1800–1914*, Stanford: Stanford University Press, 1978.

TWENTIETH CENTURY

Avins, Carol. *Border Crossings: The West and Russian Identity in Soviet Literature, 1917–1934*, Berkeley: University of California Press, 1983.

Balina, Marina, Condee, Nancy and Dobrenko, Evgeny (eds) *Endquote: Sots-art Literature and Soviet Grand Style*, Evanston, Illinois: Northwestern University Press, 1999.

Barta, Peter I. (ed.) *Metamorphoses in Russian Modernism*, Budapest: Central European University Press, 2000.

Beaujour, Elizabeth Klosty. *Alien Tongues: Bilingual Russian Writers of the 'First' Emigration*, Ithaca: Cornell University Press, 1989.

Booker, M. Keith. *Bakhtin, Stalin, and Modern Russian Fiction: Carnival, Dialogism and History*, Westport, Connecticut: Greenwood Press, 1995.

Brandist, Craig. *Carnival Culture and the Soviet Modernist Novel*, London: Macmillan; New York: St Martin's Press, 1996.

Brintlinger, Angela. *Writing a Usable Past: Russian Literary Culture, 1917–1937*, Evanston, Illinois: Northwestern University Press, 2000.

Brown, Edward J. (ed.) *Major Soviet Writers: Essays in Criticism*, London and New York: Oxford University Press, 1973.

Brown, Edward J. *Russian Literature since the Revolution* (revised and enlarged edn) Cambridge, Massachusetts: Harvard University Press, 1982.

Clark, Katerina. *Petersburg: Crucible of Cultural Revolution*, Cambridge: Cambridge University Press, 1995.

Clowes, Edith W. *Russian Experimental Fiction: Resisting Ideology after Utopia*, Princeton: Princeton University Press, 1993.

Dewhirst, Martin and Farrell, Robert (eds) *The Soviet Censorship*, Metuchen, New Jersey: Scarecrow Press, 1973.

Dunham, Vera S. *In Stalin's Time: Middleclass Values in Soviet Fiction* (enlarged and updated edn) Durham, North Carolina: Duke University Press, 1990.

Erlich, Victor (ed.) *Twentieth-Century Russian Literary Criticism*, New Haven: Yale University Press, 1975.

Erlich, Victor. *Modernism and Revolution: Russian Literature in Transition*, Cambridge, Massachusetts: Harvard University Press, 1994.

Ermolaev, Herman. *Censorship in Soviet Literature, 1917–1991*, Lanham, Maryland: Rowman and Littlefield, 1997.

France, Peter. *Poets of Modern Russia*, Cambridge and New York: Cambridge University Press, 1982.

Glad, John. *Russia Abroad: Writers, History, Politics*. Tenafly, NJ: Hermitage; Washington, DC: Birchbark Press, 1999.

Graham, Sheelagh Duffin (ed.) *New Directions in Soviet Literature*, London: Macmillan; New York: St Martin's Press, 1992.

Harris, Jane Gary (ed.) *Autobiographical Statements in Twentieth-Century Russian Literature*, Princeton: Princeton University Press, 1990.

Hayward, Max. *Writers in Russia, 1917–1978*, ed. Patricia Blake, London: Harvill Press; San Diego: Harcourt Brace Jovanovich, 1983.

Hingley, Ronald. *Russian Writers and Soviet Society, 1917–1978*, New York: Random House; London: Weidenfeld and Nicolson, 1979.

Hodgson, Katharine. *Written with the Bayonet: Soviet Russian Poetry of World War Two*, Liverpool: Liverpool University Press, 1996.

Kelly, Catriona and Lovell, Stephen (eds) *Russian Literature, Modernism and the Visual Arts*, Cambridge: Cambridge University Press, 2000.

Loseff, Lev. *On the Beneficence of Censorship: Aesopian Language in Modern Russian Literature*, Munich: Sagner, 1984.

Lowe, David. *Russian Writing since 1953: A Critical Survey*, New York: Ungar, 1987.

Marsh, Rosalind. *Images of Dictatorship: Portraits of Stalin in Literature*, London and New York: Routledge, 1989.

—— *History and Literature in Contemporary Russia*, London: Macmillan; New York: New York University Press, 1995.

Maryniak, Irena. *Spirit of the Totem: Religion and Myth in Soviet Fiction, 1964–1988*, Leeds: W.S. Maney, 1995.

McMillin, Arnold (ed.) *Under Eastern Eyes: The West as Reflected in Recent Russian Emigré Writing*, London: Macmillan, 1991; New York: St Martin's Press, 1992.

—— *Reconstructing the Canon: Russian Writing in the 1980s*, Amsterdam: Harwood Academic, 1999.

Nilsson, Nils Åke (ed.) *Studies in 20th Century Russian Prose*, Stockholm: Almqvist & Wiksell, 1982.

Pike, Christopher (ed.) *The Futurists, the Formalists, and the Marxist Critique*, London: Ink Links, 1979.

Pomorska, Krystyna. *Russian Formalist Theory and its Poetic Ambiance*, The Hague: Mouton, 1968.

Porter, Robert. *Four Contemporary Russian Writers*, Oxford: Berg, 1989.

Proffer, Carl R. (ed.) *Modern Russian Poets on Poetry*, Ann Arbor: Ardis, 1976.

—— *The Widows of Russia and Other Writings*, Ann Arbor: Ardis, 1987.

Seyffert, Peter. *Soviet Literary Structuralism: Background, Debate, Issues*, Columbus, Ohio: Slavica, 1983.

Shentalinsky, Vitaly. *The KGB's Literary Archive*, trans. John Crowfoot, London: Harvill Press, 1995.

Shneidman, N.N. *Soviet Literature in the 1970's: Artistic Diversity and Ideological Conformity*, Toronto: University of Toronto Press, 1979.

Sicher, Efraim. *Jews in Russian Literature After the October Revolution*, Cambridge: Cambridge University Press, 1995.

Slonim, Marc. *Soviet Russian Literature: Writers and Problems, 1917–1977* (2nd revised edn) London and New York: Oxford University Press, 1977.

Vishevsky, Anatoly. *Soviet Literary Culture in the 1970s: The Politics of Irony*, Gainesville: Florida University Press, 1993.

Ziolkowski, Margaret. *Literary Exorcisms of Stalinism: Russian Writers and the Soviet Past*, Columbia, SC: Camden House, 1998.

ANTHOLOGIES

Brown, Clarence (ed.) *The Portable Twentieth-Century Russian Reader*, New York and Harmondsworth: Penguin, 1985.

Chukhontsev, Oleg (ed.) *Dissonant Voices: The New Russian Fiction*, London: Harvill Press, 1991.

Collins, Christopher and Gary Kern (eds) *The Serapion Brothers: A Critical Anthology*, Ann Arbor: Ardis, 1975.

Crouch, Martin and Porter, Robert (eds) *Understanding Soviet Politics Through Literature*, London: Allen and Unwin, 1984.

Erofeev, Viktor and Reynolds, Andrew (eds) *The Penguin Book of New Russian Writing: Russia's 'Fleurs du mal'*, Harmondsworth and New York: Penguin, 1995.

Fetzer, Leland (ed. and trans.) *Pre-Revolutionary Russian Science Fiction: An Anthology (Seven Utopias and a Dream)*, Ann Arbor: Ardis, 1982.

Ginsburg, Mirra (ed. and trans.) *The Fatal Eggs and Other Soviet Satire, 1918–1963*, New York: Macmillan, 1963; London: Quartet, 1993.

—— (ed. and trans.) *The Ultimate Threshold: A Collection of the Finest in Soviet Science Fiction*, New York: Holt, Rinehart and Winston, 1970; Harmondsworth: Penguin, 1978.

Glad, John and Weissbort, Daniel (eds) *Russian Poetry: The Modern Period*, Iowa City: University of Iowa Press, 1978.

Goscilo, Helena and Lindsey, Byron (eds) *The Wild Beach and Other Stories*, Ann Arbor: Ardis, 1992.

Jacobson, Helen Saltz (trans.) *New Soviet Science Fiction*, New York and London: Macmillan, 1979.

Johnson, Kent and Ashby, Stephen M. (eds) *Third Wave: The New Russian Poetry*, Ann Arbor: University of Michigan Press, 1992.

Korovin, Valentin (ed.) *Russian 19th-Century Gothic Tales*, Moscow: Raduga, 1984.

Langland, Joseph, Aczel, Tamas and Tikos, Laszlo (eds and trans.) *Poetry from the Russian Underground: A Bilingual Anthology*, New York: Harper and Row, 1973.

Luker, Nicholas (ed. and trans.) *An Anthology of Russian Neo-Realism: The 'Znanie' School of Maxim Gorky*, Ann Arbor: Ardis, 1982.

Magidoff, Robert (ed.) *Russian Science Fiction, 1969: An Anthology*, New York: New York University Press; London: University of London Press, 1969.

Milner-Gulland, Robin and Dewhirst, Martin (eds) *Russian Writing Today*, Harmondsworth: Penguin, 1977.

Minto, Marilyn (ed. and trans.) *Russian Tales of the Fantastic*, London: Bristol Classical Press, 1994.

Mortimer, Peter and Litherland, S.J. (eds) *The Poetry of Perestroika*, trans. Carol Rumens and Richard McKane, Cullercoats: Iron Press, 1991.

Moss, Kevin (ed.) *Out of the Blue: Russia's Hidden Gay Literature, an Anthology*, San Francisco: Gay Sunshine, 1997.

Obolensky, Dimitri (ed.) *The Penguin Book of Russian Verse*, Harmondsworth: Penguin, 1965; as *The Heritage of Russian Verse*, Bloomington: Indiana University Press, 1976.

Pomorska, Krystyna (ed.) *Fifty Years of Russian Prose: From Pasternak to Solzhenitsyn*, 2 vols., Cambridge, Mass.: MIT Press, 1971.

Proffer, Carl R. (ed.) *From Karamzin to Bunin: An Anthology of Russian Short Stories*, Bloomington: Indiana University Press, 1969.

—— *Russian Romantic Prose: An Anthology*, Ann Arbor, Translation Press, 1979.

Proffer, Carl R. and Proffer, Ellendea (eds) *The Ardis Anthology of Recent Russian Literature*, Ann Arbor: Ardis, 1975.

—— (eds) *Contemporary Russian Prose*, Ann Arbor, Ardis, 1982.

Rayfield, Donald, Hicks, Jeremy, Makarova, Olga and Pilkington, Anna (eds and trans.) *The Garnett Book of Russian Verse*, London: Garnett Press, 2000.

Richards, David (ed.) *The Penguin Book of Russian Short Stories*, Harmondsworth and New York: Penguin, 1981.

Russian Literature Triquarterly [*RLT*], Ann Arbor, 1–24, 1971–91 [journal of literature in translation and criticism].

Rydel, Christine (ed.) *The Ardis Anthology of Russian Romanticism*, Ann Arbor: Ardis, 1984.

Rzhevsky, Nicholas (ed.) *An Anthology of Russian Literature from Earliest Writings to Modern Fiction: Introduction to a Culture*, Armonk, New York: M.E. Sharpe, 1996.

Soviet Literature, Moscow, 1946–91 [journal of literature in translation].

Struve, Gleb (ed.) *Russian Stories*, New York: Bantam, 1961; as *Russian Stories: A Dual-Language Book*, New York: Dover, 1990.

Zalygin, Sergei (ed.) *The New Soviet Fiction: Sixteen Short Stories*, New York: Abbeville Press, 1989.

ADDITIONAL BIBLIOGRAPHICAL SOURCES

Lewanski, Richard C. *The Literature of the World in English Translation*, vol. 2, *The Slavic Literatures*, New York: New York Public Library, 1967.

Moody, Fred (ed.) *10 Bibliographies of 20th Century Russian Literature*, Ann Arbor: Ardis, 1977.

Proffer, Carl R. and Meyer, Ronald. *Nineteenth-Century Russian Literature in English: A Bibliography of Criticism and Translation*, Ann Arbor: Ardis, 1990.

Terry, Garth M. *East European Languages and Literatures*, vol. 1, Oxford: Clio Press, 1978; vols. 2–6, Nottingham: Astra Press, 1982–94.

INDEX